Irish Women's Fiction
FROM EDGEWORTH TO ENRIGHT

Irish Women's Fiction

FROM EDGEWORTH TO ENRIGHT

HEATHER INGMAN

IRISH ACADEMIC PRESS
DUBLIN

First published in 2013 by Irish Academic Press

8 Chapel Lane
Sallins
Co. Kildare, Ireland

© 2013 Heather Ingman

British Library Cataloguing in Publication Data
An entry can be found on request

ISBN: 978 0 7165 3148 7 (cloth)
ISBN: 978 0 7165 3153 1 (paper)
ISBN: 978 0 7165 3190 6 (ebook)

Library of Congress Cataloging-in-Publication Data
An entry can be found on request

Printed in Ireland by
SPRINT-print Ltd.

'What the women have is words, Ma said.'
(Dorothy Nelson, *Tar and Feathers*, 1987)

Contents

ACKNOWLEDGEMENTS

Books are never the sole achievement of the writer whose name appears on the title page but the outcome of years of conversations and discussions. My formation as an academic goes back to Professor Malcolm Smith of London University who first taught me the importance of clarity and to Professor Marion Shaw of Hull University who oversaw my first foray into writing about interwar women's fiction. I am very grateful to Professor Nicholas Grene of Trinity College, Dublin who gave me the opportunity to teach a course on Irish women's writing which, many years later, became this book. I also owe a great debt to the enthusiasm of the students at Trinity College, both undergraduate and postgraduate, to whom I have taught Irish women's writing over the years and to their lively and challenging questions. I am fortunate to work in the School of English at Trinity which contains so many acknowledged experts in the field of Irish writing. I have learned much from their writings, lectures and conversations. I would also like to thank the staff in Trinity College library, particularly the Early Printed Books section, and the staff at the National Library of Ireland for their unfailing courtesy and helpfulness. I am grateful to the two anonymous readers at Irish Academic Press for their insightful comments. Finally, this project owes a great deal to the enthusiasm of my editor, Lisa Hyde, who has provided a constant source of encouragement and support along the way. To Ferdinand, Sebastian and Theo, as usual, thank you for your forbearance.

PREFACE

'Who are the Irish women novelists?' This question is posed by Anna Kelly Sweeney in Éilís Ní Dhuibhne's novel *Fox, Swallow, Scarecrow* (2007).[1] Anna, an author of children's fiction, asks her question at a glittering party held in Dublin to honour the publication of a book of essays by Seamus Heaney. The launch is attended by many of the leading Irish authors of the day, and Anna's women friends, all of them writers of some description, stand a little apart from the golden circles of celebrated male writers. In response to Anna's question Anita, Anna's feminist friend, reels off the names of Edna O'Brien, Jennifer Johnston, Clare Boylan, Evelyn Conlon, Deirdre Madden, Anne Enright and Anne Haverty, before running out of steam. In my experience, this is a longer list than people generally produce when asked about Irish women writers. And I am talking not only about the general public but also about scholars, even sometimes scholars in the field of Irish Studies where, too often, women's writing and feminist literary criticism are regarded as of marginal interest. In addition, the novel itself has until recently frequently taken second place in Irish criticism to the genres of poetry and drama so heavily promoted at the time of the Irish Literary Revival. One of the aims of this study is to attempt an introductory one-volume work in answer to the question: who are the Irish women novelists?

The title of this book contains two contentious elements, namely the notion that literature can be divided by nationality and the idea of privileging one gender over another. Good writing escapes such categories. However, one must start somewhere and the division of literature by nationality has had the merit of establishing a solid canon of Irish fiction from Jonathan Swift to John McGahern. Within this canon of brilliant male work, however, Irish women writers, with such notable exceptions as Maria Edgeworth and Elizabeth Bowen, often end up drifting in what Clíona Ó Gallchoir has called 'no man's land: the place of the Irish woman writer'.[2] Time after time in interviews, Irish women writers complain that men rarely read their work and that publishers fail to keep their books in print.[3] Why has Julia O'Faolain's *No Country for Young Men*, a challenging and subversive reworking of the Gráinne myth, been unavailable for so long? Why has no publisher brought back into print Pamela Hinkson's *The Ladies' Road*, an evocative, modernist portrayal of the effect of the First World War on a group of Anglo-Irish? Why has Kathleen Coyle's *A Flock of Birds*, a powerful portrayal of a mother's lament for her son facing execution, been forgotten? Why has more critical attention not been paid to Frances Molloy's tragi-comic *No Mate for the Magpie* (1985) describing the life of a working-class Catholic girl growing up in Northern Ireland in the 1950s and '60s? Why do women writers repeatedly disappear from Irish literary history?

One of the reasons must be that Irish women's literary history remains an emergent field. This is despite the fact that nowadays the researcher's task is much aided by the joint University College, Dublin and University of Warwick 'Database of Irish Women's Writing, 1800–2005', as well as such reference works as volumes four and five of *The Field Day Anthology of Irish Literature* (2002) and the *Dictionary of Munster Women Writers, 1800–2000* (2005). Pioneering critical work has been done by Ann Owens Weekes (*Irish Women Writers: An Uncharted Tradition*, 1990), Christine St Peter (*Changing Ireland: Strategies in Contemporary Women's Fiction*, 2000), Rebecca Pelan (*Two Irelands: Literary Feminisms North and South*, 2005), as well as useful essay collections edited by Kathryn Kirkpatrick (*Border Crossings: Irish Women Writers and National Identities*, 2000), Patricia Boyle Haberstroh and Christine St Peter (*Opening the Field. Irish Women: Texts and Contexts*, 2007), Patricia Coughlan and Tina O'Toole (*Irish Literature: Feminist Perspectives*, 2008), Heidi Hansson (*New Contexts: Re-Framing Nineteenth-Century Irish Women's Prose*, 2008) and Elke d'Hoker, Raphaël Ingelbien and Hedwig Schwall (*Irish Women Writers: New Critical Perspectives*, 2011).

These are only a handful of studies and I would argue that scholarship is still in the preliminary stages of developing a body of critical work on female Irish novelists. *The Field Day Anthology* is concerned with historical, sociological and cultural questions as well as purely literary topics while Weekes's ground-breaking study centres on six major Irish women writers. Other studies are limited by period: Pelan looks at feminist writing between 1970 and the mid-1990s and St Peter concentrates on fiction of the 1980s and '90s. The essay collections are more wide-ranging in date and varied in theoretical approach but tend to discuss individual women writers, or groups of writers and are not necessarily focussed on fiction. Before further, much-needed, work is done on individual women writers it therefore seemed important to produce a general overview of Irish women's fiction that might point the way to future research, discussion and debate.

Despite these stimulating critical works, to which I am much indebted, there is the further point that female novelists still struggle to make their presence felt in general discussions of the Irish literary canon. John Wilson Foster's pioneering survey, *Irish Novels, 1890–1940: New Bearings in Culture and Fiction* (2008), redresses the balance in respect of the popular novel in which Irish women wrote in such numbers. Following on from this, though, Derek Hand's *A History of the Irish Novel* (2011) does not pick up on, for example, the substantial number of *fin de siècle* New Woman novels discussed by Foster. It seems that for every step forward in critical discussion of Irish women's fiction there is a step backwards. Women writers may now have entered the mainstream of Irish literary life but still too often their names are omitted when it comes to Irish literary history.

Rather than adducing, as Anna's friend Anita does, some patriarchal plot to explain the lack of prominence given to Irish women writers, a simpler explanation may be that these writers do not register with many scholars of Irish writing primed to look for certain topics in Irish fiction connected with wars, the land, the nation and religion. In *Irish Literature in the Celtic Tiger Years, 1990–2008* (2011), Susan Cahill argues that women writers often engage with Irish history in a different way from male writers and points to the fact that a large number of women's novels set in the Celtic Tiger years have been passed over by critics who insist that there is no Celtic Tiger fiction.[4] Much of this Celtic Tiger writing by women is conscious of the need to entertain and amuse their readers, as well as to inform, and this may have prevented them from being taken seriously by scholars. A similar point is excellently made by Heidi Hansson in relation to nineteenth-century women's writing which, she argues, requires a different approach from the standard, ideologically charged Irish critical context that measures all writers against the aesthetic values of writers like Yeats, Joyce and Beckett.[5] There is, in short, often a blind spot on the part of Irish literary critics, as demonstrated, notoriously, by the absence of many women writers from the first three volumes of *The Field Day Anthology of Irish Writing* (1991), overseen by an all-male editorial board.[6] The debate organised by Queen's University, Belfast to discuss the representation of Irish women's literary history in *The Cambridge History of Irish Literature* (2006) suggests that the difficulty of acknowledging women's cultural centrality has not gone away.

Women writers often resist insertion into ready-made Irish identity constructions and it is partly for this reason that I have taken a conscious decision not to focus specifically on the conflict between nation and gender on which I have written elsewhere.[7] Nevertheless the theme remains an important one: more often than not, and well before the advent of postmodernism, Irish women's novels question essentialist notions of national identity that frequently operate to women's disadvantage. In the nineteenth century the Anglo-Irish origin of many women authors has created difficulty in inserting them into the narrative of the Irish nation. Characteristic features of Irish women's fiction are its acknowledgement of competing voices within the Irish nation and its prioritising of private narratives as sources of truth over public histories. Moreover, many Irish women's novels, both in the early and late periods, are set outside Ireland, thus posing a challenge to the concept of Irishness as a territorially based or nationally defined identity. Though national themes will inevitably intrude, the emphasis in this study will be on gender, on the open-endedness of women's writing and the way it often asks more questions than it answers, refuses fixed gender roles and resists easy definitions of what a woman, or indeed an Irish person, might be. I make no claim to have uncovered a single female tradition: Irish women's fiction is too diverse for that and has suffered too much in the past from facile and limiting definitions, particularly around the Big House tradition to which Irish female novelists have often been confined.

Anne Fogarty has pointed to the way in which the increased visibility of women writers in general studies of Irish writing may in fact mask a lack of detailed attention to their work: 'the strategic use of work by contemporary women to generate a metacommentary about the present state of Irish society and of Irish fiction runs the risk of submerging it in a critical discourse that has recourse to abstract notions of the female artist but fails to accord serious, close attention to her individual productions.'[8] For this reason, and others outlined in the previous paragraph, I have decided to take these writers on their own terms and look at what they are actually writing about, rather than attempting to scrutinise their work for identifiable Irish themes. I am concerned above all within the parameters of a single volume, to draw an outline of Irish women's fiction from the nineteenth century onwards, the title 'Women's Fiction' allowing space for inclusion of writers who are routinely ignored in more general literary histories.

While believing it important to trace, where possible, connections between writers, and between writers and their times, I have resisted the temptation to corral them into any feminist grand narrative. Some of these writers have defined themselves as feminists, many of them definitely have not. Feminism itself is a politics that has altered over time and for that reason it is always important to attend to the historical and political context of women's writing: many of the New Woman writers would not be accepted as feminist in the contemporary sense. Equally, there are some writers discussed here who would reject the category 'woman writer', or indeed 'Irish writer', altogether. To these, and their shades, I apologise in advance for my 'strategic essentialism', to borrow Gayatri Spivak's phrase.[9] I understand that these writers may be writing as women only some of the time and as Irish women even less of the time.

There is another point to stress: the fact that I have chosen to deal with Irish women novelists as a separate group is simply a means to highlight their presence and establish a heritage. It should not in any way be taken to intend that I read their writing as a kind of supplement to the work of male novelists. Neither do I position their work as constituting an alternative counter-canon: Emer Nolan has a pertinent warning that the recovery of Irish women's writing does not necessarily produce a more subversive literary canon.[10] With the obvious exceptions of Maria Edgeworth and Sydney Owenson in the earlier period by and large, until the contemporary era, Irish women novelists tended to keep within the confines of the realist novel, adapted as needs be to include features of modernism, the Gothic, or satire. What makes their work interesting, original and sometimes radical is their use of the realist mode to explore women's lives and the female consciousness in a way that often implicitly and sometimes explicitly challenges the religious and political orthodoxies of their society. I believe that those interested in Irish writing have a right to hear these other voices. While Irish women's novels may not always be feminist, especially in the earlier period, they are of interest to the feminist critic because of their exploration of women's lives in all their complexity and contradictions.

For clarity the study is arranged chronologically rather than thematically. Where writers had long careers, as in the case of writers like Elizabeth Bowen and Kate O'Brien, for example, discussion of their work has necessarily extended over several chapters. This has the advantage of demonstrating the changing contexts in which they produced their fiction as well as facilitating comparisons with different kinds of authors in the course of their careers.

Naturally, a single volume study such as this cannot hope to be comprehensive. In order to keep within the limits, I have omitted, except in very rare cases, discussion of Irish women's short stories.[11] I have also omitted children's literature, an area in which the dominance of women writers is owed separate consideration.[12] As regards the novels, I have necessarily had to be selective, particularly in the earlier period. At the same time, I aim to cover as many women novelists as possible from the late nineteenth century onwards who have something of interest to say on gender and related issues. I have included discussion of single-book authors, vital in the case of women writers whose careers, especially in the mid-twentieth century, often suffered from domestic and other disruptions. In the case of very prolific novelists, usually from the earlier period, I have not attempted to survey the whole of their career but simply selected one or two of their better-known and more easily available novels in the hope that future scholars will take up the baton and look at their work in more depth than is possible here. Rather than provide premature conclusions, one of the main purposes of a general survey like this must be to open up areas of inquiry. It is my hope that on the foot of this study scholars will look again, not only at the still underresearched area of nineteenth-century women's fiction, but also at those twentieth-century authors like Julia O'Faolain, Pamela Hinkson, Kathleen Coyle, and Frances Molloy, whose work has undeservedly fallen out of critical discourse.

Where appropriate I have grouped together writers either born in Northern Ireland or whose work deals predominantly with that region. Novelists like Deirdre Madden whose work and themes are more wide-ranging have been taken out of that category altogether. I have also included discussion of popular novels often written in large numbers by women and a useful source of social commentary on women's lives. The aesthetic quality of these popular novels varies considerably but they frequently provide illuminating points of comparison with the major literary works. Women writers' use of popular genres does not necessarily go hand in hand with conservative views, particularly as regards the role of women. Naturally readers may disagree with the inclusion of particular novels under the heading 'popular'; in the end these kinds of judgement are subjective. More detailed examination of these secondary texts than I have been able to give here may yield further points of interest. Again, in this context, the study aims to open up rather than close down future discussion.

What I hope this study demonstrates is that, far from being identified with particular themes, the subject matter of Irish women's fiction is as diverse as that of their male counterparts. Some authors emphasise female experience and write about marriage, domesticity and motherhood. Others focus instead on politics, social problems, travel, art and a myriad other subjects. Above all, what interests me are the concrete circumstances of these writers' lives, where and why they began writing, how they went about getting published, what they conceived the writer's life to be. In other words, as Elizabeth Bowen puts it in 'Pictures and Conversations', the relationship between 'living and writing'.[13]

Chapter 1

THE NINETEENTH CENTURY: LITERARY FOREMOTHERS

MARIA EDGEWORTH

*M*aria Edgeworth (1767–1849) was the most influential Irish writer in the early decades of the nineteenth century and the best-known woman writer in Britain and Ireland, yet her writing life, like that of Jane Austen, took place in the family sitting room. One of the most vivid descriptions of Edgeworth's writing methods comes from the travel writer Anna Hall (1800–81). Hall explains that the library at Edgeworthstown was used as a general sitting room and Maria Edgeworth sat on a sofa in a corner of the room behind a small table constructed for her by her father on which rested a pen presented to her by Sir Walter Scott on his visit to Edgeworthstown in 1825. Edgeworth would occasionally interrupt her work to fetch a toy for one of her numerous half-siblings or to bring down a book that might explain a topic under discussion, before seamlessly resuming her writing: 'She had a singular power of abstraction, apparently hearing all that was said, and occasionally taking part in the conversation, while pursuing her own occupation, and seemingly attending only to it. In that corner, and on that table, she had written nearly all her works.'[1] This busy domestic scene is emblematic of many nineteenth-century Irish women writers' lives.

Maria Edgeworth was born on her mother's family estate in Oxfordshire. When she was six, her mother died and, after a brief sojourn in Ireland, she was sent away to boarding school in Derby. In 1781 she attended a school in London, staying with Thomas Day, a friend of her father, and learning at first hand Day's admiration for Jean Jacques Rousseau's views on women. In 1782, Sir Richard Lovell Edgeworth brought his family back to Ireland, determined to succeed as a reforming landlord. Now a teenager, Edgeworth moved to Ireland with her family and thereafter, apart from intermittent trips abroad, remained in the family circle at Edgeworthstown, County Longford, working with her father on educational treatises, educating some of his twenty-two children by his four wives and eventually taking over management of the estate. Together, father and daughter made Edgeworthstown a place of renown, as Hall noted in 1842: 'Edgeworthstown may almost be regarded as public property. From this mansion has emanated so much practical good to Ireland, and not alone to Ireland, but the civilised world.'[2] Nineteenth-century women's writing may dwell on the confinement of women to the domestic sphere but it is important to bear in mind what this domestic sphere actually comprised: among the upper classes in this period, household management involved overseeing a large staff and running what amounted to a small business. Edgeworth's emphasis on women's primary role as wives and mothers fits into the framework of the prevailing domestic ideology but, reflecting her own life, in her fiction this domestic space is often expanded to include a role in the management of estates.[3]

Notwithstanding her close collaboration with her father, the tendency in recent criticism on Edgeworth has been to downplay his influence on her writing life and to demonstrate the extent to which she sought advice on her writing from female friends and relatives.[4] In this context it is significant that her first published work, *Letters for Literary Ladies* (1795), defends women's right to education and training in rational thought against the ideas of Rousseau and of his disciple Thomas Day. Following Rousseau's ideas on female education expressed in *Émile* (1762), Day believed that women's essential nature was emotional rather than rational and that their education should focus on making them submissive and pleasing to men. Day expressed horror at Richard

Edgeworth's encouragement of his daughter's reading and of her ambitions to become a writer. Two of Edgeworth's *Letters* ventriloquise the arguments between Day and her father concerning women's education but the volume also contains 'An Essay on the Noble Science of Self-Justification', a brilliant parody of Rousseau's views on women expressed through an uncompromisingly subversive feminine voice and addressed to a female readership. Adopting the guise of an educational manual, the essay outlines the horrors of a marriage conducted along Rousseau's lines, employing irony, wit and false logic to subvert Rousseau's sentimentality about women. If *Letters for Literary Ladies* demonstrates the extent to which Edgeworth's feminism was moulded by her father's Enlightenment belief in the cultivation of reason in both sexes and in the advancement of society through education, this witty parody of Rousseau indicates that she was finding her own authorial voice. It is perhaps not too fanciful to trace a direct line from this subversive female voice protesting against Rousseau's treatment of women to the voice of the colonised subject, Thady, in Edgeworth's best-known work, *Castle Rackrent* (1800).[5]

Maria Edgeworth's career as a fiction writer, like that of Sydney Owenson discussed below, flourished in the period between the Act of Union (1801) and Catholic Emancipation (1829), a time when, as Clíona Ó Gallchoir has argued, both Irishness and femininity became unstable constructs.[6] This instability opened up an opportunity for the woman writer, and the tendency in recent criticism has been to emphasise the subversions latent in Edgeworth's work. In *Castle Rackrent*, she crosses gender, class and cultural boundaries to adopt the voice of a Catholic male servant, 'honest' Thady. Earlier readings of *Castle Rackrent* that interpreted it as the work of a conservative social thinker seeking the reformation of the landlord class rather than its overthrow had trouble accommodating the full impact of the story of the Rackrents' colonial misrule as told through the unreliable narrative voice of their servant, Thady, whose son, representative of the rising middle class, works successfully to usurp the Rackrents' land and power. The trend in recent criticism has been to highlight the text's ambivalences.[7] Despite his professed loyalty to the Rackrent family, 'honest' Thady's account of their doings reveals their greed, extravagance and incompetence as landlords and the text gives rise to more questions than answers. Is Thady a colonised servant or a disaffected Catholic in league with his son? To what extent is his role of faithful retainer a performance?

Not only the text but also the textual apparatus that surrounds it suggests Edgeworth's ambivalence over the Union and adds to the confusions over nation and identity inherent in the narrative. The editorial apparatus of glossary and footnotes composed by Edgeworth – in Marilyn Butler's words, the tone of 'the masculine Royal Academy style'[8] – attempts to control Thady's voice but ends up as another form of ventriloquism. In other words, this seemingly impersonal scholarly authority may too be read as a performance; it has, for example, many internal contradictions and is inconsistent in tone, being sometimes that of folklore collector, sometimes lofty commentator, sometimes comic.[9] In *Letters for Literary Ladies* Edgeworth used a subversive female voice to support her father's views on education; by contrast, taking text and textual apparatus together, *Castle Rackrent* suggests a daughter's ambivalence over whether her father's vision of an Ireland won over by reforming landlords will ever succeed.

In these interpretations, the reader is left to decide with whom the ultimate authority in *Castle Rackrent* rests, with Thady or the editor. Or does the meaning perhaps lie somewhere in between, in the cross-cultural dialogue itself? And is such a dialogue possible? Edgeworth's preface, written in collaboration with her father, endeavours to control interpretation of the novel by placing the action back in the eighteenth century of misrule and disorder in order to suppress the notion that present-day landlords may not be amenable to reform. The subtitle, *An Hibernian Tale taken from Facts and from the Manners of the Irish Squires before the Year 1782*, underlines this. But for all its attempts to control the meaning of the tale, the preface suggests that reconciliation between landlords and tenants may not easily be achieved: 'For the information of the IGNORANT English reader, a few notes have been subjoined by the editor, and he had it once in contemplation to translate the language of Thady into plain English; but Thady's idiom is incapable of translation.' A later admirer of Edgeworth's work, Edith Somerville, commented: 'The more Thady Quirk's memoirs are studied, the more remarkable as an achievement do they appear to be. The book is in a class by itself in originality of design, and – as far as any one save Thady Quirk himself can judge – in successful realisation of point of view.'[10] Thady's voice, attractive and subversive, was an important precursor for Somerville and Ross in their depictions of Irish life.

Attention to gender reveals further subversion concealed in the text. In her pioneering study of Irish women's writing, Ann Owens Weekes highlights the domestic plots of *Castle Rackrent*, overlooked by previous commentators but underlined in the preface which establishes the priority of personal, domestic narratives as sources of truth over public histories. Weekes points out that despite Thady's suppression of the wives' stories, there are opportunities for parallels to be drawn between the Rackrents as bad landlords and as bad husbands. Weekes sees Edgeworth in *Castle Rackrent* as reversing the conventional romance plot, namely the female quest for love that ends in marriage or death. The Rackrent wives' stories begin in marriage but end with their escape with their fortunes intact, having neglected their duty to provide a male heir.[11] Open-ended in many different ways, *Castle Rackrent*, like much later Irish women's fiction, evades the predictable closure of the romance plot.

Castle Rackrent is not as much of an anomaly in Edgeworth's *oeuvre* as it might appear. On the surface, Edgeworth's Irish tales – *Ennui* (1809), *The Absentee* (1812), *Ormond* (1817) – constitute an active intervention in the debate about Ireland's future, not in order to emphasise Ireland's difference but to stress the possibility of union between the two nations, based on the reform of Irish estates through the Anglo-Irish gentry coming to learn about Ireland and about their role in order to exercise responsible leadership. However, these seemingly didactic texts embody contradictory voices, at times insisting on essentialist national identities, at others undermining binary structures of thought to posit the fluidity and hence constructedness of national identity. In *The Absentee*, Lord Colambre's English education ensures that, despite his Irish birth and unlike his mother, he can pass in England as an English aristocrat. Similarly, in *Ormond*, Dora, an Irish Catholic, passes as a French woman of fashion and in *Ennui*, Lord Glenthorn, apparently the personification of an indifferent Anglo-Irish landlord, is revealed to be low-born and Catholic. Son of an Irish nurse, Ellinor, who swapped him at birth, unknowingly he has been masquerading as a landlord. The novel raises questions as to whether Glenthorn's decadence is the result of his Anglo-Irish upbringing or of his native birth. Conversely, the rightful landlord, Christy O'Donoghoe, is unable to keep up the performance of landlord and squanders his estate. Is this because of his peasant upbringing or because of his Anglo-Irish heredity? Such ambivalences raise questions in readers' minds about the notion of an essential Anglo-Irish identity and, with it, that class's mandate to rule.

At other times, Edgeworth's fiction, though always expressing her desire for reconciliation between the English and the Irish, hints at an innate Irish identity that is resistant to being absorbed into Englishness. In *Ennui*, this identity is seemingly so powerful that it causes Glenthorn in England to lapse into a serious depressive illness. In *Ormond*, the young Ormond before his Enlightenment education idolises Corny O'Shane who rules Black Islands as a Gaelic chieftain; later he learns to have more admiration for Herbert Annaly's modern and utilitarian estate management. Yet, as Vera Kreilkamp points out, it is Corny's Black Islands that Ormond purchases for the site of his future home, suggesting, despite his education, the persistence of Ormond's yearning for a romanticised Irish life and raising doubts in the reader's mind as to whether he will be able to impose a modern system of estate management on this feudal society.[12] Rather than any explicit questioning of the colonial system, Edgeworth's anxieties express themselves in such ambiguities and fractures in her narratives and in their open-endedness.[13]

In spite of herself, Edgeworth seems to recognise that Ireland is too disorderly and eccentric to be amenable to English reason and good sense, and that there is something attractive, even energising, in that difference. Sometimes that difference is embodied in Irish women like Lady Geraldine in *Ennui* or the wild Irish girl Dora O'Shane in *Ormond*, to whom the heroes are attracted before settling for more solidly Anglo-Irish alliances. Thus Edgeworth's sense of unease over the possibility of an easy alliance between the Irish and the English feeds into ambivalence about the romance plot. In *The Absentee*, Grace is connected through her mother to the French St Omars and a Catholic, Jacobite ancestry, and through her putative father to a Jacobite. She only becomes acceptable as wife of the Anglo-Irish Lord Colambre when she renounces her mother's potentially troubling ancestry and swaps her stepfather's surname, Nugent, with all its associations with dissident Irish nationalism, for the name of her newly discovered English father, Reynolds. Robert Tracy sees Edgeworth here, as elsewhere in these Irish tales, toying with Owenson's theme of an alliance between Anglo-Irish and ancient Irish Catholic families only to draw back from it.[14] Several critics have noted that if Grace's marriage to Colambre is intended as an allegory of the Act of Union, it is significant that what is supposed to be a sign of political resolution is portrayed in an ambivalent light, barely concealing the violence to women and to Ireland that lies beneath it.[15] Moreover, the promised romantic union never actually takes place within the novel, which is more open-ended than it appears, concluding only with the promise of marriage and the hope that Lord Colambre's return will lead to an amelioration in the lives of his tenants.

Edgeworth's novels not only express anxieties around nationality, they also challenge gender binaries: Lady Isabel's femininity in *The Absentee*, for example, underlines the potential instability of gender by highlighting its performative aspects. The overt message of the series of novels in Edgeworth's *Tales of Fashionable Life* is conservative: educate women to become more rational wives and mothers and domestic happiness, such as the eponymous heroine of *Belinda* (1801) finds in the Percival family, will follow. In this anti-Rousseau *Bildungsroman* centred on Belinda's quest to find a suitable husband amid the dangers of London's social scene, Belinda demonstrates, in the tradition of Enlightenment feminism, a prudence and a capacity for rational thought beyond her years.[16] She is confronted with several warning examples about appropriate feminine behaviour. Harriet Freke, who dresses in masculine clothes and runs around the countryside mouthing radical statements causing damage whenever she appears, is a 'dasher'.[17] With her revolutionary slogans, Harriet may have been intended as a parody of Mary Wollstonecraft's emphasis on the rights of women (as opposed to the duties stressed by Edgeworth), but she is not an authentic feminist in the Wollstonecraft mould: she cynically declares that all virtue is hypocrisy, emphasises physical freedom as opposed to intellectual equality and is ironically incapable of sustaining a reasoned argument with Mr Percival about equal rights. 'Freke' in 1800 meant whim or caprice and it is Harriet's recklessness and irrational behaviour that are emphasised. An opposing warning model for Belinda is Virginia St Pierre, whose dangerous innocence results from being raised by Clarence Hervey in seclusion from the world. Like his real-life model, Thomas Day, Hervey has been led astray by Rousseau's pronouncements on femininity and must learn to distinguish between innocence and ignorance.

Belinda's mentor, the fashionable and spirited Lady Delacour, is herself a warning to Belinda of the danger of seeking happiness in the social sphere rather than in the domestic circle. With her flirtations and her neglect of her daughter, Lady Delacour stands for much that Edgeworth abhorred. However, it is arguable that, like Thady in *Castle Rackrent*, Lady Delacour escapes authorial control. She emerges as the most vivid character in the novel and her lively speech patterns apparently reflected Edgeworth's own.[18] She is not killed off, as

Edgeworth originally intended. Instead, she orchestrates the final scene of the novel and is given the last word, drawing attention, as she has done at various points in the novel, to the fictive nature of the romance plot. Lady Delacour cannot easily be contained within the domestic ideology the novel apparently endorses and may be read as indicating Edgeworth's own ambivalence about that ideology: she recognised that Belinda's cautious adherence to domesticity had turned her into a dull character.[19] Such instability in the text reflects tensions between Edgeworth's support for a domestic role for women and her own entry into public life through her writing.

Edgeworth's work raises questions not only about nation and gender but about fiction-writing itself. Edgeworth was aware of the low intellectual status of the novel. Novel-reading had initially been forbidden by her father, under Thomas Day's influence, as liable to arouse dangerous emotions in a young girl, and it is significant that the wayward Julia in *Letters for Literary Ladies*, who is guilty of an excess of sensibility at the expense of sense, proclaims her enthusiasm for reading romances. Edgeworth was conscious of the need to defend her chosen form: her 'Advertisement' to *Belinda* is explicit in offering her novel to the public as 'a Moral tale – the author not wishing to acknowledge a Novel'. And a preface by Richard Edgeworth to the first volume of his daughter's *Tales of Fashionable Life* emphasises the didactic nature of these tales, 'intended to point out some of the errours to which the higher classes of society are disposed'.[20] By portraying Belinda as an example of how a rational woman ought to behave, Edgeworth was endeavouring to persuade her readers that the novel form was not simply an excuse for indulgence in sentiment, as in the romances Virginia and her mother read. In her hands the novel form was intended as a moral guide, extending her commitment to the role of educator exemplified in her children's stories and in the treatises on education written with her father. Challenging Rousseau's view of women, *Belinda* is intent both on raising the status of women to rational beings and the status of the novel form. But ambivalences remain. Edgeworth continually emphasises the fictive nature of *Belinda* and in the ending specifically draws attention to the romance plot's status as fiction. She seems to want it both ways: to write an engaging story at the same time as encouraging her readers to distrust romance.

The rise of Daniel O'Connell's radical, populist campaign to repeal the Union and deprive the gentry of their traditional leadership roles rendered

Edgeworth's novels about moderate reforming landlords politically irrelevant. She recognised, too, that the advent of a populist democracy would undermine the aristocratic woman's reforming social influence that features so strongly in her novels. Henceforward political representation in parliament would be the key to power and, since they were excluded from standing or even from voting, women lost all hope of direct political influence. In 1834, Edgeworth published *Helen*, her final, full-length work of fiction. Most critics have read this novel as a psychological portrait of the domestic life of the English aristocracy and gentry in which, perhaps influenced by Edgeworth's reliance on the support of her younger sisters and favourite aunt in writing it, the bonds between women and the dangers for women living in a patriarchal society are emphasised. Significantly, Helen's rescue at a moment of danger comes from Esther, a single woman living in Wales and thus financially and emotionally independent of men, inhabiting the margins of both English society and the patriarchy. In Clíona Ó Gallchoir's reading, the novel becomes something more: a recognition that in the 1830s the emerging Catholic nation was edging women out of political life and silencing women's public voice. In *Helen*, Lady Davenant retreats from exercising direct political influence into the role of a politician's supportive wife, and in a series of nervous fits her body registers physical symptoms of the mental cost of such a withdrawal.

Edgeworth's uncertainties over the novel form, ambivalence over the romance plot, and concern about the reduced role for women in the emerging Irish nation are all themes that will be picked up and developed subsequently by Irish women writers.

SYDNEY OWENSON

At first sight, the more lowly born Sydney Owenson, later Lady Morgan (?1776–1859), could not be more different from Edgeworth. Owenson defied the prevailing domestic ideology to position herself squarely in the public eye as a professional writer and her flamboyance contrasted sharply with Edgeworth's reserve. While Owenson wrote her memoirs, Edgeworth refused even to write prefaces for her books, arguing that her life, being wholly domestic, held nothing of interest for the reader. If Edgeworth's writing and philosophy of life grew out of her domestic circumstances and early collaboration with her father on educational treatises, Owenson had to fashion her own life and she did this not by emphasising Ireland's susceptibility to reform but by stressing Ireland's difference. Owenson herself had a divided heritage. Her actor-manager father, Robert Owenson, was an Irish Catholic who claimed kinship with the ancient tribes of Galway, whereas her mother was an English Protestant whose family had disapproved of the match. It was her father's love of Irish history and song, rather than her mother's hostility to the Irish, which influenced their daughter.

After his wife's death in 1789, Robert Owenson, who had made his name in England performing the stage Irishman, sought to keep his daughters away from the theatre. He sent Sydney and her younger sister Olivia to the fashionable Huguenot boarding school at Clontarf House where conversation was carried on in French. According to her highly romanticised memoirs, Owenson thrived at this school and her professional ambitions began early. It was while she was at another school, a less amenable Dublin finishing school, that she wrote to her recently bankrupt father explaining that she had nearly completed two novels, one set in France and one an imitation of Goethe's *Sorrows of Young Werther*: 'Now, if I had time and quiet to finish them, I am *sure* I could sell them; and observe, Sir, Miss Burney got three thousand pounds for *Camilla*.'[21] In contrast to the imperatives underpinning Edgeworth's writing life, Owenson justifies her fiction to her impecunious father not for its ethical or educational purpose but for its monetary value. In very different ways, therefore, both women's early writing life was shaped by their fathers' values. In her notebook, Owenson left a description of her working life which, like Edgeworth's, was carried out within the domestic circle, albeit one that was more democratised than Edgeworth's, in a lodging house amid servants performing domestic chores:

> We are seated at our little work-table, beside a cheerful turf fire, and a pair of lights; Livy [her younger sister] is amusing herself at work, and I have been reading a work of Schiller's to her, whilst Molly is washing up the tea-things in the background, and Peter is laying the cloth for his master's supper.[22]

Before finding success as a writer, Owenson was obliged to work as a governess in order to support her father and her sister. Governessing at that time was frequently little more than drudgery, and Owenson continued to be inspired by Fanny Burney's financial success as an author; however, on publication of her first novel, *St Clair: or, The Heiress of Desmond* (1802), she received in remuneration only four complimentary author's copies. She learned to be more proactive. In 1805, she took the ferry to Holyhead to present the manuscript of her next novel, *The Novice of St Dominic*, in person to her London publisher, Sir Richard Phillips. Phillips accepted the book after persuading Owenson to cut it down from six volumes to four. A letter dated October 1805 reveals Phillips's enthusiasm for works about Ireland but expresses doubts over Owenson's use of the novel form for purposes of instruction (and incidentally sheds light on Edgeworth's struggle to rehabilitate the form):

> The world is not informed about Ireland, and I am in a situation to command the *light* to shine! I am sorry you have assumed the novel form. A series of letters, addressed to a friend in London, taking for your model the Turkish letters of Lady M.W. Montagu, would have secured you the most extensive reading. A matter-of-fact and didactic novel is neither one thing nor another, and suits no class of readers.[23]

The letter goes on to show Phillips endeavouring to encourage this wilful novice to conform to the demands of the marketplace:

> I assure you that you have a power of writing, a fancy, an imagination, and a degree of enthusiasm which will enable you to produce an immortal work, if you will *labour it* sufficiently. Write only on one side of your paper and retain a broad margin; your power of improving your first draught will thus be greatly increased.[24]

A model of tact, he adds that her second and third drafts will be greatly improved by this method too. Having met the author, Phillips shows some insight into her character when he insists that while 'this drudgery' may be 'painful to endure for a few weeks ... you will reap a harvest, for years, of renown and fortune'.[25] If Owenson did not have a Richard Edgeworth to oversee her first literary efforts, she at least had a perceptive publisher.

Encouraged by Phillips, Owenson embarked on research for the work that was to make her name, *The Wild Irish Girl: A National Tale* (1806). By this time she had become more adept at dealing with publishers, pitting Phillips against a rival publisher and forcing him to increase his price for *The Wild Irish Girl* from two hundred and fifty pounds to three hundred. Nor was she above changing publishers when offered a better deal. Even after her marriage to Charles Morgan, the family surgeon of her aristocratic patrons, the Abercorns, Owenson was careful to retain control of her earnings, which were about five thousand pounds at the time of her marriage.

Owenson is often described as the first professional Irish woman writer.[26] This came at a price: by entering public life, she was perceived to pose a threat to the prevailing ideology that confined women to the home. John Wilson Croker, writing in *The Freeman's Journal* (15 December 1806), specifically related his criticism of Owenson to her trespass into the public domain. A writer who earns her living by her pen, he argued, lays herself open to attack in a way she would not have done if she had had her work privately printed and circulated. Owenson had her revenge: in *Florence Macarthy: An Irish Tale* (1818), Croker is portrayed in the thinly disguised Conway Crawley, a land agent's son. Crawley's remarks about Florence Macarthy's writing are taken word for word from Croker's description of Owenson in the *Quarterly Review* as 'a mere bookseller's drudge'. In the novel, Crawley is accused by General Fitzwalter of unmanliness: 'are you applying such language to a *woman*?'[27] With a sleight of hand, Owenson manages both to play the gender card *and* claim equality in the male terrain of writing. The *Quarterly Review* and other journals continued to attack Owenson's work and she continued to respond by appealing over the heads of the professional critics to the general public. Such behaviour was highly unusual for a woman writer in this period and earned from her fellow countrywoman and Catholic novelist Julia Kavanagh the label 'aggressive'.[28] Nonetheless, in 1837, in recognition of her status as a professional writer, Owenson became the first woman to receive a literary pension from the British government, of three hundred pounds a year. Two years later, she published a feminist history, *Woman and Her Master*, with the aim of demonstrating that women are spiritually superior to men.

As a professional writer, Owenson crossed boundaries of class and gender, but this was not the only public role she embraced. Ironically, in view of her father's wish to keep her away from the stage, after the huge success of *The Wild Irish Girl* Owenson found acceptance in fashionable London circles by performing the part of her own heroine, the princess Glorvina.[29] Owenson's impersonation of a wild Irish girl had mixed results: like Edna O'Brien later, her identity as a writer became caught up in the publicity surrounding her novels. Owenson was well aware of the dangers of being turned into a reductive artefact for an English audience. In *Florence Macarthy*, her novelist heroine admits: 'With Ireland in my heart, and epitomising something of her humour and her sufferings in my own character and story, I *do* trade upon the material she furnishes me; and turning my patriotism into pounds, shilling and pence, endeavour, at the same moment, to serve her and support myself.'[30] Owenson was conscious of the moral ambiguity of making monetary use of her country's plight, an ambiguity she attempted to assuage by taking up spinning along with her writing, since spinning could more easily be linked to a female and Irish heritage.[31] Despite this, Owenson remained, like her novelist heroine and foreshadowing the New Woman writer at the end of the century, a subversive figure, destabilising her society's notions of the proper – that is domestic – sphere for women.

The Wild Irish Girl fulfilled Owenson's dreams of commercial success, running to nine editions in England and America in its first two years. Through her portrayal of Glorvina, the Irish princess, Owenson retrieved ancient Gaelic history and culture in a bid to establish Ireland's identity as Gaelic and Catholic at a time when that identity seemed in danger of being obliterated by the Act of Union. Glorvina is presented as an amalgam of nature – formed by the sublime Irish wilderness in which she has been raised – and of culture (she has been educated by Father John in the 'male' subjects of philosophy, science, history, Latin and Greek). Owenson expands the possibilities of womanhood beyond the confines of the domestic as her heroine performs the role of instructor, tutoring the English visitor Horatio in Irish language, culture and history so that he comes to acknowledge Ireland's separate national identity.

Drawing heavily on the work of the antiquarians of the late eighteenth-century Celtic Revival referenced in the copious footnotes to *The Wild Irish Girl*, Owenson makes a virtue of Ireland's otherness to England, exploring its sublime landscape, customs, folklore, history and language. Like Edgeworth in *Castle Rackrent*, Owenson employs scholarly apparatus to explain Irish culture to her English readers, at the same time shoring up, through quotations of mainly male sources, her version of Irish identity and her own authority to describe it. However, whereas the scholarly apparatus in *Castle Rackrent* provides a gloss on Thady's tale that sometimes undermines it, in *The Wild Irish Girl* the footnotes invariably support the claims of Glorvina and her father, the Prince of Inismore.[32] Indeed, so attractive was the picture of Gaelic culture painted through the words of Owenson's heroine that Dublin Castle officials feared its influence. Not without cause: the book sparked a media frenzy of a sort that today's authors of Irish chick lit would envy as Anglo-Irish ladies began buying harps, wearing Glorvina brooches and sporting Glorvina hairstyles.[33]

As in Maria Edgeworth's fiction, in *The Wild Irish Girl* the English visitors to Ireland, Horatio and his father, Lord M, are taught their duties as landlords, and the hoped-for reconciliation between the Gaelic and Anglo worlds that the Act of Union was supposed to bring about is signalled by a marriage. But Owenson's emphasis is very different from Edgeworth's imposition of enlightened management on Ireland: not only has Horatio to give up his prejudices about Ireland, he has to recognise his own otherness in Ireland, excluded as he is by the language and lack of knowledge of the culture and traditions. Union between himself and Glorvina can take place, not by Ireland becoming more enlightened, as in Edgeworth's fiction, but by both sides, the Prince of Inismore and Horatio and his father, acknowledging their differences and prejudices, as Lord M's final letter makes clear. In this letter, Lord M envisions that the alliance of Horatio and Glorvina will overcome 'national and hereditary prejudice', putting an end to 'the distinctions of English and Irish, of protestant and catholic … with hope to this family alliance being prophetically typical of a national unity of interests and affections'.[34] This conclusion rests awkwardly, however, with the entire thrust of the rest of Owenson's novel which has been not to underline similarities between Ireland and England but to point out their differences. Derek Hand has noted that national difference surfaces later in the letter when Lord M quotes Robert Emmet on his hopes for 'the day-star of national virtue' to rise again, suggesting that nationalism not union is the future for Ireland.[35] Dublin Castle was right to be worried. Owenson's national tale making ancient Gaelic history and culture the origin of Irish identity reinforced the idea of an essential Irishness, one that excluded both the Anglo-Irish and Ulster Protestants.

Sir Richard Edgeworth wrote to Owenson to congratulate her on *The Wild Irish Girl*, praising 'the just character which you have given to the lower Irish' as well as her skilful incorporation of passages of Irish history, 'related in such a manner as to induce belief amongst infidels'. He added some oblique criticism of her florid style: 'Maria, who reads (it is said) as well as she writes, has entertained us with several passages from *The Wild Irish Girl*, which I thought superior to any parts of the book which I had read. Upon looking over her shoulder, I found she had omitted some superfluous epithets.'[36] Rather rashly, Sir Richard suggests that, had Owenson been present, she would have agreed with his daughter's omissions.

It was not just Owenson's style Maria Edgeworth objected to. In contrast to Owenson's defiant positioning of Irishness and femininity at the centre of her work, Edgeworth played down her nationality and her gender in order to avoid marginalisation (and in doing so, attracted less criticism from the male literary establishment). Her correspondence records her hostile reaction to Owenson's portrait of the successful woman writer in *Florence Macarthy*:

> My general feelings in closing this book are shame and disgust – and the wish never more to be classed with *novel* writers when the highest talents in that line have been so disgraced.
>
> Oh that I could prevent people from ever naming me along with her – either for praise or blame – Comparisons are indeed odious – God forbid as my dear father said I should ever be such a thing as that –
>
> It was for want of such a father she has come to this.[37]

Edgeworth implies that Owenson badly lacked the training in the Enlightenment principles of order and rationality that she received from her own father. Fluidity of identity is the hallmark of Owenson's Florence Macarthy, her very name signalling uncertainty over gender since it is also her father's name. Like Glorvina, Florence is educated in 'male' subjects, philosophy, science, history, Latin and Greek, but she is of more fluid nationality than Glorvina, being of Spanish-Irish parentage and possessing several different names including one, Lady Clancare, which links her to fashionable metropolitan life. She appears frequently in disguise, her fluidity connected in the novel to the ever-changing Irish scene, as she confesses:

> I sometimes almost lose my own identity for I am absolutely beyond my own control, and the mere creature of circumstances, giving out properties of certain plants, according to the region in which I am placed ... The strong extremes and wild vicissitudes of my life have perhaps given a variegated tone to my character, and a versatility to my mind, not its natural endowments.[38]

Fluidity of identity is a strand that runs through Irish women's writing: Somerville and Ross remembered the name of Owenson's heroine and in their *Irish RM* series made it masculine again when they gave it to the chameleon-like trickster, Flurry McCarthy Knox, whose identity, like that of Owenson's Florence, straddles several cultural divisions. It may have been this romantic changeability that aroused Edgeworth's hostility yet we have seen that themes around fluid identities are not absent from her own work and this poses the question: are these two influential literary foremothers, Edgeworth and Owenson, so far apart? Attention to the gender politics in their work suggests Edgeworth's interconnectedness with Owenson, a writer with whom she would otherwise seem to have little in common. Like Grace Nugent in *The Absentee*, Glorvina is contained by a marriage which acts as a sign of political resolution but does not erase the reader's sense of unease over the fact that in order for the marriage to Horatio to take place, Glorvina has to forgive her family's murderers. Both Edgeworth and Owenson use the romance plot in an effort to close down contradictions and conflicts in the Irish situation that their work has exposed, but the doubts, ambiguities and intractability inherent in the political situation remain.[39]

Though it engages with the romance plot, *The Wild Irish Girl* suggests an Edgeworthian distrust of romantic fiction. Eager to advance Glorvina's sentimental education, Horatio lends her romances like Rousseau's *Julie; or the New Héloïse* (1761). She devours them with an eagerness that leads Horatio to wonder whether their influence has been too extreme and to worry that this romance reading may arouse in her sentimental feelings for other men. Like Edgeworth, Owenson betrays anxiety over her chosen fictional form, employing the label 'national tale' to describe *The Wild Irish Girl* in order to underline the didactic element and distance herself from a straightforward romance. Some of the didactic material in the lengthy footnotes to *The Wild Irish Girl* leaks into the text so that the book becomes an unstable mixture of fiction and essay that further indicates a lack of trust in fiction adequately to represent Irish national identity.

Like Edgeworth, Owenson lived long enough to see her vision for Ireland overtaken by political events. The Morgans' house on Kildare Street had been an important meeting place for Catholic and liberal Protestant groups but, like Edgeworth, Owenson regarded Daniel O'Connell as a dangerous demagogue and believed her vision of an Ireland revived by an ancient Catholic gentry in alliance with the Protestant aristocracy had been debased into the revolutionary hopes of the general populace. *The O'Briens and the O'Flahertys: A National Tale* (1829) expresses something of Owenson's disillusionment. From 1837 onwards she lived in London, silenced as much as Edgeworth by the conditions of Irish life and by the newly emerging bourgeois Catholic nation. In contrast to the weary note sounded in Edgeworth's famous 1834 letter to her brother on the condition of Ireland, Owenson's farewell to Ireland in her diary is couched in characteristically aggressive tones: 'You have always slighted, and often persecuted me, yet I worked in your cause, humbly, but earnestly. Catholic Emancipation is carried! It was an indispensable act – of what results, you fickle Irish will prove in the end.'[40]

The work of these two literary foremothers, Edgeworth and Owenson, exposes flaw lines in their age's conceptions of nation and gender and, despite attempts at reconciliation, what their fiction leaves us with are fissures and ambiguities. Fluidity around gender, a critique of limiting definitions of nationhood and the novel's resistance to closure are all themes that will be picked up by later generations of Irish women writers.

POPULAR NOVELISTS

The Writing Life

As the life of Sydney Owenson reveals, it took a degree of determination for a young Irish woman in the nineteenth century to become a published author. Charlotte Riddell (1832–1906), born Charlotte Cowan in Carrickfergus,

County Antrim, moved to London in 1855 with her widowed mother to try to establish herself as a writer. She recounted her experiences in an interview for Helen Black's *Notable Women Authors of the Day*:

> We did not know a single creature! During the first fortnight, indeed, I really thought I should break my heart. I had never taken kindly to new places, and, remembering the sweet hamlet and the loving friends left behind, London seemed to me horrible! I could not eat; I could not sleep; I could only walk over the 'stony-hearted streets' and offer my manuscripts to publisher after publisher, who unanimously declined them.[41]

Riddell's semi-autobiographical novel *A Struggle for Fame* (1883) echoes this description of the difficulties faced by Irish women writers in nineteenth-century London. The family estate in Ulster having been lost, Glenarva moves to London and resolves to earn money to support herself and her father by publishing a three-volume novel. Glenarva's ignorance of the publishing world – 'She did not know how books were printed or published. She had not met an author; more, she was not acquainted with any person who ever had met one'[42] – allows Riddell to introduce the neophyte reader to the vicissitudes of a nineteenth-century novelist's life. Glenarva's story is paralleled with that of Barney Kelly, a more knowing and worldly-wise Irishman who negotiates his way around 1850s literary London with greater ease. Business, money, property and class are Riddell's recurring preoccupations as a novelist and, by the end of *A Struggle for Fame*, the reader has learned a good deal about the literary and publishing world of nineteenth-century London, masculine condescension towards female authors, the rapid changes in literary fashions, the unreliability of publishers and the perseverance needed to establish oneself as an author. Glen discovers that there is little demand at this period, just after the Great Famine, for books with an Irish flavour and despite the fact that she wishes to be an Irish author, she is obliged to set her novels in England.[43] Nevertheless, though she transposes her fiction to Yorkshire to suit her publishers' requirements, Riddell's heroine never forgets that she is an Irish woman.

Although she published some forty novels and seven short story collections, apart from one short-lived period in the mid-1860s Riddell never earned a lot of money from her writing and what money she made usually went to pay off her husband's debts. After the latter's death she did not remarry and the widowed Glenarva's refusal of Ned's marriage proposal in *A Struggle for Fame* has been read as a sign that Riddell felt domestic life to be incompatible with sustained literary achievement.[44] In an article full of fascinating details about the historical context of Riddell's publishing career, Margaret Kelleher outlines her battles with a series of publishers, her short-lived period of fame and her decline into poverty. Kelleher observes:

> In the very last years of her career, as efforts were made by some fellow authors to secure for her some financial support from the Society of Authors and from the Royal Literary Fund, she was to acquire a curiously representative status as an author who had temporarily achieved success in the literary marketplace but was now marginalised by changing trends.[45]

A major stumbling block to becoming an author was that an Irish girl born in the mid-nineteenth century, even to a relatively well-off family, could expect little in the way of education. Augusta Gregory describes being taught by 'a procession of amiable incompetent governesses' but only music, French and scripture since her mother 'did not consider book learning as of any great benefit to girls ... Religion, courtesy, and holding themselves straight, these were to her mind the three things needful'.[46] The lack of sympathy displayed by Gregory's mother towards her daughter's desire for education was not unusual at the time and it cut through boundaries of class and religion. Katharine Tynan (1861–1931), born into a literary Catholic bourgeois household, learned early on to separate herself from the domestic-bound life of her mother absorbed in raising eleven children. Whereas Tynan's mother often censored her reading, it was her father, an affluent gentleman farmer, who brought books into the house and encouraged her to read widely. 'I look back on those years as a series of encounters in which I fought for reading and my mother, at times, frustrated me. She thought my prayers should be a satisfactory substitute for my reading.'[47] Tynan read Maria Edgeworth, Jane Austen and Fanny Trollope, as well as penny story-papers. She spent three years at the Sienna Convent, Drogheda, where she found the reading matter disappointingly limited to spiritual works, before being withdrawn at the age of fourteen to become her father's companion, and accompanying him often to the theatre. Her early reading was influenced by her father's romantic nationalism, and before her marriage and relocation to England she was very much part of the beginning of the Irish Literary Revival through her friendship with W.B. Yeats.

Though her father disapproved of his daughters earning money, in recognition of her talent he allowed Tynan a room of her own in the family home where she could write and receive friends. Tynan's literary earnings gave her independence and the opportunity to travel and she was able to establish social and literary contacts in London even before her marriage in 1893 to Henry Hinkson, a Protestant Irishman. Tynan became a hugely popular author in a career spanning from 1885 to her death in 1931. As well as poetry, anthologies, autobiography and journalism, she published over a hundred novels. Though enjoying her life as wife and mother to her three children, and insisting that women's primary duties lay in the home, she also, exceptionally for the time, took on the role of family breadwinner, earning prior to the First World War a good salary from her novels and her journalism. Some idea of her industry is gleaned from her memoirs:

> I had a prodigiously industrious winter and spring, 1892–93, writing all manner of things, increasing my already large correspondence, for ever striking out in new directions, writing in new places, making new friends. I was writing for the *Speaker*, the *National Observer*, the *British Weekly*, *Good Words*, the *Magazine of Arts*, *Atalanta*, the *Woman's World* (of which Oscar Wilde was editor), *Sylvia's Journal* … besides my American, Catholic, and Irish papers and magazines.[48]

Such industry was by no means unusual among nineteenth-century women writers of popular fiction, and Tynan is characteristic of many women writers of this period who, through choice or circumstances, embraced elements of what might be classed as feminism in their lives while remaining wedded to conventional views on women's role as wife and mother.[49]

Feminist?

As always in the nineteenth century there is a problem of how to define feminism. Is the simple act of taking up one's pen sufficient to be regarded as a feminist? Writers like Selina Bunbury (1802–82) began their careers producing anonymous religious tracts before progressing to publishing proselytising fiction. As Heidi Hansson has argued, this association with religious works sanctioned women's entry into the marketplace but also limited their subject matter.[50] The life of Marguerite Power (1789–1849), later Lady Blessington, contravened the prescribed sexual morality for women and from 1830 she supported herself and her family through her writing but in her novels written for a mass readership she does not seriously challenge the gender roles of the day, though her running subject of women unjustly ostracised by society does form some sort of protest. Lady Oriel in Blessington's *Grace Cassidy; or, The Repealers* (1833) is one such example, another is Clara Mordaunt in *The Governess* (1839), a novel that inaugurated the theme of the exploitation (and also sexual vulnerability) of governesses which was to be picked up later by writers such as Hannah Lynch, Maura Laverty and Kate O'Brien.[51] How to categorise Cork-born author Margaret Hungerford (1855–97), who gained an international reputation with an astonishing number of romantic novels set in fashionable society? After her second marriage, Hungerford settled in Bandon and some of her novels, including her best-known work, *Molly Bawn* (1878), have Irish settings. Hungerford approached her novel-writing as a professional, allotting three hours every morning and often writing to commission, but her light romantic fiction is careful not to contravene the boundaries of Victorian femininity even in a novel like *Lady Verner's Flight* (1893) where she toys with such New Woman themes as divorce, domestic violence and women's work.[52]

Yet, as we saw in the case of Edgeworth whose fiction on the surface endorses the domestic ideology of her times, by setting aside contemporary definitions of feminism and paying attention instead to the social and political context of nineteenth-century women's novels more complex attitudes to gender may be detected. Women in the nineteenth century wrote popular fiction in a wide variety of genres – melodrama, sensation, romance, history, evangelicalism, silver fork – consequently the reader finds gender themes in unexpected places. Women's retrospective accounts of the famines of the 1840s, for example, are often fruitful sources of gender observations, as Margaret Kelleher has pointed out.[53] Margaret Brew's (fl 1880–86) Catholic-inflected *The Chronicles of Castle Cloyne* (1886) finds space in its panoramic view of Irish society during the Famine for several meditations on the lives of single women. These range from Grace, plain and fragile daughter of the Catholic Dillons of Castle Cloyne, to women obliged by economic circumstances to earn their own living, such as the English Catholic Sydney Dacre, who works as a governess in London, and Oonagh MacDermott, an Irish peasant woman, who after the loss of the family farm finds employment as a dairy maid and then as a pedlar. The lives of these single women come to constitute an alternative mindset that pits Catholic values of duty and fidelity and honesty against a greedy and self-seeking world. The narrator comments:

> There are many women in the world like Oonagh … although the world knows them not. It does not sound their praises, nor glorify them, nor does it, in fact, notice them at all, because it cannot understand them. This is in no way strange. Their forgetfulness of self, their fidelity to duty, their untiring devotion … are all silent though emphatic protests against the hollowness and self-seeking of its creed. The world utterly ignores such women while they live, and forgets them when the grave has closed over them.[54]

The novels of Tipperary-born Julia Kavanagh (1824–77), set abroad in London, France and Italy, are similarly at pains to portray the Catholicism of her independent-minded heroines like Rachel Gray (*Rachel Gray*, 1856) as a solace in their lonely, disregarded lives, much as later, Agnes in Kate O'Brien's *The Ante-Room* finds religion a support in a time of crisis.[55] Though Irish women writers were subsequently to submit Catholicism to a rigorous critique, in the case of nineteenth-century women, the importance of religion as a source of personal comfort in a masculinist world and its power to provide an alternative discourse should not be underestimated.[56]

In the popular Victorian novel, philanthropy is often upper-class women's substitute for direct political action. In *Castle Daly* (1875) by Annie Keary (1825–79), the work done by Cousin Anne and Ellen Daly among the poor inevitably brings them into conflict with the agent at Castle Daly and such tensions reveal the potential for a clash between female reforming instincts and masculinist politics. *Castle Daly* depicts philanthropy as providing a bond of sympathy and emotional support between Anne and Bride, two single women of very differing political views, and giving them the opportunity to lead larger lives than might otherwise be possible in a society organised around heterosexual marriage. For reasons such as these, the philanthropic novel is sometimes regarded as a forerunner of New Woman fiction, with philanthropy taking the place of the New Woman's career.[57] In famine and land-war fiction, however, women's efforts were liable, like those of Anne and Ellen, to be cut short by political events. In Letitia McClintock's (fl 1857–81) *A Boycotted Household* (1881), Ellen Hamilton's classes and cottage visits are halted on the orders of her father, who fears the dangerous state of the roads during the land league campaigns. On the other hand, in Elizabeth Hely Walshe's (1835–69) *Golden Hills: A Tale of the Irish Famine* (1865), published by the Religious Tract Society in London, Lina's school for poor children prospers during the Famine years due to the fact that she gives them breakfast, and the embroidery skills she instils in the local girls provide their families' only source of support. Yet Walshe's novel is by no means on the side of social reform: Lina's philanthropy is set squarely within her evangelical Christian beliefs and her acceptance of women's intellectual inferiority.

Rosa Mulholland

Rosa Mulholland (1841–1921) was part of a group of upper middle-class Catholic, mainly female, novelists associated with the Dublin-based *Irish Monthly* founded in 1873 by the Jesuit Matthew Russell, with the specific intention of countering English publishing influence by serialising Catholic fiction set in Ireland. In certain of these female novelists, as James H. Murphy has shown, the unstable political situation in Ireland during the land war becomes entangled with issues of gender.[58] His classic example is Mulholland's novel *Marcella Grace*, serialised in the *Irish Monthly* in 1885 and published in book form in 1886.

Mulholland was the daughter of a Belfast physician whose family identified themselves as Irish and Catholic and yet believed in the international advantages gained by the union with England. She became Lady Gilbert when her husband was knighted in 1897. Katharine Tynan got to know Mulholland before her marriage when Mulholland was living with an aunt in Sherrard Street, north Dublin. Tynan, then only at the start of her career, was in awe of her friend, who had been praised and published by Dickens and who in her initial career as a painter had attracted the attention of Millais.[59] Tynan describes how Mulholland established a room of her own in her aunt's house as a kind of religious retreat and set a strict rule of life for herself, even foregoing dancing, which she loved, because the archbishop forbade it. Mulholland was tempted by convent life and Tynan describes a trip they made to Tipperary in the spring of 1888 when Mulholland turned their hotel room into a nun's cell with sacred picture and votive lamp. 'No nun could have been half so much afraid of passion as she was … She was absurdly, embarrassingly innocent,' comments Tynan.[60] In Tynan's opinion, marriage in 1890 to Sir John Gilbert, a historian and scholar, came too late to uncramp Mulholland's life: this middle-aged marriage, founded on a mutuality of intellectual interests, was childless.

In *Marcella Grace*, Marcella, daughter of a poor Dublin weaver, inherits estates in the west of Ireland from a wealthy relative, Mrs O'Kelly. In contrast to Mrs O'Kelly's absenteeism, Marcella's upbringing in poverty has equipped her to understand her tenants' needs and she is determined to be a good landlord. Yet what the novel depicts is benevolent paternalism, Marcella lavishing kindness on her tenants as if they were her children. The tenor of the novel is in keeping with Mulholland's desire for the Protestant Ascendancy to be replaced by benevolent Catholic landlords whose tie to the peasants through religion would, she hoped, calm disturbances in the countryside and lead to peaceful co-existence between landlords and tenants. Marcella stabilises the situation but because this novel is a romance, equal time is taken up with the heroine's romantic involvement with her Fenian neighbour, Bryan Kilmartin, whom she eventually marries and to whose authority she submits. It seems that female authority is allowed exceptionally in times of social instability but when order returns so does the patriarchy. James Murphy comments: 'Ultimately, Mulholland's protofeminist inclinations are always sacrificed to the interests of her class agenda.'[61] Nevertheless, Mulholland's stories for girls are full of independent-minded young women like Tabby, the half-Irish heroine of *A Girl's Ideal* (1905), who uses her unexpected inheritance to revive her ancestors' weaving factory in Dublin. Though the romance plot is also in evidence, it is impossible to calculate the influence on Mulholland's young readers of depicting a world of work with a woman in charge, employing other women (and some men) and, in the traditions of nineteenth-century philanthropy, ensuring good conditions for her workers.

M.E. Francis

Another novelist associated with the *Irish Monthly* was M.E. Francis (1859–1930), a pen name devised by Mary E. Sweetman from her own initials and the first name of her husband, Francis Blundell. Sweetman was born into a Catholic landowning family near Dublin. The Sweetmans were a literary family, and her brother and two of her sisters were writers. Her account of their early life, *The Things of a Child* (1918), corroborates many of the features of a Big House upbringing found in later fiction writers. In the large, rambling house, the nursery quarters were separate from the main part of the house and nursery food was plain in the extreme: bread and milk or stirabout for breakfast and supper, roast mutton and plain pudding for dinner at two, milk and bread and butter at five. 'Sweets and cakes were practically unknown.'[62] This kind of food was later to feature in Molly Keane's *Good Behaviour*. Occasionally the Sweetmans' mother would send up a note to the nursery to invite her children to tea in the library at five when they were expected to wear their best clothes. Education for the four girls of the family was a succession of governesses followed by a spell in a convent school in Dublin modelled on a French order. Their mother became so shocked by their underfed appearance, their bad French and shocking brogue that she took them away. After more governesses, Francis's education was finished off in convents in Brussels (an experience on which she draws in *Miss Erin*) and Switzerland, followed by her marriage into English Catholic gentry and relocation to Lancashire.

Francis began publishing in England in 1884 after her husband's death and became one of the best-known women novelists of her day. Though she can hardly be classed as a New Woman novelist due to the explicitly Catholic and moralising tone of her novels (indeed contemporary reviewers contrasted her novels favourably with the more provocative work of the New Woman writers), many of Francis's works are dedicated to women and feature female protagonists.

Miss Erin (1898), an allegory of relations between Ireland and England, is part of the attempt by Catholic novelists associated with the *Irish Monthly* to adjust to a more nationalist Ireland. Erin Fitzgerald is the daughter of an Irish peasant girl and an Irish patriot from the gentry class exiled to America after the 1848 rebellion. Orphaned, Erin is brought back to Ireland, taken in initially by the Nolans, an Irish peasant family, and then, like Owenson's Glorvina but unusually for a woman of this period, educated in the classics by her uncle, Louis Fitzgerald of Glenmor, and in Irish history by the local Catholic priest. Her uncle's eviction of the Nolans for non-payment of rent politicises Erin and she grows up to become an Irish patriot, working to help evicted tenants, publishing patriotic poetry, and maintaining her Irish patriotism and loyalty to the Irish peasant class even after she falls in love with Mark Wimbourne, an English Tory MP opposed to home rule. The middle section of the novel is set outside Ireland, in Brussels and in Lancashire where Erin stays at the home of her best friend, Joan and there are some Edgeworthian contrasts between the relationship of landlords and tenants in England and those in Ireland. In *The Things of a Child*, Francis admits to having been greatly influenced by Maria Edgeworth's writings, though her novel moves away from Edgeworth's Anglo-Irish landlord to an alignment of the Catholic upper middle class with the nationalist cause.

If Erin's politics challenge those of her class, her behaviour subverts gender expectations and here the romance plot, which generally requires female submission, conflicts with the national tale.[63] Erin's 'unfeminine' behaviour in leading the tenants' fight against evictions, justified, as in Mulholland's *Marcella Grace*, by the extremity of the Irish political situation, offends Mark, who dislikes hearing women express political sentiments. Conversely, Erin cannot accept Mark's views on Ireland nor his commitment to fight the election on an anti-home rule ticket. The dilemma between them is resolved by their mutual failures: Erin has her first taste of violence and is repulsed, while Mark fails to get elected. If the romance plot is finally resolved by Mark consenting to live in Ireland while Erin agrees to tone down her political commitment, the nationalist tale remains unresolved since Mark, like all of Erin's English friends, remains unconvinced by her work for the nationalist cause. *Miss Erin* is one of those nineteenth-century texts by Irish women that, as Heidi Hansson has argued, resist neat political categorisation.

May Laffan Hartley

In contrast to the Catholic agenda of writers associated with the *Irish Monthly*, the novels of May Laffan Hartley (1849–1916) satirise the gaucherie of the rising Catholic middle classes. Laffan was born in Dublin into a mixed marriage, her father a Catholic, her mother a Protestant from higher up the social scale. Laffan herself went on to marry a Protestant, Walter Hartley, lecturer at King's College, London and later at the Royal College of Science in Dublin, and mixed marriages are a constant theme in her work.

Laffan's most successful novel, *Hogan, MP* (1876), published anonymously, is a portrait of the Catholic middle classes in the aftermath of the Catholic Emancipation Act and has points of comparison with the novels of Kate O'Brien. Like O'Brien's *The Land of Spices*, *Hogan, MP* opens in a Dublin convent school and portrays a similar mixture of snobbery and triviality among the girls. The novel has some interesting comments on the lives of Irish Catholic women, particularly about the drawbacks of convent schools educating their girls simply for marriage in contrast with Protestant schools which pursue a more rigorous curriculum. Laffan had attended Sion Hill convent school and felt herself to be under-educated.[64] Fannie Gallaher (fl. 1880–88) was to make a similar point in *Thy Name is Truth* (1884) where Gallaher is a passionate advocate for high educational standards for girls, sending her heroine, Aileen, to Pallas College (Alexandra College) and wishing there were comparable institutions for Roman Catholic girls.

Many of the ideas about female education expressed in *Hogan, MP* come straight from the pages of Mary Wollstonecraft, and Laffan puts into the eponymous Hogan's mouth Wollstonecraft's endorsement of co-education. The professional woman writer makes a brief appearance in the shape of a certain Mrs Stryper, who is said to be earning good money from her novels (the sum of one thousand pounds is mentioned). Drawing on Laffan's own experience, the portrait of Nellie Davoren gives a glimpse into the social life of a middle-class Catholic daughter at home, revolving around church, dances, Sunday walks, lectures and the theatre. However the novel's main focus is not on women but on the Faustian tale of Hogan's efforts to get elected MP for Peatstown (Tipperary) on a home rule platform.

Education is a theme that runs through Laffan's later novels. Lacking funds to pay for private education and despising the local national school, Helena Ferrard's father, Lord Darraghmore, in *The Honourable Miss Ferrard* (1877) has allowed his unruly offspring to run wild. Various attempts are made to educate Helena – by her aunts in Bath and by the wealthy Englishman John Satterthwaite, who regards it as his mission to civilise the Irish. None of these efforts make much headway until the wild Anglo-Irish girl is tamed by Jim Devereux, a local Catholic farmer. Within the framework of the romance plot, social and political questions about Ireland are debated, particularly around Laffan's perennial interests of education and class. The vulgarity and pretensions of the rising Catholic middle classes are embodied in the family of the local solicitor Perry and his family, while Mrs Really and Satterthwaite discuss the Catholic Church's control over education and the failure of the national schools to attract good teachers, especially for girls. Nor is private education much better: the governess hired by Helena's aunts to teach her music, languages, English, drawing and needlework is interested not in education but in how much money she can fleece from her employers.

Christy Carew (1880) portrays the limited possibilities open to the middle-class Catholic daughter at home: marriage or the convent, as Christy's more submissive friend Esther puts it. At school Christy won prizes but she sees no reason for taxing her brains further since, as a young woman, nothing is expected of her and she envies the opportunities of young male students like her brother Lanty: 'They have something to do, and a good reason for doing it. It's not so with us. Where is the good of our doing anything? There's nothing to come of it,'[65] a complaint that will be echoed years later by Lois in Elizabeth Bowen's *The Last September* (1929). The lively and rebellious Christy is taken in hand by Anthony Sugrue whom she eventually marries (another mixed marriage) and lives with in London: like Kate O'Brien's heroines, Laffan's young women often find a wider future outside Ireland. However, Laffan's persistent theme of rebellious girls tamed by wiser men is not so much proto-feminist as an echo of Jane Austen's *Emma*. In this, a comparison may be made with Mrs Alexander's novel *Kitty Costello*.

Mrs Alexander

Daughter of a Dublin solicitor, Annie French (1825–1902) was taught at home by governesses but derived most of her education, as she told Helen Black, from reading books 'no doubt a good deal beyond my grasp' to a blind Scotsman.[66] In 1844, her father lost money and the family transferred to Liverpool and subsequently to London. In 1858, French married Alexander Hector who disapproved of her writing and during their marriage she published her work anonymously. After his death in 1875, she supported her four children by writing under the pseudonym 'Mrs Alexander'. She was a strong believer in education, maintaining that 'girls, as well as boys, should be trained to follow some definite line in life'.[67] She sent her youngest daughter to train as an artist in Paris.

As Mrs Alexander she published over forty novels, most of them set in England, a country which she felt inspired her most as a writer.[68] In one of her best-known, her posthumous *Kitty Costello* (1904), the elderly Alexander looks back to her experiences as a young Irish girl arriving in England. Kitty comes to Westpool (Liverpool) in the 1840s to stay with her mother's sister, who was estranged from her family for many years because of her marriage to an English businessman. Kitty thus goes from an aristocratic Big House, Coolavin, whose finances have been severely depleted by the famines, to the prosperous but 'unknown region of English commercial life'.[69] Kitty retains an aristocratic contempt for the tradespeople among whom she moves but is gradually won over by her uncle's younger brother Dick, who functions like many of Laffan's heroes as a sort of Mr Knightley figure to her Emma and eventually tames 'this proud, high-spirited wild Irish girl'.[70] Despite the liveliness of its heroine, the main aim of this novel is not to highlight gender issues but to contrast the feckless Anglo-Irish with the solid worth of the English business classes.

NEW WOMAN PRECURSORS

L.T. Meade

Philanthropy, as noted earlier, often takes the place of careers for women in Victorian fiction. In L.T. Meade's popular novel *A Princess of the Gutter* (1896), philanthropy and careers for women are linked in a negative way through the hostile comments of Joan Prinsep's rackrenting landlord. The landlord tells Joan, graduate of Girton College, Cambridge and inheritor of three thousand pounds a year which she has spent on rebuilding slum properties and running girls' clubs, that: 'The craze for colleges for women, and all that sort of nonsense, is just as objectionable as the philanthropic craze of the age.'[71]

Elizabeth Thomasina Meade Smith (1850–1914), who wrote under the gender-free name of L.T. Meade, was born in a rectory in Bandon, County Cork. At the age of twenty-one she moved to London and became one of the few Irish women authors living in England to achieve wealth from her writing. Despite marriage and three children, she managed to publish around three hundred novels in various genres including crime fiction, science fiction and children's fiction. She founded the periodical *Atalanta* (1887–98), aimed at middle-class girls between the ages of fourteen and twenty-five to encourage them in independence and other traits associated with the New Woman. However, where the theme of the New Woman appears in her fiction it is often compromised by Victorian sentimentality and by Meade's need to make money.

The Cleverest Woman in England (1898) opens with a promising portrayal of the life of a New Woman of Swedish descent, Dagmar Olloffson, who lives in London and is a brilliant public speaker on women's issues. She gathers a group of followers around her and the emotional bonds between women in this novel are so strong as to verge for the modern reader on lesbianism but probably represent no more than Victorian sentiment.[72] Early in the novel, Dagmar disappoints her friends (and the reader) by marrying Geoffrey Hamlyn, who is actively hostile to the women's movement. Despite Dagmar's insistence that she will be able to maintain her independence and her career after marriage, she becomes increasingly torn between her work and her duty to her husband and the novel lapses into Victorian sentimentality centred on themes of female suffering and self-sacrifice. It is hard to avoid the conclusion that Meade's interest in the New Woman theme arose from its commercial viability rather than from any firm ideological commitment, though again, as in the case of Mulholland, this statement about Meade's adult fiction has to be tempered by the impossible-to-calculate influence of her schoolgirl stories where girls band together against adults and disobedience becomes a positive trait.

Ella MacMahon

Ambivalence over the New Woman is a hallmark of Ella MacMahon's novels. Born in Dublin, MacMahon (1864–1956) was daughter of the chaplain to the lord lieutenant of Ireland. After being educated at home, she moved to London to work in the British civil service. In *A New Note* (1894), MacMahon portrays a New Woman, Victoria Leathley, who receives permission from her father, much to the disapproval of his relatives, to embark on a career as a professional musician. The novel is set in England but an Irish connection is maintained through Fitzgerald Annesley, an Anglo-Irishman who proposes to Victoria. She, being a New Woman dedicated to her art, rejects him. The novel reveals she is right to, for though Fitzgerald tells Victoria that marriage to him would leave her free to pursue her career, the narrator comments: 'in his heart he believed that marriage would cure her of all desire for a career.'[73] Victoria's elderly cousin Dora, who disapproves of women performing in public, warns Victoria: 'The new order of young woman ... will be no happier in the new world of her own creating than in the old world which God created for her.'[74] The novel endorses Dora's view to the extent that embracing the new order of things does not guarantee personal happiness for MacMahon's heroine. Like many New Women, Victoria falls in love with the wrong man, a fellow musician Louis Loevio, who turns out to have children by another woman. In a sisterly ending, characteristic of New Woman writing, Victoria forms a bond with Loevio's mistress and advises Loevio, whose real name turns out to be Joseph Higgins, to marry her.

If the New Woman is portrayed more or less sympathetically in *A New Note*, the screeching Augusta in MacMahon's *A Modern Man* (1895) seen through the eyes of Merton Byng, the eponymous modern man, is casually summarised as 'sex feminine – er – at least, hybrid'.[75] In MacMahon's *A Pitiful Passion* (1895), Magdalen is a New Woman to the extent that she is an independent woman earning her living through her painting, but her Victorian notions of duty and her strong religious beliefs impel her to give up her art in order to look after her friend Georgie Fitz-Roy, an alcoholic whose marriage is falling apart. From a New Woman story of a woman finding self-expression and fulfilment through her art, the novel transforms itself into a portrait of a woman who defines herself by self-sacrifice. In their portrayal of New Women, MacMahon's novels remain torn between modernity and the Victorian philanthropic novel.

Anxieties over the novel form and ambiguities in treating the romance plot found in the earlier work of Edgeworth and Owenson give way in later less literary nineteenth-century female novelists to an urgent desire to portray both women and Ireland with particular political, religious or class agenda in mind. Concerns over form are superseded by the desire to present Irish women's lives in as straightforward a manner as possible, using familiar narrative structures, engaging characters and an accessible prose style, in a way that would appeal to the widest reading public. Many of these novelists, among them Katharine Tynan, Charlotte Riddell, Mrs Alexander, and L. T. Meade, were their family's sole breadwinner. For this reason their fiction often serves up happy endings even when these are manifestly against the grain of Irish circumstances and Irish women's lives and when, as in the case of Rosa Mulholland's *Marcella Grace* or M. E. Francis's *Miss Erin*, romantic closure threatens the inner coherence of the texts. Ella MacMahon's treatment of the New Woman theme, however ambivalent, gave her a way out of the romance plot.

Popular novels of the nineteenth century by Irish women remain of interest because of their exploration of women's lives and, while many of these novelists were not ideologically minded enough to be defined precisely as feminists in the modern meaning of the word, some of them implicitly interrogate gender roles, demanding better education for girls and portraying Irish women actively engaged in various sorts of work, usually in the safely permitted feminine sphere of philanthropy.

In a sense almost any woman who succeeded in maintaining a career as a professional writer in the nineteenth century might be regarded as blazing a trail for subsequent Irish women writers but it is now time to turn to the more explicit challenging of gender stereotypes in the work of the New Woman writers.

Chapter 2

BICYCLES AND TROUSERS: THE NEW WOMAN WRITER

INTRODUCTION

*T*he characteristic bicycling, smoking, trouser-wearing New Woman was born in the middle years of Queen Victoria's reign and came to public notice in the *fin de siècle* period. The New Woman writer's engagement with women's rights and with challenging fixed gender roles has attracted critical attention in studies by Elaine Showalter, Sally Ledger, Lyn Pykett and Ann Heilmann, among others.[1] Yet, despite the fact that it was an Irish writer, Sarah Grand, who in 1894 coined the term 'New Woman', it is only recently that the New Woman writer has been set in an Irish context by scholars such as Tina O'Toole, Anne Fogarty, Gerardine Meaney, John Wilson Foster and James H. Murphy.[2] The Irish context has been partly obscured because New Woman writers were cosmopolitans who settled abroad, often in cities like London which they found offered a more vibrant cultural life, wider publishing opportunities and more extensive literary networks than Ireland.[3] Like Sydney Owenson earlier in the century and Charlotte Riddell mid-century, they crossed the Irish Sea in search of publishers and London became a centre for New Woman writers, several of whom – George Egerton, Sarah Grand, Beatrice Grimshaw – were Irish in origin. Living abroad inevitably affected their writing, and the foreign settings of their fiction, as John Wilson Foster and others have pointed out, is one reason why these writers were ignored by the Irish Literary Revival.

The New Woman was largely an urban phenomenon: for the first time women could walk out freely in public, go to restaurants, go shopping: 'The late Victorian city – specifically London – was the centre of much feminist activism during this period. By the 1890s … women of the middle and upper classes were seen for the first time walking unaccompanied down city streets, emerging at last from the private sphere to take buses and trams, to go shopping and to stroll with friends.'[4]

An Irish writer, however, might experience London differently from an English woman. Tynan, who largely enjoyed her busy and productive life as a professional writer, wife and mother in London during the 1890s, nevertheless registered the difficulty of making friends with neighbours if one were literary and Irish: 'The respectable suburb is not sure of the literary person … Then, if you are Irish and do not go to the recognized churches – one or other of them – things look black indeed.'[5] London may have offered her a wider literary network but after mixing in Ireland with writers of the Literary Revival, Tynan found the market-orientated conversation in London literary circles tiresome: 'the 'nineties had given me a surfeit of it; prices per thousand and biggest circulations, and all the crowded rooms shrieking like the parrot-houses at the Zoo, and the gist of it the making of books and the prices to be obtained for them.'[6] In *The Winds of Time* (1934), Edith Gordon, raised in Kerry, describes how difficult she found it to adapt to London initially: 'The winter of 1897 was one of more or less continuous yellow fog which depressed and suffocated me.'[7] She soon began to earn a 'fairly lucrative' income as a contributor on women's topics to *Outlook* and the *Ladies' Field* and when she had earned enough money to be able to afford a house in Kerry, 'Life in London became less irksome for the feeling that within a sixteen-hour journey lay an enchanted land to which one could repair at any time.'[8]

KATHLEEN MANNINGTON CAFFYN

'One of the very best novels we have read for many months' (*Westminster Gazette*), 'unmistakably the book of the hour' (*The Weekly Sun*), 'a work of genius remarkable for novelty of plot, force of diction, grace of literary style, and subtlety of psychical analysis' (*Daily Telegraph*) – these were some of the reviews that greeted the publication of Iota's novel *A Yellow Aster* in 1894. Iota was the pseudonym of Kathleen Mannington Caffyn (c.1855–1926), novelist and short story writer, born in County Tipperary. Kathleen de Vere Hunt, as she was then, was educated by English and German governesses and moved to London in her early twenties to train as a nurse. In 1879 she married a doctor, Stephen Mannington Caffyn, and emigrated with him to Sydney in 1880. She wrote this first novel while living in Australia but by the time of its publication she had moved back to London with her husband and son. *A Yellow Aster* was followed by some fifteen other novels over the course of the next twenty years, her last being *Mary Mirrilies* (1916).

A Yellow Aster was extraordinarily successful, going through four editions in the first month. Part of its success must have been due to its lively tone and readability, and part to the fact that while it examines New Woman themes, the overall emphasis of the novel is conservative in its underlying Christian ethos and its distrust of the intellectual life for women. *A Yellow Aster* opens with a portrait of the Warings' marriage. Cyril, a fellow in mathematics at Cambridge, has had to give up his fellowship on marriage but has managed to recreate the atmosphere of a Cambridge college in his home where he and his wife Grace spend their time discussing and writing about mathematical problems. If this seems like a New Woman opening, the thrust of the novel is to portray the deleterious effects of such absorption in intellectual work on Grace's capacities for mothering.

Grace and Cyril, both sceptics, look on their two children Dacre and Gwen as experiments and aim to bring them up without any instruction in Christianity. As a result, Gwen grows up to be a beautiful but heartless young woman who expresses herself in New Woman terms. She is physically energetic, appalled at the language of the wedding service, and calls herself 'a yellow aster' to illustrate her resistance to the stereotype of the frail, passive woman: "'I am free, free!" she cried, "my body is my own again, and my soul, and my brain! I am myself again, Gwen Waring, a self-respecting creature, with no man's brand on me.'"[9] This is misleading: the novel is not about a woman finding freedom, but about a woman finally learning that her highest calling is to be wife and mother. The prefatory quotation to the novel suggests that yellow asters may be a scientific curiosity but they do not make for happiness or improve on nature.[10] Gwen's husband Humphrey believes that nature will eventually catch up on Gwen and so it proves. The dangerous illness suffered by her baby son breaks open Gwen's womanly heart and by the end of the novel she has, after many vicissitudes, brought herself to love Humphrey. No wonder the novel was popular: it deals with New Woman themes such as companionate marriage and a woman's yearning for freedom, and then reveals the dangers. Gwen's upbringing has been so idiosyncratic that the novel could have no lessons for those women who in real life were trying to claim freedoms for themselves, and the novel's insistence that women's highest calling lay in being wives and mothers was discouraging.

Some of the contemporary arguments against the New Woman are rehearsed by the dilettantish Max Morland in Mannington's novel *Poor Max* (1898). *Poor Max* is set partly in Ireland at a time of famine but the Irish scenes are less important than the interrogation of gender roles posed by the lives of Max and his wife Judith, who live in London. Whenever he encounters obstacles in his life as a painter, journalist and novelist, Max vents his frustration in a series of misogynist statements about women: "'This rampaging greed for work is the present-day curse. Directly she joins in it, a woman slips from her throne into the gutter.'"[11] Women writers are a particular target: "'Think of the unnatural strain put upon her in following an art – literature, I'm inclined to think, is the one least becoming to woman.'"[12] Max's dilettantism does not, however, put bread on the table and the novel traces Judith's development into a writer, albeit one who has to conceal the success of her money-making novels from her husband. When Max discovers what his wife has been up to, he rails:

> 'To break into print with that unutterable herd! It's a monstrous interference with nature. It – it seems,' he cried, watching her critically, 'as though the you in you – had died there, before me, and a short-haired shriek with *pince-nez* and a beastly little note-book in her lean paws – there were three of them in Dawson's office yesterday – stood in your stead.'[13]

Poor Max, a telling juxtaposition of the male aesthete with the professional, and prolific, female writer, reveals the extent of society's hostility towards the New

Woman writer and indeed to the challenge to Victorian gender identities posed both by the New Woman and by decadent male artists such as Oscar Wilde and Aubrey Beardsley. Despite the frequent association of the New Woman and the dandy in the public mind as examples of modern degeneracy, as *Poor Max* demonstrates, male decadent writers were not necessarily interested in the causes dear to New Woman writers.

Judith's obstacles are not only external; years before Virginia Woolf, Mannington portrays the psychological barriers to becoming a woman writer. Judith, an essentially conservative woman surrounded by conservative men, resents her role as family breadwinner and dismisses her novels as 'three horrid little books'.[14] Meanwhile, Max struggles to fit into the Victorian masculine role and acknowledges that he would have made a better woman than a man. Recognising this, Judith tries to build up Daniel, the son who most resembles his father, into an Anglo-Saxon male by supplying him with the books of 'Kipling, Stevenson and Sir Walter in his most blood-thirsty and inspiring moods'.[15] The novel is realistic about the extent to which it is possible to resist cultural expectations around gender: Judith fails to bolster her son's masculinity, Max dies believing he has failed as a man, Judith fails as a New Woman because her writing career stalls and she is no longer able to support her family. She more or less sells herself to the predatory Churton Graves in order to safeguard her sons' future. Nevertheless, despite internal and external obstacles and until she runs out of inspiration, Judith earns a good living by her novels and Max's jealousy illustrates contemporary male anxiety over women's dominance of the fiction market.

EMILY LAWLESS

Emily Lawless (1845–1913), daughter of Lord Cloncurry, was born at Lyons Castle, County Kildare into a family who were fairly recent recruits to the Protestant Ascendancy and sometimes despised on this account. Family members had been involved with the United Irishmen and in the campaign for Catholic Emancipation and Lawless's own national identity was always somewhat fluid, combining nationalist and unionist sympathies. Though she never went so far as to favour home rule, she was highly critical of British policy in Ireland. This critical unionism made her writing popular for a while, especially outside Ireland, and in her lifetime she was well known in Irish and English literary circles, though after Independence her writing was dismissed as conservative and fell into neglect.

Lawless deserves a prominent place in any narrative of Irish women's writing, not only on account of her own fiction but also because in 1904 she published a biography of Maria Edgeworth. Published, ironically, in an 'English Men of Letters' series, Lawless's biography was an important recognition of a female line of Irish writing. Lawless focuses on Edgeworth's life as a professional writer, drawing on Hall to describe how she wrote in the family living room, amid family chatter and the children's lessons. Ever alive to the commercial aspect of an author's life, Lawless includes a detailed list of Edgeworth's literary earnings. Like many biographers before and since, Lawless blames Richard Edgeworth for his daughter's didacticism: the numerous quotations from Maria Edgeworth's letters are given less for biographical purposes than to illustrate her lively style when freed from her father's restraining influence. Lawless finds in these letters echoes of what she regards as Edgeworth's finest work, *Castle Rackrent*.

Though this biography may seem to indicate Lawless's feminist leanings, or at least a Woolfian recognition of the importance of establishing a literary foremother, in fact in the area of gender politics, as in the sphere of nationalism, Lawless is not easily categorised. She was proficient in several disciplines usually at that time restricted to men: not only was she a poet, novelist and biographer, she was also an amateur botanist, entomologist, geographer, geologist and marine zoologist, and in *Major Lawrence, F.L.S.* (1887) and in her historical novel *With Essex in Ireland* (1890) she writes with accuracy of military matters. She was New Woman enough to adopt a business-like approach to her career and take a keen interest in the commercial side of publishing. Nevertheless, despite these feminist credentials, Lawless declared herself anti-suffrage and, though she was aware of the restrictions on women's lives and put women at the centre of her novels, her heroines often renounce their careers in favour of marriage. According to the Countess of Fingall, Lawless's outward appearance gave little impression of a New Woman: 'No one was ever less like her work than Emily Lawless. She gave one no idea of the passion and power within her. She was pale and flaccid, with half-closed, near-sighted eyes and limp white hands. Her speech was slow and she was very delicate and rather hypochondriacal and untidy in her dressing.'[16] It may be that playing the role of lady in a drawing room drove Lawless into this apathetic state. Lennox Robinson, describing Lawless out of doors, paints an entirely different picture: 'She was very tall with red-gold hair, full of laughter and humour. An artist, a great walker, a horse-woman and a swimmer, diving deeply into the wild Atlantic and bringing to the surface strange sea-creatures and sea-plants no Clare fisherman had ever seen.'[17]

Lawless's early fiction illustrates the difficulty of characterising her as a straightforward feminist. Her first novel, *A Chelsea Householder*, published anonymously in 1882, opens with what seems a promising account of the New Woman artist. Muriel Ellis, twenty-two, is an independent orphan living on the fifteen hundred pounds a year she has inherited from her brother and working, Lawless is at pains to make clear, as a professional artist. The novel presents the first of Lawless's characteristic pairings of a lively woman with a more conventional one, embodied here by Muriel's companion Elizabeth Prettyman, who believes that it is improper for a young girl to possess as much independence as Muriel. Significantly, Elizabeth's talent is as a copyist, rather than an original artist. At the other end of the spectrum is Kitty King, Muriel's frivolous friend with a masculine hairstyle, who has adopted the life of an art student simply as a cloak for her bid for independence from her family and a life of flirtation and pleasure. Muriel's task would seem to be to hold the mean between Elizabeth's conservatism and the rather negative take on the New Woman embodied by Kitty.

Since the novel announces itself from the outset as 'a romance', it is hardly surprising that it ends in marriage yet, like many subsequent female writers, Lawless uses the romance plot to raise questions about women's lives. In the end Muriel fails to value her artistic vocation, though encouraged in it by Mr Wygram who holds out to her the offer of a companionate marriage in which husband and wife would both devote themselves to their art. Muriel rejects Wygram's offer because she does not love him but also because she has begun to be dissatisfied with art as a way of life and with personal achievement as her goal. What began seemingly as a portrait of the New Woman artist ends with Muriel laying aside personal ambition and internalising her society's association of femininity with philanthropy. She is encouraged in this by the curate, Stephen Halliday, whom she eventually marries. Halliday, whose brand of masculinity is more domineering than Wygram's, is a Mr Rochester type figure, aloof, elusive and finally tamed by illness. For his sake, Muriel abandons Chelsea and the Academy, if not her paintbrushes, though, when pressed by Halliday, in the end she agrees she could do without those too. This conservative ending was pounced on by contemporary reviewers as a welcome counterbalance to contemporary portrayals of the New Woman: 'as happy a corrective of the artistic young woman of recent fiction as can be desired'.[18]

A Chelsea Householder was followed by *A Millionaire's Cousin* (1885), a slight single-volume novel that did not sell well. Though the narrator, Adolphus Bell, is male, the novel's Algiers setting naturally gives rise to discussion of Muslim women, and Bell's conversations with the elderly Madame de la Hoche position him on the side of female emancipation, as a supporter of Miss Bonson's desire to earn her living as a painter in London. However, Bell is an unreliable narrator, self-centred and obtuse about the mutual love between Miss Bonson and his wealthy cousin, John Hargrave, and when Miss Bonson chooses Hargrave over himself, he reverts to making misogynist statements about women. Since Miss Bonson is portrayed as not deriving any pleasure from her work as an artist, the reader assumes that she will abandon it after her marriage. Like Muriel, she begins as a New Woman but ends as a married one. Lawless's pitting of characters with conservative views on women against those holding more liberated opinions suggests that she was using these early novels to work out her own views on the woman question.

If Lawless's early novels contribute towards the New Woman debate it is in their suggestion that Victorian gender roles are not easily left behind. This is made clear in *Major Lawrence, F.L.S.* (1887). Eleanor Mordaunt first appears as a spirited twelve-year-old girl whose physical courage shows up the effeminacy of her companion, Algernon. Five years later, Eleanor has turned into a shy, awkward young woman whereas Algernon has come into his own as an orchid-collecting dandy. The gender roles are reversed but the reversal, in Lawless's reading, is all to Algernon's advantage. Like Mannington in *Poor Max*, Lawless portrays the way that adopting a capable, strong, and in terms of the time, masculine role in the face of a passive, effeminate male can disempower a woman. Paradoxically, Eleanor becomes reduced by Algernon's peevish dandyish ways to the self-abnegation of a Victorian Angel in the House. Like Judith in *Poor Max*, Eleanor finds she can only recover her true self in the company of a hyper-masculinised soldier figure, here the eponymous Major John Lawrence.

Poor Max and *Major Lawrence* both reveal women's anxieties about the dandy figure and indicate that simply reversing fixed gender roles did not necessarily result in liberating women.

Masculinity is again scrutinised in *With Essex in Ireland*, supposedly extracts from the diary of Henry Harvey, fictional secretary to Robert Devereux, Earl of Essex, recounting Essex's mission to Ireland in 1599 to subdue the rebellion of Hugh O'Neill, Earl of Tyrone. So authentic did this account seem that many readers, including W.E. Gladstone, believed it to be a genuine sixteenth-century account. What is of most interest to the modern reader is the way in which Lawless shows both Harvey and his master, Essex, changed by their encounter with Ireland. This may be historically inaccurate but it allows Lawless to pose certain questions about English methods in Ireland. Essex comes under the spell of Irish songs and the Irish landscape and gradually reveals his doubts about the colonising project.[19] Essex's Elizabethan gender categories also become destabilised. That Essex is in Ireland on the orders of a woman, Queen Elizabeth, is already a complicating factor in terms of sixteenth-century ideology that positioned women as subject to men. Heroic masculinity, as embodied in the war-hungry and callow Frank Gardner, is shown to be self-defeating: Frank dies early on in the novel in an unimportant skirmish. Essex's awakening compassion for the murdered rebels is perceived by him as womanly weakness, yet Lawless shows that it is when Essex is at his most feminine he is most honourable, a trait usually associated with masculinity both in the period in which the novel is set and in which it was written. Essex's thinking on both nationalism and gender is challenged by his encounter with Ireland and in the end he cannot complete his mission. As Heidi Hansson observes in her pioneering study of gender and nation in Lawless's work: 'Most of Lawless's writings are characterised by the double voice of a writer reluctant to provide an easy solution or a final answer.'[20]

Lawless's best-known novels are *Hurrish* (1886) and *Grania: The Story of an Island* (1892), the latter appearing on a list published in the *Irish Homestead* in 1900 of the one hundred books indispensable for assembling a village library. Set in the Burren at a time of agrarian rebellion, *Hurrish* illustrates Lawless's double vision of women but between Hurrish's dominating mother urging her son to violence for the sake of Mother Ireland, and his self-sacrificing niece Alley, there is little room for the New Woman to appear. In her most accomplished novel, *Grania*, the west of Ireland setting encouraged Lawless to step outside her own culture to portray an uneducated peasant woman in a way that has some resonance with the figure of the New Woman. James Calahan suggests that Lawless's more feminist stance in *Grania* compared with her earlier work came about partly because of the novel's west of Ireland setting and her heroine's interaction with it.[21]

Set in the 1860s on the island of Inis Meáin, anglicised in the novel as Inishmaan, *Grania: The Story of an Island* was based on research Lawless gathered on a trip to the Aran Islands in the mid-1880s, many years before J.M. Synge's first visit in 1898. The title encapsulates Lawless's approach: this is both the story of a community – with detailed descriptions of the geography and geology of the island and the way the peasants, their beliefs and way of life are moulded by the environment – and an account of the life of one Aran Island woman who cannot fit into this community. *Grania* is the first Irish novel to focus on the Aran Island peasant women, presenting the reality of their daily lives rather than seeing them through the lens of Revivalist myth. In its foregrounding of active female characters it overlaps with New Woman writing and counteracts Synge's presentation in *The Aran Islands* (1907) of active men and passive or aestheticised women.

The loving relationship between two sisters, Honor and Grania, is at the heart of the novel and this pairing of a conventional with a rebellious woman again illustrates Lawless's ambivalence on gender issues. However, in this island setting the cultural constraints of Victorian femininity are irrelevant even for conventional women: Honor is often called to stand in for the priest, who lives on the larger island of Aranmore. Partly because her mother was 'a foreigner', that is, from the mainland, Grania is regarded by the other inhabitants of the island as 'a very wild queer girl, and a bold one too'.[22] Grania barely articulates her rebellion, though she does assert her right not to obey priests. Rather it is her physical strength that disturbs the island's gender roles: she goes out fishing 'just like a man'.[23] In her relationship with Murdough Blake, she is the one who does most of the hard physical labour.

Grania's bid for independence does not end happily. Her confession of love to Murdough shocks his sense of decorum. His wish to marry is from entirely pragmatic reasons to do with the farm, the cow, Grania's money and her capacity for hard work. True to his culture, he has no interest in romance and is unable to cope with Grania's adult sexuality.[24] Though she is portrayed as fitting better into the natural environment than her fellow islanders, her independence and integrity truer to the spirit of the island than the lives of those around her, Grania finds no easy place in her culture and a trip to Galway reveals that women's lives on the mainland are no freer. Grania's drowning indicates her inability to find a place either in her island culture or on the mainland. However, it is also possible to read this return to nature in a more positive way, as a sign of Grania's proto-feminist liberation from a misogynist culture.[25] Lawless's work is consistent in its ambiguity on the woman issue.

GEORGE EGERTON

The life of George Egerton (1859–1945) illustrates the New Woman's cosmopolitanism. Born Mary Chavelita Dunne in Melbourne, Australia to an Irish Catholic father and a Welsh mother, and adopting the first name George as a tribute to her heroine George Eliot, Egerton lived at various times in Ireland, New Zealand, Wales, Chile, Germany, Norway and New York. From the age of eight to her mid-teens she lived in Dublin where, after her mother's death in 1875, she cared for her younger siblings. Never able to rely on her improvident father for support, over the next ten years she worked in Germany, New York and London. In 1887, she eloped to Norway with Henry Higginson and came under the influence of the Scandinavian modernists, Ibsen, Strindberg and Hamsun. After Higginson's death, she left Norway and eventually settled in Millstreet, County Cork in 1892 with her first husband, the Canadian novelist George Egerton Clairmonte.

Egerton did most of her work in the short story form and her first collection, *Keynotes* (1893), was an immediate success, reprinted twice in the first six months of publication and subsequently translated into seven languages. It marked Egerton out as a New Woman writer and after the publication of her second collection *Discords* (1894), she moved to London where she frequented Decadent and Aesthetic circles, publishing in the first issue of *The Yellow Book*, the journal at the centre of the Decadent movement. Her autobiographical novel, *The Wheel of God*, was published in 1898 but, after the disappointing reception of her subsequent story collections *Symphonies* (1896), *Fantasias* (1898) and *Flies in Amber* (1905), and her marriage to the theatrical agent

Reginald Bright, she turned to writing plays. *His Wife's Family* was accepted by Bernard Shaw and performed in London in 1907, but she had little success thereafter and the death of her son in the First World War effectively ended her literary career. Egerton's story 'The Well of Truth' (*Fantasias*) registers a protest against publishers' increasingly conservative attitudes in the aftermath of Oscar Wilde's trial and conviction in 1895 which directly affected New Woman writers whose work had been allied in the public mind with the Decadents: 'All the windows were filled with Nursery Idylls,' Verita finds, 'the subject of man and woman had become positively indecent.'[26]

This 'indecent' subject of relations between women and men was very much Egerton's chosen theme. In *Keynotes* and *Discords*, she set out to explore the female unconscious and female sexuality, arguing that women should enjoy the same sexual freedoms as men. Inspired by her reading of Ibsen, her stories portray women who disdain conventional morality which, Egerton believed, had been constructed by men and imposed on women, narrowing their lives. Her heroines refuse to be contained by male definitions of womanhood: in 'The Regeneration of Two', the heroine's recognition of her society's false views of women and marriage leads her to propose entering into a free union with her lover. In 'A Cross Line', a story with an Irish setting, daringly erotic passages describe Gypsy's dreams and sexual fantasies. In stories where women do cave in to convention ('An Empty Frame', 'Her Share'), they are portrayed as leading emotionally sterile lives. 'Virgin Soil' is a forerunner of Mary Lavin's story 'The Nun's Mother' in depicting the disaster that follows a mother keeping her daughter ignorant about sexual matters. Married off at seventeen to a wealthy older man, the daughter returns to berate her mother and opts for a solitary life over the 'legal prostitution' of an unhappy marriage.

Egerton was by no means an equal-rights feminist, however. Her writing displays indifference towards women's education and equal opportunities in professional life. For Egerton, women's capacity for feeling was the key to the female self and the source of women's moral superiority over men. Her belief in the superior spiritual powers of women, rather than being co-opted for feminism, may be regarded as characteristic of 1890s *fin de siècle* circles generally,[27] and her writing has often been interpreted as essentialist for presenting motherhood as the fulfilment of womanhood.[28] Stories like 'Wedlock' and 'Gone Under' reveal the dangers of thwarted maternity. The heroine of 'Gone Under' is seduced at sixteen and forced to give birth in the sort of establishment that makes sure the baby is registered as a stillbirth. Listening to her tale, the young Irish girl comments: 'I think the *only divine* fibre in a woman is her maternal instinct.'[29] Years before she encountered Freud, Egerton was probing the psychological cost of the forced repression of maternal and sexual instincts. In her essay on *Keynotes*, she commented: 'If I did not know the technical jargon current today of Freud and his psycho-analysts, I did know something of complexes and inhibitions, repressions and the subconscious impulses that determine actions and reactions. I used them in my stories.'[30]

In stories like 'A Psychological Moment at Three Periods' (*Discords*), Egerton, anticipating Joyce's *Dubliners*, employs realism to critique the snobbery and materialism of Dublin society, its shallow piety and the dependent position of Irish women. In *Flies in Amber* (1905), the central image of flies trapped in amber aptly reflects Egerton's portrayal of women's lives. Two of the stories have Irish settings. 'Mammy' is a sympathetic portrayal of the lives of Dublin prostitutes while 'The Marriage of Mary Ascension' portrays convent-educated Mary whose life is constrained both by the power of the priests who collude with her relatives to prevent her from marrying the Protestant man she loves, and by her religious upbringing which suppresses her natural sexual instincts. Her story has striking parallels with that of Esther in Laffan's *Christy Carew*.

Egerton's only novel, *The Wheel of God* (1898), like Grand's *The Beth Book*, draws heavily on her own life to present a *Bildungsroman* of the New Woman. George O'Brien has described the *Bildungsroman* as 'arguably the most important genre of the Irish novel' and certainly it is a dominant feature in Irish women's fiction.[31] *The Wheel of God* opens in a manner characteristic of New Woman writing, presenting the young Mary Desmond as an avid reader, especially of *Jane Eyre*. Since this is an account specifically of an Irish New Woman, Mary is also enthralled by stories of Daniel O'Connell and Robert Emmet. The novel contains a great deal of realism in the description of Mary's early Dublin life: reflecting Egerton's own circumstances, when Mary's mother dies and her feckless artist father is imprisoned for debt, Mary is left to look after her siblings. She emigrates to the US where she finds office work but eventually moves to London to be near her father, contrasting her positive experience of working in America with life in London where, like many Irish women before and afterwards, 'she felt the racial difference keenly'.[32]

Nevertheless, London is presented as a city that has advantages for a single woman trying to make her way in the world. 'The Society for the Employment of Women' finds Mary a post as a copyist and later she comes into contact with other likeminded independent women, such as the journalist Miss Ingleton. Of Irish descent, Miss Ingleton lives in a boarding house, smokes and discusses women's issues with Mary. Mary's independence does not prevent her, however, as with so many New Woman heroines, from making an unfortunate marriage. The feckless Englishman Cecil Marriott marries her to get his hands on her money and set himself up in medical practice. In middle-class Buckinghamshire, Mary finds the social gulf between herself and the English widen. After Cecil's death in a drunken accident, Mary finally achieves self-realisation, not in marriage, but through joining a New Woman's commune with likeminded women including Miss Ingleton and 'John Morton', a celebrated woman author who, like Egerton herself, goes under a male pseudonym. In writing beyond the romantic happy ending and in its refusal to cave in to Victorian sentimentality about women's lives, *The Wheel of God* is an authentic New Woman novel.

Sarah Grand

Sarah Grand (1854–1943) was the pseudonym of Frances Clarke (later McFall) who was born in Donaghadee, County Down and spent the first seven years of her life in Ireland where her father was a naval lieutenant. After his death, the family moved to England. At the age of sixteen, Grand married a 39-year-old naval surgeon, living with him in Hong Kong and the Far East, Norwich and Warrington before separating from him in 1890 and moving to London to write. She lived for many years in Tunbridge Wells and Katharine Tynan describes her as 'a green oasis in the arid waste of Tunbridge Wells'.[33] Revealing her conservatism on gender issues, Tynan adds: 'I had thought of her as something militant; I found her soft-voiced, gentle, delicately feminine, and most lovable.'[34] Grand shared Egerton's vision of equality between the sexes, though with an emphasis not on women's sexual freedom but on women's sexual purity, and the necessity for men to live up to the same sexual standards as women. Unlike Egerton, Grand's most significant work was in the novel form, particularly her feminist trilogy *Ideala*, *The Heavenly Twins* and *The Beth Book* featuring a circle of reforming women in the fictional town of Morningquest.

Ideala (1888) is essentially a portrait of an emerging New Woman seen through the eyes of a male narrator (Lord Dawne) who is in love with her but never declares his love. Ideala becomes the mouthpiece for many of Grand's own views on the woman question: 'The women of my time are in an unsettled state, it may be a state of transition.'[35] Ideala is not in sympathy with women who struggle for political equality with men: having married a jealous and tyrannical man who is unfaithful and violent, Ideala feels that women have been let down by men. The modern man, she proclaims, is morally inferior to women, whereas men should be women's superiors: 'For the prayer of every woman worth the name is not, "Make me superior to my husband", but "Lord, make my husband superior to me!"'[36] Grand's espousal of the New Woman cause, like Egerton's, cannot be straightforwardly aligned with equal-rights feminism. However, Ideala's feminism comes through when she decides to devote herself to working for women ostracised by society.

In *The Heavenly Twins* (1893), described by Elaine Showalter as 'stylish, assured, and strikingly original',[37] Grand's didactic purpose of demonstrating the evils of keeping young girls like Edith and Evadne in ignorance about sexually transmitted disease is much enlivened by the portrait of Angelica and Theodore ('Diavolo'), the cross-dressing eponymous heavenly twins who delight in wrong-footing the adults around them. There are two parallel and overlapping stories – the twins' growth to maturity and the warning tales of Edith and Evadne. Edith is entirely conventional but Evadne is a New Woman in embryo, educating herself from books lying around the house. Both women are, fatefully, sexual innocents. Evadne's mother proclaims: 'I am indeed thankful to think that at eighteen she knows nothing of the world and its wickedness, and is therefore eminently qualified to make someone an excellent wife.'[38] Like the heroine of Egerton's 'Virgin Soil', Evadne's dangerous ignorance of the world leads her into an early marriage. Major Colquhoun, Irish on his mother's side, turns out to be infected with syphilis and Evadne refuses to consummate the marriage, believing that men should be held accountable to a higher standard of sexual control. *The Heavenly Twins* portrays Evadne's life as irretrievably damaged not only by this marriage but also by Colquhoun's refusal to allow her to engage in meaningful public work: 'Evadne had been formed for a life of active usefulness; but now she found herself reduced to an existence of objectless contemplation.'[39] The mental damage caused by being thwarted of active occupation persists into Evadne's second, happier marriage to Dr Galbraith, one of the male characters in the novel who demonstrate their moral integrity by sympathy with the women's cause.

As for the naughty twins Angelica and Diavolo, gender prejudices cause their lives to diverge in adulthood. Whereas Diavolo receives education and training at Sandhurst, Angelica is left behind and makes an early marriage to a kindly but older Mr Kilroy, another Mr Knightley figure. She is able to express her desire for a larger life only by dressing, like Princess Davorska in Katherine Thurston's *Max*, as a boy, a guise that allows Grand, like Thurston, to expose the performative aspects of gendered behaviour. Angelica's story is more hopeful than Evadne's for she reappears in *The Beth Book* as part of a circle of women working for social reform.

If *Ideala* and *The Heavenly Twins* contain only a few Irish traces, Grand's final novel in the trilogy, *The Beth Book* (1897), places an Irish woman at its centre. The subtitle gives notice of Grand's aims: *Being a Study from the Life of Elizabeth Caldwell Maclure, A Woman of Genius*. *The Beth Book* is a novel that encompasses many subjects in a polemical and didactic fashion and, like Grand herself, Beth grows into a woman who champions books with a message over those that merely attract attention for aesthetic reasons: 'Manner has always been less to me than matter. When I think of all the preventable sin and misery there is in the world, I pray God give us books of good intention – never mind the style!'[40] George Eliot becomes Beth's literary role model.

Beth is born in Northern Ireland in 1861 into what Edna O'Brien would later classify as the typical Irish family, where the father is alcoholic and unfaithful and the mother worn out by constant child-bearing. The early part of the book describes Beth's spasmodic education, first in the north and then in the west of Ireland. Any money that there is goes to educate Beth's brothers. Foreshadowing Virginia Woolf's liberating five hundred pounds in *A Room of One's Own* (1929), Beth is left a legacy by her great aunt Victoria for her education. Though she is persuaded by her mother to hand the money over to her brother, she is allowed to keep the room her aunt leaves her and this becomes the first of a series of rooms of her own.

Still innocent, she marries Dr Daniel Maclure who, she later discovers, works at a Lock Hospital where prostitutes are forcibly detained and treated for venereal disease. To compound his sins he also turns out to be a vivisectionist.

The novel is thus situated in the context of two prominent nineteenth-century campaigns: the antivivisectionists and Josephine Butler's Campaign for the Repeal of the Contagious Diseases Act (1869–86).[41] Despising her husband, Beth is gradually drawn into a circle of women who are determined to bring about social reform. Characters from the earlier novels reappear: Ideala, Angelica, Mrs Orton Beg, Lady Fulda Guthrie and what Beth's husband refers to as 'the whole of that advanced woman's party at Morne, always interfering with everything'.[42] Time spent with these women makes Beth realise 'the awful oppression of her married life'.[43]

Thrown out of the family home by her husband, Beth finds another room of her own in London and starts to write non-fiction aimed at improving women's lives. Chapter 50 contains much detailed description of Beth securing cheap lodgings in a good neighbourhood, furnishing her room from second-hand shops and learning to feed herself cheaply. All in all, this chapter provided a useful guide for Grand's readers to living as a single professional woman of modest means in London at the end of the nineteenth century. Published anonymously, Beth's book turns out to be a success and she becomes, like Grand herself, a precursor of women's later literary successes: 'Beth was one of the first swallows of the woman's summer.'[44]

Though Grand's novels sold in large numbers, *The Beth Book* became notorious when it was first published for its depictions of domestic violence, alcoholism, male philandering, and a young girl's dawning sexual awareness. What shocked contemporary readers above all, perhaps, was its portrayal of a heroine who learns to assert her own interests. *The Beth Book* remains of enduring value for its psychological portrait of the artist as a young woman.

Hannah Lynch

Born in Dublin, Hannah Lynch (1859–1904) was raised in a middle-class Catholic family that was intellectual and nationalist but cosmopolitan as well: Katharine Tynan describes Lynch and her sisters as having a wider outlook on life than herself due to their convent-school education in France.[45] Lynch worked as secretary for the London branch of the Ladies Land League, governessed in several European countries, wrote novels and earned her living through journalism and travel writing for English and American markets, finally settling in Paris where she ended her days in sickness and poverty.[46] *Autobiography of a Child* was serialised in *Blackwood's Edinburgh Magazine* (1898–99) and published in book form in 1899. It appeared in French translation in *La Revue de Paris* (1902) and Lynch was described in *Harper's Bazaar*, somewhat extravagantly, as 'the most gifted woman Ireland ever produced'.[47]

Until more is known about Lynch's life, it is uncertain whether *Autobiography of a Child* is to be read as a confessional novel or as a representative portrait of Irish girls' lives. The novel draws on the childhood memories of an adult narrator who styles herself, in tribute to a childhood split between Ireland and England, Angela of Lysterby. The *Autobiography* is notable for its extraordinarily vivid portrait of Angela's mother who is by turns neglectful and physically violent to all her children, bearing a particular animus towards Angela. For the first seven years of her life Angela, a passionate little girl with similarities to Maggie Tulliver, is fostered out to 'kindly Irish peasants' whose home is decorated with pictures of Robert Emmet in the dock and Mary Stuart bidding farewell to France. These formative years nourish the rebel in her, and when she is sent away to a convent boarding school in Lysterby in Warwickshire where the children are beaten and starved (here the echoes are of *Jane Eyre*), Angela asserts her Irish nationality in the face of the nuns' contempt. The *Autobiography* ends when Angela is twelve but, reflecting bitterly on her life and the lives of those around her, the middle-aged narrator comments on the waste of Irish women's energies and talents:

> In Ireland – the very wretchedest land on earth for woman, the one spot of the globe where no provision is made for her, and where parents consider themselves as exempt of all duty, of tenderness, of justice in her regard, where her lot as daughter, wife and old maid bears no resemblance to the ideal of civilisation – a dozen girls are born for one boy.[48]

This is a society that kills off a young girl's artistic ambitions (Angela had early showed some talent as a singer), and J.W. Foster has described the *Autobiography* as 'a reverse *Portrait of the Artist as a Young Man*'.[49] Even Angela's mother is cultured and clever, her violence born out of a sense of frustration at a life confined to domesticity. She thus becomes one in a line of cruel mothers in Irish women's fiction whose abusive behaviour towards their children stems from the limiting social context in which they live.

The *Autobiography* ends with the suggestion that Angela's middle age has not lived up to the hopes of her youth and there is a strong hint that, reflecting Lynch's own family circumstances, the family has descended into poverty on account of her stepfather's easy-going hospitality. Angela has been obliged to support other family members as well as herself and there is a powerful outburst of sympathy for 'the army of inefficient Irish governesses and starving illiterate Irish teachers cast upon the Continent'.[50] These Irish women, Lynch writes, presumably from personal experience, are sent out ill-equipped for their task and, moreover, are expected to send much of their salary home. The situation had not much changed by the early 1920s, the period in which *Mary Lavelle*, Kate O'Brien's portrayal of Irish governesses in Spain, is set.

Lynch wrote several more novels and in the context of New Woman writing, *Daughters of Men* (1892), set in Greece which she visited in 1885, is notable for the portrait of Photini, a renowned pianist of Greek and German descent who initially scandalises the naïve young hero, Rudolph, by the masculine freedoms of her life – she drinks, smokes, reads French novels, wears her hair short and has affairs. In some respects Photini resembles what we know of Lynch herself: Katharine Tynan recalls Lynch and her sisters reading George Sand at home in the original French[51] and her bohemian lifestyle in Paris seems to have shocked the American writer Gertrude Atherton.[52] But Photini is not so much a model for the New Woman as an eccentric genius sprung from the backstreets of Athens, half-educated, except in music, and ill at ease in polite society. The novel is predominantly a portrait of Greek life, as well as a critique of various forms of masculine behaviour.

KATHERINE THURSTON

Katherine Cecil Thurston (1875–1911) was born in Cork, daughter of P.J. Madden, a banker who was a friend of Charles Parnell and later became mayor of Cork (1885–86). The exploration of gender in her fiction has recently attracted critical interest.[53] The theme of gender roles must have had a personal resonance for Thurston: in divorce proceedings, reported in the *Irish Times* of 8 April 1910, her husband, the writer Ernest Temple Thurston, whom she had married in London in 1901, 'complained she was earning more than he was', that 'her personality was dominating him, and that he must get away from her'.[54] In reality he was already living with another woman.

John Chilcote, MP (1904), retitled *The Masquerader* for its US publication, displays Thurston's characteristic interest in identity as performance. Chilcote, a morphine addict and weary both of his marriage and of politics, swaps places with John Loder, an unsuccessful lawyer. The novel deals with several *fin de siècle* themes such as drug addiction, the double (Stevenson's *Dr Jekyll and Mr Hyde* is referenced in the novel) and the Darwinian theme of the survival of the fittest, the code by which Loder lives until he finds it tempered by his love for Chilcote's wife, Eve.

The political environment of *John Chilcote, MP* is well described, possibly due to Thurston's observation of her father's work as mayor and his political association with Charles Parnell, but the novel also reveals the influence of Anthony Trollope's Palliser novels. Like Phineas Finn, but more successfully, Loder faces a decisive speech in parliament on which his career depends. Eve Chilcote sees it as her role to be a supportive companion in her husband's career but, as with Trollope's Lady Laura Standish, there is more than a suggestion that, if society permitted it, she would have preferred a career of her own. She tells Loder (masquerading as Chilcote): "'You will always despise your opportunities, and I suppose I shall always envy them … That's the way with men and women.'"[55] The novel is well plotted and in the scenes with John Chilcote touches on the still relevant question of whether people in public life can ever have a private life. *John Chilcote, MP* remained on the *New York Times* bestseller list for two years, was four times made into a film, beginning with a silent version in 1912, and was later turned into a stage play, opening on Broadway in 1917. A hair-raisingly patronising account in the *Irish Times* of a women writers' dinner held in 1905 gives us a glimpse of Thurston at this period of her life:

> The Assembly numbered one hundred and eighty-five, and was a most representative gathering, including novelists, minor poets, and journalists. What with pretty frocks, flower-wreathed heads, and glittering diamonds, to say nothing of coloured sequins, the large room presented a most brilliant appearance … One of

the most remarkable figures was Mrs Katherine Cecil Thurston, author of *John Chilcote, MP*, that most talked of book. She is a tall, handsome woman, and was becomingly gowned in rich rose-red satin, a shade between pink and red, something the colour of a tea rose. She has such a striking personality that it would be impossible to pass her by without asking who she was.[56]

Thurston's *Fly on the Wheel* (1908) anticipates Kate O'Brien's fiction in its depiction of outlaw passion set against the background of the stultifying routine of a provincial town (here Waterford), and the Irish Catholic *bourgeoisie* with their silver, their Waterford crystal, their well-laden tables and their convent-educated daughters. Like Tom in O'Brien's *The Last Summer*, Stephen Carey has been forced too early to assume responsibility as head of the family: abandoning his dreams, he turns himself into a prosperous businessman and chooses his wife with care. In full New Woman flight, the omniscient narrator comments:

His idea of a wife had the faint savour of Orientalism so frequently to be found in his country and his class. A wife, in his opinion, was useful – possibly attractive as well, but fundamentally useful; a chattel, a being to be clothed and fed and housed to the best of man's ability, but beyond that hardly to be considered; and he had looked round his little world much as the Eastern might have studied the slave-market.[57]

Stephen, however, desires more for his life. He reads Spencer, Huxley and Kant and, in a parallel with Joyce, these are the writers he sets against the Gaelic League embraced by his brother-in-law Tom and by Father Cunningham: "'If you want advancement, let it be educational by all means; but let the education be modern! Souse the country with modern thought – Spencer and Huxley, Haeckel and Kant – and be hanged to sentimentality!'"[58] This small-town atmosphere is the background against which the illicit love between Stephen and Isabel, lively and rebellious and recently returned from convent school in Paris, is played out. Thurston underlines how few options are available in Ireland to young women like Isabel: if a girl has not married by the age of twenty-eight she loses her popularity in the marriage market and is faced with the choice of entering a convent or earning her living in a society that looks unfavourably on the female worker: 'In no country in the world does the feminine mind shrink more sensitively from the stigma of old maid than in Ireland, where the woman-worker – the woman of broad interests – exists only as a rare type.'[59] Stephen's wife Daisy does not believe that 'a nice woman ought to know anything outside her home'.[60]

Isabel may be a modern woman but her tragedy is that she can envisage a future for herself only in terms of her love for Stephen whom she believes could be a great man in a larger environment such as England or America. As trapped as any of Ibsen's characters, Stephen and Isabel attempt to defy fate by going for a drive in his car, anticipating the fascination of modernist writers like Elizabeth Bowen with speed as liberation: 'they fled on, gaining speed with the flying moments. It was a mad drive.'[61] In the end, the pull of convention is too strong: Stephen returns to his passive wife and Isabel melodramatically drinks the poison she had intended for him, a modern woman defeated by circumstances of her life.

In Thurston's next novel, *Max* (1909), Princess Davorska's adoption of a male persona makes her more successful than Isabel in asserting her temperament against her environment. Disguising herself as Max enables the Russian princess to transcend boundaries of both nation and gender: 'he belonged to no country, to no sex.'[62] Princess Davorska asserts her belief in the right to choose which sex to be, rejecting the drawbacks she sees in femininity and associating masculinity with freedom, confidence, adventure and the power to pursue her vocation as an artist. Masquerading as Max, she tries to establish a friendship of equals with Edward Fitzgerald Blake, an Irishman in Paris, much as Angelica's masculine disguise in *The Heavenly Twins* enables her to converse freely with the Tenor. Yet gender conditioning is not easily resisted and the Princess feels that she has lost something by becoming male. She determines to 'materialize' as Max's sister, Maxine, in order to conquer her despised femininity once and for all. Blake, whose nascent homoerotic feelings for Max trouble him, finds loving Maxine is more straightforward: he tells Max that love trumps friendship. For the Princess Davorska, however, a woman's body spells entrapment, and marriage for women entails loss of identity until Blake convinces her that for men also marriage is about compromise. As in Kate O'Brien's *As Music and*

Splendour, music leads the heroine into an understanding of love. Though *Max* delivers the required romantic ending, it also ends on a vision of equality between the sexes similar to that found in Egerton's writing.

ETHEL VOYNICH

Born in Cork to the mathematician George Boole and his wife, feminist philosopher, mathematician and educationalist Mary Everest Boole, Ethel Voynich (1864–1960) married the Polish revolutionary Wilfred Voynich in 1891. Ethel Voynich became well known in Russian émigré circles and her best-known novel, *The Gadfly* (1897), deals with revolutionary politics in 1840s Italy. The novel was immensely popular in Soviet Russia on account of its revolutionary politics and was twice made into a film. From the New Woman point of view, *The Gadfly* provides an interesting reversal of gender stereotypes: the revolutionary Arthur Burton is delicate-looking and possesses a feminine sensibility while his comrade in arms, Gemma Warren, is calm and rational and goes by the nickname of Jim. However, the main focus of the novel is not on gender issues but on the politics of the Risorgimento and the intense relationship between Arthur and his unacknowledged father, Cardinal Montanelli.

BEATRICE GRIMSHAW

Beatrice Grimshaw (1870–1953), daughter of a prosperous Belfast merchant, was educated at home, at Caen in Normandy and at Victoria College, Belfast, but early broke away from her comfortable middle-class upbringing:

> I was governessed and schooled and colleged. I was taught to ride and play games. I was taught to behave. To write notes for Mamma. To do the flowers. To be polite but not too polite to Young Gentlemen ... But I was the Revolting Daughter – as they called them then. I bought a bicycle, with difficulty. I rode it unchaperoned ... The world opened before me. And as soon as my twenty-first birthday dawned, I went away from home, to see what the world might give to daughters who revolted.[63]

Grimshaw moved to Dublin where she worked as a journalist and then to London where she persuaded the *Daily Graphic* to commission her travel writing. In 1904 she left for the South Seas, visiting the New Hebrides and the Solomon Islands, before finding her home in Papua, New Guinea until 1934. On 6 May 1922, under the heading 'In Cannibal Areas: Wanderings of Irish Novelist', the *Irish Times* announced that: 'Miss Beatrice Grimshaw, the well-known Irish writer, reached Plymouth yesterday after fifteen years' solitary wanderings in little-known parts of the world. She spent several years in the cannibalistic areas of New Guinea, vast tracts of which have never been explored.'[64] Grimshaw published a steady stream of popular novels, stories and travel books that for a while ensured her a good income, though she eventually died in poverty in New South Wales.

Like so many of these precursors of modern-day feminism, Grimshaw remains an ambivalent figure: while her extensive travels would seem to qualify her as a New Woman, her fiction is of the popular romantic Mills & Boon variety (indeed several of her novels were published by that firm). Her views on marriage were staunchly Catholic and she believed in male superiority and the racial superiority of Europeans. Her most complex novel, *When the Red Gods Call* (1911), exposes these ambivalences. *When the Red Gods Call* opens in British New Guinea at the end of the nineteenth century with Hugh Lynch, an Irishman from County Clare, in prison for manslaughter. Hugh, who has something of the wildness of Heathcliff about him, is a planter and trader, and through him Grimshaw gives a detailed account of British New Guinea and its opening up to white settlers. The novel is therefore partly travel writing, dealing with the modernist theme of the primitive in the style of nineteenth-century realism, and there are similarities with the English novelist Rose Macaulay (1881–1958), who was fond of using the contrast between so-called civilised and uncivilised peoples as a satirical device to point out the flaws of contemporary society.

Embedded in the travel writing is a New Woman theme that sees Hugh's second wife Stephanie, 'a delicate young English girl',[65] develop into a worthy companion during the course of the novel. Stephanie's initial reaction to Hugh's arrest is to abandon him and return to England with her father. Nine years later, matured by suffering and on the advice of a Catholic priest, she returns to New Guinea to search for her husband. In the course of this her conventional social veneer of governor's daughter is eroded: 'Something of what Carlyle would call "husks and wrappages" had been stripped away in those few days; what was left was the real me, and I knew that, being thus found, it would never be lost again.'[66] Though the novel endorses a firmly Catholic view of marriage as an indissoluble sacrament,[67] Stephanie's voyage out turns her into a pioneer and in that sense she may be regarded as a New Woman.

SOMERVILLE AND ROSS

Gifford Lewis locates Edith Somerville and Martin Ross 'in that very first wave of New Women to be independent of men and to have successful professional lives'.[68] Edith Somerville (1858–1949) was born into a large Anglo-Irish family based at Drishane, County Cork. She was educated at home by governesses but spent a term at Alexandra College. She initially trained as an artist in Düsseldorf and Paris and her novel *French Leave* (1928) draws on her experiences as an art student in Paris in 1884 and 1885. Like Somerville, Anglo-Irish Patsey Kirwan observes that her younger brother's freedoms increase as he gets older while hers decrease. Patsey's dilemma is paralleled in that of a male from the lower classes, George Lester, who also wishes to be a painter despite a similar lack of funds and parental opposition: Somerville anticipates Woolf's remark in *A Room of One's Own* that women and working-class men face similar educational and professional barriers. An inheritance of forty pounds from her grandmother helps Patsey to fulfil her ambitions and the novel's most interesting scenes give a rare and vivid insight into the daily lives of Irish women artists in 1880s Paris.

   Somerville lived most of her life in County Cork running the family estate after her mother's death in tandem with her sister Hildegarde for fifty years. Her professional life encompassed not only writing and painting but also cattle breeding, schooling horses, estate management and acting as master of the West Carbery Hounds. The men in her life, especially her eldest brother Cameron, often depended on her to untangle their finances. Although Somerville remained, especially in sexual matters and in her reluctance to challenge male authority directly, very much a Victorian, such a life naturally predisposed her to favour equality between the sexes. After all, hunting was one of the sports in which women could compete on equal terms with men: 'The playing-fields of Eton did not as surely win Waterloo as the hunting-fields and lawn-tennis grounds of the kingdom won the vote for women,' she wrote in '*Not* the Woman's Place'.[69]

Martin Ross (1862–1915) was born Violet Martin into the Anglo-Irish Martin family whose estate was at Ross House, County Galway. When her father died in 1872, Ross House was closed up and Martin and her mother went to live on Dublin's northside while she attended Alexandra College. She embarked on journalism but her literary career blossomed after the meeting, in 1886, with her second cousin Edith Somerville. From 1888 onwards she was also heavily involved in helping her mother restore and run Ross House. After her mother's death in 1906, Martin lived mainly at the Somerville home in Castletownshend. Though both women ploughed much of their income back in to their family estates, their writing did allow them to take breaks from their families and travel abroad. Gifford Lewis has estimated that between 1898 and 1922 they earned over six thousand pounds from their writings.[70]

Feminism was part of both women's lives: they belonged to the Munster Women's Franchise League, founded in 1910, and in 1911 Somerville became its first president and Martin one of the vice presidents. Somerville was vocal in her conviction that the taxation of women without corresponding political representation was indefensible. While not being anti-family (she could hardly be that since so much of her energy and finances, like Martin's, went into keeping the family estate going), Somerville valued the strong bonds between professional women:

> The outstanding fact, as it seems to me, among women who live by their brains, is friendship. A profound friendship that extends through every phase and aspect of life, intellectual, social, pecuniary. Anyone who has experience of the life of independent and artistic women knows this.[71]

For Somerville, one of the most valuable features of the Suffrage movement was, as she said in her first speech to the Irish Women's Franchise League (IWFL), that it taught women 'to believe in and to stand by each other'.[72] The last work Somerville and Ross wrote together before Martin's death was a suffrage pamphlet commissioned by Lady Robert Cecil about the war work being done by the movement. In *Irish Memories* (1917), Somerville wrote: 'it pleases me to think that our work together was closed and sealed with this expression of the faith that was and is in us.'[73] After Martin's death, Somerville's meeting with the composer and feminist Ethel Smyth in 1919 introduced her to younger members of the women's movement associated with Lady Rhondda's *Time and Tide* in London. She read Vera Brittain's book on marriage with approval, though she could not get on with either Brittain's *Testament of Youth* nor with her friend Winifred Holtby's novel *South Riding*, finding both too earnest.

The New Woman is arguably as important a strand running through the fiction of Somerville and Ross as the more discussed theme of relations between the Anglo-Irish and their tenants. Somerville was familiar with New Woman writers: Sarah Grand's *The Heavenly Twins* was read and discussed at Drishane[74] and both Martin and herself read Olive Schreiner's *The Story of an African Farm*. The two authors were aware of women writers who had gone before them, Maria Edgeworth being a particular influence. Martin possessed correspondence between Edgeworth and their great-grandmother, who had been a close friend. In *Irish Memories*, Somerville explained that their aim in their fiction had been to follow in Edgeworth's footsteps, rather than adopt the rollicking stage Irishry of Charles Lever with whom they were often classed: 'Miss Edgeworth had the privilege, which was also ours, of living in Ireland, in the country, and among the people of whom she wrote.'[75] They aimed at exactness in reproduction of Irish speech patterns, neither exaggerating nor poeticising it like the Literary Revival writers. When Elizabeth Hudson, compiling a bibliography of their works, classed their writing with that of Maria Edgeworth and Charles Lever, Somerville wrote back replacing Lever with Jane Austen as a more appropriate comparison, not only for stylistic reasons but also on account of their gender: 'I hope you don't mind that I have substituted Jane Austen's name for Lever's. She also was "a chronicler of her time" and being a woman it seems suitable to bracket her with Maria Edgeworth *and* ourselves!'[76] Like Woolf, whose *A Room of One's Own* she found admirable, Somerville was aware of the importance of literary foremothers. She anticipated later arguments around the *Field Day Anthology of Irish Literature* when she waxed indignant against the series 'Every Irishman's Library' for issuing complete works by William Carleton and Charles Lever but only selections from the work of Maria Edgeworth. For Somerville, Edgeworth was by far the greater writer, especially in 'that extraordinary *tour de force, Castle Rackrent*'.[77]

Encouraged by the success of an article on Youghal, accepted in 1887 by Oscar Wilde as editor of *Woman's World*, Somerville and Ross embarked on their first novel, *An Irish Cousin*. Their writing method is described in Chapter 11 of *Irish Memories*. The two women would have a discussion and the result would be written down by whoever happened to be holding the pen at the time, leaving a left-hand margin for corrections. Then Somerville, who had the neater hand, clean copied their work. Not until 1906 did she employ a typist. They often passed around their manuscripts to relatives and friends and read out their stories to their families for criticism and comment. Their relatives were not at first inclined to take their efforts seriously and Somerville famously complained about the difficulty of establishing themselves as professionals in face of family demands on their time: 'all our writing was done in casual scraps. We had no consideration for ourselves and still less did anyone else show consideration for us.'[78] To Martin she wrote: 'To attempt anything serious or demanding steady work is just simply impossible here, and I feel sickened of even trying – we are all so tied together – whatever is done must be done by everyone in the whole place and as the majority prefer wasting their time, that is the prevalent amusement.'[79]

An Irish Cousin was referred to in family circles as The Shocker, referencing the Shilling Shockers, light thrillers then in vogue. The family did not much like the book, and on her mother's suggestion Somerville added in some romantic scenes. Their relatives' attitude changed to one of respect, however, when the pair began to earn money from their writing. The London publisher Richard Bentley offered them twenty-five pounds on publication of The Shocker and a further twenty-five on sale of five hundred copies. It was Martin who did the lion's share of the work in negotiating prices with publishers and drumming up publicity. After the novel was written, she wrote to Somerville:

> I think the two Shockers have a very strange belief in each other, joined to a critical faculty – added to which writing together is – to me at least – one of the greatest pleasures I have. To write with you doubles the triumph and enjoyment having first halved the trouble and anxiety.[80]

An Irish Cousin (1889), published under the names of Geilles Herring and Martin Ross, is most definitely an apprentice piece, written by two young women desperate to establish themselves as professional writers. Their eye on the marketplace may partly account for the Gothic excesses of the novel, for *An Irish Cousin* is a combination of the Big House genre and the romance plot, Gothicised under the influence of Sheridan Le Fanu's *Uncle Silas* and Charlotte Brontë's *Jane Eyre*. Theodora, shortened in the novel to the gender-free Theo, is a proto New Woman, a rational voice in an irrational world. Her uncle Dominick, owner of the Sarsfield family's Big House, Durrus, is clearly labouring under a guilty conscience and also has sinister designs relative to the future of his niece, an innocent outsider to Ireland, on a visit to Durrus from the US. The Anglo-Irish landlord is not just irresponsible, as in Maria Edgeworth's fiction, but criminal in his complicity in his brother's death, which has cheated Theo of her rightful inheritance.

Dominick's past relationship with his illegitimate cousin and servant Moll Hourihane results in her insanity, making her one of a long line of women whom life in the Big House renders insane, such as Cousin Nettie in Elizabeth Bowen's *The Heat of the Day* and Miss Pidgie in Molly Keane's *Two Days in Aragon*. The costs of miscegenation and sexual exploitation descend to the next generation since Dominick is most likely the father of Mad Moll's beautiful daughter Anstey, the peasant girl who lives in the gate lodge and falls passionately in love with her half-brother Willy. Willy belongs to the Gothic part of the novel; by contrast, the romantic hero, Nugent O'Neill, whose sister Henrietta is a suffragist, represents the modern man. The plot creaks in places: for such a lively heroine, Theo is exceptionally obtuse over the mystery of her father's death. Nevertheless a review in the *Observer* highlighted what the two authors had taken most pains over, namely faithfulness to Irish speech patterns: '*An Irish Cousin* is quite one of the best Irish novels of the generation. The texture of the story is slighter than *Hurrish*, but the truth to detail is more striking, and the dialect more faithfully reproduced than by Miss Lawless.'[81]

Their subsequent novel, *Naboth's Vineyard* (1891), dealing with romance, greed and treachery among the Land Leaguers, is a thin and melodramatic work but it inspired an interesting review in the *Daily Graphic*:

> The issue of a new story by the two clever ladies who gave us *An Irish Cousin* serves to remind us of the instructive fact that Irish fiction is practically in the hands of Irish women, and, let us

hasten to add, in very safe hands too. Gerald Griffin and Samuel Lover, Charles Lever and Sheridan Lefanu have left no literary descendants in the male line ... for faithful pictures of Irish home life and Irish scenery we must go to the author of *Flitters, Tatters, and the Counsellor* [May Laffan], to Miss Lawless's *Hurrish*, and to the admirably vivid pages of *Naboth's Vineyard*.[82]

For once, Irish women's fiction was being recognised.

The Real Charlotte (1894), begun in 1889 but not completed until 1893, is Somerville and Ross's masterpiece and generally regarded as one of the most technically accomplished of Irish nineteenth-century novels. Its portrayal of an entire society is facilitated by the fluid social status of the 'land grabber' Charlotte Mullen, daughter of a national schoolmistress and granddaughter of 'a barefooted country girl', who moves between classes, invited to Bruff, the local Big House, while also collecting rents from the 'savage' washerwomen at Ferry Row. Somerville's account in *Irish Memories* makes clear that of all the characters, Charlotte's young cousin Francie was closest to the authors' hearts,[83] but it is the portrait of Charlotte, greedy and obsessed with power, that provides the focus of the book. Her unrequited sexual passion for Roderick Lambert, for which Somerville drew on two youthful affairs of her own, is as ugly as any of Balzac's portraits of characters in the grip of an obsession.

Despite Somerville's endorsement of the life of the single, professional woman, there is little sympathy for Charlotte trying to make her way in the world, and her modernity in reading French novels and 'yellow paper-covered volumes' is portrayed as a threatening force. In fact, Charlotte and her young cousin Francie are not so much New Women as women positioned between tradition and modernity. Both have to establish themselves in the world using the limited resources available to them. Whereas the pretty and lively Francie can rely on her looks and personality to secure a marriage, Charlotte, squat and Caliban-like in appearance, with a large jaw and thick lips, has to rely on cunning, bullying and manipulation. If she is a New Woman, the class bias of Somerville and Ross against the rising middle classes, as well as Somerville's personal grudge against Emily Herbert, the real-life model for Charlotte, results in a far from admirable character.

Yet, a novel that begins with confusion over the gender of a cat remains fascinating for its gender politics. Unjustly excluded from power by class and gender, Charlotte would have made a better land agent than the weak and self-indulgent Lambert and a more efficient landowner than the lethargic heir to Bruff, Christopher Dysart. If there is criticism of those who fail to fulfil their proper gender roles – Charlotte is treated as an honorary man while Christopher is regarded as unmanly, even effeminate – there is also humour when the Dysarts' tutor, James Canavan, modelled on James Tucker, a hedge schoolmaster who tutored the Martin children, cross-dresses as Queen Elizabeth I. There is contempt for those who, like Mrs Lambert, play up to the expected wifely role and lightly sketched compassion for the daughter at home, Pamela Dysart, whose capacity for self-sacrifice makes her mid-way between an Angel in the House and one of Molly Keane's victimised daughters. The gender politics in *The Real Charlotte* are far from straightforward.

There is more than a touch of Jane Austen in the Lismoyle matrons' recognition of Christopher Dysart's eligibility and in Francie's determined pursuit of 'those heroes of romance, "the Lismoyle officers"',[84] in the use of social events like picnics to reveal character, and in the intertwining of marriages with money. Unlike a Jane Austen novel, however, *The Real Charlotte* writes beyond the romantic ending into a marriage of convenience for Francie and finally the young heroine's death. The novel as a whole is pessimistic about Ireland: the Anglo-Irish are in a state of irresponsible lethargy, the rising middle classes are venal and the peasants ill-educated. It ends appropriately with Norry's cry of despair and grief. Only the beauty of the Irish landscape redeems the country.

The Real Charlotte attracted negative reviews at the time, readers finding it too depressing. A review in the *Lady's Pictorial* is characteristic:

> The next time that E. OE. Somerville and Martin Ross combine to write a novel of Irish life, I hope they will keep to the fun, with the undercurrent of sadness which is so typical of the Irish race, and devote their clever and graphic pens to the task of delineating men and women who are brave, generous, and noble, instead of wasting their powers upon elaborately finished pictures of the sordid-minded Charlotte Mullens and Roddy Lamberts, whose ill-spent lives need no historian.[85]

The reviewer fretted that 'English people who read this novel will be confirmed in their mistaken idea that Ireland is a nation of barbarians.' These hostile notices puzzled the two authors since they knew that *The Real Charlotte* was their best work. A handful of writers, including Andrew Lang and W.B. Yeats, praised the novel, and in 1921 the Protestant Nationalist MP Stephen Gwynn, in an extensive review of the work of Somerville and Ross, called it 'the best novel ever written about Ireland ... it is the only book of theirs where sex-psychology is boldly handled. They make us feel how big, how ugly and how dangerous a force sex is in Charlotte who desires love none the less because she is physically repulsive.'[86]

The New Woman continued to be an important strand in the writing of Somerville and Ross. In *The Silver Fox* (1897), the building of a railway line is used, as in several English novels of the period, to explore issues of tradition and modernity. Somerville and Ross complicate the theme by employing it in the context of those who understand Ireland and those who do not. One of the former is the Anglo-Irish Slaney Morris, a proto-New Woman, who sympathises with the local legend of the silver fox that appears whenever the land is tampered with. Among the latter are Lady Susan French, an Englishwoman who has married Slaney's brother, and her would-be lover Wilfred Glasgow, builder of the railway. The vulgarity of the English in this novel and their lack of understanding of Irish customs will be echoed by Elizabeth Bowen in her portrayal of English army wives in *The Last September*. One of the striking elements in *The Silver Fox*, noted by Declan Kiberd, is the overcoming of class and national barriers in the tentative sisterhood that develops between Slaney and Lady Susan and between Lady Susan and the peasant woman Maria Quin.[87] Perhaps mindful of criticism of *The Real Charlotte*, Somerville and Ross gave this New Woman a satisfactorily romantic ending.

It was at this time that Somerville and Ross embarked on their *Irish RM* stories where the New Woman makes an appearance in the guise of the rising Dublin middle-class woman Larkie McRory, a more successful Francie Fitzpatrick, whose victory on the hunting field so impresses Major Yeates in *In Mr Knox's Country* (1915). In the last complete novel written jointly by Somerville and Ross, *Dan Russel the Fox: An Episode in the Life of Miss Rowan* (1911), the New Woman is an Englishwoman, the independent and wealthy Katharine Rowan who earns her living as a writer. The novel opens in Aix-les-

Bains, with an E.M. Forster-like evocation of the English abroad, but quickly transfers to Ireland where Katharine, for the first time in her life, makes her acquaintance with the Irish hunting scene and becomes obsessed by it, much to the disgust of her writer friend Ulick Adare who, though Irish himself, follows the hunt on his bicycle. Katharine determinedly pursues the fox that in the end, like John Michael Fitz-Symons with whom she fancies herself in love, eludes her pursuit. As in *The Silver Fox*, there is a distinct sense of Ireland, an ancient and mysterious land, escaping English comprehension. The novel is one of the weaker Somerville and Ross works but it may have provided a stimulus for the young Molly Keane: there are several echoes of *Dan Russel* in Keane's apprentice novel *The Knight of Cheerful Countenance*.

There has been much debate on the exact nature of the relationship between Somerville and Martin.[88] From letters and diaries Gifford Lewis deduces that their relationship was emotional and intellectual rather than physical, with Somerville and her sister Hildegarde treating Martin as their 'third sister'.[89] They certainly shared a bed on occasion and Elizabeth Bowen remarked that the nature of the two writers' intimacy would, at the time in which she was writing (1970), have given rise to speculation. Bowen, however, dismissed the notion of a physical relationship on the grounds that the Anglo-Irish inclined as a class, she felt, to sexlessness. Instead she defined their partnership as a rare case of 'interlocking creative imaginations'.[90]

This is not to deny the importance of the emotional, creative and perhaps sensual bond between the two women. On Martin's death in 1915, Somerville wrote to her brother, Cameron: 'No one but she and I can know what we were to one another … Half, and the best half, of my life and soul is torn away and there are no words and no tears that can cure my trouble.'[91] For Somerville, Martin's death did not mark the end of their literary partnership: regarding Martin as her spiritual collaborator, she continued to publish work under both their names. In the final chapter of *Irish Memories* she summed up their friendship: 'two lives that made the world a pleasant place for each other'.[92]

Somerville's words may stand as a tribute to the pioneering efforts of all the New Woman writers who struggled in this early period to give a voice to Irish women, from the ambivalences of Kathleen Mannington Caffyn and Emily Lawless to the confident didacticism of George Egerton and Sarah Grand and the subtler probing of gender, identity and performance found in Katherine

Thurston's *Max* and Somerville and Ross's *The Real Charlotte*. Of the authors discussed, Emily Lawless, George Egerton and Somerville and Ross show most interest in consciously shaping their narratives and the interiority of Egerton's writing as well as of Thurston's *Max* points forward to the modernist novel. Nonetheless, in this pre-modernist period, when not specifically dealing in the sensational or the Gothic, Irish women writers continued to adhere to the realist form, however fractured and contested, as most suited to conveying their messages about Ireland and women.

Chapter 3

1910–1939: DISILLUSIONMENT

*I*n May 1910, the Corinthian Dinner Committee gave a banquet for Irish women writers presided over by Lord Aberdeen. Twelve women writers, including Edith Somerville, Violet Martin, Augusta Gregory, Eva Gore-Booth, Emily Lawless, Susan Mitchell and Katharine Tynan were invited to the Gresham Hotel along with two hundred guests and the next day their photographs were in the *Irish Times*. This banquet is something of a highlight in the story of Irish women's writing and reflects the optimism of the early years of the twentieth century which in Ireland saw a ferment of political activity in which women played a crucial part, speaking in public not only on suffragism but on issues of nationalism and labour.

More clearly than in the earlier period, philanthropy is linked to feminism as, for example, in Susanne Day's novel *The Amazing Philanthropists* (1916). Born in Cork, Susanne Day (1876–1964) was both a philanthropist and a suffragette and she collaborated on plays with her fellow Cork suffragist Geraldine Cummins. *The Amazing Philanthropists* arose out of Day's work as a Poor Law Guardian and takes the form of a series of lively letters written by Lester Martin detailing her work on the Ballybawn Board of Guardians, during which she comes up against the sexism of the locals ranging from the Church of Ireland canon to the editor of the *Ballybawn Blazer*. As well as demonstrating Day's feminism, the novel is a mine of information on the work of Ireland's Poor Law Guardians. Together with another female board member, Mrs Maguire, Lester is able to make some advances on the issues of sanitation and infant welfare. However, the power of women to effect change in Irish public life was to be gradually eroded during the course of the following decades.

ROSAMOND JACOB

Rosamond Jacob's life is paradigmatic. Born in Waterford to a cultured Quaker family, Jacob (1888–1960) was educated partly at home and partly in Quaker and Protestant schools in Waterford. Though sharing her parents' agnosticism, Jacob remained deeply influenced all her life by the Quakers' pacifist and anti-imperialist attitudes. From 1909 onwards, she made frequent visits to Dublin to participate in feminist, nationalist and language revival activities and, after her mother's death in 1919, she moved to Dublin, sharing lodgings initially with Hanna Sheehy Skeffington and later with Dorothy Macardle. At this stage Jacob was optimistic that Ireland was about to enter a new phase of political and cultural life in which women would play a central part. However, increasingly her nationalism came into conflict with her feminism. She joined Sinn Féin but, wary of the dangers of identifying Irish suffragism with the English movement, was reluctant to commit formally to membership of the IWFL. She joined Cumann na mBan, founded as an auxiliary to the Irish Volunteers, but the lack of assertiveness among nationalist women caused her much irritation.

Jacob's novel *Callaghan*, published in 1920 under the gender-free pseudonym F. Winthrop, is unusual in making the question of Irish suffragism at least as important as Irish nationalism. The novel opens in 1913 and traces the evolution of the nationalist and the suffragette movements in the course of the years leading up to 1916. The conflict between feminism and nationalism is outlined in a scene in Dublin where the heroine, Frances Morrin, and her friend Una attend a meeting of the Irish Women's Franchise League. Frances joins the IWFL and begins selling copies of the *Irish Suffragist* on the street whereas Una is closer to Jacob's own position when she exclaims of the suffragette who tries to recruit them: 'She speaks as an Englishwoman throughout!'[1] Although she is willing to help Frances sell suffrage papers, Una, like Jacob, refuses to commit formally to the suffragists because she does not want a vote given to her by the British parliament.

Callaghan portrays the choices facing politically active women at this time when Frances falls in love with Andy Callaghan, a republican activist. Though Frances supports Irish nationalism, she is not prepared to have a relationship with Callaghan unless he admits her equality. Callaghan takes a while to comprehend her seriousness on this point but eventually he manages to come to grips with 'this idea that a woman might have public duties which seemed to her as important as a man's'.[2] Politically, the novel is left open-ended – in 1920, it could hardly be anything else. Romantically, the novel ends in closure and Leanne Lane reads the ending as re-establishing gender hierarchies, Frances's marriage and the raid of Callaghan's home by the police shifting the focus away from suffragism onto nationalist concerns.[3]

A review of *Callaghan* in the *Irish Times* (14 January 1921) praised it as 'an unusually well-written novel'. 'It has been a quite unexpected pleasure, after wading through many ill-conceived, dull tales about things Irish,' wrote the somewhat jaded reviewer, 'to come on a story so fresh and sincere and thoroughly independent in its point of view.' This reviewer guessed that F. Winthrop was a militant suffragette. Daniel Corkery, on the other hand, reviewing the novel for *Banba* (July 1921), took the author to be male, focused entirely on Callaghan, and objected to the word 'sexual' as aping the vulgarity of English writers. Nevertheless, Corkery concluded that *Callaghan* was one of 'the most convincing novels that have been written about the Ireland of our days'.

Jacob's next novel, *The Troubled House* (1938), was written in the early 1920s but not published till the following decade, probably because of the volatile political situation. Its date of composition is important, marking the novel as belonging to the years when it was still possible to be optimistic about the opportunities for Irish women's lives. Subtitled *A Novel of Dublin in the Twenties*, it is a portrait of a family riven by political and religious differences. *A House Divided* had been the original title, emphasising the Cullen family's metaphorical role as symptomatic of the schisms in Irish society. The father, Jim, a Catholic, supports the Irish Parliamentary Party and believes in peaceful efforts for home rule. The eldest son, Theo, defining himself as a pacifist republican influenced by the Quakers, argues for a policy of passive resistance against the British. The mother, Maggie, is a Unitarian. While recognising the ethical superiority of Theo's viewpoint, Maggie shares the republican sympathies of her middle son, Liam, and secretly helps him when he is on the run. Drawing on Jacob's own experience, *The Troubled House* captures the atmosphere of Dublin during the War of Independence with British Army raids and sounds of gunshot in the streets. It ends in tragedy when Jim is mistakenly shot in an ambush by Liam, symbolising the removal of the colonialist older generation by the younger generation of Sinn Féin. Jim's apology to Liam for his past physical violence towards him suggests the final defeat of the colonial system of abuse and domination.

As in *Callaghan*, the nationalist theme of *The Troubled House* does not preclude attention to women's lives. Unusually in Irish fiction, Maggie refuses to be confined by motherhood. At the beginning of the novel, she is returning to Ireland from Australia where she has spent three years nursing her sister in order to free her niece for her studies. She feels it has been good for her sons to learn to be independent of her and she rejects special privileges for mothers, responding to her sister-in-law's comment that 'It's a hard thing to be a mother in Ireland now' with 'Mothers must take their chance like other people.'[4] Josephine and her partner Nix, both New Women and artists, provide a counterbalance to Maggie's life and suggest more varied possibilities for women's lives. Maggie admires them for their dedication to their work but believes that such dedication is only possible without a husband and children, an interesting corrective to the optimism of New Woman writing.

Despite her refusal to define herself by her motherhood, Maggie gets drawn into the ideological conflicts in her family in a way that subsumes her sense of self:

> It came into my mind … what a queer thing it was that my life should spend itself thus, almost entirely in love and care and fear and thought and anxiety over three men and a boy. Was I nothing but a being relative to them, without real existence of my own? … It seemed absurd, futile, unworthy … My energy had all gone into one channel; I could not liberate myself enough of it to

> concentrate on any life of my own ... Was it necessary for wives
> and mothers to be like that? I could not believe it.[5]

Maggie's situation reflects how it was all too easy for feminist concerns to
be relegated to the margins by political events. Despite her wish to remain
detached and objective as a mother, the violent political situation affects
Maggie's attitude to her sons, a fact that perhaps goes some way to explaining
why, irrespective of Catholic ideology, Irish mothering of sons has often been
unusually intense.

Unpublished manuscripts by Jacob reveal her interest in exploring sexuality
and the extent to which she was obliged to engage in self-censorship in her
published work. Among the papers held by the National Library of Ireland is
an unfinished story by Jacob written in 1924 about a love affair between Nix
and Theo.[6] The sexual scenes between them are described with a frankness that
would have made publication impossible and which owe not a little in tone
and vocabulary to Jacob's reading of D.H. Lawrence (in fact Nix is reading
Lawrence). The couple discuss sadism, masochism, phallic imagery and the
beauty of the naked male body. Nix has painted a male nude without disguising
the penis and has had her painting rejected by the RHA on that account.[7]
During the 1920s, Jacob was also working on her unpublished novel, 'The
Third Person Singular'.[8] The plot has echoes of Thurston's *The Fly on the Wheel*
and is set in the same county, Waterford, though among Protestant rather than
Catholic middle classes. The manuscript is less interesting for the love story
between Hugh and the married Violet than for its portrayal of Constance
and Emily, two independent women living together. Constance, who is partly
the mouthpiece for Jacob, displays an interest in sexuality and the masculine
form explored more daringly in 'Theo and Nix'. Confessing her love for Hugh
to a shocked Emily, Constance admits: "'I know I take too much interest in
masculinity – because I'm starved of it – but I'm nearer the right and normal
than you are, with your vacant cavity where sex ought to be.'"[9] The passage
reveals both Jacob's dissatisfaction with her single status and the way in which
her writing might have developed had censorship, and perhaps her own fears,
not inhibited her.

Jacob's life after 1922 was, like that of many republican women, a series
of withdrawals from the equal citizenship and purposeful activity she desired.

In Jacob's case this marginalisation was exacerbated by her single status in a state increasingly premised on motherhood and family and by her failure to get her fiction published. Her affair with the IRA activist Frank Ryan petered out in the mid-1930s and her Quaker upbringing made her feel alienated by the Catholic ethos of the new state. In an effort to carve out a space for herself Jacob continued to espouse increasingly counter-cultural left-wing and feminist causes, as well as turning her attention to international issues.

In 1957, Jacob published *The Rebel's Wife*, a fictionalised account of the life of Matilda Tone in which Jacob is at pains to stress the equality of the marriage between Wolfe Tone and Matilda. Contemporary reviewers however focused on the male political figures and the book did not sell well, though in 1958, the Women Writers' Club made *The Rebel's Wife* their Book of the Year and Jacob was guest of honour at their silver jubilee banquet. Mention of the Women Writers' Club recurs in Jacob's diaries and as an example of supportive networks between women writers it certainly merits future research. Jacob clearly found the club an important support during the years when her work remained unpublished. Founded in 1933 by Dorothy Macardle and Blanaid Salkfield, the Women Writers' Club was a means for Irish women writers to meet in one another's homes in order to read and discuss work in progress as well as debate wider social and political issues. As Gerardine Meaney observes of this period: 'One does not really need to see photographic and newspaper evidence (though it helps) of Jacob, O'Brien, Macardle and Sheehy Skeffington sitting down to dinners and awards ceremonies together to postulate a critical culture that was woman centred, dissident, active and well aware of its political limitations.'[10]

Jacob's biographer sees her final years as ones of increasing marginalisation: 'as a single woman with limited formal education, she was forced increasingly to live on the fringes of society.'[11] In this, Jacob's life was representative of the fate of many previously influential women in the newly independent Irish state.

SOMERVILLE AND ROSS

Edith Somerville's feelings of marginalisation in twentieth-century Ireland had more to do with class and religion than with gender. After 1916 she became increasingly critical of the English for their handling of the Irish situation and felt that they had not done enough to protect the position of the Anglo-Irish. *Mount Music* (1919), published, despite Martin's death, under the joint name of Somerville and Ross, opens in the authors' favourite period, the 1890s, and portrays the decline of the once-powerful Talbot-Lowry family through a combination of political circumstances, personal failings and the social ambitions of the middle-class Catholic Dr Mangan. *The Enthusiast* (1921), set in 1920, deals with the Troubles head on. Despite the difficult times, Anglo-Irishman Dan Palliser, possibly based on Horace Plunkett, founder of the Irish Co-operative Movement, is determined to dedicate himself to enriching his country by introducing new farming methods. As one would expect, the novel is knowledgeable about local Irish politics and rural affairs and it seems at first that Somerville's message, possibly aimed at English readers, was that, despite the Troubles, everyday life was continuing in Ireland. The scenes at the Rural District Council and the Agricultural Show possess some of the humour of the *Irish RM* stories. However, both author and protagonist become overwhelmed by the Irish situation: Somerville strives for a humorous tone but her subject matter is too dark and Dan ends up defeated and distrusted both by his Anglo-Irish counterparts and by the native Irish. In his review of the work of Somerville and Ross in the *Edinburgh Review* (October 1921), Stephen Gwynn observed that in *An Enthusiast* and *Mount Music* Somerville and, he added tactfully, 'her comrade' were attempting to get to grips with what amounted to a social revolution in their lives.

The Big House of Inver (1925), though written by Somerville, famously had its genesis in a visit by Violet Martin to Tyrone House, home of the once-powerful St George family, and her encounter with the last, illegitimate descendant of the family, the elderly Miss St George.[12] Set in 1912, *The Big House of Inver* is a powerful and dark portrait of the way in which heredity plays itself out through the various members of the Prendeville family whose motto ('Je Prends') suggests their status as land grabbers. *The Big House of Inver* follows in the tradition of the comic grotesque of *Castle Rackrent* but the central character here is a woman, Shibby Pindy, an illegitimate daughter of the Prendeville line. In Shibby, a monomaniac intent on returning the legitimate Prendeville heir, her half-brother Kit, to the Big House and its demesne, Somerville creates a portrait second only in power to Charlotte Lucas. In her discussion of these later novels, Vera Kreilkamp argues persuasively that the death of the more politically conservative Martin freed Somerville to take a sharper look at the Anglo-Irish and the extent of their responsibility for accelerating their own decline.[13] The Big House, rather than its inhabitants, stands for civilisation in the novel and Shibby finally realises that none of the Prendeville family have ever nor will ever live up to the promise implied in its architecture: 'There was too much pride and wickedness long ago, destroying the ones that came after.'[14] It is Somerville's damning indictment of her class's failure to perform its socially mandated role.

THE POPULAR NOVEL

Obliged to take account of the turbulent times, popular novels of the period by Irish women tried to effect reconciliation between the warring factions generally by means of the romance plot.

B.M. Croker

Daughter of an Anglican rector, Bithia Mary Sheppard (1847–1920) was born in County Down, educated in England and France and, after her marriage to Lt. Col. John Stokes Croker, lived in India and Burma for fourteen years. It was there that she embarked on her career as a prolific and commercially successful novelist of Anglo-Indian romances. In *Lismoyle: An Experiment in Ireland* (1914), Croker employs the well-worn theme of the visitor to Ireland in the shape of Rhoda, daughter of an Irish mother but raised outside Ireland. Invited by her aunt to Lismoyle, Rhoda encounters an Ireland of ruined estates and unemployment but is impressed by the hard work of Niel and his sister Bryda in keeping the estate going. Love soon ensues and with the aid of Rhoda's fortune, but also of a Romney found in the attic, Lismoyle will be restored. Such a novel published at this time about Ireland could only be intended as escapism. However, Croker does make some interesting comments on the emptiness of the Irish countryside and on the lack of entertainment for Catholic country girls in particular. Whereas the men have football matches and cards to amuse them, the girls do nothing but attend mass and sit at home. 'No wonder they go off to Australia and America,' comments one character.[15] Rhoda's first meeting in Ireland is with a group of girls emigrating because there are no jobs for them, an anticipation of a problem that was to grow in the middle decades of the twentieth century.

Annie M.P. Smithson

Until the arrival of chick lit in the 1990s, Annie Smithson (1873–1948) could be counted as one of the most successful Irish romantic novelists. She published nineteen novels, all of them bestsellers, as well as an autobiography, *Myself and Others* (1944). Born in Dublin into a Protestant middle-class family, Smithson trained as a nurse and midwife in London and Edinburgh and then devoted herself to Dublin's poor. After an unhappy love affair with a married man, she converted to Roman Catholicism at the age of thirty-four, whereupon she was disowned by her family. She became an ardent nationalist and campaigned for Sinn Féin in 1918, nursed the wounded during the Civil War and was briefly imprisoned by the Free State in 1922. Edna O'Brien attests to the popularity of Smithson's 'painful and breathlessly sad' novels in 1930s and '40s rural Ireland: 'Always the "Via Dolorosa" until the excruciatingly happy ending, until the miracle of everlasting love occurred.'[16] In Evelyn Conlon's semi-autobiographical *Stars in the Daytime*, about growing up in rural Ireland in the late 1950s and '60s, Smithson's novels are still regarded as 'handy books for a growing girl', a shorthand way for mothers to induct their daughters 'into a woman's terrible world where romance was all she could ask for and marriage was all she could get'.[17]

Smithson's first novel, *Her Irish Heritage* (1917), opens in 1913 and leads up to the events of 1916. Dedicated to the memory of those who died in the Easter Rising, the novel is unashamedly patriotic and sentimental but also, more interestingly, draws on Smithson's work as a nurse in the Dublin slums. Clare Castlemaine, daughter of an Irish mother and an atheist English businessman, and orphaned at the age of twenty-two, is invited over to Ireland by her maternal uncle. The Blakes, an impoverished middle-class family living in Rathmines, introduce Clare, 'brought up to consider the Irish as a sort of second-rate English',[18] to a range of Irish life. One of the Blake sons, Shamus, is a Gaelic Leaguer and republican, Ursula is about to enter the Poor Clares while Bride is a social worker. Clare becomes familiar with the lives of the nurses in St Columba's Home and with their work in the Coombe. Impressed by the way the faith of the Catholic convert Mary Carmichael pulls her through a tragic love affair (possibly based on Smithson's own), Clare moves towards being received into the Catholic Church. A novel that ends in 1916 with a chapter titled 'The Call of the Dark Rosaleen' can have only one viewpoint: ashamed of her nation, Clare is relieved that marriage to Anthony Farrell will make her entirely Irish.

Katharine Tynan

Katharine Tynan returned to Ireland in 1911 when her husband was appointed resident magistrate (RM) for Mayo. Not only was Tynan returning to a very different Ireland from the one she had left, an Ireland where the voices of nationalism and labour were growing increasingly louder, but her years in England among the middle classes had marked her to the extent that while she remained an Irish nationalist, she also felt loyalty to England. She supported the British in the First World War and both her sons enlisted as soon as they were old enough. After her husband's death in 1919, at odds with republicanism, Tynan resided mostly abroad, in England, Germany and France.

In her autobiography, Tynan describes her literary output during her time in Ireland: 'During my three years and a bit in Mayo I have, as a mere matter of book-making, written nine novels besides *Lord Edward: A Study in Romance*, which is something more than a novel: two volumes of reminiscences, three volumes of poetry, two school-books, besides a great number of short stories, articles, etc.', adding poignantly, 'I am not specially proud of this facility of mine; it has produced a good deal of honest work, with, of course, a good deal of necessary pot-boiling.'[19] Seemingly incapable of living on the pay of an RM, Tynan and her husband relied on the income from her writing to an extent that, as she was aware, damaged the quality of her work.

Much of Tynan's fiction in this period uses the popular novel to urge reconciliation. *The Golden Rose* (1924) opens in 1917 with Ireland divided between the supporters of the First World War and those who support 1916. After the executions of 1916, the people turn against Dr Anthony O'Reilly, a Catholic, whose four sons are fighting at the front. The doctor's daughter Carmel is engaged to Beaufoy Molyneux, Protestant son of the local Big House. Beau returns from the trenches shell-shocked and, after many vicissitudes, in the final reconciliation scene Carmel opens her arms to him in an embrace that is as much maternal as lover-like. Tynan ends with an image of a conciliatory Mother Ireland similar to M.E. Francis's *Dark Rosaleen*, but Tynan's sympathies in this novel lie less with the Catholic Irish than with those Irishmen who fought in the First World War.

A later novel from this period, *The River* (1929), depicts the bitterness of the Anglo-Irish after independence and their sense of betrayal by the British: 'It was very sudden,' remarks Lady McGregor. 'England – all they should have given us was a little time.'[20] Tynan again uses romance as a vehicle to promote reconciliation, and *The River* ends with a series of marriages between those of different religions, portrayed as the Anglo-Irish crossing the river to marry Catholics, thus bringing in new blood to run the old estates and embedding the Anglo-Irish more firmly in Irish life.

The Playground (1930) opens in a Dublin tenement though the novel speedily moves out of the tenements as John Tracey is taken under the wing of the Anglo-Irish Barton family and trains to be a gardener. As in Jacob's *The Troubled House*, a divided family represents the nation divided: John fights in the British Army during the First World War, Christopher, also with the British Army, is killed in Dublin in 1916, whereas their brothers, Pierce and Fergus, fight with the Volunteers and are imprisoned after the Rising. Like Maggie Cullen, Mrs Tracey becomes a mother torn between her sons though, revealing where Tynan's sympathies now lie, the two Sinn Féiners turn their backs on violence after their release. Several love stories work themselves out through the course of the novel and this mixture of socio-political themes with romance was evidently commercially successful. Tynan's novels were marketed as 'clean, wholesome love stories, free from intrigue and sensationalism, and containing well-drawn characters and good dialogue'. They are also full of repetitions, digressions and sentimentality.

Jessie Louisa Rickard

Jessie Rickard (1876–1963), who wrote a large number of popular romances, comedies and detective fiction under the name Mrs Victor Rickard, was born Jessica Louisa Moore, daughter of a Church of Ireland clergyman, and brought up in Mitchelstown, County Cork. Her second husband, Victor Rickard, fought with the Munster Fusiliers and was killed in 1915. The First World War is the subject of Rickard's novel *The Fire of Green Boughs* (1918), which has some parallels with *Non-Combatants and Others* (1916) by the English novelist Rose Macaulay in its criticism of the attitudes of non-combatants.

The Fire of Green Boughs opens in London where Dominic Roydon, who has been invalided out of the fighting, is well aware that the old order is changing and that the future of young women like his cousin Sylvia, brought up in the Victorian era and trained to do nothing in particular, is precarious. Sylvia acts as unpaid companion to Dominic's mother, Lady Roydon, and takes on war work as a badly paid clerical worker before being shipped out to Ireland after Lady Roydon's death, to live in the family's rambling house on the Kerry coast. The novel is thus able, like Elizabeth Bowen's Second World War fiction, to provide a contrast between the two countries during wartime.

For the city-bred Sylvia it is the loneliness and silence of rural Ireland that strikes her after wartime London and she comes into her own, inspired by the landscape and by the spirits of the Lynches, the original owners of Ballinadree. Her view of the war changes also. She feels a common bond with the younger generation involved in the fighting, and when a dying German sailor turns up at Ballinadree, she hides him from the police. The novel draws on the conventions of the thriller as well as the romance plot, for what Sylvia and her Irish friends see as an act of compassion is taken by non-combatants in London to be an act of treachery. *The Fire of Green Boughs* ends with Sylvia's marriage to Willie Kent (a Kerry MP), but not before it has explored the labyrinthine intricacies of Irish allegiances during the First World War.

Geraldine Cummins

Geraldine Cummins (1890–1969), born in Cork, was co-founder, with Edith Somerville and Susanne Day, of the Munster Women's Franchise League. Cummins's novel *The Land They Loved* (1919) is set during the First World War and, like Tynan's fiction, has a mission to reconcile those Irishmen who fought in the British Army with those who died during the Easter Rising. The division is represented in the Turpin family by Michael, killed in France, and his brother Steve, who died during the Easter Rising. Kate Carmody, who has been friendly with both, is haunted by the thought that the hostility between the brothers will continue after their deaths: Cummins's interest in spiritualism is evident in the novel.

The Land They Loved opens with 33-year-old Kate returning to the family farm in County Cork after five years working in domestic service in the US. Kate is a modern woman who reserves the right to choose a husband for herself, as distinct from the prudent marriage made by her half-brother Denis in the interests of the family farm. Finding the Irish countryside denuded of its young men away fighting or looking for jobs, Kate moves to Dublin to work in domestic service and there are some interesting accounts of the city in the aftermath of 1916 as Kate, in search of her masculine ideal, cuts a swathe through the Dublin Military Police. She eventually returns home to marry the determinedly non-political third Turpin brother Eugene, who has found his mission running a Co-Operative Society. The narrator comments: 'where there is division in a nation the people perish both mentally and spiritually.'[21]

Cummins's later novel *Fires of Beltane* (1936), set in rural Munster and covering the first three decades of the twentieth century, eschews political events in favour of a clichéd romance plot in which a playboy from the city, John Louis St Blaise, seduces the pious country girl Norah Keogh. The romance plot is a peg for Cummins to hang her interest in the supernatural. Norah, who sees visions – of the Virgin Mary, of the pagan Sky Queen – and is prone to be led astray by 'fancy', easily falls for Louis's tale that he is descended from a French count. The novel creates a Yeatsian divide between dreamers like Norah and Owen the fiddler, and hard-headed materialists like Norah's aunt Abina. Norah's many trials eventually persuade her that facing facts is better than relying on fancies. The style of the novel works against this message, however, being pervaded by both Catholic and pagan imagery. Atheism, on the other hand, is associated with the cities, where 'Cheap, popular, pseudo-scientific books had destroyed belief and made a desert-solitude of the universe.'[22]

Miriam Alexander

Miriam Alexander (1879–?) was born in Birkenhead but spent a brief period at Alexandra College in Dublin and became known for publishing historical novels with Irish settings. *The Green Altar* (1924) opens in Munster in the 1890s and traces political events up to the Civil War through the lives of the small community of Dunkyle, ranging from the inhabitants of the local Big House, Ballas Court, through the manor house of Killeenullick to the farming classes, the Spillanes and the MacCarthys, and the cabin-dwelling outlaws, the Cassidys. The Ballas family, prejudiced against Catholics and nationalists, lead unhappy lives isolated from the surrounding countryside by the high walls of Ballas Court. Like the Naylors in *The Last September*, they possess a hybrid identity: 'They considered it bad form to be Irish, and the barrier of birth and blood prevented them ever becoming English.'[23]

The novel focuses on three members of the younger generation, Morna, daughter of the gentry at Killeenullick, Ailill, son of the farming Spillanes, and Peg, adopted daughter of the MacCarthys who, in contrast to the Ballas family, dream of Irish independence and equality between the classes. The novel depicts the effect on the community of the arrival of a Gaelic League teacher to promote the Irish language, Irish dances and Irish history. Ailill, Peg and Morna are inspired by a performance of Yeats's 'Caithleen Ni Houlihan' at the Abbey Theatre to dedicate themselves to Ireland. However, the First World War intervenes. Stephen Ballas is killed in the trenches and Ailill, who joined up hoping that England would reward Ireland after the war, becomes a republican gunman on the run. As the burning of the Big Houses begins, Morna finds herself caught between loyalty to her brother and love for Ailill. Increasingly the novel gives prominence to the voices of nationalists like Morna who support independence but are opposed to violence. Morna proves her love for Ireland by sacrificing her life to save Ailill's and the novel ends on a bleak note amid scenes of chaos and looting brought about by the Civil War. The gentry are leaving Ireland and the cabin-dwelling Cassidys have replaced the Ballas family at Ballas Court. The tourist trade has been hit and Ireland faces a period of austerity. Ailill, a supporter of the Treaty, is disappointed in his fellow countrymen feeling they have yet to learn the meaning of citizenship, but in the end he and Peg decide to stay and work for a new Ireland. The novel ends poised between hope for Ireland of the future and despair over a country in the throes of civil war.

Other women writers of the period besides Miriam Alexander specialised in historical fiction. In 1925 *The Diary of a Young Lady of Fashion in the Year 1764–65* was published under the name of Cleone Knox. This combination of Big House tale and Grand Tour novel caused quite a stir since it was at first supposed to be a genuine eighteenth-century diary. Subsequently its author was found to be nineteen-year-old Magdalen King-Hall (1904–71), who went on to have a successful career as an historical novelist in the following decades.

Bridget Boland

Bridget Boland (1913–88) was born in London, daughter of an Irish barrister who represented Kerry as an MP between 1900 and 1918. Boland spent several years in Daniel O'Connell's home at Derrynane, a fact that she claimed as an influence on her writing.[24] *The Wild Geese* (1938) is an epistolary novel set between 1733 and 1746 and portraying life under the Penal Laws when Catholics were excluded from education and training for the professions and forbidden to practise their religion or own land. To get around these prohibitions, the Kinross family use their Protestant cousin Garrett Ahearne to hold land for them and they secretly send their sons Maurice and Brandan to be educated by the Jesuits in France. After their father's death, Brandan returns to Ireland to take over the farm whereas Maurice joins the Irish Brigade and fights as a mercenary in Europe. The story is skilfully handled, as befits a future film scriptwriter (Boland worked on, among others, *Gaslight*, *War and Peace* and *Anne of a Thousand Days*), and is full of well-researched detail about the vulnerability of Catholics in eighteenth-century Ireland, the famines, the Jacobite struggle, and the Irishmen who went abroad and became known as the Wild Geese.

Norah Hoult

Norah Hoult (1898–1984) employed the popular novel for feminist protest. Born Eleanor Lucy Hoult in Dublin to an Irish Catholic mother and an English Protestant father, Hoult attended English boarding schools after her parents' deaths. She worked as a journalist for the *Sheffield Daily Telegraph* but after the success of her short story collection *Poor Women!* (1928) she became a full-time writer. She returned to live in Ireland in 1931 but left again to live in New York and then in England (1939–57), before finally settling in Ireland.

Holy Ireland (1935) opens in 1898 with nineteen-year-old Margaret O'Neill forced to meet her English Protestant lover Clem in secret because of her father's opposition to marriage with a Protestant. The middle-class O'Neills, based on Hoult's maternal relatives, live on the north side of Dublin and the novel's vivid portrait of Dubliners' daily lives at the turn of the century owes much to Joyce, particularly in its depiction of Dubliners under the sway of their priests. Margaret is the occupationless daughter at home with a father who, like the priests, interferes in every aspect of his grown-up children's lives. This applies particularly to their sexual lives and Hoult is at pains to underline the sinister side of this Catholic obsession with sexuality: Margaret is conscious that her father's feelings border on the incestuous, while a visiting priest tries to kiss her. Though the novel is set in the early years of the twentieth century, it has been read as a critique of 1930s Ireland and the new state's legalistic approach to religion.[25]

Holy Ireland contains a protest too against the waste of women's talents: "'The way we go on putting up with things,'" Margaret tells her mother. "'You know, getting married and settling down and having heaps of children and never doing anything else. Why should it be that way?'"[26] Margaret intends to be a writer. Her models are Emily Brontë and George Eliot, but the novel also mentions New Woman writers associated with the *Yellow Book*. By 1903, however, married to Clem and living in Dollymount with two children and another on the way, she recognises that motherhood has put paid to her ambitions. *Holy Ireland* is a powerful protest about the constraints on women's lives and one woman's failed bid for freedom. The sequel, *Coming from the Fair* (1937), picks up the lives of the O'Neill family after the father's death but Hoult's feminism is much less in evidence in this novel. Instead, she concentrates on Margaret's brother Charlie, and, spanning the years 1903 to 1933, the novel registers a general protest against the new Irish state in which – the mourners at Tommy Langland's funeral agree – 'there's too much censoring, books, films, and, Holy Smoke, the price of drinks is enough to make any country sober and sorry'.[27]

Ella MacMahon

Ella MacMahon's publishing career extended beyond the era of the New Woman. *Wind of Dawn* (1927), set in 1921, is one of her better novels. Less confined to the Big House than Bowen's *The Last September*, *Wind of Dawn* features Roman Catholic priests and Protestant canons, Catholic and Protestant servants, and sympathetic portraits of both unionists and Sinn Féin supporters. Romance does feature but, unusually for MacMahon, the novel ends with a death rather than a marriage and much of the book is not about love but about the state of Ireland at a time of confusion. There is a sympathetic portrayal of Thomas Wilson, a self-educated Sinn Féiner from the Dublin slums, as well as a – slightly unrealistic – depiction of the grandson of a unionist peer, Dermot D'Arcy, who emerges from fighting in the First World War a Sinn Féiner complete with kilt and conversion to Roman Catholicism. 'It – it seems so extraordinary that in such a beautiful country – so soft and tender to look at, that there should be such hardness,' remarks the English Miss Bellamy.[28] Elizabeth Bowen would remember these words and have Hugo Montmorency echo them in *The Last September*.[29]

ELIZABETH BOWEN

Elizabeth Bowen (1899–1973), one of the most outstanding and accomplished writers of the twentieth century, began her writing career in the 1920s. Born into an Anglo-Irish family who had lived in Bowen's Court, County Cork for generations, she was later to describe the Anglo-Irish as 'a class that, potted at by the Irish and sold out by the British, has made an art of maintaining its position in vacuo'.[30] Bowen was the only child of Henry and Florence Bowen and therefore, in the absence of males, the heir to Bowen's Court. Her memoir, *Seven Winters* (1942), with its rhythm of winters spent in Dublin and summers at Bowen's Court, captures the very enclosed Protestant world in which Bowen grew up, a world of governesses, walks in Stephen's Green, and dancing classes. This safe, secure world was shattered when she was seven and her father had a prolonged nervous breakdown. The official reason given was overwork, but family members knew that mental instability ran through the Bowen family. Henry Bowen had himself certified and was treated at a mental hospital outside Dublin. In 'Pictures and Conversations', the unfinished autobiography that she was writing at the time of her death, Bowen glosses over this period: she came out of it, she says, with nothing worse than a bad stammer. Nevertheless, a glimpse of what was surely a traumatic episode for the young child emerges in her description of 'the tensions and mystery of my father's illness, the apprehensive silences or chaotic shoutings'.[31]

On the doctors' advice, Bowen and her mother left the family home and went to live in a series of villas along the Kent coast. As an outsider she was able to judge this society, and England, Bowen speculated in 'Pictures and Conversations', may have made her a novelist. Mary Lavin was to feel similarly about her transplantation from Massachusetts to Athenry at the age of nine. In 1912, the cosy feminine world of mother and daughter, recreated in Bowen's novel *The Little Girls*, was destroyed by Florence's death. This devastating blow was summed up by Bowen in a single sentence no less powerful for its brevity: 'I could not remember her, think of her, speak of her or suffer to hear her spoken of.'[32] Bowen was cared for by her maternal aunts while attending first Harpenden Hall and then Downe House boarding school in Kent. The summers she spent at Bowen's Court with her father, by now recovered and remarried. So began for Bowen a life split between Ireland and England: she was later famously to say that her home was 'somewhere in the middle of the Irish Sea'.

After the first seven years, Bowen's upbringing was turbulent: in addition to her father's breakdown and her mother's death, the First World War impacted on her schooldays, and in Ireland she encountered the hostility of once-friendly neighbours. Beneath the polished surfaces of her novels these traumas emerge obliquely: confession was never her aim and indeed would have been regarded by her as the height of bad manners. 'I am dead against art's being self-expression,' she was to write.[33] Nevertheless, Bowen's art is not impersonal. She saw her fiction as arising from a personal source but transformed by aesthetic considerations, 'transposed autobiography' but 'at so many removes as to defeat ordinary recognition'.[34] Though perhaps her novels were not always at as many removes as she intended: when Charles Ritchie read *The Death of the Heart*, he instantly recognised 2 Clarence Terrace in the Quayne household and Thomas Quayne as 'an unsparing portrait of A. [Alan Cameron]'.[35]

The characteristic Bowen themes of displacement, dispossession, instability of identity, sexual repression, treachery, hauntings, dreams, and an edgy distrust of language reveal the anxieties beneath the surface of her world that have in the last decade or so attracted the attention of scholars. Born into a class on the edge of ruin, she turned to art for a sense of stability and a reinvention of

self. As she explained in 1948 in answer to the question 'Why do I write?':
'My writing, I am prepared to think, may be a substitute for something I
have been born without – a so-called normal relation to society. My books
are my relation to society.'[36] Bowen's fiction may dwell on the private lives
of her characters, with few of her female, or even male, characters, with the
exception of Emmeline in *To the North*, depicted in a place of work, but these
private lives are very much shaped by social and historical processes. In her
introduction to *English Novelists* (1942), Bowen wrote: 'The relation of man
to society is an integral part of the concept of any novel.'[37] 'Fiction with the
texture of history' is how she described *The Last September*.[38]

After leaving Downe House, Bowen briefly attended art school in London
but that was no more than a cover, she admitted, for her ambition to become
a writer:

> Nothing made full sense to me that was not in print. Life seemed
> to promise to be intolerable without full sense, authoritative
> imaginative knowledge. Feeling what a book could do, and what
> indeed only a book *could* do, made me wish to write: I conceived
> of nothing else as worth doing.[39]

She began to write short stories. In her 1949 preface to the reissue of *Encounters*,
her first published volume of stories, Bowen gives one of the most accurate
accounts of what it feels like to embark on a writing career. She began writing
in a room at the top of an aunt's house in Harpenden: 'Embarking on my first
story, "Breakfast" (not the first I had started, but the first that I had finished),
I felt this to be, somehow, a last hope. I was twenty; already I had failed to
be a poet; I was in the course of failing to be a painter.'[40] She describes the
novelty of the sensation of writing and the way an apprentice writer becomes
hyperconscious of her physical surroundings: 'The room, the position of the
window, the compulsive and anxious grating of my chair on the board floor
were hyper-significant for me: here were sensuous witnesses to my crossing
the margin of a hallucinatory world.'[41] She wrote by hand on lined writing
paper, finding the lines an aid to clarity of thought. She does not disguise
the difficulty: 'as an occupation writing enthralled me, which made it suspect,
but also killed me, which made it in some way "right".'[42] She affirms what

many writers have felt, that writing does not get any easier with practice. Sean O'Faolain, disturbing Bowen at her desk one day, was surprised to see beads of sweat on her forehead.[43] Later, in the throes of what was to become in the view of many her most important novel, *The Heat of the Day*, she wrote to Charles Ritchie: 'I discard every page, rewrite it and throw discarded sheets of conversation about the floor. Is everything you do as difficult as that? I imagine so. From rubbing my forehead I have worn an enormous hole in it, which bleeds.'[44] Such struggle would be pointless, she felt, without publication as a goal, not for the glory so much as for validation, to be sure she was not being 'prey to delusions',[45] an interesting choice of words given, according to her own account in *Bowen's Court*, her family's proneness to self-aggrandising fantasies and mental illness. Like Virginia Woolf, Bowen was aware of the thin line between sanity and insanity an imaginative writer often has to tread.

The story of Bowen's path to publication illustrates the benefit of female literary networks. Through the intermediary of her former headmistress at Downe House, Olive Willis, Bowen met Rose Macaulay who encouraged her to publish and introduced her to Nancy Royde-Smith, then editor of *The Saturday Westminster* where her first short story appeared. In 1923, *Encounters* was published and in the same year, Bowen married Alan Cameron. There has been much speculation around the Cameron marriage, which was probably not consummated, either on account of Alan's homosexuality or because of wounds he suffered during the First World War. At the beginning Alan was senior partner in the marriage, instilling confidence in Bowen and advising her on sartorial and financial matters. For the rest of their life together, he provided a secure base for her professional and emotional life. For ten years the Camerons lived in Oxford where Alan was Secretary for Education for the city, moving back to London in 1935 when he was employed by the BBC. They lived in London until 1951, with long periods spent at Bowen's Court, which Bowen had inherited on her father's death in 1930.

The Hotel (1927), Bowen's first novel, portrays a collection of English people on the Italian Riviera. It came out of a winter she had spent in Italy with her aunt Edie, unhappily aware that she was about to break off her engagement to a young British Army lieutenant stationed near Bowen's Court, an episode that features in *The Last September*. Though displaying Bowen's literary influences – Jane Austen, Henry James, E.M. Forster, and Virginia Woolf of *The Voyage*

Out – The Hotel is nonetheless accomplished for a first novel, with witty and pointed dialogue and powerfully drawn characters. The focus is on women's lives and the novel introduces us to what were to become some of the most characteristic themes of Bowen's fiction: the young girl (Sydney) on the brink of adult life, the malign older woman (Mrs Kerr), and the knowing schoolgirl (Cordelia). There is a romance plot but, like Woolf, Bowen writes beyond it, not with her heroine's death, as in *The Voyage Out*, but with Sydney's engagement to the middle-aged clergyman Milton broken off and Sydney (one hopes) returning to her medical studies. Indeed, the novel contains strong questioning of the heterosexual romance plot for women's lives: 'It seemed odder than ever to Sydney, eyeing these couples, that men and women should be expected to pair off for life.'[46] During Milton's proposal, she has a feeling of a bell-glass descending.

The novel opens and closes with scenes between two women, Miss Fitzgerald and Miss Pym, suggesting the priority of female friendship over the romance plot. There is a lesbian colouring to these scenes and the question of Bowen's lesbianism has intrigued critics. She rejected advances from Nancy Spain and Carson McCullers but she is known to have had a brief affair with May Sarton when staying at her house in Rye in May 1937 and she may have had other lesbian encounters. Lesbianism, and more especially the emotional bonds between women, is a recurring theme in her work but in her own life Bowen seems to have treated lesbianism lightly. The friendship with Sarton continued until the mid-1950s when Bowen abruptly dropped her, possibly because she had become too demanding.

What Bowen seems to be most at pains to convey in her work is a modernist awareness of the fluidity of sexual identity, which sometimes tips over into lesbianism (Clare in *The Little Girls*, for instance) but at other times remains uncategorised. Charles Ritchie understood this: 'she puts the case in her new book [*The Little Girls*], E. does, that many people's feelings are undifferentiated and have to be forced into some pattern, whether it suits the owners or not; and sexual love is the usual pattern for feeling.'[47] In *The Little Girls* Dinah remarks:

> People are glad to feel anything that's already been fabricated for them *to* feel, haven't you noticed? … There's a tremendous market

for prefabricated feelings: customers simply can't snap them up fast enough. They feel they carry some guarantee. Nothing's so fishy to most people as any kind of feeling they've never heard of.[48]

It was precisely these unheard of, uncategorised emotions that Bowen, like Woolf, tries to pin down in her work.

Like Sydney, nineteen-year-old Lois in Bowen's best-known novel *The Last September* (1929) regards the adult world in which she has to live with a sceptical eye. The genesis of this novel, which Bowen described as of all her books the nearest to her heart, had, she wrote, 'a deep, unclouded, spontaneous source'.[49] The source was her life at Bowen's Court seen from a distance of eight years and a different country (she wrote it in Oxford) and, she was careful to stress, 'at many, many removes from autobiography'.[50] Yet sense of place is important in *The Last September*, as it is in all of Bowen's novels. 'Am I not manifestly a writer for whom places loom large?' she was to say. 'As a reader, it is to the place element that I react most strongly: for me, what gives fiction verisimilitude is its topography ... Characters operating *in vacuo* are for me bodiless.'[51] In Bowen's work, character is inextricably shaped by physical environment, and this is especially the case with the inhabitants of Danielstown aware that the Big House has written the script for their lives.

The Last September is set in Ireland in 1920 during the War of Independence and Lois, seeing through the pretence of her aunt and uncle, the Anglo-Irish Naylors, that everything will carry on as it is, recognises that the particular pattern into which she has been born is in the process of disintegrating. However, just as the new Irish state has not yet come into being, so Lois has not yet found her path in life.

She is first presented to us as performing with accuracy the part expected of a young girl in an Anglo-Irish household while at the same time conscious that it *is* a performance: 'Lois stood at the top of the steps looking cool and fresh; she knew how fresh she must look, like other young girls.'[52]

This emphasis on Lois's performance of her role as niece of the Big House is repeated several times in the novel and her life in Danielstown strikes Lois as quite as vacant as this performance suggests. Her vacancy is partly gendered: her cousin, Laurence, who is similarly *désoeuvré*, does at least have Oxford to look forward to. For Lois, aware that exciting developments are going on around her as the Irish wage their war against the British, her gender is a trap. When Gerald, the young English officer who hopes to marry Lois, mentions the recent burning of an army barracks by Irish nationalists, Lois explodes in frustration at the feminine role she is expected to play:

> Do you know that while that was going on, eight miles off, I was cutting a dress out, a voile that I didn't even need, and playing the gramophone? [...] How is it that in this country that ought to be full of such violent realness, there seems nothing for me but clothes and what people say? I might just as well be in some kind of cocoon.[53]

Bowen never idealised young people: she remembered her own youth at Bowen's Court as mainly a time of 'impatience, frivolity, or lassitude. I asked myself *what* I should be, and when?'[54] The younger generation, Lois and Laurence, have no clear vision of what they would put in place of the traditions of Danielstown that they both in their different ways deplore. The atmosphere is one of apathy and paralysis akin to Beckett's plays, a picture of the Anglo-Irish young embalmed alive in the routines of the Big House and, as Margot Backus puts it, 'colonialism as a pervasive historical system that appropriates the sexuality and lives of Anglo-Irish children'.[55]

The vacancy Lois perceives in herself is matched by the vacancy she senses in Danielstown: 'after every return – or awakening, even, from sleep or preoccupation – she and those home surroundings still further penetrated each other mutually in the discovery of a lack.'[56] In *Bowen's Court* (1942), charting the rise and decline in the fortunes of the Bowen family, Bowen describes the Anglo-Irish Big Houses as alien structures imposed on the colonised Irish countryside. In *The Last September*, Danielstown is just such an alien in the Irish countryside:

> The house seemed to be pressing down low in apprehension, hiding its face, as though it had her vision of where it was. It seemed to gather its trees close in fright and amazement at the wide, light, lovely unloving country, the unwilling bosom whereon it was set.[57]

Lack of contact with their Irish neighbours exacerbated the unreality of the Anglo-Irish way of life, Bowen argues in her family memoir. They had nothing to sustain them but a certain standard of behaviour that living in the Big House imposed on them. Unsure of their status in Ireland, the Anglo-Irish put their trust in style to protect themselves against an inner uncertainty.[58]

Lois's aunt and uncle can only preserve their identity by clinging to the past and ignoring the rise of the nationalists. But this is just what Lois cannot do. Though aware of the attractions of living in a pattern, she also chafes against its constraints, determined to keep her identity fluid and open-ended. When she overhears Lady Naylor and Francie Montmorency discussing her, she takes her water jug and bangs it down into the basin to get them to stop:

> But when Mrs Montmorency came to: 'Lois is very—' she was afraid suddenly. She had a panic. She didn't want to know what she was, she couldn't bear to: knowledge of this would stop, seal, finish one. Was she now to be clapped down under an adjective, to crawl round lifelong inside some quality like a fly in a tumbler? Mrs Montmorency should not![59]

Lois's awareness of the flaws in the role both her gender and her class require her to fulfil opens her to the possibility of difference and leads her to take an interest in the nationalists who haunt the Irish countryside and hide guns in the woods. Bowen draws a series of parallels between Lois and the rebels: both, for instance, tend to be ignored by the older generation of Anglo-Irish unless circumstances force them upon their attention. Lois knows her invisibility is partly a consequence of her youth but also of her class and her gender: it is not proper for 'a lady' to attract attention. Lady Naylor is ruthlessly determined not to notice the relationship that has formed between Lois and the unsuitable Gerald until remarks by her old friend Francie Montmorency force her opposition to the match into the open. Similarly, Lady Naylor's response to the Troubles is to play them down as far as possible. Caught in their divided loyalty between their Irish tenants and the British Army, and fearful of their position in the Ireland of the future, the Naylors adopt a self-protective policy of not acknowledging the ambushes, arrests and raids going on around them. In doing so they are, in Neil Corcoran's words, evading a 'total war in miniature'.[60] When Lois spies a man in a trench coat hurrying through their demesne, she realises that it is pointless to tell the other inhabitants of Danielstown about her exciting encounter since they will not listen. Here, Lois's fate and that of the nationalists merge in the Naylors' determination 'not to know'. Conversely, for the IRA man Lois is an irrelevance.

Lady Naylor is one in a long line of powerful older women in Bowen's work, women who, confined to the domestic sphere, find an outlet for their unused abilities in dominating those around them. These older Bowen women are not always Anglo-Irish but in Lady Naylor's case her exercise of power fills a vacuum left by the loss of power and status of the Anglo-Irish male. Sir Richard Naylor is a particularly emasculated, ineffectual landlord. Fictional accounts and memoirs of Anglo-Irish childhoods are full of such dominating women: in Bowen, the portrait of Lady Naylor is lightened by touches of Wildean comedy, her speeches about Gerald's Surrey background recalling Lady Bracknell's horrified reaction to Jack's lack of family in *The Importance of Being Earnest*. In the end, though, Lady Naylor's interference in Lois's engagement is redundant since Lois herself comes to realise that life with the unimaginative Gerald will be as constraining as life in Danielstown and that she cannot foreclose her future by marrying him. Later, Irish nationalists, probably tenants of the Naylors, shoot him. After his death, Lois connects Gerald's love with his politics: 'He loved me, he believed in the British Empire.'[61] Gerald's sense of chivalry impels him into a protective attitude towards both Lois and Ireland. For both Lois and Ireland, though, the price of his protection – loss of freedom to act – is too high. Gerald's kiss in the drawing room at Danielstown seals his fate, prompting in Lois feelings of loneliness and homelessness, reminding her of the times when she has been 'locked in misery between Holyhead and Kingstown'.[62] Lois's gender identity and her national identity combine to cause her confusion. As a member of the Anglo-Irish caste, her identity is forever hyphenated, torn between Ireland and England. As a woman, Lois remains unaroused by Gerald's kiss. She longs to escape both gender and nationality. Nationality when she desires to be 'enclosed in nonentity, in some ideal no-place'.[63] Gender when she tells Marda: 'I hate women. But I can't think how to begin to be anything else.'[64]

The influence of Jane Austen is evident in scenes where Lois and her friend Livvy go into Clonmore in search of the society of soldiers. Unlike Livvy, who displays a sentimental adherence to romance and pragmatism as to how to achieve her ends, manoeuvring the bewildered David into an engagement, Lois challenges the romance plot: 'All that fuss, if you know what I mean, about just somebody.'[65] In a gender-divided society, such as that depicted in *The Last September*, it is older women who provide clues for Bowen's young heroines as to how to live. It is this, rather than the sexual ambivalence stressed by some critics, which in my view prompts Lois to look to the older Marda for a sense of her identity.[66] When Lois tries on Marda's fur coat, she is experimenting with a different identity and when she plies Marda with questions, she is in effect asking her how to go about beginning to be a woman. Through observing Hugo Montmorency's infatuation with Marda, Lois becomes aware of the nature of sexual passion: that it is not the respectable indifference she feels for Gerald but, as always in Bowen, something violent and unpredictable. In the abandoned mill, Lois comes up against two realities simultaneously: the reality of conflict in her nation as the IRA man's gun goes off, and the reality of sexual passion in the violence of Hugo's reaction to Marda's wounding. 'I had no idea – I was too damned innocent,' she comments.[67]

Unlike Marda, who will capitulate to her society's gender and class expectations by marrying the dull-sounding Leslie Lawe, Lois's future, like Ireland's, is left uncertain. After Gerald's death, she is packed off to France to perfect her language, an apparently random choice by her aunt which has little to do with Lois's own wishes or plans. Art school and Italy are what have been talked of for most of the novel. None of these options will provide a real future for Lois. She knows that she does not draw well. In the eyes of her Anglo-Irish family, she has in fact only one destiny – marriage to someone of her own class – but the burning down of Danielstown subsequent to her departure underlines the fact that there can be no return to the fixed patterns of the past for Lois. Whereas Lois's mother lingers in the text like some kind of trapped ghostly presence, haunting Danielstown with her scratching on the walls, her rotting trunks and the memory of her unappeased rages, by the end of the novel Lois has escaped the paralysis of the Anglo-Irish Big House. Her future is left open-ended, her identity perpetually in question: 'every time she would wonder: what Lois *was* – She would never know.'[68]

Lois's fears to some extent reflect Bowen's own in her early twenties:

> Motherless since I was thirteen, I was in and out of the homes
> of my different relatives – and, as constantly, shuttling between
> two countries: Ireland and England ... Though quite happy, I
> lived with a submerged fear that I might fail to establish grown-
> up status. That fear, it may be, egged me on to writing: an author,
> a grown-up, must they not be synonymous?[69]

In the novel, Lois's future is left in doubt. Bowen solved her problem by
becoming a writer. By the time *The Last September* was published she was living
in Oxford with Alan and getting to know writers like John Buchan, David
Cecil, Maurice Bowra, Cyril Connolly and Isaiah Berlin. 'Here I was, living
a life dreamed of when, like Lois, I drove the pony-trap along endless lanes.
Civilization (a word constantly on my 1928 lips) was now around me, I was
in company with the articulate and the learned.'[70] She struck up friendships
with other women writers, notably Virginia Woolf, who was already a literary
influence: the music sheet flapping in Gerald's empty room after his death
recalls the air that causes the curtain to swell in Jacob's empty room at the end
of *Jacob's Room* (1922). Bowen always remained a little in awe of Woolf though
she found Woolf's feminism in her fiction 'a bleak quality, an aggressive streak,
which can but irritate'.[71] Bowen visited the Woolfs' home in Rodmell and
Virginia and Leonard Woolf spent a night at Bowen's Court during their trip to
Ireland in 1934. Not understanding the Anglo-Irish compulsion to struggle on,
Woolf was scathing about its shabbiness. After Woolf's death in 1941, Bowen
wrote in a letter to William Plomer that what she chiefly remembered about
Woolf was her laughter, an important counter to the portrayal of Woolf as a
tragic victim. A year later when Bowen spoke about Woolf to Charles Ritchie,
he recognised how deeply Woolf had influenced her: 'An influence I can still
feel alive in her.'[72]

Given the circles in which she was now moving, it is hardly surprising that
Bowen's next novels show her wanting to establish herself in the mainstream of
European literature, though, as one critic has recently argued, even in novels
set in Paris and London, there are themes associated with Bowen's Anglo-Irish
upbringing, and times of war would always bring her fiction back to Ireland.[73]

In an interview in *The Bell* she explained: 'I regard myself as an Irish novelist. As long as I can remember, I've been extremely conscious of being Irish – even when I was writing about very un-Irish things such as suburban life in Paris or the English seaside.'[74] Despite their domestic settings, Bowen's novels always point to the larger political scene. This is obvious in relation to *The Last September* but it is also relevant for reading her novels with English settings: 'Domestic crisis,' she wrote in 1936, 'only becomes important where there is a lively sense of what lies beyond its stage.'[75]

Friends and Relations (1931), perhaps Bowen's least successful novel, observes tangled relationships and inconvenient passion among the English upper middle classes. At times *Friends and Relations* comes close to Yeats's contempt for the middle classes as Bowen reveals the vacuum at the heart of English life. There are faint echoes of Frances Cashel Hoey's (1830–1908) novel of romantic entanglements *All or Nothing* (1888), particularly in the opening scene of a marriage that is clearly doomed from the outset, suggesting that Bowen's reading of earlier popular female Irish novelists would bear examination. The novel may be a (relative) failure but it contains some brilliant set pieces in the portrait of the girls' school, the passionate bully, Theodora, and the perceptive child, Anna.

In *To the North* (1932), Bowen's talent for Wildean social comedy is much in evidence. There are familiar Bowen characters – the interfering, Wodehousian aunt, the annoying schoolgirl, Pauline, and in the story of Emmeline, an innocent who falls violently in love with the predatory and worldly Markie, the first outing of what Sean O'Faolain was to term 'the kid and the cad' theme in Bowen's writing. Irony is much in play in the fact that Emmeline owns a travel agency but in her love affair with Markie loses her bearings completely. The interwar vogue for travel is central to this novel, as is Bowen's own fascination with speed, which brings about the final tragedy. In their love affair, Emmeline travels further in passion than Markie wishes to go and his rational view of life is revealed to be insufficient as Gothic melodrama (a touch of Anglo-Irish literary tradition) erupts into the lives of the English upper middle classes.

The House in Paris (1935) has attracted critical attention recently for its depiction of the Jew as outsider and its portrayal of English and French anti-semitism in the interwar period. Karen Michaelis's English mother positions Max, the Jew, as the demonic other, while in Paris Max is manipulated by the despotic Madame Fischer. When the Englishman Ray crosses cultural boundaries to bring home Max's son, he undermines Madame Fischer's monstrously oppressive control and his intervention has been interpreted as rescuing a part-Jewish child from fascist Europe.[76]

France had played a large part in Bowen's consciousness as a young girl.[77] It was a country she associated with her mother and her aunts, all fluent French speakers and, though herself a weak linguist, she began reading Flaubert when she embarked on her career as a novelist and continued reading French novels for the rest of her life. The portrait of Max the outsider may also, though, owe something to Bowen's own ambivalent position as an Anglo-Irish woman in England. *The House in Paris* contains a crucial interlude set in Ireland, a country that gives Karen a feeling of 'troubling strangeness'.[78] Though engaged to the reassuringly conventional Ray, Karen begins to realise that Max is someone who makes her deeply unhappy and, in the example of her aunt Violet, learns to dread a woman's life lived passively and conventionally. 'Something in Ireland bends one back on oneself,' she writes to Ray.[79] She returns to England knowing that she must come to terms with her feelings for Max. As in *The Heat of the Day*, Ireland functions as the foreign space in which re-evaluation takes place. This may seem the reverse of much Irish writing where abroad is often a welcome escape from the constraints of Irish life, but it does draw on a consistent trope in popular fiction by Irish women writers such as B.M. Croker, Annie Smithson, Katharine Tynan and Geraldine Cummins, in which the heroine, brought up outside Ireland, becomes changed by her stay in that country.

The Death of the Heart (1938) is set, like Bowen's previous novels, among the English upper middle classes, in a house overlooking Regent's Park that Charles Ritchie recognised as Bowen's own. The novel returns to one of the themes of *The Last September*, namely the portrayal of a motherless young girl spying on the adult world in an attempt to locate her place in it. In order to interpret the complex text of life in her sister-in-law's house, sixteen-year-old Portia commences a diary, reflecting the connection that Bowen made in her own life between her fear of failing to become an adult and writing as means of overcoming that fear and entering the adult world on her own terms. 'Writing … what it could do!' Bowen declared in a radio broadcast. 'That was the revelation; that was the power in the cave … The power of the pen.'[80] Wielding her pen to devastating effect on the lives of the adults around her, Portia is able to re-align the balance of power between the generations. Whether in the Anglo-Irish Big House or in a London townhouse, Bowen's heroines in this period struggle for selfhood in domestic spaces that define and confine them. Bowen's modernist techniques and her exploration of dislocated states of mind provide a welcome expansion of the realism adhered to by her less literary contemporaries.

PAMELA HINKSON

Katharine Tynan's daughter, Pamela Hinkson (1900–82), appears in the background of her mother's autobiography, writing poetry and stories.[81] She also features in Leland Bardwell's memoir *A Restless Life*, where Bardwell observes the close relationship between Hinkson and her mother.[82] Hinkson's *The Ladies' Road* (1932) is an elegiac portrait of two houses, Winds in Southern England and Cappagh in County Mayo, based on Brookhill, the house Hinkson lived in as a child when her father was RM. Permeated with echoes of Bowen and Woolf, and influenced by modernist experiments with stream of consciousness, Hinkson's novel is superior in literary quality to anything her mother wrote and, like Bowen's work, provides a counterbalance to the realism embraced by popular novelists.

The inhabitants of the two houses are interrelated and the story moves from a pre-First World War idyll in Cappagh, an Anglo-Irish world of shooting, fishing and tennis parties that recalls *The Last September*, through the First World War to the War of Independence and the Civil War in Ireland during which Cappagh, like Danielstown, is burned down. The First World War is chiefly recounted through the voice of Stella, an English girl at boarding school during the war in which many of her male relatives and friends are killed or injured. Like Rose Macaulay's heroine in *Non-Combatants and Others* and like Lois in *The Last September*, Stella resents the fact that her gender excludes her from an understanding of what men go through in wartime: 'All the men she knew – Francis, Alan Goff, Maurice Liddell – were silent and liked quietness. They sat for hours and hours saying nothing and you couldn't guess their thoughts, shut out from an experience you had not shared.'[83] Like Vera Brittain in *Testament of Youth*, when David, the brother to whom Stella is closest, is reported missing, life seems to come to an end for her.

If comparisons may be drawn between *The Ladies' Road* and English women's First World War writing, the novel also echoes *The Last September* in its portrayal of the Anglo-Irish inhabitants of Cappagh caught between Irish and English identities: 'Edmond Urquhart looking on at this life had seen the world between two worlds in these grey stone houses dropped down by the conquerors in the land they had conquered.'[84] The Naylors are unwilling to recognise that their time is drawing to a close but in Hinkson's novel Irene, an Anglo-Irish neighbour of Stella's family, does acknowledge the ending of their class: 'Looking towards the barrier that shut her world in, she knew that it would go down soon, that in another generation their world too would have gone, and there would be only Ireland.'[85] Like Lois, Stella is caught between two loyalties – to the British soldiers she plays tennis with and to the gunman she spies in the woods. The greater space given in Hinkson's novel to the First World War and to the losses sustained by the Anglo-Irish in it provides a different emphasis from Bowen to the burning of the Big House. In *The Ladies' Road* the burning down of Cappagh becomes only the final straw for a class and a generation already devastated by the First World War: 'There would be, as Irene had thought, for the next generation, no world between two worlds, but only Ireland. And none of this really concerned them, because they had spent everything in the War.'[86]

As a moving portrait of the Anglo-Irish in their final stages, *The Ladies' Road* deserves to stand beside *The Last September*.

MOLLY KEANE

Molly Keane (1904–96) stayed at Bowen's Court on several occasions. 'Clever as a bag of monkeys' was Bowen's verdict, 'but her cynicism and pessimism are quite terrifying. She makes me feel quite a blobby old idealistic optimist by contrast.'[87] In this Bowen was right: Keane's portrayals of the Anglo-Irish are bleaker and more cynical than anything Bowen wrote. They are often regarded as belonging more to the satiric tradition of Jonathan Swift and Maria Edgeworth (of *Castle Rackrent*) than to the realist novel, though Annabel Davis-Goff, whose sister Julia stayed in Molly Keane's childhood home in Kildare, testified to the authenticity of Keane's portraits: 'Her tough, accurate descriptions of Anglo-Irish life can even now make me shiver with the recognition of long-forgotten associations.'[88]

Keane's first novel, *The Knight of Cheerful Countenance* (1926), was published under the gender-neutral pseudonym M.J. Farrell. The pseudonym was necessary, she later claimed, because anything in the way of literary prowess would have been frowned upon in the hunting circles in which she moved: 'For a woman to read a book, let alone write one, was viewed with alarm. I would have been barred from every respectable house in County Carlow.'[89] This statement must be taken with a pinch of salt for Keane's mother, Moira O'Neill, was herself a poet and author of *The Songs of the Glens of Antrim* (1900). By becoming an author, Keane was in a sense following in her mother's footsteps. However, mother and daughter did not get on and Keane later claimed that her mother neglected her children: 'My mother didn't really like me and the aunts were ghastly to me and my father had absolutely nothing to do with me.'[90] In typical Anglo-Irish fashion, Keane was raised mostly by nannies and governesses before being sent, at the age of fourteen, to boarding school in Bray where she felt isolated and deeply unhappy, an experience, she later said, that went to forming her as a writer. Her unhappiness must have been more than was usual, even in an Anglo-Irish childhood, for Keane eventually left home and went to live with family friends in County Tipperary. There she began to move in more literary circles and met Bobby Keane whom she later married.

As a young woman Keane fully immersed herself in the hunting set, even claiming that this was why she wrote: 'The only thing I thought about writing was that it would give me some money so that I could go on having lots of fun and going to horse shows and hunting.'[91] It was a society, she said, 'in which I wanted to get on jolly well'.[92] This early enthusiasm for Ascendancy social life is reflected in *The Knight of Cheerful Countenance*, a girlish hunting and romance story set in an Anglo-Irish framework with none of the black comedy of her later work. The novel endorses without irony the Anglo-Irish myth of themselves as honourable and civilising Empire boys and girls, and the characters, of the younger generation at least, are both attractive and good: such characters are very thin on the ground in Keane's later work.

Nevertheless, even in this first novel, there are indications of Keane's later preoccupations: Rachel Sealy Lynch interprets Major Hillingdon's loss of nerve as representing the Ascendancy's declining prestige.[93] In the treatment of the Major's successor as master of foxhounds, Johnny St Lawrence, socially inferior and accepted into Anglo-Irish society only because of his marriage to the daughter of a Big House, Keane exposes the cruelty and snobbery of the Anglo-Irish world. Despite his education at a prestigious English public school, Johnny's son Dennys is unable to overcome the handicap of such a father. *Young Entry* (1928) repeats the hunting and romance formula but in Keane's third novel *Taking Chances* (1929), the tone darkens, the characterisation is a little deeper, and the comedy less light-hearted. Aunt Edythe, a despot and a bully, becomes grotesque in her efforts at rejuvenation. There are two attempted abortions in the novel and no happy ending, at least for Maeve Sorrier whose husband is stolen by the predatory Mary and whose beloved elder brother dies on the hunting field trying to overcome his loss of nerve.

Mad Puppetstown (1931) marks a move away from the enclosed Anglo-Irish world of Keane's 1920s novels to underline the way the fate of the Big House inhabitants was becoming increasingly linked with the lives of their tenants: Patsy Roche, the boot boy and ghilly who plays cards with the child of the Big House, Easter Chevington, also drills with the Volunteers. The novel opens in 1908 and establishes an apparently timeless picture of the Big House and its occupants. With the death of Easter's father in the First World War, this pre-war world turns into a golden age for the Big House occupants and especially for aunt Dicksie, left alone in decaying Puppetstown when Easter and her cousins flee to England during the War of Independence. Both Ballyrankin, Keane's parents' house, and Woodruff, the house in Tipperary where Keane spent long periods before her marriage, were burned down in the Troubles but *Mad Puppetstown* is, like *Treasure Hunt* (1952) and *Time After Time* (1983), about the survival of a Big House and its adaptation to the modern age. Challenging the myth of the Big House's inevitable ruin, Keane dwells instead in the latter stages of the novel on how Puppetstown may be resurrected (Easter's name is significant) as a modern commercial enterprise.[94] In *Good Behaviour* (1981), Keane will suggest that the decline of the Big House and its inhabitants is deserved, but here she is more ambivalent, indicating that there is something heroic about aunt Dicksie's obsessive love for Puppetstown and Easter's commitment to a new way of life for the house.

Conversation Piece (1932) continues this ambivalent attitude. It is the aesthetic delights of Big House architecture, landscape and interiors and their appropriateness to the Irish setting that strike the English artist Oliver on a visit to his Irish cousins at Pullinstown. 'Exercising their horses, Willow and Dick Pulleyne seem an integral part of the Irish landscape. The happy, self-contained household at Pullinstown is, however, threatened by the darker side of Anglo-Irish life represented by Templeshambo, home of Cousin Honor and Cousin Beauty. Fairy legend, the Gothic and Anglo-Irish guilt are woven into Keane's description of this Irish Big House which for a time menaces the stability of Pullinstown as the two sisters engage in a tug of war with Sir Richard Pulleyne for Willow's affections. Even in the apparently harmonious Pullinstown, intensity and madness lie just beneath the surface.

Devoted Ladies (1934) must surely have disorientated early readers expecting an Anglo-Irish hunting romance. The novel opens with a sophisticated 1930s party at the London home of Sylvester Browne, a fashionably jaded playwright. The reader would have been further disorientated by the sadomasochistic relationship between the South American heiress Jane and her bullying and violent partner Jessica. George Playfair, an Anglo-Irish innocent who takes a fancy to Jane, would have been more reassuring, and in fact after the first chapters the novel does move to Ireland where Sylvester's Anglo-Irish cousins Hester and Piggy live in a dilapidated house, Kilque, 'with a mildly leaking roof and mildly defective drainage'.[95] The reader is back on familiar ground.

Devoted Ladies has been reclaimed for a lesbian tradition of Irish writing. Jessica, as Moira Casey notes, bears a striking resemblance to Radclyffe Hall's mannish lesbians, a reminder that the publication of Hall's book *The Well of Loneliness* and the subsequent trial for obscenity six years earlier had done much to make the lesbian more visible, at least in England.[96] However, the relationship between Jane and Jessica is hardly an inspiring one and indeed functions mainly as an obstacle to be overcome before Jane can marry the manly and straightforward George Playfair. Ireland is positioned as a place of innocence in contrast to the decadent, 'rotten' and 'deathlike' society Sylvester surrounds himself with in England. For all her shallowness and lack of self-knowledge, Jane recognises that Ireland is not a place where her homosexual manservant Albert can carry on an affair. In Ireland, the lesbian characters become erased,

Piggy and Jessica by death, Jane by absorption into heterosexual marriage. However, Ireland's innocence, like George's in his forthcoming marriage with Jane, comes at the price of excluding certain kinds of knowledge. In Keane's following novel *Full House* (1935), the playwright whose fondness for corduroy jackets marks her out among the ladies of Owenstown as a lesbian is ignored by the daughter of the house, Kitty, who finds her friendship acceptable in London but not in Ireland.

Like *Devoted Ladies*, *Full House* is written in a light-hearted manner with lots of pointed and witty dialogue employing contemporary slang. 'Ladies and Gents talk like people in Dublin slums,' sniffed Edith Somerville.[97] But the novel also gestures towards Anglo-Irish Gothic in its depiction of a strain of inherited insanity running through two Anglo-Irish families and in the suggestion that Silverue is a house saturated by ancestral unhappiness. *Full House* is notable both for its portrayal of the Bloomsbury artist Eliza and, in Olivia, the first in a long line of selfish mother figures who are a danger to their children. In *Full House*, Olivia's dangerous selfishness is mitigated through the efforts of her friend Eliza; in later novels, the children of the Big House will not get off so lightly. In Keane, as in Bowen, the infantilism of the Anglo-Irish is tied to their paralysing dependency on a past golden age: in this novel, Eliza acts as the agent of change, moving the younger generation forward from dependence on their mother and the past.[98]

There has been much debate about the origins of Keane's matriarchal tyrants. She freely confessed in interviews that she and her mother did not get on: as a child, she had adored her mother but displays of emotion were forbidden and later, as Keane mingled among young people in less repressive Big Houses, she became 'everything that she [her mother] thought was wrong'.[99] Keane's matriarchal tyrants are linked to the Big House theme through her 'reimagining of Anglo-Ireland as a repressive matriarchy'.[100] Like Bowen's Lady Naylor, Keane's maternal tyrants exercise power inside the home as a response to the Anglo-Irish male's loss of power in the external world. Both mother and Big House exert a dangerous glamour over the lives of the younger generation, yet both also reinforce the habits and style of living of an older generation that are unhelpful for the future. In *Full House*, Olivia's unnatural youthfulness, obtained by a strict beauty regime, symbolises the unnatural wish of the Anglo-Irish to hold on to the past.

One of Keane's most accomplished novels, *The Rising Tide* (1937), is a sustained treatment of successive generations of Anglo-Irish in a Big House, Garonlea, which exercises a malevolent effect on its inhabitants. In *The Rising Tide* the theme of the matriarchal tyrant also comes to the fore. The novel opens in 1900 with Garonlea ruled over by Lady Charlotte French-McGrath whose malignant cruelty crushes the life out of her four daughters. It is the domestic setting of the Big House which gives Lady Charlotte her dominance: 'She had a strange sense of her own power, made real indeed by a life spent chiefly at Garonlea with her obedient husband, frightened children and many tenants and dependants. Here she had lived and suffered and here she was supreme.'[101] When Desmond, Lady Charlotte's only son, introduces his young wife Cynthia, an early forerunner of a Twenties Bright Young Thing, into this Gothic atmosphere, the stage is set for a clash of wills between two very different sorts of tyrants. Cynthia succeeds in banishing Lady Charlotte's malign influence from Garonlea only to see it brought back by her own son, Simon. The novel portrays unspeakable cruelties perpetrated by two very different mothers on their children – Lady Charlotte from perversity, Cynthia out of indifference. It is in *The Rising Tide* that Keane gets closest to Sheridan Le Fanu's use of the Gothic to suggest the racial guilt of the Anglo-Irish, though here the Gothic specifically takes on female form; indeed Garonlea, 'this habitation of glorious Gothic', was originally built 'out of a rich wife's money'.[102]

A chronological reading of Keane's novels from the 1920s and '30s reveals her developing her powers as a writer and gradually locating her theme in the dark history of the Big House and its destructive effect on the weak and powerless. Like Bowen's modernism, Keane's use of Gothic and melodrama expands the realist mode employed by many of their contemporaries.

BETTY MILLER

The novels of Betty Miller (1910–65), born in Cork to Jewish Lithuanian and Swedish parents, are interesting both for their exploration of gender themes and their portrayal of the lives of outsiders. Miller's father, Simon Spiro, was a prosperous store-owner in Cork and a Justice of the Peace, a position that brought difficulties for the family when the Troubles began since he was involved in sentencing IRA prisoners. In 1920 Miller's mother moved her children back to Sweden for a couple of years before settling in London. After her marriage to the psychiatrist Emanuel Miller, Betty Miller lived for most of her life in London, becoming part of Olivia Manning's literary circle. *The Mere Living* (1933), a stream of consciousness novel with echoes of Dorothy Richardson and Virginia Woolf, recounts a day in the life of the immigrant Sullivan family from Cork. The novel also includes an interesting debate on the merits of realism versus modernism, concluding that both modes are necessary to provide a comprehensive view of life. In *Farewell Leicester Square*, completed by 1935 but not published until 1941, Miller joins other Irish writers of this period – Elizabeth Bowen, Olivia Manning – in highlighting pre-war English anti-semitism. Through the consciousness of her protagonist Alec Berman, Miller gives a sensitive and convincing portrayal of a character uncertain of his acceptance in English society and insecure over his national identity.

NORTHERN IRELAND

Olga Fielden

Island Story (1933) by Belfast-based novelist and playwright Olga Fielden (1903–73), is an elemental tale of life on the island of Rathnaheena (probably Rathlin): 'A heartbreaking island of endless toil, dour and abrupt as her people, but opening into exquisite loveliness in her short sudden summer as her people open all too rarely into passionate heroic heat.'[103] Most elemental of all is the island woman Jane McCormick, a huge, energetic figure who dominates her three children by two different fathers and runs her farm single-handedly. Jane meets her match in her younger, citified relative Jim Cole. They marry but the power struggle between them continues, with tragic consequences for all around them. Jane's spirit however remains undefeated: 'Her teeth were clenched, her whole body taut, but her head was thrown back, and on her face was the old high look of defiance, as if she had seen Death coming and dared him to do his worst.'[104] The portrait of the tough peasant woman moulded by her environment recalls Lawless's *Grania*.

Agnes Romilly White

Agnes Romilly White (1872–1973) also depicted rural Ulster in her commercially successful novels *Gape Row* (1934) and its sequel *Mrs Murphy Buries the Hatchet* (1936), based on White's experience of living in Dundonald between 1890 and 1913 when her father was rector at St Elizabeth's. The novels portray life in Gape Row, a distinctive row of whitewashed cottages (demolished in 1934) lining the Newtownards Road and a tram ride away from Belfast. White's modern editor, Roy McFadden, likens her writing to that of Sam Hanna Bell and Michael McLaverty, and there are similarities in White's portrayal of her characters' everyday lives using the dialect of the region.[105]

Partly as a result of an economic situation where men have to go abroad to find work, in Scotland and America, Gape Row is a matriarchal community. However, the women's decisions are often thwarted by outside events and there is much wasted potential, summed up in the figure of Tam Murphy who despite his thirst for knowledge ends up a labourer all his life. In the sequel, *Mrs Murphy Buries the Hatchet*, Tam's potential is fulfilled through his son Ned, who, with the aid of scholarships and money his sister Mary sends back from America, succeeds in getting to Queen's University, Belfast.

Like Fielden's Rathnaheena, Gape Row is not a community unaffected by outside events. At the end of the first novel, the First World War breaks out and Mary's fiancé Michael joins up. There is also much coming and going of the characters between Gape Row and Belfast, America and Scotland. White gives us no rural idyll but a community in touch with and changed by events from outside. *Mrs Murphy Buries the Hatchet* ends with the arrival of a telegram announcing Michael's death at the front.

D.G. Waring

The family of Dorothy Grace Waring (1891–1977) had lived in Lisnacree House, County Down since the late eighteenth century. She published popular novels under the gender-free name of D.G. Waring, perhaps to underline the fact that she wrote in a variety of genres: Big House, romance and spy fiction. During the First World War, Waring served in the British Red Cross, in the late 1920s she was involved with the Ulster Women Fascists and in the early 1930s she joined the anti-Catholic Ulster Protestant League.[106] Not surprisingly, it is the unionist point of view that finds expression in her light-hearted romance *Nothing Irredeemable* (1936), featuring Sir Desmond Loughlin, 'one of the Southern loyalists, broken when the Free State took over'.[107] Sir Desmond has been badly wounded in an IRA ambush, burned out of his home, Castle Loughlin, and is now slumming it in seedy lodgings in south London. The plot turns upon Sir Desmond's relationships with his wife Sylvia, who is planning to divorce him, and with the spoiled and selfish Patsy Markham who comes to live in his lodgings for a bet. The romance plot is conventional and the endless Cockney dialogue tedious, but real emotion shines through the passages describing the fate of loyalist sympathisers: 'Thousands of Irish, whose only fault had been loyalty to the Mother Country, were driven penniless from their homes, and with them went Sylvia and Desmond, bearers of ancient title, to begin life anew on the princely Disbandment Pension of one hundred pounds a year.'[108]

Waring's spy novel *Fortune Must Follow* (1937) is a very readable story of an Ulsterman, Neil M'Crane, who has been captured and held prisoner by the Germans while working for British Intelligence. Released by the Germans but unable to work undercover again, Neil returns to his native Ulster to manage Miss Arnfield's estate in south Down and the novel becomes a portrait of an Ulster Protestant farming community. With his experience in Intelligence, Neil is soon able to put a stop to a cross-border cattle-rustling scheme. *Fortune Must Follow* reveals the influence of Kipling and Buchan and also, in the German scenes, of Waring's sympathies with fascism.

Kathleen Coyle

Kathleen Coyle (1883–1952) was born in Derry. Owing to dwindling family fortunes she moved to England in 1906, working first in a library in Liverpool and then in a newspaper office in London. In 1911, she returned to Ireland and became involved in the socialist movement. She married Charles O'Meagher in 1915 and had two children before separating from him in 1919 and returning to London. Thereafter she lived in Paris and the US.

Possessing the interiority of Hinkson's *The Ladies' Road*, *A Flock of Birds* (1930) is a sustained meditation on death through the consciousness of

Catherine Munster, a middle-class Protestant woman whose son Christy is to be hanged in Belfast for shooting a man during an IRA ambush. Since everything is filtered through Catherine's consciousness, the novel is deliberately vague about dates but it is set during the later years of the First World War. The Munster family is not nationalist: they live in a Big House, Gorabbey, outside Dublin and neither of Christy's siblings shares his politics. Catherine, a believer in 'life before death', challenges the idea of giving one's life for a political cause. Christy has accepted guilt for the shooting even though it may not have been his bullet that killed the man, but what he regards as heroic martyrdom, she sees as waste: 'What fools they were these young men, these weavers of wreaths!'[109]

The main interest of the novel lies not in politics, however, but in the depiction of Catherine's consciousness, her memories of Christy as a child, of her travels and of her unrequited love for her cousin Mitchell. Above all there is her concern for her three very different adult children and her sense of their strangeness now that they are grown up and the mothering task is over. The novel teeters on the brink of sentimentality but the power of the writing draws it back. Coyle is particularly skilful in showing the difference between Catherine's apparently calm demeanour and her inner turmoil. As everyone around her frantically tries to garner enough support to save Christy from the hangman, Catherine resists false optimism and her thoughts remain focused on Christy in his cell. She plans to keep vigil the night before his execution so that Christy can take courage from her prayers; then she will go abroad and become 'a ghost of all the mothers whose sons had been taken'.[110] Not only the nationalist struggle in Ireland but also the First World War shadows this powerful portrayal of a mother grieving for her lost son.

Olivia Manning

Olivia Manning (1908–80) was born in Portsmouth, daughter of a Northern Irish mother and an English naval officer. Her mother came from a prosperous County Down family and Manning spent much of her childhood in Bangor. One might expect nostalgia to have glamorised Manning's portrayals of Northern Ireland; instead much of her writing views Ireland through the critical eyes of a stranger. In short stories from the 1930s, such as 'The Children' and 'Two Birthdays', warring parents, hostile Catholic neighbours and the decline in her family's status are all portrayed through the eyes of a child. Manning moved to London to train as an artist and her first novel under her own name, *The Wind Changes* (1937), was published with the help of Stevie Smith.[111] *The Wind Changes* is set in June 1921, in the period leading up to the Anglo-Irish truce, and the novel already conveys the sense of displacement and alienation that will become Manning's great themes in the novels based on her wartime experiences, the *Balkan Trilogy* (1981) and the *Levant Trilogy* (1982), on which her literary reputation largely rests.

As in this later work, politics in *The Wind Changes* is filtered through the consciousness of selected individuals and their relationships with one another. Sean Murtaugh is a young revolutionary who looks to Riordan to instigate a second rising but depends on the middle-aged Englishman Arion to maintain his self-confidence. Arion, a novelist and journalist, is in Dublin to report on the Troubles. The young woman with whom both men have a relationship, Elizabeth Dearborn, is an impoverished artist born in Northern Ireland but raised in England before becoming an art student in Dublin. The novel draws upon Manning's lengthy childhood stays with her grandmother in Northern Ireland, her early training as a painter and her three-year affair with Hamish Miles, a married man and Edward Garnett's assistant at Cape, with whom she visited Dublin, Galway and the Aran Islands, all of which feature in the novel.

The Wind Changes is shot through with a haunting sense of the loneliness of the three protagonists: Sean faces death from the consumption that has already claimed the lives of his grandfather and two of his brothers; Arion, whose coldly intellectual novels reveal nothing about himself, is elusive, non-committal and ultimately indifferent to the fate of his two friends and of their country; Elizabeth, one of Manning's deracinated heroines, looks on Dublin with the eyes of an outsider: 'She had been born near all the enterprise of Belfast and had lived much of her childhood in London, so Dublin, with its lost air and lost wealth, had often seemed pathetic to her.'[112]

The novel is notable for its painterly descriptions of Ireland's landscapes, reflecting Manning's early ambition to be an artist. There are also vivid descriptions of Dublin as a city under threat, with shops barricaded, a ten o'clock curfew, random gunfire from snipers, and houses burned down by the Black and Tans or by their Sinn Féin opponents:

People lay in bed and listened to the sound of rifle fire, exploding bombs, the rumble of armoured cars, and saw waving across the night sky the white arms of the searchlights on the Crossley tenders. There was no knowing what news of death and destruction the morning would bring.[113]

In 1939, Olivia Manning married R.D. Smith and travelled with him to Bucharest where he was a British Council lecturer. During the war, the couple fled to Greece, Egypt and Palestine and from 1941 Manning worked for the British Council in Jerusalem. After the war, they returned to England. Manning's subsequent novels are set outside Ireland, though several contain secondary characters of Irish extraction, often eccentrics such as Quintin's emotionally unstable wife Petta in *The Doves of Venus* (1955), the unforgettable rogue Yakimov in the *Balkan Trilogy* and the Anglo-Irish rake Lord Peter Lisdoonvarna in the *Levant Trilogy*. Perhaps as a result of her fractured Ulster identity, Irishness often becomes in Manning's fiction a marker of marginalisation and alienation.[114] In *Artist Among the Missing* (1949), set in wartime Palestine, the painter Geoffrey Lynd, who undergoes an existential crisis as a result of the pressure of his involvement in a war in which he does not believe, is Irish.

Helen Waddell

Helen Waddell (1889–1965) was born in Tokyo where her father was an Irish Presbyterian missionary. She spent the first eleven years of her life in Japan before her family returned to Belfast. She was educated at Victoria College for Girls and Queen's University, Belfast and then studied for her doctorate in Oxford. In London, where she was vice-president of the Irish Literary Society, Waddell gained an international reputation as a translator, editor and scholar. Her single novel, *Peter Abelard* (1933), combining exploration of philosophical questions with the romance plot, foreshadows Iris Murdoch's later use of the genre.

Margaret Barrington

Margaret Barrington (1896–1982), daughter of an RIC inspector, was born in Malin, County Donegal and spent her early years there on her maternal grandfather's estate. Later she moved to her parents' home in County Tyrone. She was educated in Dungannon, Dublin and Normandy and attended Trinity College, Dublin. In 1922, she married the historian Edmund Curtis and taught French and German in Dublin schools. In 1924 she left Curtis for the writer Liam O'Flaherty. They lived together in England, marrying in 1928 and separating in 1932. Barrington's first-person novel *My Cousin Justin* (1939) draws on many of these early experiences.

Part Big House novel, part war novel and part romance, *My Cousin Justin* centres around Anne Louise Delahoe (Loulie) whose family are Protestant mill owners in the Lagan. Faced with the rise of the Ulster Volunteer Movement, Loulie's father, who is of French Huguenot descent, tries to maintain his political detachment but the increasing polarisation of political attitudes in the North forces him to take sides. Loulie herself resembles one of Manning's deracinated heroines: having spent part of her youth with her grandfather, aunt and cousin Justin in their Big House in County Donegal, Loulie has come to understand Catholic bitterness at being dispossessed from the land. As a consequence, she feels an outsider among Lagan Protestants. Her political awakening continues in Dublin where, as a student at Trinity College during the First World War and later as a journalist, she becomes a supporter of James Connolly and shelters republican gunmen on the run. Loulie is no great supporter of the fighting, however, favouring Connolly's socialism above Irish nationalism and, like a Kate O'Brien heroine, increasingly suspicious of the bourgeois Catholic state de Valera aims to establish.

The First World War shapes the romance plot as Loulie is torn between her feelings for her cousin Justin and for Egan O'Doherty, both of whom are traumatised by their experiences in the trenches, Justin as an officer, Egan as a private. The two men represent opposing political attitudes. Justin is Oxford-educated, wealthy, co-owner with Loulie of the house in Donegal, whereas Egan fights on the republican side during the War of Independence and the Civil War. Despite her opposition to violence, Loulie eventually marries Egan, though the marriage turns out to be a failure. She returns to Donegal with Justin, now increasingly alienated, misanthropic and cynical about Ireland, especially for Protestants like themselves:

> Times are changing, Loulie. Wherever we go, we are lone wolves,
> outcasts. In England because we are Irish. The English hunt in

a close pack. Here in Ireland because we do not belong to the people. We are thrown out by both sides. We no longer have any power. We no longer serve any purpose. We are an unhappy race, nothing is left us but our personal life and our emotions.[115]

My Cousin Justin resonates with many of the themes found in Irish women's fiction in this period: like *The Wind Changes*, Barrington's novel portrays an Ulster woman alienated from much of Irish life and depicts through her eyes the violence in Dublin in the early 1920s. Like Bowen and Hinkson, Barrington registers the displacement of Big House Protestants in the new Ireland and, like Kate O'Brien, she views the Ireland born after independence as insular and sectarian.

KATE O'BRIEN

Kate O'Brien (1897–1974) was born in Limerick into a prosperous Catholic middle-class family, much like the wealthy and self-confident Catholic families that feature in her novels. Her mother died when she was five and she was sent to be with her older sisters in Laurel Hill boarding school in Limerick city. Significantly, in view of O'Brien's European-centred novels, Laurel Hill was run by a French order of nuns intent on forming their girls into European Catholic ladies. In adult life, O'Brien moved away from the Catholic faith but she nonetheless retained an admiration for those who embraced the religious life. Nuns – the teachers at Laurel Hill, her aunts in the Presentation Convent in Limerick – functioned for her as models for the possibility of living a vocation outside marriage and motherhood. Pervaded by Catholic imagery, O'Brien's novels display understanding of the life of a believer while maintaining a stance of intellectual and moral dissent from Catholic doctrine. Her portrayal of independent-minded Catholics owes much, her biographer Éibhear Walshe believes, to O'Brien's exposure to English Catholicism.[116]

In 1916, with the aid of a county council scholarship, O'Brien went to study English and French at University College, Dublin (UCD), one of a privileged handful of female students. After receiving her degree, she embarked on a journalistic career in England and, after spending a year as a governess in Spain, she married a Dutch journalist, Gustaaf Renier, in London in May 1923, a marriage that ended after eleven months. Renier's 1933 biography of

Oscar Wilde was, however, to influence O'Brien's portrait of Henry Archer in *The Land of Spices*.[117] O'Brien began her writing career with plays; the first, *Distinguished Villa*, was performed in London in 1926 and became a commercial success, touring the English provinces. After several less successful plays, O'Brien turned to the novel form and wrote *Without My Cloak* (1931) while living in Kent with her first female partner, Margaret Stephenson.[118] She wrote slowly, rarely revising, and her preferred routine was to begin in the evening and write through the night.[119]

Without My Cloak is an account, loosely based on O'Brien's own antecedents, of three generations of the Considine family who, through hard work and thrift, rise from horse thieves to Catholic middle-class respectability in Mellick, a stand-in for Limerick. Set between 1789 and 1877, *Without My Cloak* takes pains to emphasise the civilised refinements of Considine family life, thereby advertising the fact that Catholic Ireland was not solely made up of peasantry but had an educated middle class as well. O'Brien's chief concern, however, is individual freedom as she depicts the entanglements of family life and the attempts of younger Considines to develop their own voices. Caroline's failure to break free is echoed in the next generation in Denis's struggle to assert his own wishes against those of a beloved but selfish father. Though the novel portrays the attractions of Catholic middle-class life, the Considine family's introspection and sexual repression, its insistence on tradition, and its crushing of individuality, become representative of what O'Brien saw as the insularity and claustrophobia of Irish life.

Despite a series of female partners, O'Brien never publicly identified herself as a lesbian; nevertheless, her portrayal in *Without My Cloak* of the bids of Caroline and Denis for sexual freedom may be read as correlative of her own situation at a time when lesbianism was viewed with hostility. Caroline's homosexual brother Eddy, living apart from his family in London, most closely mirrors O'Brien's own situation. Eddy's incestuous love for his sister, his love of his friend Richard, and the adulterous love between Caroline and Richard are represented as loves that are all equally 'out of order'. Though not in this first novel finally acted upon, they give notice of what will be important themes in O'Brien's work, namely the essential amorality of desire and the variety of outlaw loves versus conventional heterosexual marriage. In this first novel, O'Brien capitulates to a happy ending by having Denis's private desires align themselves finally with his father's wishes. Nevertheless, the costs of the patriarchal family romance are evident in these stories of transgressive desire suppressed. *Without My Cloak* was warmly received, winning both the Hawthornden and James Tait Black prizes.

By the publication of *The Ante-Room* (1934) O'Brien was living in Bloomsbury and mixing with such writers as Anna Wickham, Dorothy Sayers and Hugh McDiarmid, but she remained drawn to her Irish past. Set in 1880, *The Ante-Room* continues the story of the Considines in the portrait of Teresa Mulqueen's family, the seeds of which are already present in Chapter 13 of *Without My Cloak*. Like her previous novel, *The Ante-Room* is realist in form but O'Brien gives space to exploring the interior consciousness of her characters. *The Ante-Room*, like its predecessor, is about thwarted desire, centring on a pair of star-crossed lovers, the handsome but moody Vincent and his sister-in-law Agnes, a devout Catholic tormented by guilt over her love for her sister's husband. The structure of *The Ante-Room*, built around three successive feast days in the Catholic Church calendar, takes us away from the romance plot, however, and in the end the novel is less about romance than about the way Agnes uses the rituals of the Catholic religion in order to preserve her sense of self and evade the romance plot in which Vincent seeks to trap her.[120] None of the prevailing discourses – Victor's romantic fantasies, Dr Curran's image of a *femme fatale*, the London surgeon's fantasy of an Irish colleen – are adequate to describe Agnes, who remains unhappily excluded at the end of the novel from the general rejoicing over her brother Reggie's marriage. Nevertheless, her Catholic faith has given her the strength to reject Victor's narcissistic fantasies in favour of the realities of her life at Roseholm and her bond with her sister. O'Brien's portrait of Agnes provides a good illustration of Myrtle Hill's argument that the centrality of the Catholic faith to Irish women's sense of self during this period has been seriously underestimated by commentators eager to dwell on the oppressive nature of Catholicism.[121]

After two historical novels drawing on her family history, O'Brien used her own experiences for her third novel *Mary Lavelle* (1936), depicting the life of an Irish governess in Spain in the 1920s. Dimly conscious of the limitations of middle-class life in Mellick, where her role is to play daughter of the house and her destiny is marriage to the nearest conventional young man, Mary Lavelle sees no possibility of another sort of life until a teacher in her convent school mentions a vacancy for an English-language governess in Spain. Irish convents in O'Brien's novels frequently have European contacts, allowing O'Brien to contrast the internationalism of these female-run communities with the intense nationalism prevalent in Ireland during this period. Mary's months in Spain as governess for the Areavaga family are intended to be no more than an interval of freedom before she becomes John's wife. However, Spain is a transforming experience, leading Mary to re-evaluate the life awaiting her back in Ireland. She takes pains to learn the Spanish language and to adapt to Spanish culture and this marks her out from the other Irish Misses who cling to Irish customs despite the fact that they are in Spain because their own country has offered them no future.

An exception to the xenophobic Irish Misses is Agatha Conlan who speaks Spanish fluently. Recalling Hannah Lynch's *Autobiography of a Child*, Agatha is clear-sighted about the position of the Irish Misses: 'We came out in our green youth because our parents had no money to spend on us, and saw no likelihood of us getting husbands … most of us have no one to go home to and no way to keep ourselves alive, if we did that.'[122] At Agatha's prompting, Mary attends a bullfight, and its violent sensuality, piercing her senses in a way John never did, introduces her to emotions from which, as a young Irish girl, she was intended to be sheltered. She becomes conscious of her potential for sexual passion and immediately after this she meets the Areavaga heir, Juanito, a married man. Their mutual adulterous passion startles her into an awareness of life's possibilities and completes her experience of Spain. By the end of the novel, Mary has learned that sexual passion is not reasonable or manageable; that, unlike her feeling for John, it has nothing to do with social convention or conformity to tradition. It cannot be legislated for and is only with difficulty restrained. This knowledge puts her at odds with her nation's view of womanhood in which the sexual purity of the Irish woman guaranteed the purity of the nation. Mary's future after her emotional awakening is left uncertain. She will return to Ireland to break off her engagement and collect her godmother's legacy and then she intends to 'go away', knowing that, whatever she may become in the future, she will no longer fit into the stereotyped role of wife awaiting her back in Ireland.[123]

Mary Lavelle is notable for its early portrayal of an Irish lesbian, Agatha Conlon, who speaks frankly of her physical desire for Mary. Agatha accepts the Catholic Church's view of her sexual orientation as a sin, but Mary places it as a sin on equal terms with her own heterosexual love affair and this, for Agatha, is tantamount to acceptance. In December 1936, *Mary Lavelle* was banned by the Irish Censorship Board on grounds of 'immorality', presumably because of the love affair between Mary and Juanito but also perhaps for Agatha's openness about her feelings for Mary. Remarkably for this period, Agatha is depicted as neither vampiric nor doomed; instead, through conversations with Mary and despite what her church tells her about lesbianism being 'a very ancient and terrible vice', she works her way from self-hatred to mature self-acceptance and a calm, if lonely, future.

O'Brien returned frequently to Spain during the summers leading up to the Spanish Civil War and in 1937, a year after the war broke out, she published *Farewell Spain*, an engaging and very personal account of her travels around pre-war Spain. O'Brien presents the aspect of Spain she felt most in tune with, Castilian and Catholic, but the republican sympathies expressed in *Farewell Spain* got her banned from Spain by Franco until 1957.

In March 1937, O'Brien chaired a lecture on Irish Women Writers given at the Minerva Club in London by Hanna Sheehy Skeffington. During the course of her lecture, Skeffington, presumably thinking of the first two novels, called O'Brien 'the Irish Galsworthy'.[124] The label does not really fit. *Mary Lavelle* already showed O'Brien moving into contemporary subjects and her following novel *Pray for the Wanderer* (1938), set in 1937 just before the publication of the new Irish Constitution, contains, through the voice of Matt Costello, some of O'Brien's most outspoken criticisms of de Valera's Ireland. Written hastily, over the course of five months, to protest against censorship at home and the worsening situation in Europe, *Pray for the Wanderer* is O'Brien at her most polemical. Matt, one of O'Brien's Irish cosmopolitans, stands for individual freedom which he sees threatened, not only by the rise of fascism in Europe but by 'the new Calvinism of the Roman Catholic' that rules in de Valera's Ireland, 'a dictator's country', where Matt's writing, like that of his creator, has been censored.[125] Matt is alarmed by the moral philosophy behind the Constitution de Valera is about to put before the Irish people: 'Founded, intelligibly enough and even as this house was, upon the family as a social unit, and upon the controlled but inalienable rights of private ownership, but offering in its text curious anomalies and subtleties, alarming signposts.'[126] The depiction of Matt's sister-in-law Una, a woman who perfectly embodies the ideal Catholic wife and mother that was shortly to be enshrined in the Constitution but whose naivety and insularity are evident, is just one of these 'alarming signposts'.[127]

Through Matt's voice, O'Brien defends the artist's freedom of expression: 'Any books, mine or Amanda Ros's, or Virgil's, exist solely to demonstrate the artist's desire and ability to write them,' he tells Father Malachi, an intellectual who is nevertheless in favour of censorship. 'They are the fruits of the creative function, as irresponsible, if you like, as other fruits of creation.'[128] Unable to find a place in Ireland despite his participation in the War of Independence, Matt may be seen as representing the many Irish men and women who, having helped to establish the new Irish state, no longer felt at home in their own country.

'Life is grim, and is likely to be grimmer in the future,' commented Edith Gordon in the final pages of *The Winds of Time* (1934).[129] Gordon ends her memoir on a picture of Ireland stagnating, pointing to rising taxation, censorship, and the retrograde influence of the Catholic Church in opposing birth control. Many women writers during this period shared this sense of anxiety about the new Irish state. Some of this anxiety related to political changes, particularly for writers like Edith Somerville from the Anglo-Irish class facing a marginalised position within the new state. Some of the pessimism, however, in authors such as Rosamond Jacob, Norah Hoult, Olivia Manning, Margaret Barrington and Kate O'Brien reflects the increasingly disempowered position of Irish women after independence.

The realist novel still features prominently in this period but to it are added the melodrama and Gothic overtones of Molly Keane's fiction and the modernist inflected works of Elizabeth Bowen, Pamela Hinkson, Kathleen Coyle and Olivia Manning with their shifting time schemes, patterns of imagery and concentration on the inner consciousness of their protagonists. Though women's fiction is not openly experimental, modernist interiority influences even the ostensibly realist novels of Kate O'Brien, notably *The Ante-Room* and *Mary Lavelle*. Romance and life in the Big House continue to dominate as subjects, particularly in the popular novel. In a more literary writer like Bowen, these themes are up-dated so that the demise of the Big House in *The Last September* represents freedom for her young protagonist who also in the end evades the romance plot. Romance lurks in the background in the novels of Hinkson and Manning but the romantic ending is resisted and in Coyle's *A*

Flock of Birds and Jacob's *The Troubled House* romance barely features. This was also the period when writers like Elizabeth Bowen and Kate O'Brien began to write openly of sexual desire and of the fluidity of sexual identity, while Rosamond Jacob's manuscripts reveal a Lawrentian frankness about sexuality that had to remain unpublished during her lifetime.

Chapter 4

THE SECOND WORLD WAR AND AFTER: STAGNATION AND UNEASE

ELIZABETH BOWEN

*A*t the fifth annual banquet of the Women Writers' Club held in June 1939 in the Gresham Hotel in Dublin where she was guest of honour, Elizabeth Bowen, as usual when addressing an Irish audience, identified herself unequivocally as an Irish writer.[1] The Second World War was to put that loyalty to the test. While feeling it was her duty to support the war effort by spending the war years in London, Bowen understood that Ireland's neutrality was, as she observed in her reports for the British Ministry of Information in 1942, vital for that country's sense of identity. These reports are the most controversial part of Bowen's career. A letter to Virginia Woolf dated 1 July 1940 makes clear that it was Bowen who, in response to the fall of France, approached the Ministry of Information in London to inquire whether there was any work she could do in Ireland. Perhaps naively, she seems to have regarded herself as well placed to mediate between England

and a newly independent Ireland; however, her reports, when they became known, damaged her reputation in Ireland.[2]

'Eire' (1941), an essay published in the *New Statesman and Nation*, shows Bowen attempting to hold the balance between the British viewpoint on Irish neutrality as 'a passively hostile and in some senses rather inhuman act' and the Irish view that neutrality was 'Eire's first major independent act' and therefore of huge symbolic significance.[3] Bowen hints at the dangers of Ireland's 'abnormal isolation' resulting in claustrophobia, censorship, and a 'lack of grasp on the general scheme of the world'.[4] Later she was to argue that in wartime Ireland 'the taboo on judgement – for if one is neutral one must not take sides – fostered a listless irresponsibility'.[5] Many of these themes of claustrophobia and intellectual and cultural stagnation appear in her stories set in wartime Ireland – 'Unwelcome Idea', 'Sunday Afternoon', 'Summer Night' and 'A Love Story, 1939' – portraying Ireland as an unreal, unchanging place cut off from what was happening in the rest of Europe.

As the war progressed and Bowen was caught up in her work as Air Raid Precautions warden in London, she became increasingly critical of Ireland's stance and her loyalties shifted in the direction of the Allies. The war stimulated her creative imagination and she was in the first, happy stages of her love affair with the Canadian diplomat Charles Ritchie. Some of her finest stories – 'Mysterious Kôr', 'The Demon Lover', 'The Happy Autumn Fields' – are set in wartime London. 'Wartime London – blitzed, cosmopolitan, electric with expectation – teemed, I feel, with untold but tellable stories; glittered with scenes that cry aloud for the pen.'[6] One senses the energy in these lines in contrast to her picture of the inhabitants of wartime Ireland as lethargic and trapped.

At the same time as, amid the chaos and danger of wartime London, Bowen wrote out her impressions of the war in her short stories, essays and the novel that was to become *The Heat of the Day*, she turned for consolation to north Cork and the world of her Anglo-Irish ancestors to give, in *Bowen's Court* (1942), an imaginative reconstruction of three hundred years of the Bowen family's residence in Ireland. Later she was to write:

> In wartime, the surface being itself uneasy, he [the writer] plumbs
> through to, and renders, unchanging and stable things – home
> feeling, human affection, old places, childhood memories, and

even what one might call those interior fairy tales … on which men and women sustain themselves and keep their identities throughout the cataclysm of war.[7]

In the same year, she also published a short memoir, *Seven Winters*, describing her happy, safe childhood in the years before her father's breakdown. Both these works reveal Bowen creating consoling myths for herself in the midst of war.

In 1949, Bowen published what many regard as her finest novel, *The Heat of the Day*, a tale of wartime espionage in which she locates treachery in the heart of English middle-class family life. The traitor's mother, Mrs Kelway, combines the xenophobia of Hannah Kernahan in Kate O'Brien's *The Last of Summer* with the ruthless egoism and will to power of Ivy Compton-Burnett's monstrous mothers. The novel portrays the tension and claustrophobia of living in London during the Blitz when death was everywhere present and ordinary life suspended, lending a dreamlike, or nightmarish, quality to people's lives. The opening scene depicts exhausted, shabby, dislocated Londoners drawn together to listen to a concert in Regent's Park, much as in the opening scenes of Woolf's *Mrs Dalloway* Londoners are united by the sight of an aeroplane. There are vivid descriptions of the atmosphere in London after an air raid, of the privations of food rationing, and reduced travel. *The Heat of the Day* is coloured by Bowen's experience of seeing her Regent's Park home bombed twice in 1941 and 1944, and by her love affair with Ritchie, to whom the book is dedicated.

Part of the novel is set in Ireland and this draws on Bowen's wartime trips back to Ireland for the British Ministry of Information. Arriving at Mount Morris, the Big House her son Roderick has inherited, Stella has 'the exciting sensation of being outside the war'.[8] However, wartime Ireland is full of ambivalences. To counteract the war and the rather rootless life he led previously with his divorced mother, Roderick looks on Mount Morris as a source of identity and continuity and is determined to preserve its traditions. In her preface to *The Demon Lover* (1945), Bowen described how the dehumanisation of war caused people to cling to personal identity in this way:

Personal life here, too, put up its own resistance to the annihilation that was threatening it – war … To survive, not only physically but spiritually, was essential. People whose homes had been blown up went to infinite lengths to assemble bits of themselves – broken ornaments, odd shoes, torn scraps of curtains that had hung in a room – from the wreckage.[9]

Stella, who by this stage has relinquished the attempt to create a home, is more sceptical. She recognises the attractions of Mount Morris as a stable repository of values and a refuge from the war but, aware of her own failure to fit in to the expected narrative for women of her class, she is conscious of the unhappy women the Big House has sheltered. Driven to the point of madness, or feigned madness, by the expectations laid upon her as mistress of Mount Morris, Cousin Nettie has voluntarily left the family home for Wistaria Lodge, a home for the mentally ill. Preferring this life in limbo to forced participation in the ascendancy narrative of wife and mother, Nettie's happiest days are when she forgets she ever had a husband and a home.

The divided loyalties of the Anglo-Irish are touched on in the portrait of the former owner of Mount Morris, Cousin Francis. Francis's shame at Ireland's neutrality leads him to offer his services to the British War Office, but when his old friend Colonel Pole makes a snide remark about Irish neutrality, he fires back a stiff letter 'fairly blowing my head off – this and that and the other in a pretty nearly nationalistic strain'.[10] Ireland is the place where Francis's old retainer, Donovan, triumphantly announces Allied victories in north Africa but where Donovan's daughter receives the news 'indifferent as a wand'.[11] A comparison may be drawn with Olivia Manning's novel *Artist Among the Missing* (1949), where Geoffrey Lynd's Irishness underlines his feeling of being an outsider to the conflicts of the Second World War. His national identity becomes, as in Bowen's wartime writing, a mark of neutrality or even treachery: Geoffrey's wife is horrified to hear him declare that he would rather have remained in Greece under Nazi occupation, provided he could continue with his art, than have joined in the war effort that has destroyed him as an artist.[12]

If wartime Ireland was a refuge, it was also a place of treachery where infiltration by spies for both sides was a problem.[13] It is at Mount Morris that Stella gains proof of Robert Kelway's treachery and, given that a proportion of Irish people favoured the German side during the war, Kelway's allegiance to Nietzchean fascism rather than to communism has been read as an Irish trace in the novel.[14] Kelway betrays his country's secrets less out of positive conviction than from despair at his loss of belief in words like honour, patriotism and loyalty. He sees in the fascists a glorification of the masculinity that both he and his father, and England after Dunkirk, have failed to achieve. Ironically, by the end of the novel the tide of war has turned in the Allies' favour.

The psychoanalytical resonances of the scenes at Kelway's home and the description of his upbringing are characteristic of women's war writing. Olivia Manning's presentation of the psychological disintegration of an Irish painter under the pressure of war in *Artist Among the Missing* has already been mentioned. In *On the Side of the Angels* (1945) Manning's friend, Betty Miller, vividly portrays the psychological effects of war on a group of civilians attached to a British military hospital, while her following novel, *The Death of the Nightingale* (1949), delineates the psychological effects of the aftermath of the war, underlining the sense of anti-climax experienced by women returning to domesticity after their war work. For Cork-born Matthew O'Farrell there is also fallout from the War of Independence to be dealt with.

The Heat of the Day explores Bowen's favourite themes of rootlessness and the fragility of identity, both themes given greater urgency by the pressures of war during which identity becomes so fragile that traitor and spy, Kelway and Harrison, who share the same first name, seem interchangeable and Louie, displaced by the war and by the loss of her home and her parents, searches for her identity in the newspapers. Under pressure, Bowen's style became even more knotted and evasive, her syntax even more jarring, an effect she particularly sought in order to portray the ambivalences and uncertainties, the entangled loyalties and the sheer strangeness of life in wartime. In a 1950 radio broadcast, she compared the structure of *The Heat of the Day* to 'the convulsive shaking of a kaleidoscope, a kaleidoscope also of which the inside reflector was cracked'.[15] In the portrayal of Stella, intelligent and articulate, for whom love has provided a refuge in time of war, yet who is vulnerable to Harrison's suggestion that if Kelway is able to conceal his treachery he may also be capable of acting the lover, the novel underlines, with Bowen's characteristic subtlety, the difficulty of knowing the truth, both in war and in love.

The shadow of the First World War hangs over *A World of Love* (1955), Bowen's portrait of 1950s Ireland set in the context of an extended ghost story. As in 'The Demon Lover', the return of a dead soldier via his letters suggests that the First World War remains unfinished business, certainly for the inhabitants of Montefort, a Big House where time has stood still since Guy's death. In her description of Montefort, Bowen conjures up a fairytale atmosphere of a Sleeping Beauty place that also, as Clair Wills has shown, invokes 1950s anxieties over emigration and the depopulation of the Irish countryside.[16] 'Ireland, small as it is, can give the effect of being a stretching continent,' Bowen wrote in 1958. 'Tract after tract of emptiness seems unbounded.'[17] The novel contains a specific message to the Anglo-Irish. Glossed with her 1951 broadcast 'The Cult of Nostalgia' and her essay 'The Bend Back' (written in the early 1950s) warning contemporary writers of the dangers of nostalgia, *A World of Love* portrays the Anglo-Irish trapped into mythologising their past, represented in the novel by Guy, inhabitant of a pre-1914 Anglo-Irish world.[18]

A World of Love also mirrors Bowen's own anxieties during the years after Alan Cameron's death when she was trying single-handedly to keep Bowen's Court going. Her writing from this period on the Anglo-Irish expresses characteristic ambivalence. In essays such as 'The Big House', published in *The Bell* in 1940, she is optimistic about the possibility of her class making a contribution to the new state, and in 'Ireland Makes Irish' (1946), she insists: 'I believe it is possible to bring these beautiful legacies of the old world into line with the more arduous ideals of the new.'[19] However, only certain types of modernity were acceptable to her: in *A World of Love*, Bowen satirises the post-war invasion of *nouveaux riches* like Lady Latterly, wealthy refugees from socialist Britain who were buying up large houses in Ireland and importing luxury and sophistication without fulfilling the kind of responsibilities to neighbours and tenants understood by the older gentry class.[20] As Antonia drily remarks, though, 'Better late than never',[21] and the ending of *A World of Love* suggests that Montefort will be revived by an input of American money.

A World of Love contains some of Bowen's most characteristic themes in the portrait of Jane, a girl on the brink of adulthood, Antonia, the disabused older woman, and the demonic child Maud. The Gothic touches, indicating Anglo-Irish entrapment in their myth of themselves, skilfully maintain the balance between realism and fantasy by employing Sheridan Le Fanu's method of mingling the supernatural with the psychologically plausible. By the end of the novel, the Sleeping Beauty spell has been broken as twenty-year-old Jane travels west to modernity in the shape of Shannon airport and her American lover, Richard Priam. The novel ends on a fairy tale note of confidence in love, all the more remarkable in that the final chapters were written during a period of emotional turmoil for Bowen when her anguish over Charles's marriage was at its height. Charles himself recognised that the novel contained their 'shared illusion of life',[22] a reference to their shared faith in love but also to their dream of one day living together at Bowen's Court. *A World of Love* was Bowen's final word on the Anglo-Irish, its forward-looking ending perhaps as much a message of hope to herself as to her readers during the years after Alan's death when she was working frantically to preserve Bowen's Court as a home for herself and Charles.

KATE O'BRIEN

The outbreak of the war found Kate O'Brien in Limerick but by October she was in England where, like Elizabeth Bowen, she stayed for the duration of the war, increasingly critical of what she saw as Ireland's isolationist stance. In London the two writers' paths crossed and they collaborated on a volume of patriotic essays, *The Romance of English Literature*, edited by O'Brien and published in 1944. But they were never friends and Éibhear Walshe posits the class difference as a reason for this, citing O'Brien's review of *Bowen's Court* in *The Spectator* of 3 July 1942 as revealing the difference of outlook between the two authors: 'Both women valorized their own class identity, Bowen seeing the Anglo-Irish as heroic and courageous and O'Brien seeing her own Catholic bourgeois as civilized, cultivated and intellectually gifted.'[23]

The Last of Summer (1943) is set in Ireland in the days leading up to Britain's entry into the war on 3 September 1939. Like Bowen, O'Brien, while acknowledging de Valera's pragmatic reasons for declaring Ireland's neutrality, portrays Ireland as an insular and complacent place, the insularity underlined by the opening scene where the French girl Angèle is mocked by local children for wearing lipstick. As in *A World of Love*, Ireland is portrayed as sleepy and abandoned. The exteriors are quiet and shut up, while interiors such as the Kernahan family home, Waterpark, with its clutter of china and glass objects, or the snug to which the younger members of the family repair, frequented by remnants of the Anglo-Irish, are claustrophobic. Two minor characters in the novel, Corney and Dotey, underline the point that neutrality is morally corrupting and perhaps even, as in Bowen, infantilising, by their willingness to live as dependents of Waterpark, interested in little more than their material comforts. In *The Last of Summer* the moral choice is to get involved in the war. O'Brien's experience of fascism in Spain must have strengthened her belief in the war against Germany as the ethical choice, but not all of those Irish who supported neutrality were as complacent as the inhabitants of Drumaninch.[24]

Ireland's withdrawal from the situation in Europe is mirrored in the Kernahan matriarch Hannah, a woman idealised by priests and some members of her family as a saintly example of Catholic motherhood but who gradually reveals herself to be narrow, selfish and uncaring about the world outside. Bowen may have drawn upon Hannah for her portrayal of Muttikins, the traitor's mother, in *The Heat of the Day*. Like Mrs Kelway, Hannah Kernahan prides herself on living in a 'backwater' and feels that 'Danzig's a long way from Drumaninch'.[25] Hannah's powerful emotional hold over her elder son Tom leads her into conflict with Angèle when, in a reversal of the Sleeping Beauty myth, Angèle comes from Paris, an upbringing by a mother who was an actress in the Comédie Française and her own nascent career in the theatre, to provide Tom's sexual awakening. O'Brien's characteristic theme of human love versus the cost and self-discipline of an artistic vocation is thrown into sharp relief by the impending war. The oedipal resonances of the relationship between Hannah and Tom are remarked upon by several of the characters but Angèle herself is not exempt from oedipal love, attracted to Tom partly because he reminds her of her dead Irish father. As in earlier O'Brien novels, the Irish family is portrayed as a locus of parental possessiveness and psychological entanglement for the younger generation, but in this novel the theme becomes part of a wider portrait of Ireland during the war. Tom's younger siblings display courage in escaping the clutches of both mother and mother country – Martin by enrolling in the French army, Jo by joining a European order of nuns.

The Last of Summer was well reviewed and translated into several foreign languages. A stage adaptation, directed by John Gielgud, was put on in London in 1944 and O'Brien signed a contract with Doubleday, her American publishers, for her next three novels.[26] O'Brien also brought out *English Diaries and Journals* (1943), part of a patriotic wartime series called *Britain in Pictures*. O'Brien's discussion of Dorothy Wordsworth's diary is particularly interesting, her suggestion that Dorothy's creativity was blocked by her brother foreshadowing later feminist work.

O'Brien's earlier novel from this period, *The Land of Spices* (1941), written in Oxfordshire amid personal financial troubles, is set between the years 1904 and 1914, at a time when nationalist ideas were taking hold in Ireland. Though there is no mention of the current war, the novel ends on the verge of the First World War and a running theme is the juxtaposition of Irish nationalism with a wider, and more sympathetically portrayed, international outlook espoused by Helen Archer, the English head of a convent school in Mellick run by a French order. In conversations between Helen and local clergy, O'Brien points to the Catholic and nationalistic ethos of the future Irish state. The bishop anticipates an Irish education system that will endorse 'the establishment of a national character'.[27] In opposition to this narrow brand of nationalism, Helen sets out her concept of transnationalism, emphasising that her order cuts across national boundaries with nuns teaching in Canada, Portugal, Poland, England, the US and South America. Helen permits her pupils to study the Irish language but as 'a choice of cultures offered to them'.[28] By educating its pupils into a European outlook, the convent encourages them to transcend local nationalisms and O'Brien's novel provides an interesting juxtaposition of masculinist Irish nationalism with a transnational female network of convents. It annoys the bishop intensely that the convent of the Compagnie de la Sainte Famille lies outside his jurisdiction. The brief presence in the novel of the English suffragist Miss Robertson underlines the link O'Brien is making between women and transnationalism by reminding us that the struggle to gain the vote was one that crossed national boundaries.

The convent school in Mellick is very like the one O'Brien attended in Limerick and Anna Murphy, who enters the school at a young age, bears several resemblances to her creator, notably in her love of language and her reserve. Portraying, over the course of ten years, Anna's growth to maturity and, in the final epiphany, pointing to her future as a writer, *The Land of Spices* is a female *Bildungsroman* with distinct echoes of Joyce's *A Portrait of the Artist as a Young Man*.[29] Reminiscent of Bowen's recurrent theme of young girls looking to older women for guidance, the pairing of Helen and Anna is also a writing back to the predominance of father–son relationships in Joyce. With a detachment very different from her own father's suffocating absorption in his daughter's future, Helen introduces Anna to the life of the intellect, art and aesthetics denied to Stephen Dedalus's sisters.

As *A Portrait of the Artist as a Young Man* reveals the 'nets' cast around Stephen Dedalus by Irish life, so *The Land of Spices* portrays the 'traps' that lie in wait for Anna, and the novel gives important insights into the constraints on Irish women's lives. Anna knows that whereas her brothers are encouraged to be independent, 'if a girl sees liberty as the greatest of all desirables, she will have to spin it out of herself, as the spider its web'.[30] The most dangerous trap facing Anna is her financial dependence on her grandmother who, though prepared to finance her grandson's university studies, does not believe in higher education for women. Whereas the nationalist nun Mother Mary Andrew hinders Anna's development in all sorts of ways, Helen opens up the future for her by supporting and facilitating her desire to go to university despite the Murphy family's opposition. In this respect, as Ann Owens Weekes has pointed out, the Compagnie de la Sainte Famille is more truly nurturing of Anna's potential than her biological family.[31] Relying on the authority invested in the convent's transnational network, Helen helps Anna take her place in the world. It is O'Brien's reply to what she saw as the narrowness and limitations of de Valera's Ireland. Ireland in turn responded by banning *The Land of Spices* on account of the brief reference to Henry Archer's homosexuality. The banning of a book so clearly coloured by Anglo-Catholic spirituality led to its championing by Sean O'Faolain and others, a debate in the Senate and eventually, in 1946, to the removal of the ban.

Resistance to tyranny of a different sort features in *That Lady* (1946), set in sixteenth-century Spain and written in Ireland where O'Brien had returned directly the war was over. Ana de Mendoza, Princess of Eboli, relies on her Catholic faith in her defence of the rights of the individual against the increasing tyranny and political dogmatism of the king of Spain. As Éibhear Walshe has argued, *That Lady* is, among other things, 'a political fable', a protest against Franco's Spain, but also against the authoritarianism of de Valera's Ireland.[32] Ana, a widow and Castilian aristocrat possessing all the pride of her lineage, comes to stand for individual freedom in the face of Philip II's growing absolutism. Taking a great deal of historical licence, O'Brien paints a detailed portrait of Philip's changing attitude towards Ana, with whom he was once in love. Against Philip's claim that all aspects of his subjects' lives belong to him, Ana insists on the right of every individual to a private life and personal moral code. Under house arrest at Pastrana, in the company of her housekeeper

Bernardina and her daughter Anichu, Ana creates a place of spiritual resistance to Philip, 'an alternative religious community' as Walshe calls it, peopled by women.[33] Though Ana's resistance to Philip is a private matter, it comes to have a national resonance as Ana is increasingly portrayed as resisting tyranny on behalf of all the people of Spain and especially on behalf of her beloved Castile. The implications for Franco's Spain, for de Valera's Ireland, or even for Hitler's Germany, are clear: rulers who try to impose a homogeneous identity on their nation cannot legislate for what goes on in the individual soul. In turn, by clearing a private space in the nation, be it a convent or a room, the individual may function as a site of dissidence on behalf of the whole nation. The novel was a commercial success but drew criticisms from the Catholic press because of its unorthodox handling of questions of morality.

In 1950, with the proceeds from *That Lady*, O'Brien purchased a large house in Roundstone, Connemara where she was to live and entertain on an extravagant scale for the next ten years. *The Flower of May* (1953) was written there and the opening scene plunges us straight into O'Brien's favourite milieu, with the extended families of the Morrows and O'Connors gathered in 1906 Dublin to celebrate Lilian Morrow's marriage to Michael O'Connor. Two women are outsiders in this family atmosphere: Lilian's mother, Julia, who yearns for her childhood home in west Clare, and Julia's second daughter, Fanny, unsure at eighteen where life will lead her. Summoned back from her beloved convent school in Brussels by her father's arbitrary decision, Fanny feels she is 'only marking time. She had no intention of going Lilian's way, and her mind would not long be contained between the two bridges that spanned the canal at either end of Mespil Road.'[34]

The novel pits the wider life represented by Europe and by the Belgian convent against the claustrophobia of middle-class Irish Catholic family life at the turn of the century. Fanny's schoolfriend Lucille is engaged in a similar battle against her wealthy Belgian family to avoid either marriage or being the daughter at home. The problem for both Fanny and Lucille is how to get a university education when reliant on their fathers' money. It is aunt Eleanor, a version of O'Brien herself in her fifties, who empowers Fanny by making her inheritor of Glasalla, the home of Fanny's maternal ancestors in County Clare, thereby putting in her hands 'a weapon of independence'.[35] She also guarantees Lucille's future, ensuring that the two young women will be able to study together at the Sorbonne. Woolf's influence is palpable in Fanny's empowerment through her maternal line and in Eleanor's creation of a space of her own in her father's house where, unbeknownst to him, she drinks sherry and smokes cigarettes. In *The Flower of May*, as in the majority of O'Brien's novels, it is women and the bonds between them that are paramount and it is this woman-centred perspective that makes her such an important voice in the decades when women's voices in Irish public life were few and far between. In the novel, the relationship between Lucille and Fanny does not progress beyond friendship and critics are divided as to whether O'Brien leaves open the possibility of a lesbian relationship in the future.[36]

In 1958, O'Brien published her most joyful, sensuous, yet also most heartbreaking novel, *As Music and Splendour*, about the lives and loves of two Irish convent school girls sent abroad at the end of the nineteenth century to train as opera singers. *As Music and Splendour* is an early example of retrieving Irish women's history: researching her novel, O'Brien spent time in Rome and other Italian cities studying the world of Italian opera and the training of Irish singers. The character of Rose has been seen as a portrait of the celebrated Irish singer Margaret Sheridan.[37] O'Brien also drew on her own extensive knowledge and appreciation of music and skilfully uses Gluck's opera *Orfeo ed Euridice* as a lens through which to focus the various doomed love affairs in the novel.

As Music and Splendour is set in the 1880s and encompasses O'Brien's characteristic theme of Irish girls finding emotional and sexual freedom, as well as financial independence, outside Ireland. The novel traces the gradual changes wrought in Clare and Rose over a period of five years, so that when Clare eventually goes back to Ireland to watch over her dying grandmother, she knows that there can be no permanent return to her own people. She and Rose have been 'refashioned altogether' by their years abroad.[38] However much Clare yearns for home – and indeed the Catholic values in which she has been raised determine her preference for sacred music over opera – she knows that she will end her days outside Ireland. *As Music and Splendour* juxtaposes the puritanism and static nature of life in Ireland, 'the simple, clean, courageous and uncomforted life',[39] with the life Clare and Rose find abroad, a series of adventures and hazards, of trials and errors, that allow for growth and development.

In the account of the joyful love affair between Clare and Luisa, lesbianism is treated more openly than ever before in Irish women's writing, without defensiveness and without polemics, as just another aspect of the variety of human loves, of which there are many in this novel. O'Brien skilfully suggests the invisibility of lesbian love by allowing the reader to believe for a while that Clare is in love with Duarte rather than with Duarte's lover, Luisa. *As Music and Splendour* acknowledges that lesbian love is sinful if you take the Catholic Church's view of things, which Clare does, but, as in *Mary Lavelle*, the point is made that lesbian affairs are no more sinful than heterosexual ones. Clare tells Thomas:

> I am, I suppose, a sinner – certainly I am a sinner in the argument
> of my Church. But so would I be if I were your lover. So is Rose
> a sinner – and she knows it – in reference to our education and
> faith ... There's no vagueness in Catholic instruction.[40]

In this novel, consciousness of guilt is not an occasion for self-humiliation but a means to growth and transformation. The scene between Clare and Thomas in Chapter 10 exposes some of the ugliness of society's attitudes towards lesbianism. 'Two silly girls kissing each other? Is that love?' asks Thomas. To which Clare replies in one of the most dignified responses by an Irish lesbian in this, or any other, period: 'I find it to be so.'[41]

Clare's struggle throughout the novel is less sexual than spiritual: she is tormented by the question of whether secular music, with its stereotyped portrayals of tragic heroines who are either mad or bad, is worth devoting her life to. Perhaps there is a faint echo here of O'Brien's own doubts about her career as a fiction writer when compared to the lives of her aunts, nuns at the Presentation Convent in Limerick, portrayed in her memoir *The Presentation Parlour* (1963). In *As Music and Splendour*, as in *The Land of Spices*, parallels are drawn between the discipline required of an artist and that of a nun and there is a reflection of Helen Archer in the cold and distant Mère Marie Brunel who, the reader learns in the final pages, fled into the convent from the emotional turmoil of her life in the world. Like Helen, Marie Brunel became an over-disciplined nun. She finds her emotional outlet in preparing girls for their operatic training.

As Music and Splendour was O'Brien's last published novel. Shortly afterwards, beset by money troubles and critical neglect, she sold her house in Roundstone and, despite living until 1974 and producing journalism, radio broadcasts and reviews, she never completed another novel. Undoubtedly her alcoholism and ill-health contributed to this lessening of creative output but she also seems to have felt that her particular brand of fiction, centring on the posing of moral problems coloured by the Catholic spirituality in which she had been raised, had gone out of fashion.

Popular Fiction

Dorothea Conyers

In her late novel *Kicking Foxes* (1948), Dorothea Conyers (1871–1949) combines her two specialities: hunting stories and detective fiction. Born Dorothea Blood-Smith in County Limerick into an Anglo-Irish family whose fortunes declined after her father's death, she married Charles Conyers of Castletown Conyers estate, County Limerick in 1892 and published her first novel in 1900, going on to produce over forty popular novels and short story collections. In *Devoted Ladies*, Molly Keane summed up the kind of entertaining but ultimately shallow novels written by Conyers and her ilk:

> ... some hysterical Irish novelist writing her seventy thousand words through which the cry of hounds reverberates continuously: where masters of hounds are handsome and eligible men and desirable young girls over-ride hounds continually, seeing brilliant hunts on incredible three-year-olds: and all – after even the hardest day – are capable of strong emotion at night.[42]

Kicking Foxes, which opens in London during the Blitz, soon sends its half-Irish heroine Felicia Flood off to Ireland and there follow many bright and breezy hunting chapters with romance mixed in for good measure. In between the lighthearted escapism, however, are glimpses of wartime Ireland that chime in with the observations of more literary writers. Fresh from London, Felicia and her friend Barbara appreciate the food, the warmth and the quiet of rural

Ireland. But Ireland is not entirely cut off from the war: in their hotel, Felicia and Barbara socialise with American airmen and come across French aristocrats who have escaped from the Germans. Anglo-Irish involvement in the war lies behind the lack of men on the hunting field and, despite her joy to be hunting again, Felicia cannot quite shut out the thought of 'Gallant men killed in tanks, crashing in planes, or perhaps prisoners in Germany and dreaming one day they would once more see Arvagh.'[43] Even in Ireland there have been changes: amid their hunting exploits Felicia and Barbara come across many ruined or debt-ridden Anglo-Irish estates, some of them already taken over by local farmers. Since this is escapist romance, Felicia's marriage to the wealthy Edgar Allardyce allows her to fulfil her dream of buying and restoring one of these estates, but not before the novel has registered the revision of political and social allegiances in post-independent Ireland.

Maura Laverty

In 1942, Maura Laverty (1907–66), journalist, playwright and broadcaster, published *Never No More*, an account of young Delia Scully's life with her grandmother on the edge of the Bog of Allen during the 1920s. Life in the village of Ballyderrig, based on Rathangan, County Kildare where Laverty grew up, is recounted in a warm, lighthearted manner that did not, however, prevent the author of *Never No More* from encountering the sort of hostility that, as Edna O'Brien was to discover, is the fate of writers who choose to write about their own locality. Though sentimental, the novel does not gloss over the hardship and poverty of Ballyderrig life: the fee-paying secondary schools that are out of reach of most of the villagers, dependence on money from relatives in America, prostitution, deaths of young people, including Delia's brother, from consumption, and deaths of women in childbirth, a consequence of delayed marriages.

What gave the novel its huge popularity during the bleak and hungry war years when commentators were prophesying the death of rural Ireland was Laverty's portrayal of the rich texture of Irish country life, its festivities and its food. Especially popular was Delia's Gran with her acts of neighbourliness and her country recipes. Larger political events are mentioned only as they impact on the lives of the villagers: a son recruited by the British Army in the

First World War, Mick Reddin's sons fighting on the republican side during the Civil War. Even the parish priest, an outsider, scarcely impinges on the villagers' lives. This is a place where faith stems from the heart of the villagers' lives rather than being imposed on them by the church. Though any young girl having a baby out of wedlock is frowned upon, the villagers accept Sarah Gorry, the local prostitute with her four children by different men.[44] The only time the story moves out of the village is in the few chapters depicting the convent boarding school where Delia is desperately unhappy and the plan for her to train as a teacher comes to nothing. *Never No More* was received with great acclaim in America and, as a letter from Brendan Behan testifies, appreciated by the prisoners of Arbour Hill Military Prison. This did not, however, prevent the novel from being banned by the Irish Censorship Board.

Laverty's sequel, *No More Than Human*, opens with eighteen-year-old Delia setting out, after her grandmother's death, for a post as governess in Spain. Like Kate O'Brien's *Mary Lavelle*, *No More Than Human* portrays the isolation of Irish governesses abroad. With no prospect of marrying and no means of returning to Ireland, their entire social life centres around tea parties:

> There was sound reason for their discontent. Good food, a lovely home and an easy time did not make up to them for their lonely unnatural life. There was no social life for governesses, no parties, no dances. The English-speaking colony cold-shouldered them. Their aristocratic employers kept them in their place.[45]

The portrait of Spain is more lighthearted than in *Mary Lavelle*, reflecting the popular readership for which Laverty was writing. The canvas is also wider, since Delia is soon sacked from her governess post. Thereafter she takes a series of jobs that bring her into contact with a variety of Spanish people, ranging from prostitutes to wealthy businessmen and political revolutionaries. Unlike *Mary Lavelle*, the romance plot concludes happily with Delia returning to make a marriage in Ireland.

Laverty's later work of this period explores her experiences of living among the Dublin poor. Like the nineteenth-century philanthropic novels by Irish women, also written for the popular market, Laverty's *Lift Up Your Gates* (1946) exposes, through the eyes of fourteen-year-old Chrissie Doyle, the wretched housing, health, education and employment prospects endured by Dublin's poor, which had become more visible during the war years.[46] In the 1950s Laverty wrote plays based on this material, *Liffey Lane* and *Tolka Row*, and in the following decade, she turned *Tolka Row* into a popular weekly series of the same name focusing on the daily lives of the Nolan family. Broadcast between 1964 and 1968, it was 'RTÉ's first important serial'.[47]

Magdalen King-Hall

After achieving early fame with *The Diary of a Young Lady of Fashion in the Year 1764–65* (1924), Magdalen King-Hall turned to journalism and historical novels. Her *Tea at Crumbo Castle* (1949) is a throwback to the Gothic Big House genre, with the young girl, Blanche, and her paralysed mother subject to the tyranny of the family patriarch, Frederick Toye. The real villain of the story is not, however, Frederick but the cunningly ruthless Emily Hogan, brought up in poverty in a Dublin suburb. The story is set in the years 1878 and '79 but framed by a visit from an Englishwoman in 1931 who encounters Emily in the sparsely attended Protestant church and is invited to tea at Crumbo Castle, where she immediately senses an unpleasant atmosphere and sees the spirit of the long-dead Blanche. Though there is some attempt at sketching in the historical context (Gladstone's Land Act, agrarian disturbances, tenant evictions), the novel, popular at the time, is an outworn raking over of the Gothic.

Barbara Fitzgerald

A subtler use of the Big House theme is found in the work of Barbara Fitzgerald Gregg (1911–82). Fitzgerald, daughter of a Church of Ireland clergyman, John Gregg, who went on to become Archbishop of Dublin (1920–39) and Archbishop of Armagh (1939–59), was educated in London and Trinity College, Dublin. After graduating in 1933, she married oil executive Michael Fitzgerald Somerville (a nephew of Edith Somerville) and lived abroad for many years, mainly in west Africa. Not surprisingly, given her background, as a writer Fitzgerald was attracted to the Big House theme. Her first novel, *We Are Besieged* (1946), was written in the Archbishop's Palace in Armagh where Fitzgerald had returned during the war with her two children. The novel portrays the state of siege felt by the Anglo-Irish after 1922, as an isolated minority in what they perceived to be a hostile state, but also reflects, somewhat didactically, her father's conciliatory policies in urging Protestants to come to terms with the new Ireland in which they now found themselves. Like Bowen, Fitzgerald emphasises the hybrid nature of the Anglo-Irish. Moira Butler, whose house is burnt down by Sinn Féin, states their choices: "'We go back to an England that has lost all knowledge of us and that can never be our home, or we may remain, as aliens besieged, in a land that has lost its welcome.'"[48] Moira's sister Helen never makes her accommodation with the new state but Helen's daughter Caroline decides to make her life in Ireland. Butler's Hill is rebuilt and will be kept going, not through rents and private income but by farming the land professionally. Like Bowen's *A World of Love*, *We Are Besieged* portrays the gradual, and sometimes painful, adaptation of the Anglo-Irish and their Big Houses to the modern world.

Though Fitzgerald's writing career was ended by early dementia, in 1955 she completed a second novel, *Footprint upon Water*, which was eventually published in 1983. A more accomplished novel than its predecessor, *Footprint upon Water* is a study of the Anglo-Irish Fellowes family through the lives of the daughters of the house. The elder daughter Katharine, 'obsessed with the consciousness of sin and the need for self-denial', continues the tyrannical rule imposed on herself and her siblings by Captain Fellowes as she presides over the decline of Fellowescourt through the First World War, the War of Independence and the Civil War. 'Hell yawned before her and she continually described its horrors to her family, hoping to terrify them into observance of the strictest rules of Puritanism.'[49] *Footprint upon Water* echoes both the generational conflicts of Molly Keane's fiction and the coruscating effects of fundamentalist Protestantism portrayed in the novels of Janet McNeill. By the closing pages, set in 1948, the decline of Fellowescourt has been halted by the tenancy of an American couple, but in the end the Big House theme is less important than the portrayal of Katharine's niece Susan finally shaking off the effects of her aunt's imposed Puritanism to achieve spiritual and emotional healing through trusting her own judgement and religious insight. In this respect Fitzgerald's novel provides a, less earnest, up-date on all those nineteenth-century novels by Protestant Irish women writers that specialised in spiritual problems.[50]

Dorothy Macardle

It is difficult to confine Dorothy Macardle (1889–1958) to the realms of popular fiction, though her first novel, *The Uninvited* (1942), was marketed by Corgi as 'a shockingly sinister tale of romance and horror'.[51] Macardle's fiction is more interesting than this description might imply, for she often employs the Gothic to express unease about the position of women in the new Irish state. Macardle was born in Dundalk into a wealthy Catholic brewing family and educated at home by governesses and then at Alexandra College, Dublin. She studied at UCD where she came into contact with feminist and nationalist circles and began to break away from her middle-class upbringing. After a spell in Stratford-upon-Avon, where she developed her interest in the theatre, she returned to Ireland in 1917 and joined both Cumann na mBan and Sinn Féin. She wrote plays, taught English literature at Alexandra College and lived for a time in Maud Gonne's house. She was a republican activist in the War of Independence and the Civil War, during which she got to know Rosamond Jacob, with whom she later shared a house in Dublin. In 1922, she was arrested and she wrote many of the patriotic and nationalist stories in *Earth-bound* (1924) while in Mountjoy and Kilmainham jails. She was a close friend of Éamon de Valera and her best-known work is *The Irish Republic* (1937), a political history of Ireland in the years between 1916 and 1923 from a republican perspective.

Although publicly associated with the Fianna Fáil party for which she served as Director of Publicity, Macardle's secular, liberal republicanism was often at odds with the Irish state's Catholic and conservative nationalism. Working for international and feminist causes, she became highly critical of the secondary status for Irish women enshrined in the 1937 Constitution. As a result, there has been renewed interest in interpreting her life and work from a feminist standpoint.[52] Gerardine Meaney suggests that Macardle's preoccupation with the Gothic and the paranormal in her fiction reflects her anxiety over the way the Irish state had developed, particularly in relation to women, an anxiety she was unable to express openly in non-fiction work like *The Irish Republic*: 'The gothic becomes an arena where the reservations that Macardle held about the state she helped form and her own uneasy freehold within it could be explored.'[53] In all but one of her novels, Macardle updates the gothic by combining it with references to psychoanalysis as a way of exploring and exorcising issues that were personally troubling to her.

In *The Uninvited*, Macardle exploits her personal interest in the occult in order to unpick idealisations of motherhood. Though the novel is set in Devon, there are many Irish resonances throughout, in the names of Pamela and Roddy Fitzgerald, who are half Irish, their maid Lizzie Flynn from County Clare and the Irish psychic researcher Ingram, whom the Fitzgeralds bring in to investigate the hauntings at Cliff End. Father Anson, the Catholic priest they consult over their haunted house, is also partly Irish and therefore, it is suggested, understands what it is like to live in a home under threat: 'Here was a man from whom people whose home had been menaced could expect understanding.'[54]

Like Kate O'Brien's *The Last of Summer* and *Pray for the Wanderer*, *The Uninvited* reflects unease over Catholic representations of motherhood. The first-person narrator, Roddy, comments on the 'cult of the sainted mother, this fixation on dead virtue, dead standards, dead taste'.[55] Though Mary Meredith is talked of in the neighbourhood as a saint, it is not this apparently virtuous and disciplined Englishwoman who turns out to be the good mother, but Carmel, the foreign, wild girl. In the characters of Mary and Carmel, Macardle plays on the Madonna/whore stereotype, though this Madonna is revealed to be a cruel and manipulative hypocrite, while the warmhearted foreigner, seduced by an unscrupulous Welsh artist, is the loving mother of Stella. Stella, who has been told that Mary was her mother, has decorated her bedroom in a way that strikes Roddy's sister Pamela as 'a shrine' to her dead mother:

> Pale blue walls – her mother's favourite colour ... Mary's pictures – Florentine madonnas ... even a statuette of her mother – a white, plaster thing. It's a *cult*. Oh, the piety, the austerity, the pure, virginal charm! Any sensitive girl would come under the spell – and I doubt if the man is born who could break it.[56]

For Stella to become an adult woman with adult sexuality, the novel suggests that Stella's lover, Roddy, must break the power of the mother and the plaster saint must be destroyed. Such passages invite comparison with Maggie's protests against idealising mothers in *The Troubled House* by Macardle's friend, Rosamond Jacob.

While posing a challenge to the view of motherhood enshrined in the Irish Constitution, *The Uninvited* also reflects Macardle's troubled relationship with her own English unionist mother, who was unsympathetic to her daughter's intellectual ambitions and republican activities. In addition, the novel expresses, in a manner characteristic of the female gothic, society's repressed fears around female sexuality, a theme that Edna O'Brien in later decades was to make her own. Daphne du Maurier's classic of the genre, *Rebecca*, had been published in 1938 but whereas in du Maurier, transgressive female sexuality as embodied in Rebecca is eventually erased in favour of the unnamed narrator's wifely submission, in Macardle's novel the monster turns out to be, not the sexual woman, but the sainted mother. *The Uninvited* was a commercial success and in 1944 it was adapted for the screen by Dodie Smith. Significantly, de Valera interpreted the film version as a pointed criticism of his 1937 Constitution.[57]

Like Elizabeth Bowen and Kate O'Brien, Macardle spent the war years in England. Since she disliked living in England, this indicates a deliberate wish to get involved in the war effort, which she did through journalism and humanitarian work.[58] Unlike Bowen and O'Brien, Macardle became increasingly sympathetic as the war progressed to de Valera's policy of neutrality, judging it to have kept Ireland stable. *The Seed was Kind* (1944) portrays a community of refugees in London during the Blitz and a daughter torn between her glamorous, fun-loving mother and her more high-minded and intellectual grandmother. Though this is one of Macardle's less successful works of fiction, the characters being used mainly as mouthpieces for varying shades of political opinion, the tensions between Diony and her shallow-minded mother Sybil, unsympathetic to her daughter's political ideals and engagement in war work, again reflect Macardle's relationship with her socially conventional mother.

Fantastic Summer (1946), written on Macardle's return to Ireland at the end of the war, returns to the paranormal with Virgilia Wilde consulting various experts over her increasingly disturbing visions. Virgilia's school friend Dr Ada Stack puts her visions down to conformity to female domestic roles: 'You over-did the dutiful daughter, marrying to please your Papa; you over-did the faithful wife, those twenty mortal years in Manchester, and now it's the self-effacing mother stuff.'[59] The novel raises this feminist interpretation only to sidestep it in favour of exploring the threat Virgilia's visions pose to her close bond with her daughter Nan. A Gothic atmosphere of foreboding is built up as

Virgilia's visions almost destroy her daughter's chance of happiness. The novel ends carefully poised between Freudian psychoanalysis – a childhood experience may have traumatised Virgilia – and the paranormal. As in *The Uninvited*, an evil mother figure, Suzette, has to be exorcised and banished before a happy ending can be achieved, indicating that Macardle had still not come to terms with the memory of her unhappy and difficult mother.

Like Macardle's short story 'The Portrait of Róisín Dhu' (*Earth-bound*), *Fantastic Summer* critiques myth-making around women through its portrayal of a sculptor prone to idealising women in his art in a way that both ruins his art and threatens the physical safety of his models when they fail to live up to his ideal.[60] The novel is also notable for its sympathetic presentation of the Travelling community and of the small boy Timeen, who has been shut up in a reformatory. Reflecting Macardle's international humanitarian concerns during and after the Second World War with issues of child welfare, *Fantastic Summer* is an early critique of Ireland's reliance on reformatories and industrial schools.[61]

In *Dark Enchantment* (1953), set in Provence, the former Resistance fighter, the Gypsy woman Terka, is persecuted as a witch by a community in the grip of superstitious hysteria. Terka does indeed turn out to be mentally unbalanced and the community returns to normal after her expulsion. Terka has been read as reflecting Macardle's increasing anxiety about her anomalous position in 1950s Ireland as a single, childless woman and a former revolutionary.[62] In this last novel, the fact that the evil spirit who has to be expelled before the protagonist can move forward to adulthood and a happy marriage is no longer the bad mother but a version of Macardle herself offers a poignant commentary on the marginalisation by the 1950s of Irish women formerly involved in Irish public life and the revolutionary struggle. Macardle's gothic novels are an important contribution to Irish women's expression of unease at the way the Irish state had developed after independence, with the silencing of women's public voices and the confinement of women's lives to the roles of wives and mothers.

MAEVE BRENNAN

A similar unease about failure to conform to her country's model for womanhood is reflected in the work of Maeve Brennan (1917–93). Dorothy

Macardle, who knew Brennan's father through his work for the *Irish Press*, briefly acted as mentor to the young Brennan in the early stage of her writing career, and Brennan's biographer, Angela Bourke, quotes a letter from Macardle to Brennan, then in Washington. The letter, written in 1937, weeks before de Valera's Constitution took effect, expresses Macardle's disillusionment in her warning to Brennan that if she returns to Ireland she must be prepared to find a country no longer interested in intellectual activity.[63]

At the time of Brennan's birth her father Robert was in prison for his part in the 1916 Rising. Before their marriage, both her parents had been involved in the Irish–Ireland movement, her mother changing her name from Anastasia to Una as a sign of her support for the Irish language. Brennan's early years were disrupted by her father's lengthy absences, either in prison or fighting, first against the British and then on de Valera's side during the Civil War. Brennan's story 'The Day We Got Our Own Back' (1953) describes, through the eyes of the child Brennan then was, the intrusion of political violence into the domestic sphere as Free Staters raid the house in Ranelagh while their father is on the run. When Brennan was seventeen, Robert Brennan was appointed secretary of the Irish legation at Washington and the whole family moved to America. After college, Brennan began working in New York on *Harper's Bazaar* and stayed on in the US when the rest of her family returned to Ireland. After *Harper's*, Brennan worked at the *New Yorker* for nearly thirty years and it was there that her stories began to appear in the 1950s. In exile, Brennan, like Joyce, endlessly recreated the petty social constraints and spiritual discontents of the Dublin of the 1920s in which she had grown up.

It was while she was working at *Harper's* that Brennan completed her novella *The Visitor* some time in 1944 or '45. It remained unpublished during her lifetime and was only discovered in 1997 among publishers' papers and published in 2000. *The Visitor* is a story of a young woman bearing the name of Brennan's mother, Anastasia, who returns to Dublin after six years' absence, looking for a home in her grandmother's house. In the novella Brennan conveys, it has been suggested, her own feelings of exclusion from the Ireland that had developed after independence – introverted and xenophobic with a narrow definition of femininity that had no place for a sophisticated professional woman like herself.[64] Anastasia's grandmother, Mrs King, narrow-minded, exclusive, religious and complacent, functions as a symbol of what Ireland in Brennan's eyes had become. Mrs King is a monster of selfishness that is concealed, as in the case of Molly Keane's monster mothers, beneath impeccable manners. Valuing her relationship with her son above that with her granddaughter, Mrs King makes it clear that she will offer no home to Anastasia, punishing her for having as a child chosen her mother over her father. *The Visitor* suggests that in Ireland the mother–son relationship will always trump the mother–daughter, but Brennan subtly challenges this by naming her heroine after her mother.

The subplot underlines Brennan's portrayal of Ireland as a chilly, repressed place in the story of Norah Kilbride, the lonely spinster forced by her domineering mother to suppress her sexuality. These Dubliners, like Joyce's, are leading lives of paralysis. The difference is that Brennan is portraying, not a colonised city, but Ireland post-independence. The novella turns on the question of home. 'Home is a place in the mind,' reflects the narrator.[65] This was to be increasingly the case for Brennan during her lengthy decline into alcoholism in the 1960s and '70s when she felt at home neither in Ireland nor America and wrote in a letter: 'The most I ever knew was that I "didn't know where I was".'[66] *The Visitor* ends with a haunting picture of Anastasia standing barefoot outside her grandmother's home singing, as if in a dream, a scrap of a once-remembered song about a happy land 'Where we have eggs and ham/ Three times a day'.[67]

MOLLY KEANE

Molly Keane continued to draw on the theme of the Anglo-Irish in her fiction. One of her most complex novels, *Two Days in Aragon* (1941), is set, like Bowen's *The Last September*, in 1920, when 'many old and beautiful houses had their last hours of life'.[68] Unlike Bowen, Keane does not confine her portrait to the Anglo-Irish but dwells in some detail on those fighting for independence, spelling out the often tangled web of Irish political loyalties. Foley O'Neill is an illegitimate descendant through his mother, Nan, of the Fox family who own Aragon. He has an affair with his cousin Grania, one of the daughters of the house, and sells horses to the British Army while also giving shelter to IRA gunmen. The novel charts the steady rise to power of Nan, a servant in the Aragon household, yet with Fox blood in her veins. Nan's ambivalent status is emphasised by the manner of her death: strung up by the rebels, she is accidentally killed by a British Army lorry. Despite Foley's wish to stay neutral, there can be no neutrals in this guerilla war where 'there was every chance of bloodshed after tea and tennis'.[69]

Keane appears to have written *Two Days in Aragon* partly in atonement for what she felt had been her earlier lack of understanding of the Irish situation and partly in rebellion against her mother, who 'couldn't think that the English had ever done anything wrong'.[70] The novel acknowledges the sensual beauties of Aragon and its demesne while also displaying the cruelties and selfishness of its inhabitants, summed up in the sadomasochistic boudoir in the basement, in the abortions regularly performed on the housemaids and the skeletons of their unwanted babies that lie scattered on the river bottom. In such an atmosphere, Nan's sadistic treatment of aunt Pidgie goes unnoticed by the rest of the family. *Two Days in Aragon* has been seen as a reworking of Edith Somerville's *The Big House of Inver*: in both novels, the illegitimate daughter of the Big House tries in vain to save the house from the ruin inflicted on it by improvident Anglo-Irish.[71] The difference is that while *The Big House of Inver* laments the decline of the Big House family, *Two Days in Aragon* exposes its cruelties and presents Nan's idealisation of Aragon and internalisation of colonial ideology as ruthless and wrong-headed.

Keane's portrayal of Anglo-Irish life is supported by the memoirs of Anglo-Irish childhoods that were appearing in this period.[72] *Bricks and Flowers* (1949) by Katherine Everett paints a particularly bleak picture of her early years growing up at Cahirnane in Kerry in the last decades of the nineteenth century at a time when her family was already in decline. Money could be found for servants and carriages but not for books or holidays, 'and our clothes were made at home of harsh Kerry frieze'.[73] Her father was kind and cheerful but she hardly saw him, and her mother was terrifying enough to feature in a Keane novel.

Keane's next novel, *Loving Without Tears* (1951), portrays a monstrous mother, Angel, in conflict with a younger generation of Anglo-Irish who must resist her possessive love if they are to have any sort of adult life. Angel's behaviour and speech patterns owe more than a little to the influence of Ivy Compton-Burnett, but Keane plays in this novel on the specifically Anglo-Irish theme of infantilism. Angel's niece Tiddley is in awe of her aunt and still reads L.T. Meade's children's stories, while Angel's eighteen-year-old daughter Slaney speaks with the vocabulary of an Angela Brazil school story. Slaney's brother

Julian, despite his three years as a pilot in the Second World War, remains childlike in his obsession with machinery and boats. Tiddley, who is in love with him, realises that he would rather mend a broken clock than make love. 'Don't you ever fear arrested development?' asks Sally, the smart and worldly American woman Julian has met during the war.[74] Sally introduces a note of modernity into the paralysed lives of Owlbeg, but for Angel she is a dangerous unknown quantity, radiating sex appeal and unwholesomeness.

Everything is relative: if Sally finds Owlbeg 'a malign gothic castle',[75] her valet is charmed, feeling that he has returned to 'a richer, kinder childhood' than his real one in the East End of London. The younger generation is unable to withstand Angel's 'destructive loving' and it falls to her land agent, Oliver, to act to ensure everyone's happiness. It might be argued that Keane's cruel, self-absorbed and amoral mothers at least resist the stereotype of the self-sacrificing Irish mother: as Anglo-Irish women they expect to hand over care of their children to nannies and get on with their lives. Yet Keane's novels are anything but affirmative of mothers. Taken as a whole, they endorse the view of mother as someone who is best grown out of: 'Life starts when mother stops' is Oliver's Freudian pronouncement.[76]

Bobby Keane died in 1946 and in 1952 Keane and her two daughters moved to Ardmore, County Waterford, where she was to live for the rest of her life. In the same year, her novel *Treasure Hunt* was published. *Treasure Hunt* originated as a hugely successful play that ran for a year on the English stage in 1949, providing much-needed escapism for an England still in the grip of post-war rationing. Keane was following in the nineteenth-century tradition of portraying stage Irishmen for the amusement of English audiences but with the difference that in her play the comic Irish are not peasants but their overlords. No wonder Keane felt at times that she had betrayed her class.

Set in 1948, *Treasure Hunt* has some parallels with Bowen's *A World of Love* in the portrait of an Anglo-Irish estate, Ballyboden, relying on farming to keep going, in the portrayal of an older generation of Anglo-Irish trapped in pointless and destructive fantasies about their glamorous pasts, and in their resentment against wealthy English interlopers who can afford to buy up castles in Ireland. The novel depicts three generations of the Ryall family. Aunt Anna Rose represents the older generation of Anglo-Irish living in a fantasy world that self-protectively blots out the reality of the changing times. In the middle generation, Hercules (called by Brigid, who nannies him, Master Hercules) and his sister Consuelo represent the glamour, decadence and infantilism of the Anglo-Irish too irresponsible to face up to the fact that their vast debts have almost crippled the estate. The younger generation, Phillip and his cousin Veronica, lack the charm of the older generations but are more practical and it is they who, like Fred in *A World of Love*, keep the estate going by farming. There is much comedy when a family of well-heeled, sophisticated English people, Eustace, his sister Dorothy and her daughter Yvonne, arrive as paying guests to a house that lacks everything in the way of modern comforts. These guests act as a catalyst for change. Eustace manages to wake aunt Anna Rose sufficiently from her Sleeping Beauty trance for her legendary rubies to be found, thus finally allowing Phillip and Veronica to run the estate in a commercial fashion. The novel dwells, however, at least as much on past glories – aunt Anna's Viennese waltzes, Hercules's and Consuelo's memories of gambling at Monte Carlo – as on the present. In *Treasure Hunt*, perhaps because it originated as a play for popular audiences, the seductive glamour of the Big House lingers and Keane is not entirely exempt here from Bowen's criticism of the Anglo-Irish as seduced by their own past.

MARY LAVIN

Mary Lavin (1912–96) was reluctant to invoke gender as an explanation of her work: 'I write as a person. I don't think of myself as a woman who writes. I am a writer. Gender is incidental to that.'[77] Despite this, Lavin has been an important trailblazer for Irish women writers. Born in the US to Irish parents, she returned to Ireland at the age of nine. She was educated at the Loreto College, Dublin and studied French and English at UCD, where she met William Walsh whom she later married. After Walsh's early death, in 1954, Lavin was left to run the farm they had bought together in County Meath as well as supporting herself and her three daughters by her writing. In contrast to many of her female literary predecessors who remained childless – Maria Edgeworth, Somerville and Ross, Elizabeth Bowen, Kate O'Brien – Lavin illustrated in her daily life that books and motherhood could be combined, often writing at the kitchen table while at her side her daughters did their homework. In the 1950s, her Dublin home, the Mews, became a magnet for young writers, many of whom she helped in the early stages of their careers. Later writers like Evelyn Conlon have claimed Lavin as a role model for Irish women writers and regretted that her works were not more widely available when they were growing up: 'young femalehood in Ireland in the sixties would have been greatly illuminated by the voice that examined the wars of relationships rather than those of countries.'[78]

Lavin's writing career was launched in the 1940s with her short story collection *Tales from Bective Bridge* (1942), and it is in the short story form rather than the novel that she is an acknowledged master. Her two novels are of interest, however, in their exploration of themes, such as female sexuality and motherhood, that were to become popular in the more overtly feminist Irish fiction of the 1970s. Female sexuality is a central theme of Lavin's much-neglected novel *The House in Clewe Street* (1945), depicting the heroine, Onny Soraghan, resisting, by means of her body, the puritanical society in which she lives. The novel is set in Castlerampart, a fictionalised version of Athenry, the twelfth-century walled town in County Galway, birthplace of Lavin's mother, to which Lavin returned from America in 1921. The stultifying middle-class values of the leaders of Castlerampart society are established from the outset of the novel. It is a world dominated by class, property and Catholicism with the Coniffe family at the centre as the largest property owners of all. Onny, who comes to work for the Coniffes and whose body exerts such a fascination over Gabriel, the Coniffe heir, lives on the outskirts of Castlerampart beyond which lie the ruined castle and wild parkland. Many of Lavin's stories feature such wildernesses outside the town walls and these wildernesses come to symbolise all that the town rejects. It is therefore significant that Gabriel's and Onny's first embrace, breaking through the class distinctions of their society that would keep them apart, takes place in the fields outside Castlerampart. For Gabriel, Onny's brightly coloured clothes express a spirit of rebellion 'in the dull walled town'[79] and the wilderness contains all the sensuality his society has tried to suppress.[80]

In Dublin, to which the couple move when the strain of keeping their relationship a secret in Castlerampart becomes too difficult, Onny's body exerts its charms over the artists among whom she and Gabriel live. Jealous of her success, Gabriel tries to assert his authority, wanting to bring Onny's outlawed and untamed body inside the Catholic Church by marrying her. Unusually in Irish fiction of this period, though by now pregnant, Onny refuses to be cowed. Rejecting ownership either by Gabriel or by the church, she asserts her rights over her own body, including her right to have an abortion. The illegal abortion is botched and Onny dies but, despite the urging of his artist friends, Gabriel will not disown her even if it means making himself, under the Irish law of that time, an accessory to murder. Remarkably for the period, Lavin portrays an Irish woman asserting ownership of her body, taking pride in it and gaining pleasure from it in a way that anticipates the fiction of Edna O'Brien. Though, like many of O'Brien's heroines, Onny comes to a tragic end, it is she who grips the reader's imagination, as she grips Gabriel's in his search for a different way of living from that in which he has been raised, and as indeed she seems to have gripped Lavin.

Lavin returned to this theme of the female body as subversive in her novella *The Becker Wives*, published the following year. The bird-like Flora, wife of Theobald Becker, uses her slender body to parody the heavy movements of the other Becker wives, all solid, middle-class women with bodies amply built for child-bearing. Flora's imitative gestures emphasise the entrapment of the Becker wives in their comfortable houses filled with heavy furniture. For a while the Becker males are entranced as Flora seems to offer the possibility of a different, more imaginative way of living. She is an artist, a photographer, in contrast to the earth mother Becker women.[81] However, Flora is revealed to be schizophrenic. The tone of the novella turns from surreal to bleak in its suggestion that the choice for women's lives in post-independence Ireland lies between conformity and insanity.[82]

As well as opening up the theme of female bodily pleasure in *The House in Clewe Street*, *The Becker Wives* and stories such as 'The Nun's Mother' (1944), Lavin's work also points to later women's fiction in its treatment of the theme of motherhood and mother–daughter relations. 'The Nun's Mother', 'The Will' and 'A Cup of Tea', all published in *The Long Ago* (1944) explore the mother–daughter relationship, and motherhood features centrally in Lavin's second novel *Mary O'Grady* (1950).[83] *Mary O'Grady* lovingly portrays Mary's life as a wife and mother who has been transplanted, as many were in this period, from her rural upbringing to life in the city. Living for the rest of her life in Dublin, sorrowing as her children grow away from her, Mary never forgets her roots in Tullamore and to the end of her life she retains her country values which are at odds with and even unhelpful in the city. Despite Mary's struggle to keep her family members safe, it is often her misjudgements that bring disaster on them, and the narrative of the various tragedies undergone by her children undermines Mary's attempt to keep the family idyll intact. Though she embodies the contemporary ideal of Catholic motherhood, towards the end of her story, Mary reveals her doubts as to whether her self-sacrificing mothering has been successful: 'She had spared neither toil nor sweat nor sacrifice, and yet life, that had been as sweet as milk and honey, was souring, hour by hour.'[84] She wonders whether her children would have done better if they had been less protected by a mother's love. In *Mary O'Grady*, Lavin, like Dorothy Macardle, Rosamond Jacob and Kate O'Brien before her, subjects idealised maternal love to scrutiny and concludes that it cannot withstand the realities of modern urban living.[85] It is perhaps no coincidence that before Lavin embarked on her writing career she began a dissertation on Virginia Woolf. Taken together, her short stories and novels from this period suggest that Lavin was a more radical writer, and a more feminist one, than is sometimes allowed.

VAL MULKERNS

Glimpses of the way in which Irish women's writing was to develop in later decades may be spied in the early work of Val Mulkerns (1925–). Born in Dublin, Mulkerns was educated by Dominican nuns and worked as a civil servant in the 1940s and as associate editor of *The Bell* in the 1950s. Her first novel, *A Time Outworn* (1951), is set during the Second World War. Apart from the quarrels between her nationalist father who fought in 1916 and his neighbour George Henderson, wounded in the First World War, the war has so far not affected eighteen-year-old Maeve Cusack, just out of convent school:

> It had meant dark bread and no oranges, and my father and George Henderson shouting at each other across a room. It had meant little more. At school we had been on an island within an island; bombs and ravaged cities and mutilated bodies had never been able to penetrate. We had listened to war news as we would listen to a ghost story told around a fire. It was all unreal and shadowy and infinitely far away.[86]

Imbued with her father's nationalism, Maeve sets off from Dublin for a post as librarian in Tipperary with the same sense of adventure that Cait and Baba will experience a decade later in Edna O'Brien's *The Country Girls* when they make the journey in reverse, from rural Ireland to Dublin. Among its various love stories, *A Time Outworn* captures the rhythm of life in 1940s rural Ireland with its weekday masses and spread of culture through the network of local libraries. The debates between Maeve and the local schoolmaster, Brian, a lukewarm nationalist opposed to compulsory Irish-language teaching in schools, highlight opposition to the government's promotion of the Irish language, while Father Tom's policing of the morals of the young people underlines the continuing strength of clerical influence. Attitudes to higher education for girls continue to be a problem: like Anna's grandmother in *The Land of Spices*, Nora's mother refuses to spend money on third-level education for her daughter, telling her that women with degrees are 'atrocities' and that in all likelihood Nora will meet some boy halfway through and drop out.[87] In Maeve's family there is no money for university.

Mulkerns's other novel from this period, *A Peacock Cry* (1954), portrays life in Irish-speaking Connemara, opening with a description of the landscape of the west of Ireland and its inhabitants that recalls the writing of Emily Lawless. Mulkerns's principal characters, however, are educated people, like the schoolmaster Peter McGlynn, and Dara Joyce who writes folk tales updated for a contemporary readership. Like Éilís Ní Dhuibhne's *The Dancers Dancing* (1999), *A Peacock Cry* reflects contemporary debates over efforts to preserve the Irish language. The fate of Dara's wife Mary, who fell in love with her husband because 'he was rare and splendid, a product of the purest and oldest form of Gaelic civilisation',[88] punctures any easy sentimentality over life in Connemara. Formerly a schoolteacher with a university degree, Mary's life is now confined to raising six children with a husband who is unfaithful.

The person Dara is unfaithful with is Ruth Willmann, an American Irish literature enthusiast who has come over to Ireland to research his work. At a literary party given by Ruth in Dublin, an unnamed young woman defends Kate O'Brien's novels as of more use to present-day Ireland than Dara's peasant tales, a genre that in her view has been done to death: 'The sort of novel that I think of most value to Ireland at the present moment is a novel in the European tradition, the sort of thing Kate O'Brien does so beautifully.'[89]

This championing of fiction that manages to be simultaneously European and Irish picks up on a characteristic of much Irish women's fiction, and the young woman's statement is an interesting early glimpse of the possibility of establishing a genealogy of Irish women writers. It is worth remembering that it was during these years that the Irish feminist literary scholar B.G. MacCarthy, a colleague of Daniel Corkery in Cork, published her ground-breaking volumes devoted to retrieving Anglophone women's fiction: *Women Writers: Their Contribution to the English Novel, 1621–1744* (1944) and *The Female Pen: Women Writers and Novelists, 1744–1818* (1947).

NORTHERN IRELAND

In July 1954, a special edition of *Irish Writing* edited by David Marcus and Terence Smith and including work by Elizabeth Bowen, Kate O'Brien, Mary Lavin and the Northern Irish writer Mary Beckett indicated that Irish women's writing was beginning to make its mark. The inclusion of Mary Beckett, known at this time for her short stories, suggests a continuity between women's writing north and south of the border that is borne out by the fiction of Anne Crone and Janet McNeill. Yet, even in this period before the Troubles, there are differences of emphasis.

Anne Crone

Born in Dublin, Anne Crone (1915–72) was educated in Belfast and Oxford and taught modern languages for many years in Belfast schools. Despite this she chose to set her novels, *Bridie Steen* (1949), *This Pleasant Lea* (1952) and *My Heart and I* (1955), not in Belfast but in County Fermanagh, her mother's birthplace. *Bridie Steen* explores the sectarian divisions of rural Fermanagh through the fate of the eponymous Bridie, daughter of a Catholic mother and a Protestant father. Bridie's hybrid identity runs counter to the duality on which her society is based. Orphaned early on and rejected by her father's Protestant family who disapproved of the mixed marriage, Bridie is raised by her maternal aunt Rose Anne, a bigoted Catholic. Rose Anne, whose character has been deformed by grinding poverty, imprints on her niece a religion as severe as the puritanical Protestantism Katharine Fellowes imposes on her niece in Fitzgerald's *Footprint upon Water*. During her harsh upbringing Bridie instinctively derives more solace from her love of nature than from her religion. The bog is Bridie's natural home and, away from the sectarian divisions of her culture, she carves out a space that gives her a freedom of spirit unobtainable from the institutional religions of her society. Like her uncle James who instructs her in local legends and folklore and who may be seen as a forerunner of the father in Deirdre Madden's novel *One by One in the Darkness*, Bridie is in touch with the spirit and ways of the land that pre-date the Christianity that has brought such divisions.

At eighteen, Bridie is summoned to live in the more prosperous home of her paternal grandmother, as dogmatic in her non-conformism as aunt Rose Anne is in her Catholicism. Though Bridie learns to love her imperious and possessive grandmother, she resists efforts to persuade her to convert to Protestantism. After many vicissitudes, searching for peace from the religious divisions that have haunted her life, Bridie flees her grandmother's house and takes refuge in the bog. She meets her death walking alone there in the dark. It is left to her lover, William, to lament the sectarian divisions that have destroyed Bridie's life. The Catholic and Protestant men who have been helping William search for Bridie hear his cry but the novel holds out little hope of change: 'The men stood rooted to the ground, compassionate, motionless, humble, acknowledging by their wet eyes that what he said was true. But helpless, each in his station doomed to play the part destiny and the social order had ordained for him.'[90] Crone's novel contains many lyrical passages describing the beauties of the Fermanagh countryside and the rhythms of rural life with a gentle leisureliness that points forward to the work of John McGahern, but its ending is a gloomy portent for the future of Northern Ireland.

Observations about the division of gender roles in rural Fermanagh become more prominent in Crone's next two novels, the omniscient narrator of *This Pleasant Lea* observing: 'the unwritten law of the countryside was that, whether by day they taught in school, served behind counters, or made hay in the fields, in the hours remaining before sleep women served men.'[91] Frank Storey, a wastrel and a gambler, takes it for granted that his mother and sisters will wait on him. There are many echoes in Crone's work of the nineteenth-century realist novels that she admired, and Mrs Storey is a foolish mother who might have stepped out of a George Eliot novel. *This Pleasant Lea* depicts the clash between those characters who belong to their environment and those who, like Frank's sister Faith and Anthony Fletcher, have been educated out of it and bring a modern sensibility to traditional ways of living.

In *My Heart and I*, the marriage of the hard-working doctor, John, and his luxury-loving wife, Christine, recalls that of Lydgate and Rosamond in *Middlemarch*. The novel portrays the materialism of rural Ulster life where marriages are contracted for pragmatic reasons rather than for love. Having made such a marriage, Grace pours all her love into her relationship with her son John, whom she raises through hard work and self-sacrifice to be a doctor. Unlike *Bridie Steen*, *My Heart and I* describes Catholics and Protestants living and working alongside one another without conflict, though the focus is chiefly on the Protestant community and on Grace's tribal loyalty and 'deep admiration for Ulster, its ideals, its steadfastness'.[92] *My Heart and I* paints a vivid picture of obsessive mother love that in the end turns to tragedy as Grace, having sacrificed her own chance for happiness, finds herself replaced by John's wife. In depicting the conflict between Grace and her daughter-in-law, the novel portrays the clash between tradition and modernity, and between rural and urban women. *My Heart and I* possesses some of the power of Mary Lavin's deconstruction of idealised motherhood in *Mary O'Grady*. On her deathbed, Grace begs for the print of Virgin and Child belonging to her Catholic neighbour to be removed: "'It isn't true, you see,' said Grace. 'It takes women in. They think it's the greatest thing in life, and it isn't after all. It's of no consequence.'"[93]

Janet McNeill

Janet McNeill (1907–94) was born in Dublin and moved to England with her family in 1913, returning to Belfast to work at the *Belfast Telegraph* (1929–33). Daughter of a Presbyterian minister, she knew at first hand the creed's potential for joylessness. *Tea at Four O'Clock* (1956) depicts the repressions and paralysis of life in middle-class Protestant Belfast and the struggle for power between the generations in a way that recalls Molly Keane's portraits of the Anglo-Irish. Like an Anglo-Irish Big House, the imperialistically named

Marathon, once symbol of the prosperity the linen industry brought to three generations of the Perceval family, is in decline, fringed with shops and housing estates. Widowed early, Mr Perceval has raised George and his two sisters, Mildred and Laura, in an atmosphere of repression as daunting as any found in Keane's novels and, as in Keane, the will to power passes down the generations: after their father's death, his elder daughter Mildred continues his patriarchal regime so that the gentler Laura knows in any given situation what Mildred would do or say.

Sexual repression is as much a part of Mildred's regime as it is a feature of women's writing south of the border. Her devaluation of sexual love has disastrous consequences for Laura, who learns to police her desires until she becomes, in the eyes of her brother George, 'a small hesitant inelegant figure, as sexless as it was possible for a woman to be'.[94] *Tea at Four O'Clock* portrays the way in which Laura's innate capacity for happiness has been stifled, first by her father and then by Mildred. The ending reveals that she has become complicit in her own repression when she rejects Mr McAlister's proposal of marriage with a cruelty that reminds him of Mildred. Like a Molly Keane character, Laura the victim grows up to victimise in turn.

McNeill was reluctant to be defined as a regional novelist and *Tea at Four O'Clock* is not overtly political but, as in the novels of Kate O'Brien and Molly Keane, McNeill uses one family to symbolise an entire class. Her portrayal of the stagnation and paralysis of Northern Protestant middle-class life led one critic to describe her work as recording 'the religious twilight of a class and a generation'.[95]

Examination of Irish women's wartime writing reveals unsuspected connections and influences, between major writers like Elizabeth Bowen and Kate O'Brien but also between more marginalised authors (at least in the context of the Irish canon) such as Olivia Manning and Betty Miller. In the hands of writers like Manning, Miller, Dorothy Macardle, Janet McNeill and even on occasion Molly Keane Irish women's fiction is becoming more explicitly interested in psychoanalytical themes. But whatever mode is employed – realism, satire, the Gothic, the psychoanalytical – Irish women's writing of this period marks women's disillusionment and unease at the way in which the Irish state has turned out. Novel after novel underlines the silencing of women's public voices, the limited opportunities for Irish women to lead positive, fulfilling lives and the damage often wreaked on their families because of this. Idealised images of motherhood are repeatedly challenged in the work of Kate O'Brien, Dorothy Macardle, Mary Lavin and Anne Crone. The search of Kate O'Brien's heroines for a wider and more satisfying life outside Ireland is representative of much Irish women's writing during these years.

Chapter 5

THE 1960S AND '70S: SEX, RELIGION AND EXILE

EDNA O'BRIEN

*I*n 1960, Edna O'Brien (1930–) burst onto the Irish literary scene with her novel *The Country Girls*. This simple and nowadays innocuous tale of two convent-bred girls leaving rural Ireland for the delights of the big city caused uproar when it was published, its depiction of female sexuality posing a challenge to Irish Catholic and nationalist pieties. O'Brien was immediately attacked for bringing shame on Irish women, she was condemned at parish masses and her local priest organised a burning of her books. Yet her novels and stories were to be enormously influential in giving young Irish women a voice. Here was an Irish woman writing not from the Big House tradition like Maria Edgeworth, Somerville and Ross, and Elizabeth Bowen, nor from the Catholic bourgeoisie like Kate O'Brien, but from the heart of Catholic rural Ireland. As Mary Dorcey put it: 'At last, a proletariat Irish woman. An inspiration.'[1]

The fact that *The Country Girls* was banned only increased its attraction and O'Brien went on to become 'one of the most commercially successful [writers] ever to come out of Ireland'.[2] O'Brien's life has been much mythologised and this, together with the highly theatrical Irish persona she adopted for her readings, gained for her, like Sydney Owenson in the nineteenth century, a notoriety that has not always been helpful for a serious critical assessment of her work. She struck Elizabeth Bowen, for instance, as 'talented but completely mad'.[3] Her age has been no bar to reviewers waxing lyrical over her appearance at the expense of serious consideration of her writing. An interview, conducted by a female novelist, published in *The Times* in 2005 gives a flavour:

> Seated on her plywood chair, as on a burnish'd throne, the High Queen of Irish letters ... is terribly beautiful, in a Yeatsian kind of way. In her scoop-neck sweater, shimmery velvet skirt, ethnic beads and stout suede walking boots, she is a minxy Mother Ireland, the kind of woman who might, if she chose, pluck a harp with one hand and milk a cow with the other.[4]

Yet O'Brien has testified to the seriousness with which she takes her work, observing that 'the novelist is the psychic and moral historian of his or her society'.[5] Certainly O'Brien's novels and short stories could be described as providing an unflinching portrait of Irish women's lives during the second half of the twentieth century. It was not until the beginning of the twenty-first century, however, that volumes of scholarly essays devoted to her work began to appear.[6]

Edna O'Brien was born and raised in Tuamgraney, County Clare. Her early life, described in her memoir *Country Girl* (2012), closely resembled that of many of her heroines: 'Money troubles, drink troubles, all sorts of troubles.'[7] She was educated at national school in Scariff and then in the Convent of Mercy at Loughrea before studying pharmacy in Dublin, where she met and in 1951 married the German-Irish novelist Ernest Gébler. Gébler was nearly twice her age and the model for many of the controlling older men in her novels. They had two sons, Carlo (now a novelist in his own right) and Sasha. In 1958, the family moved to London, where O'Brien has lived ever since. The beginning of her writing career forms a backdrop to Carlo Gébler's memoir *Father and I* (2000): 'All through that first London winter, from the end of 1958, when we arrived, through to the spring of 1959, while I was at school in the daytime, my mother wrote in the bedroom at the back of the house that I shared with my brother.'[8] As O'Brien's career blossomed, Ernest Gébler's reputation as a writer declined. He became increasingly bitter about this and in 1964 they divorced.[9] Invoking Joyce as her model, O'Brien has said: 'I realise now that I would have had to leave Ireland in order to write about it. Because one needs the formality and the perspective that distance gives in order to write calmly about a place.'[10]

Much of O'Brien's work centres on the theme of women routinely crushed and defeated, not only by their menfolk but also by the constraints of the rural society in which they grow up and the puritanical form of Catholicism they imbibe from an early age. *The Country Girls*, a deceptively simple tale, has given rise to varied readings centred on nationalism, sexuality, food, clothes, the abject, the family, all of them connected with Irish women's lives. It opens with a portrait of two families. That of Caithleen Brady fits O'Brien's iconoclastic description in *Mother Ireland* (1974) of the typical Irish family: 'the martyred Irish mother and the raving rollicking Irish father'.[11] Caithleen and her mother live in fear of violence and abuse from the alcoholic and feckless Mr Brady but, since the family unit is inviolate, the abuse cannot be publicly acknowledged. Mr Brady is thought of in the neighbourhood as 'a gentleman, a decent man who wouldn't hurt a fly'.[12] In her portrait of Caithleen's mother, a woman who does not even possess a name of her own, being simply referred to as 'Mama' throughout, O'Brien underlines the drudgery and isolation of rural women's lives during the 1940s and '50s. Mrs Brady and the labourer Hickey are left to do most of the work on the farm, yet she is almost entirely dependent on her husband for money and is powerless to prevent him from squandering the family income on drink. Moreover, Mrs Brady's vulnerability is not only financial but sexual: she is prey, like her daughter, to the random sexual attentions of various males in the neighbourhood. Jack Holland fondles Mrs Brady's knee in exchange for presents of candied peel and chocolate, and fourteen-year-old Caithleen is expected to kiss Hickey, Jack Holland and other assorted adult males. Caithleen, whose relationship with her mother is stiflingly symbiotic, absorbs from her lessons on the vulnerability of females in Ireland during the 1950s.[13]

The portrait of the family of Caithleen's friend Baba provides a different perspective. In the Brennan family, it is the mother, Martha, who has the upper hand, beating the maidservant and concealing the best food from her husband. If Mrs Brady is the downtrodden saint, Martha is regarded in the neighbourhood as fast because she drinks in the Greyhound Hotel. Later in the novel, Martha loses confidence, gets religion and becomes the submissive wife. Nevertheless, she passes on to her daughter a more positive role model than does the martyr mother Mrs Brady, who instils in her daughter a passivity bordering on masochism, together with a fear of sex.

The convent school which Caithleen and Baba attend after Mrs Brady's death, based on O'Brien's own convent-school experience, continues their initiation into their nation's gender divisions. The nuns' repressive attitude to the female body manifests itself in anorexic attitudes to food and in their stress on modesty and concealing female flesh.[14] Naturally Baba, looking for something that will get them expelled, alights precisely on this equation of Irish girlhood with modesty. At the age of seventeen, she and Caithleen are expelled from the convent for writing 'a dirty note'. The young women's subsequent eager embrace of single life in the city provides a counter-narrative to the nationalist construct of Ireland as a family-centred, rural nation. Caithleen and Baba have become outsiders to this ethos, a fact stressed when they lodge with a foreign landlady. Caithleen's unconsummated romance with Mr Gentleman, who attracts her precisely because he is a foreigner and an outsider, confirms her sense of otherness.[15] Though Caithleen and Baba resist the Catholic values in which they have been raised and the equation of Irish girlhood with chastity, they are increasingly trapped in other discourses, that of metropolitan consumerism, the heterosexual romance plot and the commodification of the female body. They become adept in the feminine masquerade, monitoring their clothes, appearance and diet in accordance with fashionable norms in order to attract men. In a world where the lucrative professions were still occupied by men, Baba looks for a man who will provide her with a comfortable lifestyle, while Caithleen, yearning to submerge herself in another, turns Mr Gentleman into an object of religious adoration.[16] To the reader it is plain that this love object is an unhappily married middle-aged man with a suspicious predilection for young girls. The ending, like much in this novel, operates through anti-climax as Caithleen's 'god' lets her down when he backs out of their planned trip to Vienna. O'Brien, often marketed and read as a straightforwardly romantic novelist, is already in this first novel questioning the illusory promise held out by the romance plot and the damage it inflicts on women's lives.[17]

For the twenty-first-century reader, sensitised to the subject of paedophilia, Mr Gentleman's behaviour towards the young Caithleen is less like seduction than 'grooming'.

In 1962, O'Brien published a sequel to *The Country Girls*, *The Lonely Girl*.[18] Caithleen, conditioned by her masochistic mother into self-abnegation and still in thrall to the romance plot, constructs another love object in the mysterious and ascetic Eugene Gaillard, a successor to Mr Gentleman and modelled on Ernest Gébler.[19] Though in fact half-Irish, Eugene is perceived by the locals as foreign due to his way of living: he is separated from his American wife and he does not attend mass. Like Mr Gentleman, Eugene is a good deal older than Caithleen and functions as a substitute for her unsatisfactory father. The plot owes much to Daphne du Maurier's novel *Rebecca*, most obviously in the fact that Eugene has a wife, the sophisticated American Laura, to whom Caithleen feels vastly inferior. When Caithleen's family and neighbours come after her, the debate is not simply about the 'immorality' of Caithleen's decision to live with Eugene, a married man; it is a tussle over the very notion of what constitutes Irish womanhood and an assertion of male ownership over definitions of the nation and women. The author of an anonymous note sent to Caithleen's father regards Eugene as a foreigner enticing Caithleen away from her rightful place as an Irish Catholic girl who should be embodying the purity of her nation but, like Clare in Kate O'Brien's *As Music and Splendour*, Caithleen has been estranged from the values of rural Ireland for too long. She knows that she never will marry 'one of her own kind'.[20] Nor is she sufficiently mature to handle the sophistication of Eugene's way of life. In the end she resigns herself to fleeing to England with Baba, a choice of destination that sums up her rebellion since in the eyes of her father and his cronies England is the other, 'a pagan place' in contrast with Catholic Ireland.

The highly ironical title of Edna O'Brien's final volume of her *Country Girls* trilogy, *Girls in their Married Bliss* (1964), underlines her critique of the romance plot as unreliable in providing narrative closure for women's lives. Caithleen, renamed Kate by Eugene who is now her husband and the father of her child, continues her maturing process. In an effort to find her path in life she experiments with different identities but is hindered in her development by her continuing entanglement with the romance plot and with prescriptions for Irish femininity. In this final volume of the trilogy, Baba's sceptical, debunking voice becomes dominant, her astringent views on Ireland and love providing a counterpoint to Kate's romantic notions about men and the Irish nation. These romantic notions eventually destroy Kate while Baba, cynical and realistic about men, motherhood and nation, survives. The affairs Kate and Baba embark on outside marriage provide a counter to the idealisation of the chastity of Irish Catholic womanhood, an idealisation reinforced by Baba's Irish husband Frank, whose Madonna/whore way of thinking leads him to suppose that Baba should be perfectly happy without sex. Losing custody of her son, Kate has herself sterilised, an act that suggests both self-punishment and rebellion in her refusal to conform to the view of both her nation and the Catholic Church that the natural vocation of Irish women is motherhood. Cheryl Herr comments: 'Abuse and misogyny are internalised in O'Brien's women and converted to self-hatred, specifically hatred of the gendered body.'[21]

The trilogy originally ended with Kate's sterilisation, but for the 1987 collected edition O'Brien added an epilogue narrated through Baba's voice twenty years later. Kate has drowned in what Baba suspects is suicide. In a conversation with Baba before her death, Kate put her feelings of depression down to the failure of yet another romance. Baba, however, has another explanation – she blames Ireland:

> Her son and I will have to take her ashes there and scatter them
> between the bogs and the bog lakes and the murmuring waters
> and every other fucking bit of depressingness that oozes from
> every hectometer and every furlong of the place and that imbued
> her with the old Dido desperado predilections.[22]

Throughout the final novel of the trilogy, Baba's voice provides a clear-sighted commentary on her fellow countrymen's sentimentality about their native land, remarking of a conversation between Irish emigrants in London: 'They covered crime, too, and unmarried mothers and the morals of England. As if the morals of Ireland were any better.'[23] Frank, who agrees with Kate about the importance of 'roots, values, not losing one's identity', promises Baba that they will go home one day, a prospect that appals her.[24] Though Baba herself cannot entirely break with the past, she does at least see the dangers of nostalgia and censures both Frank and Kate for being so caught up in the myth of a unique

Irish identity that they have failed to embrace emigration as an opportunity to break out of fixed patterns of thought. In O'Brien's subsequent novels, the force of Baba's astringent commentary will be increasingly replaced by a more conservative nostalgia about Ireland and a feeling that there is in fact an essential Irish identity tying Irish women to their home country, which is impossible to overcome.

Faced with an outcry over her trilogy in her native land, O'Brien insisted she was not attacking the Irish nation. In an interview, she said: 'Nobody outside this country considers that I write a condemnation of Irish life; they just take it for granted that I am writing about a set of people in Ireland.'[25] O'Brien was surely being disingenuous: her choice of subject matter in *The Country Girls*, namely the growth to maturity of two young Irish girls in the 1950s, allowed her to give a detailed critique of nationalist pieties about family life and the construct of Irish womanhood. This critique becomes overt in the final volume of the trilogy through the use of Baba's voice and is underpinned by the epilogue. In O'Brien's depiction of Ireland there is no room in the life of the nation for women who do not conform to its construct of femininity.

In *August is a Wicked Month* (1965), a novel that, despite its superficial *Cosmopolitan* glamour, is pervaded by imagery of disease and death, O'Brien again associates Irish Catholicism with punitive attitudes towards sex. Ellen, who has spent time in a Magdalen laundry in Ireland, equates sex with sin and shame: 'She had been brought up to believe in punishment; sin in a field and then the long awful spell in the Magdalen laundry scrubbing it out, down on her knees getting cleansed.'[26] In England, where she is introduced to the world 'of ideas and collective thought and flute music' by her husband, a successor to the free-thinking Eugene Gaillard of *The Country Girls* trilogy, Ellen remains haunted, like all O'Brien's Irish emigrants, by her childhood in Ireland: 'It all sounded grand. Except that it wasn't enough and he didn't buoy her up when she hankered after the proverbs and accordion music and a statue of the Virgin hewn from blackthorn wood.'[27] Abroad, Ellen has found no new identity to set against the Irish one she has only partly outgrown: internalising her society's religious and social values, she regards a venereal infection as punishment for sex and her son's death as a judgement on her for her failings as a mother.

If Ellen's life is coloured by attitudes inculcated into her during her upbringing in Ireland, it is also shaped by the heterosexual romance plot:

'The great brainwash began in childhood. Slipped in between the catechism advocating chastity for women was the secret message that a man and a man's body was the true and absolute propitiation.'[28] Lacking a secure sense of self, Ellen goes out to the south of France yearning to lose herself in love, but the men in the sophisticated circles she encounters desire new and ever-more physically perfect women to prey on with the same jaded appetites as they seek out exotic food and drink. In turn the women starve themselves and feverishly invest in clothes and cosmetics in an effort to remain attractive.[29] In this fourth novel, O'Brien combines a continuing critique of Irish religious and nationalist constraints on women with a more general and transnational portrayal of the commodification of the female body and female sexuality during the sexual revolution of the 1960s.

O'Brien continued to portray men and women as casualties of their sexual relationships. Set in London, *Casualties of Peace* (1966) retains an Irish link since the protagonist, Willa, is an emotionally damaged Irish woman. Though she tells Patsy and Tom stories about her childhood in Ireland, Willa has become completely detached from her country and confused as to her identity: 'What are you? she thought. A person who does not love her country, a person who cannot love a man, a person without child who babbles on about love.'[30] As an Irish woman, Willa fails on all counts, being neither wife, nor mother, nor patriot. Like many O'Brien protagonists, and reminiscent of Lois in *The Last September*, Willa is conscious of using clothes as a way to escape the self, or, in Willa's case, the lack of self: 'She said that her neck, the thin earring chains that tapered to an oval stone, the dress with sacramental sleeves were things donned in an attempt to escape her true self and assume another self: "You see before you another me,"' she tells her lover.[31] As in *The Country Girls* trilogy, there is a pairing of two women, Patsy, a survivor like Baba, and Willa who, like Kate, is a victim of her relationships, though by now, even the passive, victimised O'Brien heroine is beginning to see through the romance plot: Willa has no desire to give her lover Auro 'Christ-like standards for which she could upbraid him when he failed'.[32] The male characters are more violent and misogynist in this novel: when Patsy announces she is leaving him, Tom plans to murder her, while Herod, a Bluebeard character, keeps Willa captive in Switzerland entangled in a relationship of victim and sadist. After the comedy of *The Country*

Girls, contemporary reviewers of *Casualties of Peace* were disorientated by the change of country and by its dark tone.[33]

A Pagan Place (1970) is another of O'Brien's ironically titled works for it is not abroad that is the pagan place but Ireland, its landscape marked out by symbols of Catholicism, its people haunted by history and superstitions. Irish Catholicism's equation of sex with shame and guilt for females is central to O'Brien's detailed evocation of the rural Ireland in which she grew up. Narrated in the second person by a young girl whose upbringing resembles that of Cait Brady (violent, alcoholic father, idealised, self-sacrificing mother), the novel adds to the mix an unmarried elder sister whose pregnancy shames the family, and a priest, another god-like love object until he sexually abuses the narrator. As in *August is a Wicked Month*, sex leads to self-punishment: taking the blame for her own seduction, the narrator performs penances on herself and further suppresses her 'sinful' female desires when she decides to join an order of nuns in Belgium. The novel ends on the mother's long howl of anguish at the separation from her daughter, re-enacting the sacrifice of the mother that underpins all of O'Brien's portraits of Ireland during these decades. In O'Brien's fiction, Irish women live under an ideological tyranny which sets them against one another and against their deeper selves through the idealisations imposed on them by church, state and society and the punishments meted out to those who fail to live up to the ideal.

During the 1970s, Edna O'Brien continued to surprise reviewers and readers with her literary experiments. Of *Night* (1972), one of her most accomplished novels, O'Brien has observed: 'it was the dividing line in my life, between one kind of writing and another.'[34] *Night* goes deeper than earlier O'Brien novels in its exploration of the female consciousness, taking the form of a monologue recounted by Mary Hooligan, a bawdy, rabble-rousing Irish woman living in England. Like all O'Brien's Irish heroines, Mary is unable altogether to forget her native land: 'Oh mine own land, a lifetime away and still near to me now and for eternity.'[35] She is haunted by memories of her recently deceased mother, Lil: 'she was going to be trailing me for the rest of my life.'[36] But Mary is also in rebellion against the stereotypes of femininity that have ruled her life till now and prevented her from asserting her full identity: 'Half a lifetime. Felt, seen, heard, not fully felt, most meagrely seen, scarcely heard at all, and still in me.'[37] Looking back over a series of lovers, she concludes that, as far as she is concerned, the romantic ideal is a failure: 'Oh shadows of love, inebriations of love, foretastes of love, trickles of love, but never yet the one true love.'[38] The ending leaves Mary poised to quit this house of memory, with its families and its couples, yet her embrace of the future still includes the possibility of an all-consuming love: 'O star of the morning, oh slippery path, oh guardian angel of mortals, givvus eyes, lend us a hand, lead us to the higher shores of life, of bolden, lawless, transubstantiating love.'[39]

For this O'Brien protagonist, the notion of finding a sacred union has not quite faded yet it is no longer tied to a particular type of romantic hero: Mary's desires are polymorphous, including lovers of both sexes, all colours, all classes and her goal is not marriage. Ultimately her fluid identity cannot be contained within patriarchal constructs of femininity, and several critics have read the novel as a challenge to Joyce's masculinist depiction of women and female sexuality in Molly Bloom's concluding monologue to *Ulysses*.[40] *Night* is an account of an Irish woman's search for a different form of selfhood in language that, to borrow O'Brien's description of Joyce's writing, is 'at once real and transubstantiating'.[41]

If the mother–daughter relationship in O'Brien's work is usually depicted from the daughter's point of view, the mother–son relationship, reflecting the trajectory of her own life, is generally portrayed from the point of view of the mother. *Johnny, I Hardly Knew You* (1977) includes both relationships. The narrator, Nora, is a daughter who has been unable to shake off her mother's values. Her upbringing has left her with a 'begging, famished self' looking for a lover to supply her with a sense of identity: 'Haven't I always been attending to a him, and dancing attendance upon a him, and being slave to a him and being trampled on by a him?'[42] Nora has a symbolically incestuous affair with her son's friend Hart, thus subverting Irish and Catholic ideologies around the family. In keeping with the romance plot, Nora turns their affair into a sacred rite to replace the Catholic religion she has long abandoned: 'It was not like love-making, it was almost passionless, almost with a breath of sanctity.'[43] The danger of making lovers into idols is revealed when an epileptic fit causes Hart's angelic features to turn ugly and devil-like. Nora, whose 'compromised female subjectivity', to use a phrase employed by Amanda Greenwood to characterise O'Brien's early heroines,[44] leads her to worship her lovers, is unable to tolerate the sight of her own neediness reflected in Hart. In keeping with the punitive atmosphere that surrounds sex in so much of O'Brien's work during these decades, the affair ends in tragedy. The epigraph from Freud's *Interpretation of Dreams* suggests that O'Brien intended her novel to pose a challenge to Freud's oversimplified view of the mother–son relationship as 'altogether the most perfect, the most free from ambivalence of all human relationships'.[45]

An analysis of O'Brien's work during the 1960s and '70s reveals her continually changing and developing as a novelist in ways that contemporary reviewers and readers often failed to keep up with and are perhaps only fully recognisable with the perspective of time. Her gradually deepening explorations of female sexual desire and female consciousness mark out new territory for Irish women's fiction.

JULIA O'FAOLAIN

Reviewing a collection of Edna O'Brien's stories in the *New York Times* (1974), Julia O'Faolain (1932–) referred to them as 'bulletins from a front on which they [feminists] will not care to engage, field reports on the feminine condition at its most acute'. The description applies just as well to O'Faolain's own work during this period: her first volume of short stories, *We Might See Sights!* (1968), was notable, in stories such as 'We Might See Sights!' 'First Conjugation' and 'A Pot of Soothing Herbs', for its exploration of youthful sexuality; indeed the 'sights' referred to in the title explicitly refer to lifting the lid on Irish sexuality.

Born in London, Julia O'Faolain is the daughter of the writer and editor Sean O'Faolain and of Eileen Gould, who wrote children's stories and edited collections of Irish myths and sagas. O'Faolain was raised in Dublin but has spent most of her adult life outside Ireland, studying in Rome and Paris and then working as a teacher and translator in Italy before moving to Los Angeles with her husband. In 1970, she brought out another collection of short stories, *Man in the Cellar*, and her first novel, *Godded and Codded*. Both novel and short stories adopt a mock-heroic tone that recalls the early Beckett of *More Pricks Than Kicks*. Set in 1956, *Godded and Codded* recounts the sexual adventures of convent-educated Irish girl Sally Tyndal, in Paris ostensibly to research for a PhD but actually to meet men.

Sally has been 'godded' from a young age, her Irish Catholicism deeply rooted: 'They got you young – from five to seventeen – and pump you with guilts, shames, uncertainties hard to exorcise later,' she reflects bitterly.[46] Like an Edna O'Brien heroine, Sally has been taught to equate 'shame with sex'.[47] Her mother, slightly more empowering than the Catholic rural mothers of O'Brien's fiction, recognises that she and Sally live in a world ruled by men. Unusually for Irish fiction of this period, she urges Sally to get a doctorate, pursue an academic career and lead an independent life. In the area of sex, however, she is a less positive role model; both she and Sally are shy on the topic:

> I scarcely know the facts of life. In fact I *don't* know them with any precision. Precautions, for instance. I've read about them – but what are they? For all her advice, Mummy never got round to them. Catholics aren't supposed to use them or get into situations where they *need* to use them and they're not available in the Republic of Ireland, so what would have been the point?[48]

In her love affair with Mesli, an Algerian student involved in his country's struggle for independence, Sally has to be instructed by her lover on methods of preventing pregnancy. Inevitably these fail and Sally becomes pregnant.

If Sally has been 'godded', she has also been 'codded' by the fiction of romantic love. Like an O'Brien heroine, Sally turns the love object into an idol: 'he has a shadowed mouth, scrolled, curling nostrils like a Byzantine saint's and the same rather fixed sombre look in his eyes that they have.'[49] Early on in the relationship it is clear that Sally takes second place in Mesli's life to the struggle for Algerian independence and their relationship dwindles into 'a domestic image of her parents' marriage. Hey diddled Dido!'[50] Sally's backstreet abortion is described in more detail than is usual in Irish writing of this period, but O'Faolain, as much as O'Brien, resists turning her fiction into a feminist tract for second-wave feminism. After the abortion, far from channelling her energies into her career, Sally remains more interested in exploring life through her sexuality than her intellect. For both O'Faolain and O'Brien, the pressures on Irish women are too complex to be solved by a straightforward equal rights agenda. Instead both writers foreground the suffering, desiring female body as expressive of Irish women's rebellion against the repressive ideologies that shaped their lives during this period. About to sleep with Mesli, Sally exults:

'She was getting truly away from Ireland, she thought, with satisfaction and terror.'[51]

O'Faolain's writing differs from that of the early O'Brien in that she includes the Irish male voice in her fiction (here that of Fintan McCann), allowing her to explore the war of sexual relationships from both sides. O'Faolain also possesses a wider canvas than O'Brien: her second novel, *Women in the Wall* (1975), is a fictional exploration of the life of Saint Radegunda, who in the sixth century founded a monastery in Gaul, a safe haven for women from the violence, chaos and lusts of the male-dominated post-Roman empire world outside. O'Faolain has scholarly expertise in this subject: in 1973, together with her husband, historian Lauro Martines, she published an anthology of writing on women, *Not in God's Image: Women in History from the Greeks to the Victorians*, that includes excerpts from the Church Fathers and later theologians, both Reformer and Catholic.

Like Helen Archer in Kate O'Brien's *The Land of Spices*, Radegunda finds that being a nun gives her authority and control over her life denied in the outside world. She stands up to the local bishops and refuses her husband's demand that she return to him. If there are gains to be found in convent life, O'Faolain is more explicit than Kate O'Brien in highlighting the dangers of suppressing the female body. As she notes: 'flesh subdued by monastic vows can and does requicken.'[52] Radegunda's pathological distaste for the flesh finds an outlet in erotic mystic transports. Agnes's inclination for life outside the convent is revealed in her love affair with the poet Fortunatus. Despite Fortunatus's self-deluding attempt to spiritualise their friendship, he is forced to recognise that 'the carnal was the real and affirmed itself in a way impossible to ignore'.[53] The suppressed body finds an outlet too in the mad reveries of Ingunda, the anchoress, an early example in Irish women's writing of *écriture feminine* representing the buried women's world of sexuality and desire. Like Edna O'Brien in this period, Julia O'Faolain was pushing Irish women's fiction in new directions.

JUANITA CASEY

Irish Catholicism is a target of Juanita Casey's first novel, *The Horse of Selene* (1971). In the previous decade, Casey (1925–), a writer from the Travelling community, published a short story collection, *Hath the Rain a Father?* (1966), portraying country life and beliefs with the knowledge of an insider. *The Horse of Selene* is a remarkable description of the birds, animals, inhabitants and tourists of the island of Aranchilla evoked in poetic language that recalls Liam O'Flaherty's combination of lyricism and humour. Casey's portrayal of country people moulded by their natural environment follows in the footsteps of Emily Lawless's *Grania*. Miceal differs from the rebellious Grania, however, in the hold Catholicism has over his spirit. Like the novels of O'Brien and O'Faolain in this period, *The Horse of Selene* portrays Ireland as a country dominated by an 'uncompromising, rigid brand of Catholicism'.[54] Ran, the renegade Irishman, tells Miceal that this Catholicism has ousted the powerful queens and goddesses of Celtic times: 'Our queens are dead, our goddesses turned into pimply saints, and we have turned our Great Mother of all the earth into an impossible virgin. The Virgin-Mother with her list of don'ts like some bloody landlady.'[55] In this respect, *The Horse of Selene* anticipates Mary Condren's ground-breaking study of Celtic goddesses and lost female power published in the following decade: *The Serpent and the Goddess: Women, Religion and Power in Celtic Ireland* (1989). Nature exacts its revenge on Miceal for his refusal to trust his instincts over the religion imposed on him: on Aranchilla only birds and horses and outsiders like Selene and Ran are truly free. The islanders are either cowed by religion, like Miceal, or materialists like his brother Paudi, exploiting the natural beauties to earn money from American tourists.

ELIZABETH BOWEN

1964 saw the publication of Elizabeth Bowen's *The Little Girls*, a novel that makes no overt reference to Ireland but in its Proustian working out of the theme of involuntary memory and the destruction of the past provides an analogy to the series of losses Bowen had sustained in recent years. Financial considerations added to Alan's health problems had obliged the Camerons to give up their London home early in 1952. They moved to Ireland intending to settle there permanently but then in August of the same year Alan died, leaving Bowen, who until then had mostly turned over financial affairs to her husband, with sole responsibility for running Bowen's Court. Traumas in Bowen always emerge obliquely. When Dinah in *The Little Girls*, helped by Sheila and Clare, unearths a coffer buried in childhood, the loss of its contents propels her into a nervous breakdown similar to that Bowen herself apparently experienced in the period leading up to the sale of Bowen's Court.

> 'Yes, but I have to get back.'
> 'Your home,' pointed out Sheila, 'won't run away.'
> Dinah examined the speaker, before saying: 'That's what it *has* done, Sheikie.' She took a shaky gulp at her drink. She added: 'Everything has. *Now* it has, you see. Nothing's real any more … We saw there was nothing *there*. So, where am I now?'[56]

The late 1950s had been a time of personal crisis for Bowen. Instead of concentrating on her fiction, she spent her energies accepting offers of magazine publication, journalism, broadcasting and lectures in order to make ends meet: 'doping myself with non-stop hard work' was how she described it in a letter to Charles Ritchie.[57] There are ominous references in her letters to meetings with her bank manager about her overdraft. By 1958 she was selling silver and jewellery to make ends meet and in a letter of 16 June from Rome she was obliged to ask Charles to send money.[58] A week later she wrote to him about giving up Bowen's Court: 'One fact I'm facing: I *can't* go on carrying Bowen's Court. I'll have to get out of it somehow … the house has become one great barrack of anxiety.'[59] By selling up not only was she, as she felt, letting down the generations of Bowens who had lived in Bowen's Court, she was also ending the dream that one day she and Charles would live there together.

For a few months in 1959 Bowen drifted from place to place staying with friends. She was to all intents and purposes homeless and, until the sale of Bowen's Court went through, in financial difficulties. Friends rallied to her support but, despite the jaunty façade she tried to maintain in her letters to Charles during this time, Bowen's loneliness and vulnerability break through. As a woman brought up in an age when women's purpose was to marry, and having relied on Alan's practical help throughout their marriage, Bowen found it difficult to cope with organising her life, as she admitted to Charles:

> I sometimes wonder whether even *you*, knowing me as well as you do, really realise my horror of my state as a *femme seule* (legal

definition). It seems to me abnormal, it fills me with a sense of ghastly injury, that I should have to organize my own life. It seems abnormal that any woman should have to do so ... Look at my life since Alan died – when I'm not with you I simply go drifting from one orbit of influence to another ... I am slightly independent in my mind, that is, in my intellectual part – but quite outstandingly the reverse in disposition and temperament.[60]

She added tellingly: 'People make a mistake when they identify the performance I give with my real being.'[61] The sale of Bowen's Court went through at the end of 1959, while she was teaching at the American Academy in Rome, and the editors of her correspondence note that Charles did not keep any of her letters written between December 1959 and November 1960. As it was Charles's habit to suppress letters he felt were too exposing, one can only guess at the emotional turmoil expressed in Bowen's correspondence at this time.

Outsiders may have seen a successful and capable professional woman, but Bowen needed someone to organise her life. Eventually friends and relations helped sort out her financial affairs, while Isaiah Berlin found a flat for her in Oxford. It was here that she finished her ninth novel, *The Little Girls*. The novel uses the tripartite structure often employed by Bowen, moving from the present to the past (1914) and back again to the present, in order to portray, in Bowen's words, 'encaged, rather terrible little girls battering about inside grown-up (indeed, almost old) women'.[62] The different vulnerabilities of the three grown women in *The Little Girls* may be read as a reflection of Bowen's own state of mind in the years leading up to and after the sale of Bowen's Court. Charles, with his usual egotism, read 'the chilly exhilaration' of the novel as 'revenge on love. Revenge on me'.[63] It is true that male characters are marginal in this novel, and though Dinah has a loyal male friend, Frank, the emotional force of the book comes from the relationship between the three middle-aged women who were friends at school, lost touch in the intervening period, and have now reached 'the days after love'.

The Little Girls is dedicated to one of Bowen's oldest women friends, Ursula Vernon, and in its middle section recreates the years between 1906 and 1912 that Bowen spent with her mother wandering from villa to villa on the Kent coast making each, as she described in 'Pictures and Conversation', 'pavilions of love'.[64] Perhaps Charles was right to read the novel as shifting the focus of Bowen's imaginative life away from the preoccupation with their love affair that had been so central to *The Heat of the Day*. The editors of Bowen's letters to Charles note: 'She had many "girl-friends" of a certain age, mainly in Sussex and Kent, some of them emotionally linked, whom she met frequently. CR was not told much about this aspect of her social life.'[65] She did tell him, however, about a trip she made to Jordan in March 1964, before the book's publication, with her friend, Jean Black:

> I've never seen Jean happier, handsomer or more thoroughly in her element. I am devoted to her, I must say, and am having a roaring time in her company. She and I *are* both very childish characters. In a way, this time here is being like an additional chapter to *The Little Girls*. I mean, our vocabulary and our recreations and our mental level seem to be about the same (as those of the Little G's, I mean).[66]

The ending of *The Little Girls* suggests that Dinah's collapse eventually produces a belated maturity, an acceptance of the past as gone forever, and a facing up to old age.

Shortly after the publication of *The Little Girls*, feeling marginalised in the pressurised academic atmosphere of Oxford, Bowen moved back to Hythe, where she had been so happy with her mother: 'I suppose I like Hythe out of a back-to-the-wombishness, having been there as a child in the most amusing years of one's childhood – 8 to 13. But I can't see what's wrong with the womb if one's happy there, or comparatively happy there.'[67] It was at Hythe that Bowen began writing her final novel, *Eva Trout: or Changing Scenes* (1968), featuring the most lost and displaced of all her heroines. Several critics have argued that in her sexlessness and inability to settle, Eva Trout incorporates aspects of the Anglo-Irish, but she also reflects Bowen's own restless life after the sale of Bowen's Court: visits to friends' houses in Ireland, lecture tours in the United States and Europe, flying to meet up with Charles wherever he was posted. Bowen's correspondence with Charles betrays the depths of her loneliness and displacement during these later years; she described it after one of their many partings as 'a feeling of being nowhere because we're not still together'.[68] Towards the end of her life she contemplated another move, from Hythe back to Ireland, possibly to Clontarf outside Dublin, but she fell ill before anything came of it.[69]

Beyond its personal resonances, *Eva Trout* is an acute portrait of Bowen's times. From 1950 until her last illness Bowen spent part of every year in the US, giving lectures and teaching on creative writing programmes. These stints on American campuses gave her a different angle on life. She identified with the restlessness and cosmopolitanism of America, writing to Charles: 'America really has come to be a sort of extra, or further dimension to my life. There are times when I think it's become, even, the norm for me. After all, what a non-attached, divided life I've led, since childhood, haven't I?'[70] Reading her students' compositions, 'the usual variation of sex themes occasionally varied by violent and lurid deaths',[71] kept Bowen up to date with what the younger generation was thinking and she became fascinated with teenagers, about whom she wrote several essays. Perhaps influenced by the stirrings of second-wave feminism in America, she modified her stance on women: in a magazine article, 'Woman's Place in the Affairs of Man' (1961), she still rejected the label feminist, taking it to imply denigration of men's achievements, but she welcomed women's emergence from the home into public life, believing women had special talents to bring to the world of work.[72]

Dealing with such themes as the unreliability of language and the fragility of human identity in a media-obsessed and consumer-driven society, *Eva Trout* represented a new departure for Bowen. Early critics, trying to force it into the mould of her previous fiction, were perplexed by the novel with its outsize, inarticulate heroine. It was a work in advance of its time, one that had to await the advent of postmodernist theory with its emphasis on surfaces, parody, interrogation of language and identity, in order to be properly understood. The wealthy heiress, Eva, left as a child in the care of foreign women hired by the various hotels around the world from where her father Willy pursues his international business interests, sent to an experimental boarding school, and in later life adopting a child seemingly on a whim, is a remarkable foreshadowing of today's celebrity lifestyles. Bowen brilliantly and comically evokes the shallowness of human identity produced by this kind of society as Eva struggles to communicate with those around her, and indeed puzzles over what exactly constitutes a human being. Her outsider status is reinforced by a childhood spent under the shadow of her father's sexual obsession with Constantine, and Tina O'Toole has drawn some interesting parallels with Henry Archer's homosexuality in *The Land of Spices* that is so damaging to his daughter, Helen.[73] Eva's own sexuality remains unformed: she is variously referred to as 'hermaphrodite', 'sexless' and dragging her sex after her 'like a ball and chain'. Like Lois, but in a more extreme form, Eva's difficulty in achieving selfhood is compounded by her failure to fit in to her society's feminine stereotypes. The lesbian theme is more overt in this later novel, in Eva's attachment first to Elsinore, then to her teacher Iseult, but the central question of Eva's alienation from the human race remains paramount.

When we first see Eva, the 'larger than life' 24-year-old is driving an enormous Jaguar (Bowen noted how many of her wealthy friends drove Jaguars).[74] Observing her, Mrs Dancey doubts whether Eva possesses sufficient language to have an inner life: '*Is* she thinking? Mrs Dancey thought not. Monolithic, Eva's attitude was. It was not, somehow, the attitude of a thinking person.'[75] Lacking any meaningful inner life, Eva buys heavily into the consumer society in a way that echoes Jean Baudrillard's definition of consumption as founded on 'a lack' in 'The System of Objects' published in the same year as *Eva Trout*.[76] Eva purchases a computer in order, she says, to learn how to think, as well as those objects advertised in 1959 as up-to-the-minute aids to language and communication. These include a large-screen television set, a radio-gramophone, a projector and screen, and a recording instrument. Since, as Baudrillard argues, consumerism can never satisfy but only stimulate desire, this bid to join the human race ends in failure.

Eva then decides to write herself into the traditional script for women's lives by adopting a child in the US, a performative act described in the novel as a 'mimicry' of motherhood.[77] Since Jeremy is a deaf-mute, he can be no help in pulling Eva into the world of language. For eight years she and Jeremy wander around the US living in a world of 'changing scenes', of images without language: Bowen likened her own experience of America to 'sitting in at a non-stop movie'.[78] Returning to England to look for a permanent home for Jeremy, Eva is distracted by her feelings for Henry Dancey. She writes herself into another script: the new bride embarking on a honeymoon with Henry as groom. However, she discounts the fact that by abandoning the wordless, pre-oedipal bond with Jeremy, she is betraying their years together. Just as Eva has a chance to move beyond the world of surfaces and appearances by becoming loved by Henry, Jeremy guns her down in a melodramatic ending that matches the cinematic quality of her life. Eva, Bowen's lost and alienated giantess, remains, like Frankenstein's monster, an incomplete human being.

Bowen's final creation, *Eva Trout*, is brilliantly prophetic about the way in which society was to evolve at the end of the twentieth century and with it comes a warning that human beings are in danger of losing their humanity. The technological future Bowen conjures up in her final novel is a far cry from the Anglo-Irish world of *The Last September*, but the same themes of identity, language and alienation continued to preoccupy her at the end of her writing life as at the beginning, even if the society she portrayed had radically altered.

IRIS MURDOCH

In an attempt to comprehend what constitutes a human being, Eva Trout visits London's National Portrait Gallery. The scene is reminiscent of Dora's visit to the National Gallery in Iris Murdoch's *The Bell* (1958). Bowen was interested in Murdoch's novels which she read and commented on in her letters to Charles Ritchie. In 1956, Murdoch, whose first novel *Under the Net* had been published two years earlier, visited Bowen's Court. A letter to Charles (3 August 1956) gives Bowen's account of the visit. Initially alarmed by Murdoch's reputation as an existentialist philosopher, Bowen took to Murdoch, characterising her as Anglo-Irish (which was only partly accurate) and a typical only child. The letter reveals a generational difference between the two writers and also perhaps the difference between a woman who has trained for a career and one who has not. Murdoch was anxious about her forthcoming marriage to John Bailey. She had already had to resign her fellowship at St Anne's College, Oxford because of the impending marriage and feared, according to Bowen, that marriage would mean 'loss of identity', a fear that Bowen, missing Alan's practical help and yearning to live with Charles full time, could not empathise with at all.[79]

Iris Murdoch (1919–99), whose father was Scots-Irish while her mother's family were Dublin Protestants, was born in Dublin but raised in England and rarely set her fiction in Ireland. *The Unicorn* (1963), however, is set in a fictional County Clare and some of the characters draw on the Anglo-Irish Vernon family whom Murdoch met while staying at Bowen's Court. Charles

Ritchie was not the only reader to see a similarity between Ursula Vernon and Hannah in *The Unicorn*.[80] The Gothic atmosphere of the enclosed community at Gaze Castle and its surrounding wilderness owes much to the influence of Sheridan Le Fanu, as Murdoch herself acknowledged. The plot, though, is characteristically Murdochian, namely a struggle between the good and the demonic, with Hannah, the unicorn of the title, a flawed saint, atoning for her guilt and taking on aspects of the suffering Christ and the Virgin Mary, both figures traditionally associated with the unicorn. 'In a way we can't help using her as a scapegoat,' the Platonic philosopher Max tells Effingham. 'In a way that's what she's for and to recognize it is to do her honour. She is our image of the significance of suffering.'[81] The arrival of an outsider, Marian, acts as a catalyst, breaking the sleeping beauty spell that has hung over Gaze Castle and its occupants for seven years. This leads, in turn, to a series of violent events the working out of which is part of the spiritual and philosophical pattern of the novel. In his study of Murdoch's work, Peter Conradi points out that *The Unicorn* was undervalued by reviewers partly because they did not understand the Gothic conventions on which Murdoch was drawing.[82] It might be added that the novel is most easily understood when set in the specific context of Irish Gothic.

Though the Troubles do not feature largely in Irish women's fiction of this period, in 1965, in anticipation of the fiftieth anniversary of the Easter Rising, Iris Murdoch published *The Red and the Green*. The novel was an unusual one for Murdoch on several counts, being set in Ireland and involving the historical events of the week leading up to the Easter Rising. It was published by an English publisher and is clearly addressed to a readership outside Ireland since so much basic information about Irish history and politics is fed through the dialogue and thoughts of the characters. In its depiction of the divided loyalties of the Anglo-Irish and its portrayal of a young girl, Frances, coming of age at the same time as the Irish state is coming into being, *The Red and the Green* reveals Bowen's influence, particularly *The Last September*. Like Lois, Frances is engaged to an unimaginative and protective British soldier but breaks off the engagement. As Lois experiences a brief attraction to the elusive Daventry, so Frances is in love with the glamorous republican rebel Pat, but her reasons for breaking off her engagement are as much political as personal: she objects to Andrew's participation in an imperial war. Like Lois, Frances challenges the restrictions imposed by her gender and by her nation: 'I think being a woman is like being Irish,' said Frances, putting aside her work and sitting up. [...] 'Everyone says you're important and nice, but you take second place all the same.'[83]

Throughout the novel, various characters express casual remarks about gender issues: Andrew's mother disapproves of mixed bathing, Andrew is afraid of women, Pat is repulsed by them, Frances resents the passive role women are expected to play, Millie scandalises with her trousers, her cigar smoking, her rumoured affairs and her shooting gallery. A destabilising character, Millie not only challenges fixed gender boundaries but, like Charlotte Mullen in *The Real Charlotte*, cuts through class and religious divisions to make friends with Catholics as well as Anglo-Irish, nationalists as well as loyalists.[84] For the male characters – Christopher, Pat, Andrew, Barney – Millie is a surrogate mother figure, providing comfort and a sense of purpose at points of crisis. *The Red and the Green* centres on the characteristic Murdochian theme of the battle between good and evil and, despite its documentary style and its inaccurate reproduction of Irish speech patterns, the novel received a generally warm reception from Irish reviewers.[85]

JENNIFER JOHNSTON

With her portraits of young girls and Big Houses, Jennifer Johnston (1930–) may in some respects be regarded as Elizabeth Bowen's heir. From the start, Johnston's deceptively slight novels aroused controversy about where to place her work in the Irish literary canon. An early article by Christine St Peter defended Johnston against accusations by critics such as Mark Mortimer and Seamus Deane that her work was limited in scope.[86] Rüdiger Imhof, reviewing *The Invisible Worm*, summarised Johnston's novels as 'fraught with artistic shortcomings'.[87] Yet many contemporary Irish authors have testified to Johnston's influence on their writing and in 2004, at the Joyce celebrations in New York, Roddy Doyle provocatively declared: 'She is the greatest Irish writer. She writes perfect books.'[88] Popular with the general reader but underrated in critical discourse, Johnston has nevertheless been the subject of several scholarly articles and chapters, her work has featured on the Irish school syllabus, she has been shortlisted for the Booker Prize and has won a PEN award.

Johnston was born in Dublin to the playwright Denis Johnston and the Abbey actress/director Shelagh Richards. Tensions soon appeared in the marriage. Shelagh had a busy life as an Abbey actress and by 1939, after several affairs, Denis had begun a second family. Shelagh and Denis finally divorced in 1945. These events may have given rise to what is a significant theme in Johnston's novels, namely young girls' yearnings for lost or dead fathers. During her early life, Johnston spent a lot of time with nannies, maids and her paternal grandparents, an experience she draws on in *Shadowstory* (2011). The number of elderly men and women that feature in Johnston's novels may be a reflection of these years spent with her grandparents.

Johnston attended Trinity College, Dublin where she joined Trinity Players but left before taking her degree. Thwarted in her ambition to become an actress, in 1951 she married Ian Smyth, a solicitor, and moved to London to raise four children but always, she has said, felt the pull back to Ireland. In 1974 she was divorced and on her second marriage to David Gilliland went to live in his ancestral home in Derry. Her life, like that of many of her characters, has thus involved crossing several national and cultural boundaries.

Growing up as a member of the Protestant minority in Ireland, Johnston felt marginalised from the mainstream Catholic population and, as she has explained, has often been classed as a Big House novelist: 'Even though my mother's parents were not immediately "big house" people, that was their sort of background and there were always undertones of that background in my life and ultimately in my writing.'[89] However, Johnston extends her range as a writer far beyond a single theme and even her treatment of the Big House is revisionist, as Eileen Battersby has pointed out:

> More than any other Irish writer, it was Johnston who took the Big House novel, with its final vestiges of fading privilege, out of the countryside and towards its inevitable, and logical, resting place – the more narrow, less romantic, and ultimately realist suburban comforts of Dalkey and Killiney.[90]

Like Bowen, Johnston interiorises the Big House theme, marrying 'the psychological with the social novel'.[91]

Johnston's novels feature a substantial amount of dialogue, reflecting her interest in the theatre: she has written several monologues and one-act plays. Her primary interest, however, is fiction. Her first novel, *Captains and Kings* (1972), was published when she was already forty-two, a fact that Johnston, though not defining herself as a feminist, has nevertheless connected to the masculinist world in which she grew up: 'The world was for men and I couldn't work out where I fitted into it. I certainly didn't see myself taking up the woman's role and in all my dreams and imaginings I was always a boy.'[92] The theme of the late-developing female artist recurs in her work. Her first novel, however, features male protagonists and depicts life in the Big House. In an interview, Johnston explained:

> When I began to write seriously a lot of my writing was set in 'big houses' which I suppose reflects on my childhood to a certain degree. The houses that I wrote about were never really very bad. They were just rather crumbly country houses that one's friends lived in, where people had time to sit down and talk to you – old men would talk to you about the First World War, for example.[93]

Critics such as Vera Kreilkamp have discussed the ideological contradictions in Johnston's treatment of the Big House, arguing that her novels at times display a Yeatsian nostalgia for its aesthetic refinements, while at other times portray the inhabitants trapped in received and unjust patterns of living from which they are powerless to escape.[94] In *The Captains and the Kings*, Charles Prendergast's emotionally starved wife is imprisoned in marriage by her financial dependence, while Charles's mother is the first of Johnston's matriarchal tyrants who find in Big House life no outlet for their talents and whose unused energy, like that of Molly Keane's mothers, turns to malice and cruelty. By contrast, the village boy Diarmid, seeking refuge from the brutalities of his home life, like Johnny in John McGahern's short story 'Oldfashioned', regards the Big House as a repository of beauty and culture.

In the relationship between Charles and Diarmid, *The Captains and the Kings* introduces Johnston's characteristic theme of an older generation of males handing on to the younger generation romantic tales of militarism. In this first novel, military romance centres on past campaigns such as the Napoleonic wars, the Crimean war and the First World War and is not subject to as much critical scrutiny as it will be in Johnston's later novels. Coming out of the Protestant tradition, Johnston's novels with their concentration on the past, on themes of liminality and ghosts, and on inherited guilt may be placed in a line of Irish writing going back to Sheridan Le Fanu and including Elizabeth Bowen. Johnston herself explained the persistent intertwining of the contemporary and the historical in her work: 'I am trying to write about the complex overlapping of history and personalities involved in being Irish in the past and at the moment.'[95] On a personal level, Charles, like so many of Johnston's characters, finds memories of the past invading his present: 'If only there was some way of disposing of the debris, leaving the mind neat and ordered, but more and more now the mess, the past, kept breaking through the barriers.'[96]

In 1973, Johnston published *The Gates*, another Big House novel that in fact was written before *Captains and Kings*. In Minnie, *The Gates* presents the first of Johnston's female characters on the cusp of adulthood and starting to interrogate the world around her. Surrounded by elderly men who relive old battles, whether in the First World War like her uncle Frank, or with the IRA, like Jim Breslin, Minnie begins to recognise how much of her identity is moulded by her past. Since sixteen-year-old Minnie is one of Johnston's younger heroines, her questioning, like her diary, never gets very far and the novel ends in stasis.

In the portrayal of Minnie's dead father whom she longs to know more about, *The Gates* introduces the characteristic Johnston figure of the Anglo-Irish rebel against his class, a theme that is continued in her third novel, *How Many Miles to Babylon?* (1974). *How Many Miles to Babylon?* is one of Johnston's best-known novels, often featuring on the Irish school syllabus and adapted for the stage by the actor-director Alan Stanford. In this novel, Johnston is more critical, both of the inhabitants of the Big House and of their tradition of fighting in the British Army. Alec's mother Alicia, who manipulates her son into the war, is one of Johnston's maternal monsters whose entrapment in the Big House results in frustration and malice. The Big House traditions are interrogated through the words of Alec's father, an enlightened landlord who goes beyond Edgeworthian tradition when he counsels his son to remember that their house has been built on land stolen from the people and that one day the land must be handed back to the people in good order. By revealing that her husband is not Alec's father, Alicia cuts her son off from his roots in Ireland, leaving him little alternative other than to embrace her British traditions.

In its depiction of conditions in the trenches during the First World War (still, at that time, a sensitive subject for Irish readers), *How Many Miles to Babylon?* rejects any romanticisation of war and the novel is remarkable for its account of the enduring friendship in the trenches between Alec, Protestant son of the Big House, and Jerry, his Catholic tenant. Johnston undermines any lingering Yeatsian sentimentality over the paternalistic bond between landlord and peasant: in this relationship, Jerry is the stronger character and his, implicitly homoerotic, friendship with Alec does not outweigh his nationalist sympathies. He is in the British Army to prepare himself for fighting with the IRA. In the end, however, both young men are destroyed by the British militarist machine: Jerry is sentenced to death for going AWOL, Alec is awaiting execution by firing squad for shooting Jerry rather than allowing him to be shot by the British. The narrative is recounted through Alec's voice as he awaits his death, making *How Many Miles to Babylon?* Johnston's earliest presentation of what was to become one of her characteristic modes of writing, namely a narrator painfully, obsessively and often uncertainly revisiting a traumatic event in the past. Johnston's preference for method over subject matter, as Robert Garratt has pointed out, focuses her novels on the psychology of the narrator and the complexities of storytelling rather than on plot and action.[97]

In *The Old Jest* (1979), the young diarist Nancy Gulliver is the central character and this novel marks the start of a series of Johnston novels that put female characters at their heart. She has always, however, rejected the label 'feminist', explaining in an interview: 'I'm a woman and I'm Irish, but above all else I'm a writer.'[98] Like Murdoch's *The Red and the Green*, *The Old Jest* is a direct literary descendant of Bowen's *The Last September*. *The Old Jest* is set in the same year (1920) as *The Last September* and, like Bowen's novel, deals with a nation and a young girl in the process of defining their identities. Like Lois, Nancy is the daughter of a Big House and parentless. Nancy's mother died giving birth to her and her father, whose identity she has never known and who may or may not be dead, haunts her thoughts. Nancy lives with her aunt Mary who, like the Naylors in Bowen's novel, survives by a policy of 'not noticing': neither Nancy's unknown father, nor the growing violence of the Black and Tans nor the family's steady slide into impoverishment may be mentioned at home. As in *The Last September*, the Anglo-Irish are presented in a state of stasis, caught between their ties with England and their unwillingness to betray their Irish neighbours: the Misses Brabazons refuse to lend their car to the rebels, but neither will they inform on them to the police.

Like Lois, Nancy feels ambivalent about the world in which she finds herself and chafes against the petty restraints imposed on her as daughter of a Big House. She loves her aunt Mary but does not want to grow up to be like her and she confesses to Harry, the rather staid stockbroker on whom she has a crush, her desire to 'know and understand'.[99] In pursuit of this, she interrogates Harry about war and sex to the point where he feels persecuted: Harry, a literary descendant of Bowen's Gerald, shares that character's views on appropriate female behaviour. On her eighteenth birthday, Nancy signals her intention to examine the world around her and her place in it by commencing a diary that records her secret rebellion against the values of the world in which she has been raised. Like Bowen's Lois and Johnston's earlier heroine Minnie, Nancy is on a quest to discover an identity larger than the one that has hitherto been forced on her.

In these early Johnston novels, protagonists form secret friendships that bring them into collision with the society around them: Charles and Diarmid, Minnie and Kevin, Alec and Jerry. Nancy's meeting with a middle-aged nationalist on the run confirms her interrogation of the world in which she has been raised. Nancy names the gunman Cassius and naturally, in view of her yearning for her lost father, converts him into a father figure. Cassius encourages Nancy to re-think her views on the fight for freedom. The parallels, largely implicit in Bowen's novel, between political rebels struggling to shape their nation's identity and a rebellious young girl's efforts to create a personal identity, become explicit here as, under the influence of her encounter with Cassius, Nancy finds herself drawn out of her sheltered life into involvement in the struggle for Ireland's independence. It is this initiation into political action that brings Nancy to adulthood. A comparison may be drawn with another Big House daughter, Sylvia Fox, in Keane's *Two Days in Aragon*, whose life is changed forever by her brief connection with and protection of the IRA officer Denny.

However, as Nancy's political activity takes off, so her writing trails away. By abandoning her diary, Nancy loses the writer's ability to interrogate the values of the struggle she has now joined. Her diary becomes a symbol of the way in which a potentially subversive, female-centred version of events becomes silenced by direct involvement in the national struggle, bearing out the foreboding of Irish women like Hanna Sheehy Skeffington who in the earlier part of the century feared that feminism would be subsumed by the nationalist conflict. Critics have provided various readings of the ending of *The Old Jest*. Shari Benstock interprets Nancy's story as overtaken by the events of Cassius's life and death.[100] An opposite interpretation is given by Ann Owens Weekes, who reads the ending as illustrating Nancy's growth in freedom from gender and class constraints.[101] Rachael Sealy Lynch, too, gives a more positive interpretation of Nancy's self-development, pointing out that Nancy is due to study history at Trinity and so will become one of the early number of Irish women to benefit from higher education.[102] *The Old Jest* was one of Johnston's most noticed novels, winning the Whitbread Award and subsequently made into a film starring Anthony Hopkins.

The Big House and rebellious young women were not the only themes Johnston tackled in this period. If her previous novels looking back at earlier periods of war may partly be interpreted as a response to the reawakening of violence in Northern Ireland, her next novel, *Shadows on Our Skin* (1977), tackled the Troubles directly. Johnston conveys the tense atmosphere of Derry during the 1970s: the constant sound of gunfire, the boarded-up shops and burnt-out houses, the soldiers patrolling the streets, the noise of British Army helicopters circling overhead. Through the mouths of two women, Mrs Logan and Kathleen Doherty, *Shadows on Our Skin* challenges nationalist ideology and the romanticisation of violence. Mrs Logan, Catholic and working class, rejects her husband's tales of heroism in the old IRA that have inspired their elder son Brendan to become involved in paramilitary activity. She has no expectation that removing the British from Irish soil will make any practical difference to her life. When her husband quotes Patrick Pearse at her, she retaliates by pointing out that the political freedom enjoyed by Catholics in the Republic does not necessarily mean freedom for working-class women like herself: 'Have they any more freedom down there than we have up here?' she asks her husband. 'Is there a job for every man? And a home for everyone? Have all the children got shoes on their feet?'[103] Working in a menial job to support the family has made Mrs Logan's priority not political freedom but economic.

As Mrs Logan challenges the male-authored text of Northern nationalism, so Kathleen Doherty, a schoolteacher from the Republic, the child of a mixed marriage, is intent on keeping an open mind about Irish politics and preserving a fluid national identity. Though Kathleen is engaged to a soldier in the British Army stationed in Germany, she tries to cut across the sectarian divide in her country by moving to Northern Ireland in order to understand what is happening there. She makes friends with young Joe Logan, a nascent poet, and attempts to maintain relations with both her soldier fiancé and Joe's IRA brother, Brendan. Her efforts to reach across sectarian divisions come to an end when Brendan finds out about her engagement to a British soldier. She undergoes a punishment beating at the hands of Brendan's mates and is forced to leave Derry. One woman's attempt at border crossing has been defeated by political intransigence and male violence.[104] Johnston's warning about the dangers of rigid versions of the past and her highlighting of the invasion of personal life by political realities foreshadow Irish women's writing on the Troubles in the following decade.

LELAND BARDWELL

Another writer on Big House themes, Leland Bardwell (1922–) was born in India into the distinguished Hone family. In her autobiography *A Restless Life* (2008), Bardwell describes her spartan upbringing in a decaying Georgian house in Leixlip where her dysfunctional family neglected her and her mother was psychologically abusive. To make ends meet, her mother took in paying guests, among them Katharine Tynan and her daughter Pamela Hinkson. They are among the few people singled out by Bardwell as kind to her in her youth, entertaining her in their room at night with Horlicks. She had no idea of Tynan's literary status, regarding her as 'just another ancient in a long black dress'.[105] She was aware of Pamela, though, working on her novels.

Bardwell eventually attended Alexandra College but her parents were unwilling to pay for her to go to university, so she trained at secretarial college and worked as a groom before taking the boat over to England in 1944 to have her first baby, given away for adoption. *A Restless Life* describes Bardwell's turbulent life: factory work in Birmingham, secretary in London during the Second World War, educating herself by reading French and Russian classics in

Paddington Lending Library, and her later frequentation of Soho literary circles. Constantly on the move in these years, between England and Ireland, and between men, poverty-stricken yet raising six children, Bardwell nevertheless pursued her writing vocation: 'while the children crawled around the floor, I typed away on my ancient machine.'[106]

A Restless Life, the female equivalent of her friend Anthony Cronin's better-known chronicle of post-war literary Dublin, *Dead as Doornails* (1976), documents Dublin literary life in the 1960s when Bardwell's damp and crumbling Lower Leeson Street basement flat played host to Patrick Kavanagh, John Jordan, Macdara Woods, Paul Durcan and Michael Hartnett, among others. While the men drank, Bardwell struggled to raise her children, cope with a violent partner and write her poems and stories: 'Yes indeed, it was an all-male society. As an unpublished writer, you were ruled, bedevilled, damned – especially if you were a woman. In all those years, I never got to know either a woman writer or a woman artist.'[107] Though she received support and encouragement from the literary friends who came round to her flat to drink whiskey after McDaid's closed, not surprisingly it was to be years before Bardwell was able to publish her first book of poems, *The Mad Cyclist* (1970). Writing about these years, Nuala O'Faolain paid tribute to Bardwell's generosity and capacity for survival: 'She was the support-system for a generation of writers, down in her basement, stirring a stew with one hand and comparing translations of Baudelaire, as it might be, with the other.'[108] Leland's basement may be compared with Mary Lavin's mews in Lad Lane that also became a gathering place for young writers. Lavin supported Nuala O'Faolain financially while she resat some college exams and Maura Laverty gave O'Faolain her first professional job. These kinds of networks of support between Irish women writers have hardly begun to be explored.

Bardwell's first novel, *Girl on a Bicycle* (1977), is set among the Anglo-Irish as eighteen-year-old Julie de Vraie goes to work as a groom at Girvan Castle. This wry, humorous novel is partly autobiographical, based on Bardwell's own three months as a groom for Lord Farnham in Cavan.[109] Like her creator, Julie is disenchanted by life in the Big House and feels she would be glad 'if the whole structure of the Anglo-Irish way of life, with the landlord class and its false mores, arrogance, self-deception, crumbled away in its senescence'.[110] In an interview, Bardwell spoke of wishing to document Anglo-Irish life because she believed it had 'destroyed so many people'.[111] *Girl on a Bicycle* is set in the early 1940s and, like the fiction of Elizabeth Bowen and Olivia Manning, portrays the sense of entrapment experienced by many in Ireland during the Second World War. Julia reflects: 'I longed to leave the country, as if the country was to blame for everything.'[112] In her memoir, Bardwell writes of her yearning to get to Paris at this period in order to study art.

Julie's boy's bicycle becomes a symbol of her quest for freedom, a quest that leads her to ignore this society's restrictions of class and gender. She fraternises with the servants, drinks with the locals and befriends an Anglo-Irish woman, Emily, cousin of Lord Girvan, whose eccentricity has led her relatives to label her insane and confine her to the care of a mental nurse. In a previous life, Emily was a skilled botanist working in South America until dragged back to Ireland by her family on the grounds of impropriety (she had been alone in the desert with a male guide). Unable to settle into the life of a country spinster (bridge, tennis, hunting, opening fetes), Emily follows in a long line of fictional portraits of women driven mad by the constraints of Big House life. Bernard tells Julie: "'People like her should never get born into that society. It's dwindling, you see, so all the members have to be counted and kept in line.'"[113]

In her drinking, her sex life and her challenge to the rules, Julie claims the right to the same freedoms as the males of her society, making her one of the more rebellious Anglo-Irish heroines in women's fiction of this period.

NORTHERN IRELAND

Caroline Blackwood

Notwithstanding Johnston's *Shadows on Our Skin*, fiction by Irish women set in Northern Ireland in this period is often located in the pre-Troubles era and is preoccupied with themes similar to that of women's fiction in the Republic. If Alicia's nature in *How Many Miles to Babylon?* is warped and perverted by life in the Big House, in Caroline Blackwood's novel *Great Granny Webster* (1977), the narrator's grandmother, like Emily in *Girl on a Bicycle*, is driven insane. Caroline Blackwood (1931–96) drew on her own family background for the novel, set in the post-war world of the late 1940s.

Blackwood was born in London into an Anglo-Irish family from Northern Ireland. Her father was the fourth Marquess of Dufferin and Ava, her mother, a Guinness heiress. Like Bardwell, Blackwood endured a dysfunctional childhood, neglected by her parents and assigned to the care of abusive nannies. Educated in Northern Ireland, Switzerland and England, she was presented as a debutante in 1949 and went on to marry in turn the painter Lucian Freud, the composer Israel Citkowitz and the poet Robert Lowell. She initially worked in journalism but, encouraged by Lowell, she turned to writing fiction in the 1970s. Her brilliantly dark novella *The Stepdaughter* (1976) is a thinly veiled account of her difficult relationship with her eldest daughter Natalya, who was to die two years later, aged seventeen, from a heroin overdose. A powerful monologue by an angry, self-absorbed woman deserted by her philandering husband and encumbered with an overweight, cake-addicted stepdaughter whose presence points up her maternal failings, *The Stepdaughter* won the David Higham Prize for best first novel. The novella reveals, at a remove, Blackwood's fears about her inadequacies as a mother and perhaps also, in the portrait of the narrator's changing view of Arnold, a wish to persuade herself that in a crisis Lowell would be capable of acting responsibly towards her daughters.

In *Great Granny Webster*, Blackwood depicts, through the voice of the unnamed seventeen-year-old narrator, a series of Anglo-Irish eccentrics living in a Northern Irish Big House, Dunmartin Hall, based on Clandeboye, the rambling old house in County Down where she and her siblings had grown up. Like Danielstown, Dunmartin Hall is depicted as a colonial imposition on the Irish countryside: 'The house had both the melancholy and the magic of something inherently doomed by the height of its own ancient colonial aspirations. It was like a grey and decaying palace fortress beleaguered by invasions of hostile native forces.'[114] The cast includes the narrator's grimly stoical Great Granny Webster, based on Blackwood's paternal great-grandmother, her frivolous but suicide-prone aunt Lavinia, and her mentally unstable grandmother. The latter is eventually driven mad by life in Dunmartin Hall and committed to an asylum by Great Granny Webster.

> In describing his pre-war visits to Ulster, the terrible state of neglect and the undefeatable damp of Dunmartin Hall had obviously chilled him [Tommy Redcliffe, a friend of the narrator's father] so much that when he tried to tell me what my grandmother had

been like I often thought he felt the house itself might well have been responsible for driving her insane.[115]

In depicting a woman driven insane by life in a Big House, Blackwood, like Bardwell, draws on a tradition of writing about the Big House that goes back to Maria Edgeworth's *Castle Rackrent* and recalls Cousin Nettie in Elizabeth Bowen's *The Heat of the Day*. The wild rages of the narrator's grandmother, though, resemble those of Bertha Mason rather than Cousin Nettie's gentle withdrawal from a world with which she does not wish to cope.

Portraying a complex network of dysfunctional relationships between women, *Great Granny Webster* is also partly a mother–daughter story but one that, like Molly Keane's *Good Behaviour*, draws on a vein of Anglo-Irish macabre humour to portray life in a grotesque and decaying Big House where it is women who wield the power. Like Lois in *The Last September*, Blackwood's narrator looks at the grown-ups around her and despairs of her future. Despite its determinedly surreal atmosphere, the grounds on which *Great Granny Webster* narrowly missed winning the Booker Prize were that it was too autobiographical to count as fiction.

Janet McNeill

In *Girl on a Bicycle*, Bernard concludes his description of the repressive Northern Irish Protestant world in which he was raised with the question: "'And what have they got to show for it? Spinsters, grey-green pimply youths hot from the dormitories of the British Public Schools.'"[116] This is the world of Janet McNeill's novel *The Maiden Dinosaur* (1964). *The Maiden Dinosaur* bears some similarities with writing from the Republic in this period: like the fiction of Edna O'Brien and Julia O'Faolain, albeit in a very different context, *The Maiden Dinosaur* explores female sexuality and the ideological constraints on Irish women. Like that of Baba and Cait, the education of Sarah Vincent and her school friends in pre-Troubles middle-class Protestant Belfast has emphasised female chastity. As Sarah's friend Addie observes: 'Modesty and duty, what do you think we expected to get out of that little lot?'[117] In Sarah's case, the sexual repression of her Presbyterian upbringing has been reinforced by the childhood trauma of discovering her father making love with her governess. Like Helen

Archer in *The Land of Spices*, under pressure from a similar shock, Sarah retreats into herself and suppresses her sexuality: 'to share my body is unthinkable.'[118]

The novel opens with 52-year-old Sarah, now a teacher, still living in her old family home: 'Thronehill, a monument to middle-class Victorian prosperity, on the north side of Belfast Lough.'[119] As a middle-aged woman who does not fit into conventional notions of femininity – her thick ankles are said to make her resemble 'a female impersonator'[120] – Sarah finds herself constantly patronised by others. She pours all her affections into her friendship with her school friend Helen, and the novel has been read as a lesbian text. However, as Emma Donoghue has pointed out, a lesbian reading is something of a disappointment since the relationship between Sarah and the clearly heterosexual Helen is always one-sided and never consummated.[121] If anything, Sarah comes to regard her love for Helen as 'dishonest', omitting as it does the physical intimacy that allows Helen's male lovers to know her so much better, Sarah eventually acknowledges, than she ever can. When the novel ends with Sarah finally preparing to risk physical love, it is not with Helen that she contemplates having a sexual relationship but with Helen's former lover, George. Tempting as it is to expand the canon of Irish lesbian writing, it may more plausibly be argued that the theme of *The Maiden Dinosaur* is not lesbianism but arrested sexual development that passes almost unnoticed in this repressive Presbyterian milieu.

If overtly political feminism is not a feature of Irish women's fiction during these years, the interrogation of the ideological constraints on women's lives by such writers as Edna O'Brien, Julia O'Faolain, Leland Bardwell, Janet McNeill, Iris Murdoch and Jennifer Johnston and the exploration of female sexuality in the work of the first four of these writers reflect the development of Irish feminism in this period and point forward to the more polemical feminist writing of the 1980s. In the 1970s, women's issues began to be discussed in the media, and Irish newspapers started feminist women's pages. Second-wave feminist book publishing in Ireland began in 1975 when Catherine Rose founded Arlen House. As well as publishing new women writers, Arlen House began to bring back into print neglected or forgotten Irish novelists such as Kate O'Brien, Norah Hoult and Janet McNeill.[122]

The 1970s was also the period when Irish women's history started to be seriously researched. The pioneering volume *Women in Irish Society: The*

Historical Dimension, edited by Margaret MacCurtain and Donnchadh Ó Corráin and published by Arlen House in 1978, provided a scholarly challenge to traditional Irish historiography by highlighting aspects of Irish women's lives from early medieval times to the present day. The study stimulated both scholarly work on Irish women's history and also the general public's interest in women's history and women's studies.[123] This interest is reflected in Irish women's fiction: both Iris Murdoch's *The Red and the Green* and Jennifer Johnston's *The Old Jest* go back into history to include women as political agents.

Popular historical fiction by women in this period is as likely to concentrate on women's lives as men's. In 1969, Beatrice Coogan (1904–97) published her historical novel *The Big Wind*, often described as an Irish *Gone with the Wind* because of its epic panorama of nineteenth-century Irish history in which famines and land wars between tenants and landlords are interwoven with events in the life of its heroine, Sterrin O'Carroll of Kilsheelin Castle, born on the night of the great storm of 1839. Eilís Dillon (1920–94) also went back into the past for *Across the Bitter Sea* (1973) and its sequel, *Blood Relations* (1977). *Across the Bitter Sea*, a saga of over five hundred pages, spans the years 1851 to 1916, taking in several generations of the same family. Opening in the post-famine years and documenting the growth of Fenianism, the Land League campaigns, the rise and fall of Parnell and the days of the Easter Rising, *Across the Bitter Sea* provides a clear and detailed introduction to the development of Irish nationalism. As well as public events, the novel also gives considerable space to the private lives of Irish women, thereby posing a challenge to male historiography.[124]

These historical novels reflect an increasing desire to give a voice to women and to demonstrate the interconnection between public and private lives. In 1960, *The Great Fortune*, the first volume of Olivia Manning's *Balkan Trilogy*, was published, followed by *The Spoilt City* (1962) and *Friends and Heroes* (1965). In the following decade, the three novels that make up her *Levant Trilogy* were published: *The Danger Tree* (1977), *The Battle Lost and Won* (1978) and *The Sum of Things* (1980). Based on Manning's wartime journey through Bucharest, Athens, Cairo and Jerusalem, and constituting a major critique of British diplomatic and military policy in Europe and the Middle East, the trilogies give at least equal weight to the experiences of Harriet Pringle.

Harriet's sceptical view of politics and the battleground frequently challenges the attitudes of the males around her, and Eve Patten has noted 'a concern with patterns of female exclusion running through both the Balkan and the Levant sequences'.[125]

Partly as a result of the political campaigns of the 1970s, more Irish women were finding their voice as fiction writers and certainly there was a demand from the reading public for stories about Irish women's lives. Towards the end of the decade the volume of women's fiction, particularly in the short story form, increased significantly, with names like Maeve Brennan, Edna O'Brien, Mary Lavin, Val Mulkerns, Julia O'Faolain and Maeve Kelly all publishing collections. Yet the ambivalence of Johnston's ending in *The Old Jest* is characteristic: the 1970s may have seen promising developments in Irish feminism but fiction dwells on the constraints of Irish women's lives. Though female sexuality began to be openly discussed, with the exception of Edna O'Brien's *Night* it was rarely celebrated. The mother–daughter relationship began to catch up with the father–son relationship as an important theme in Irish writing but, again, the bond was rarely seen as a source of strength and in fact it was not until the 1990s that Irish women's fiction was to become openly celebratory of Irish women's lives.

Arguably it is in the area of style rather than theme that Irish women's fiction of this period gives cause for optimism as it begins to move away from reliance on realism and becomes more interested in artistic form. The opening up of Ireland to modernity, wider publishing opportunities and increased access to secondary and higher education unleashed women's creative energies. From Edna O'Brien's constant experiments with literary forms in the 1970s, to Bowen's postmodernism, Jennifer Johnston's impressionism, Iris Murdoch's Gothic fable, and the black comedy of Caroline Blackwood, there is a greater richness and variety now in Irish women's fiction that foreshadows developments in the following decades.

Chapter 6

THE 1980S AND '90S: FROM FEMINISM TO POSTMODERNISM

JULIA O'FAOLAIN

*A*fter the public visibility of feminism during the 1970s, the 1980s was, at least on the surface, a decade of regression. Julia O'Faolain's tragi-comic reworking of the Gráinne and Diarmuid myth *No Country for Young Men*, published in the first year of the decade and shortlisted for the Booker Prize, emphasises, through the thoughts of her protagonist Grainne, the progress Irish women still needed to make:

> Laws here had not changed, nor people's attitudes underneath. Not for women. Like a group riding the last steps of an escalator, Ireland moved with the times but stayed in the rear. Women could now live openly with their lovers but legal protection lagged. There was no divorce. Alimony – if you obtained one abroad – was hard to collect.[1]

No Country for Young Men locates the roots of present-day violence in the North in the War of Independence and highlights the involvement of American republican sympathisers in both conflicts (O'Faolain wrote the novel while living in the United States). *No Country for Young Men*, a work of historiographical metafiction, lends itself to a gendered analysis of the Troubles, the events of 1921 and 1922 being recounted in flashback by Sister Judith Clancy, an elderly trauma victim living in 1970s Dublin and cared for by Grainne, who tries to uncover her great-aunt's secret history. As Grainne's present-day life is dictated by her (unhappy) marriage and motherhood, so Judith's life in the earlier period was shaped by the active part her family played in the War of Independence and on the anti-Treaty side in the Civil War. Both women have grown up in a society where violence is applauded as heroism but where female sexuality and the female body are distrusted.

The events of 1921 and 1922, with the visit of Sparky Driscoll, an Irish American supporter of the IRA, his romance with Judith's sister Kathleen and its repercussions on the Clancy family, find their echo in the 1970s story of James Duffy, the Irish American who comes to Dublin to make a patriotic film about the IRA and embarks on an affair with Grainne. Owen O'Malley's anti-Treaty republicanism is paralleled in the IRA politics of his son Owen Roe, a lustful, menacing figure with whom Grainne has had an affair in the past. In 1922, Sparky, a supporter of the Treaty, is murdered by Judith to prevent him from influencing American donors against Owen and to preserve the engagement between Kathleen and Owen O'Malley whom she naively admires for his die-hard republicanism. In the 1970s, James Duffy is murdered by Patsy Flynn, a simple-minded IRA supporter whose nationalist version of history makes him a fanatical follower of Owen Roe. Recurring imagery pits the ideological rigidity and sexual repression of characters like Owen, Patsy and Judith against the indeterminacy of the bog representing, among other things, memory, female sexuality, the ambivalence of language and the multiple layers of Irish history.

As Owen O'Malley silenced Judith by shutting her away in a convent and submitting her to electric shock therapy in order to destroy her memory, so his son Owen Roe continues to prevent Judith's voice from being heard and works to end the affair between Grainne and James. The novel exposes the destructive patterns of certain versions of Irish myth and history, empowering men like Owen O'Malley and Owen Roe while controlling women like Judith and her sister Kathleen by confining them to convent and home respectively. Though ostensibly a freer agent in the 1970s, Grainne's Catholic upbringing and familial entanglements leave her vulnerable to Owen Roe's machinations. She distrusts the pleasure her affair with James brings: 'Raised to believe the world "a vale of tears", Grainne had a sneaking sense that only the crass took satisfaction in it.'[2] Her spell working in a home for battered wives in London highlights the theme of women's continued vulnerability in the face of male violence. The novel leaves Grainne searching for the body of her dead lover, and her story, like Lois's in *The Last September*, remains open-ended: she may opt for freedom or she may decide to return to her husband and the O'Malley clan (if she does, Judith's recovered story awaits her). By interweaving stories from the 1920s and the 1970s, the novel reveals the extent to which Irish independence did little to free Irish women from colonisation: Judith and Grainne remain trapped by familial bonds and by masculine scripts – religious, mythic, national – for their lives.

In O'Faolain's following novels from this decade, *The Obedient Wife* (1982) and *The Irish Signorina* (1984), it is the romance plot that prevents progress in women's lives. In both novels, the Italian Catholic family may be read as a stand-in for the Irish Catholic family. *The Obedient Wife* focuses on the twin training into obedience of Carla, wife and mother, and Leo, the Catholic priest with whom she falls in love. Times are changing: American mores are fluid, Italy has brought in divorce and even the Catholic Church has loosened the rules governing annulment – but Carla was raised in an older dispensation. In Los Angeles, she attempts to bring up her son Maurizio along traditional Italian lines and to perform the traditional wifely role. Ironically she does this in the face of her bullying husband's self-deluding insistence that he no longer wants this kind of subservience from her: 'the conditions you were reared for are gone,' Marco tells her.[3] Leo's training has also been too thorough: he leaves the priesthood but Carla recognises that his priestly training has left him emotionally immature and unable to connect properly with another person.

A central theme of the novel is the dysfunctional nature of the modern family unit highlighted by families like the Steeles and the Briggs. Terry Steele proclaims Christian family values on his radio show but can hardly bear to spend time with his five children and resents the Catholic Church's teaching on contraception that has given rise to them in the first place. Meanwhile his wife Sybil contemplates adultery. Dysfunctional families endanger the children in them. The Briggs family situation – a violent father and an unfaithful, abused wife – puts the young girl Evie in danger, just as Marco's absence confuses and terrifies Maurizio. Reflecting on her situation, Carla observes:

> Her life had been structured by rules as easily tested as a recipe for sauce. Now what? What did happen to a family when the mother gave these up? Surely it must collapse like an umbrella with a broken spine? Like a belly released from a corset or a stern old society robbed too suddenly of hierarchy and belief?[4]

Without a defined role in the family unit, Carla fears loss of identity: 'Not a wife, not a mother, who was she?'[5] In an ending that was criticised by feminists, but which skilfully highlights both the depth of Carla's colonisation and her own awareness of it, she returns to her husband and the ordered structures of family life.

In *The Irish Signorina*, Anne Ryan retraces her mother's footsteps after her death by staying at the Tuscan home of Marchesa Niccolosa Cavalcanti where, twenty-five years earlier, nineteen-year-old Eithne was employed as chaperone to the marchesa's daughter. The novel examines obsessive love, from the Platonic to the lustful, against a background of political violence in Italy, which allows O'Faolain to draw several parallels with the IRA campaign in Ireland. Anne becomes involved in these events when, despite her resistance to the romance plot and ambivalence about her mother's romanticisation of a past love affair with an Italian, she falls in love with Guido, the middle-aged son of the marchesa. Determined not to relive Eithne's life of thwarted love, by the acting of falling in love with Guido, whom she subsequently discovers to have been her mother's lover, Anne finds herself completing her mother's interrupted love story. Her rebellion has resulted only in bringing her full circle into her mother's inheritance, and the claustrophobic and narcissistic nature of the family unit is underlined by Anne's final discovery that she is in fact Guido's daughter.[6] With their messages that the romance plot, the maternal legacy and family ties are difficult to resist, these three 1980s novels by O'Faolain do not hold out much hope for change in women's lives. In this they reflect the increasingly conservative ethos of Irish society during this period.

MOLLY KEANE

In 1961, the failure of her play *Dazzling Prospect* on the London stage had caused Molly Keane to retreat into a life of domesticity in Ardmore but she returned to public view in 1981 with her novel *Good Behaviour*. Her rediscovery as a writer caused a literary sensation and the novel was shortlisted for the Booker Prize. The themes of *Good Behaviour* bear a resemblance to Keane's earlier novels, namely the decadence of the hunting and shooting Anglo-Irish, the decline of the Big House, and a fractious mother–daughter relationship that in this novel deteriorates into black farce and eventual matricide. *Good Behaviour* demonstrates a technical advance on the earlier novels in its use of a first-person unreliable narrator, Aroon St Charles, unloved and unlovable daughter, whose unreliability as narrator exposes the self-deluding fictions by which the Anglo-Irish live.

Unlike *Two Days in Aragon*, *Good Behaviour* focuses exclusively on the inhabitants of the Big House whose collapse comes from within. This collapse is marked by the way their bodies let them down at crucial moments, running counter to Anglo-Irish codes of good behaviour based on evasions and euphemisms about bodily functions.[7] The St Charles family's adherence to an empty code of good manners is further undermined, as Éibhear Walshe has demonstrated, by the middle-class governess Mrs Brock, whose system of education destabilises Anglo-Irish notions of manliness through fostering Hubert's homosexuality and counters Anglo-Irish indifference to domesticity by encouraging Aroon's predilection for middle-class cosiness and comfort.[8] The novel ends with the remnants of the St Charles family moving out of Temple Alice into middle-class suburbia where Aroon is able to shape her environment to suit herself. The romance plot is subverted as the abused and neglected daughter of the Big House becomes empowered, not through marriage, but by gaining control over the family finances.[9]

Aroon's access to power is achieved at the expense of her mother and, as often in Keane's work, the abused turns into the abuser, as Aroon exerts control over Mummie and Rose. As in *The Country Girls*, the theme of food in *Good Behaviour* is closely tied to issues of femininity and lack of maternal nurturance. Aroon diverts her thwarted sexuality into an obsession with eating that ensures her body shape, unlike that of her anorexic Mummie, challenges the acceptable norm for women in the 1920s and '30s. Far from indicating a loss of control, food becomes Aroon's way of establishing an identity for herself in opposition to her mother.

After the success of *Good Behaviour*, Keane went on to publish two more satirical novels about the Anglo-Irish, *Time After Time* (1983) and *Loving and Giving* (1988). *Time After Time* portrays the cruel manoeuvring for power between the last remaining members of the Swift family of Durraghglass, an Anglo-Irish family stranded in modern Ireland and whose surname underlines the satiric tradition in which Keane is writing. Jasper and his three elderly sisters are all in some way physically or psychologically maimed – Jasper has lost an eye, April is stone deaf, May has a deformed hand, while the youngest, Baby June, at sixty-four, is stunted, practically illiterate and in love with the farmhand who helps her run the farm that supports them all. All four have been injured by childhood neglect, yet they remain in thrall to long-dead Mummie: 'a miasma of overdraft and mismanagement abetted Mummie's wishes, holding brother and sisters captive for year past forgotten year, locked in inviolable small conflicts and old adventures.'[10] Cousin Leda's unexpected arrival acts as a catalyst. Leda, interpreted by some critics as representing Keane herself, treacherously rips through the veils of nostalgia and self-deception that hang over these Anglo-Irish lives, allowing them to move forward.[11] Released from the past, they begin to engage with contemporary Ireland. The dominance of Catholicism is indicated as April retires to a convent and Jasper recruits monks from the neighbouring monastery to keep his garden going. Class structures are shaken up as May goes to work in an antique shop, while Baby June allies herself with a Traveller. As Elizabeth Bowen advised years earlier, Keane's Anglo-Irish learn, belatedly, how to let go of myths about their own past and are happier for it.

Loving and Giving, with its theme of misguided and unrewarded acts of love, suggests continued Anglo-Irish delusions regarding Ireland. As in all three of these final Keane novels, death and decay comes from within the Big House itself: the protagonist, Nicandra, is killed by falling through a rotting floor in Deer Forest while her aunt Tossie, one of those 'widowed aunts' who, according to Keane, 'were an accepted part of any ascendancy family',[12] lives to see her fortune dissipated by Deer Forest. However, like Aroon, aunt Tossie survives by moving out of the Big House and contriving a new life for herself.

Deer Forest itself will be restored by the new owner, Robert, a businessman whose plans for the house make aunt Tossie feel like a primitive: 'This talk from a stranger of dry rot and habitable bedrooms was curiously hurtful. Well as she recognised the horrid truth of what he said, she felt herself to be some sort of aboriginal, and Robert a species of white settler.'[13] Keane's attitude to the Anglo-Irish turns on ambivalence: just when her satire seems at its most acute and merciless she evokes sympathy for these Big House inhabitants, often abused and neglected as children and now stranded in the new order.[14] Taken together, Keane's three novels of the 1980s suggest however that, victims of history though they may be, it is time that as a class the Anglo-Irish recognised their era is at an end.

LELAND BARDWELL

The search for a way out of an oppressive identity shaped by religion and class is the theme of Leland Bardwell's beautifully written novel *The House* (1984). Cedric Stewart spends much of his life running away from his emotionally repressed Protestant family but discovers in the end that he loves both his hard-working solicitor father and the large house in Killiney his father purchased in an attempt to establish a family line; though Cedric also knows that this will not stop him running away from both house and father again. Less savagely than Molly Keane's portraits of the Anglo-Irish, *The House* depicts the Protestant middle class at the tail-end of the British empire as constrained by a code of manners and adherence to a particular form of 'good behaviour' that militates against open expression of emotion and individual self-fulfilment. Each of the five Stewart siblings reacts in a different way: James by running away, Cedric by taking refuge in history and travel, Richard by leading a life of utter conformity, Jess by converting to Catholicism and Maria by burying her thwarted artistic life in an obsession with hunting. 'This is not strictly speaking the story of Cedric,' the narrator warns, it is about 'what a house and a family does to everyone, how lives are shaped and generations shoved into each other like the bellows of a concertina'.[15]

In her autobiography, *A Restless Life* (2008), Bardwell explains that *The House* fictionalised the lives of her mother's four Collis siblings: 'I have always been pleased with this novel, because I think I have captured the characters of the five siblings and their parents with a slant of accuracy in my endeavour to portray the Protestant professional middle classes in all their ambiguous relationships with the new Catholic state, while emphasising the chill of the Church of Ireland ethic.'[16]

Irish women's fiction was becoming more outspoken in the 1980s. This was the decade when Bardwell, who suffered domestic violence during the 1960s and wrote about it in her short stories, was finally able to get these stories published: 'Whenever I sent out stories of family violence to David Marcus [literary editor of the *Irish Press*], they were rejected. Not until the eighties were the citizens of holy Ireland allowed to read such calumny.'[17] Domestic violence in rural Ireland is central to Leland's less successful novella *There We Have Been* (1989).

DOROTHY NELSON

Dorothy Nelson (1948–) made domestic violence and child sexual abuse the central subjects of her searing and stylistically experimental novels *In Night's City* (1982) and *Tar and Feathers* (1987). In *In Night's City*, Sara's sexual, physical and mental abuse by her father, with the collusion of her mother, Esther, is a memory Sara finds so hard to deal with that she creates a stronger and darker *alter ego*, called Maggie. While Sara may excuse her father's violence, Maggie will not; yet in a country that does not acknowledge the facts of incest, Maggie's voice remains unheard. The novel also gives Esther's point of view and registers a strong protest, as earlier women writers like Dorothy Macardle had done, against Catholic idealisations of motherhood:

> The people who preached that word didn't know the meaning of it. If they lived what they preached they would have found out that motherhood wasn't a thing to be welcomed with open arms but sleepless nights followed by thrashings and beatings that left no place for dignity or reverence or whatever it is they wanted you to believe 'motherhood' was.[18]

The effects of living with Joe's physical and emotional abuse are so severe that they distort Esther's personality to the point where she is unable to help or even empathise with her daughter.

In *Tar and Feathers* the narrative voice, as in the earlier novel, moves back and forth between the characters, highlighting the claustrophobic nature of the dysfunctional family unit. 'So even without money,' Ma tells her son Ben, 'there was a way to keep your self respect, as long as the words were your words, rearranged in your own way.'[19] The trouble with Ben's mother is that many of the words in her head are not her own but planted there by her abusive husband. Nelson's novels vividly recreate the private hell of living in deeply dysfunctional and traumatised families.

Maeve Kelly

Domestic violence is the subject of Maeve Kelly's (1930–) *Necessary Treasons* (1985), hailed by one reviewer as 'a landmark in Irish feminist writing'.[20] *Necessary Treasons* traces Eve's awakening feminist consciousness as she becomes involved in the struggle to establish a refuge for battered women in Limerick. The novel, which draws on the author's own experience of working with battered women, parallels the situation of Irish women in the twentieth century with Ireland's dispossession of land, language and independence by the English in the seventeenth. The response of Eve's fiancé Hugh to family papers detailing the defeat of Honora and her family, betrayed by one of Hugh's ancestors ingratiating himself with the English in order to ensure his own survival (a 'necessary treason'), highlights Hugh's own collusion in colonising attitudes. His hostility to Eve's increasing involvement in campaigns for women's rights leads Eve to break off their engagement. However, as the novel's title indicates, political idealism is not always possible and there are times when life forces a necessary compromise. Hugh's sister-in-law Eleanor exemplifies this. In the past, Eleanor gave up her training as a medical doctor to marry Hugh's brother, who turned out to be violent and abusive. Despite being a major figure in educating Eve into a feminist analysis, Eleanor seems likely to repeat the same mistake at the end of the novel, falling in love with Adrian, an avowedly misogynist Irish-language poet and giving birth to their son just as one of the battered women at the refuge she has founded is stabbed. Treasonous it may be, but Irish women will continue to desire relationships with men and to bear their children. *Necessary Treasons* ends on an ominous note with Adrian walking contentedly through the hospital full of mothers and their newborn babies, and feeling, 'Everything was very well organized.'[21] Kelly's novel suggests that in 1985 Irish women had still some way to go in their battle to secure justice and protection for victims of domestic violence.

In common with many Irish women in the late 1940s, Kelly went over to London to train as a nurse in the newly formed National Health Service and she draws on that experience in her novel *Florrie's Girls* (1989). Limited opportunities in Ireland (the family farm in Kerry is due to be inherited by a brother) oblige the narrator, seventeen-year-old Cos, to emigrate. Along with other Irish girls, she travels to London to train as a nurse in a Catholic hospital and the novel opens with a pointed observation on Ireland's treatment of its young women: 'I arrived at Euston with all the other emigrants, like refugees from a war.'[22] Neither does Cos feel at home in London, where she encounters anti-Irish prejudice and is made to feel like an outsider. *Florrie's Girls* is remarkable, not only for its detailed account of the life of an Irish nurse in London, but also for its ending in which Cos, anticipating French feminist theory, yearns for a different language and a different way of thinking: 'I would like to learn a language so different from my own that it would be like starting all over again, with different thoughts and different ideas.'[23]

EVELYN CONLON

In keeping with the explicitly feminist themes of much Irish women's fiction of the mid-1980s, *Stars in the Daytime* (1989), a semi-autobiographical novel by feminist campaigner Evelyn Conlon (1952–), portrays its protagonist, Rose, rebelling against the restrictions of her impoverished rural Irish upbringing in the 1950s and '60s. Observing the social and sexual repressions of women's lives, Rose is determined to live her life in a different way from her mother and grandmother. Education seems likely to provide a route out, but when she arrives at university she realises that this is not the place to learn the kind of knowledge about life she is seeking. In an effort at self-education she takes on various menial jobs, experiments with sex, marries briefly, has a miscarriage and goes travelling in an effort to free herself from the last lingering constraints of her upbringing. Yet even abroad she does not entirely break her links with Ireland: 'Rose felt the need [...] to do something about her own country. Let it do something for her.'[24]

When she becomes pregnant by a stranger, her family's horrified response is predictable. Rose retreats to one room with a 'half-door' in order to reflect on Ireland and determine whether her country, whose morals are 'those of a sneaky bunch of men who had always been old',[25] will have a place for herself and her baby. The mention of the half-door interestingly echoes a letter by Louie Bennett of the Irish Women Workers' Union to Éamon de Valera protesting against the proposed Articles 40 and 41 of the Constitution:

> In country homes, the housewife often finds it necessary to keep the house door open, but it is usual then to put up a half door as a safeguard against unwelcome intrusions. If you must keep this particular door in the Constitution open, put up a guard against Fascist intrusions.[26]

As Rose uses the half-door to shield herself from the 'unwelcome intrusions' of people who seek to mould her life so Bennett warned de Valera that, unless he introduced safeguards, Irish women's lives risked being defined by marriage and motherhood as a consequence of Articles 40 and 41 of the Irish Constitution.

Rose is eventually persuaded to emerge from behind the half-door having re-negotiated her relationship with her family and rethought her attitude towards her country so that she is now able to re-enter family and national life on her own terms. The epilogue reveals Rose living in Ireland as a single mother, raising her child and working her way towards finding 'some sort of woman's truth that could be stitched together with what was already there to make a whole truth'.[27]

Mary Leland

In *The Killeen* (1985), Cork-born novelist and journalist Mary Leland (1941-) adopts the 'killeen', a graveyard for unbaptised babies, as a symbol of an Ireland resistant to alternative viewpoints. *The Killeen*, set in 1930s Cork just as the identity of the new Irish state is starting to coalesce, recreates the stifling atmosphere of a homogeneous country where priests dream of a racially pure Ireland uncontaminated by the outside world, men like Earnán are committed to continuing the unfinished struggle for a united Ireland, and the sisters of the dead hunger striker Maurice

Mulcahy plan to train up a new generation of 'freedom fighters'. Those who do not fit into this ethos are ostracised or forced into exile – like Maurice's widow, Julia, who rejects his brand of violent republicanism, or Michael Coakley, who turns his back on a society that has consigned his sister's illegitimate baby son to an unmarked grave. *The Killeen* leaves it to the reader to draw the appropriate parallels with 1980s Ireland.

In Leland's subsequent novel *Approaching Priests* (1991), Claire Mackey, like Rose in *Stars in the Daytime*, contests narrow definitions of Irishness and works from the margins to open up her nation to other voices. As a lapsed Catholic and journalist, Claire stands apart from her society, an observer of its political, cultural and spiritual life, a stance for which she finds authority, interestingly, in Somerville and Ross's novel *Mount Music*. A genealogy of Irish women's fiction was starting to be established, though it was not until the following decade that the first academic study of Irish women's fiction, by Ann Owens Weekes, appeared.

Approaching Priests is an account of Claire's spiritual and political growth over a span of twenty years set against the background of a nation divided between those who welcome Ireland's opening up to outside influences and those who wish to preserve the homogeneity of Catholic Ireland. Part One, set in the 1960s at the moment when the reforms of Vatican II are being introduced to dubious Irish Catholics, shows Claire attempting to maintain dialogue with both sides: she remains friendly with Damien Sebright, a Catholic priest, but criticises the pope's encyclical '*Humanae Vitae*', prohibiting the use of contraception. Similarly, she argues with those who, like her friend Leon, insist on the unique identity of the Irish nation and the Irish language. Claire's family connections emphasise that Irish identity is not homogeneous: her sister Angela has married an Irish Protestant whose relatives fought in the British Army and the girls' own grandfather served in the British Army in India. Claire rejects the element of compulsion behind the commitment of Sinn Féiners like Anselm Daunt to the Irish language and to a nationalist agenda that turns its back on the modern, pluralistic world in which she hopes to live.

In Part Two of the novel, set in the 1980s during the Troubles when Daunt has become the public mouthpiece of the IRA, Claire remains unaligned, on the borders of nationalist discourse, hating the violence in Northern Ireland, hating those in the Republic who give it tacit support, yet feeling compassion for the hunger strikers. When her gentle sister Angela is murdered by paramilitaries, Claire momentarily loses faith in her country before deciding to stay in Ireland and test her conviction that it is possible to live there and evade the traps set by nationalism and Catholicism. Unlike the poet Jarleth Tattin, whose faith in the Irish language is destroyed by the political uses to which violent nationalists in the North are putting it, Claire does not, ultimately, lose faith in her country. Unaligned, she maintains her dialogue with it. As a result she has become, she realises, 'one of the stories that make up this country'.[28] The novel ends with Claire, like Conlon's heroine, committed to a heterogeneous Irish nation of the future.

CLARE BOYLAN

Clare Boylan (1948–2006) lived for most of her life in Dublin, working as a journalist with the *Irish Press*, editor of *Image* magazine, short story writer and novelist. In the 1980s and '90s she published a series of novels dealing with the tragi-comedy of, generally, lower middle-class Irish Catholic family life in Dublin. In some ways her fiction may be seen as a quirky successor to Maeve Brennan's urban realism, with husbands often at odds with family life and wives trapped in small houses and weighed down by the responsibilities of marriage and motherhood. The bleakness of the context is always offset in Boylan by humour, and the feminist theme is more apparent than in Brennan as Boylan examines the way the pressures of the family unit impact particularly on mothers and daughters, with daughters yearning for a larger life and fending off their mothers' attempts to make them conform to stereotypes of femininity.

Holy Pictures (1983) depicts a selfish and self-protectively weak mother who tries to mould her daughter to fit in with the middle-class values of 1920s Catholic Ireland. Nan's mother is financially dependent on her husband and when he dies her one idea is to find another male protector for herself, even if it means virtually selling her daughter to do so. Nan's father may be a terrifying patriarch whose factory produces corsets designed to force female bodies into acceptable shapes but her mother colludes in her society's equation of femininity with marriageability and is no help to Nan, who wishes to resist this equation by opting instead for university. Boylan's training as a journalist encouraged her to research from original documents and her novel provides a detailed insight into young women's lives in 1920s Dublin.

Boylan's other novels from the 1980s explore single motherhood (*Last Resorts*, 1984) and, unusual in this period, the life of a black woman in Ireland (*Black Baby*, 1988). In the following decade, Boylan published *Home Rule* (1992), a prequel to *Holy Pictures*, covering the period from the late 1890s to the establishment of the Free State and focusing on the domestic trials of six-year-old Daisy Devlin (Nan's mother in *Holy Pictures*) and her eight siblings. Like many of Boylan's mothers, Daisy's Mama has a powerful sense of herself but is placed in a situation that disempowers her. She preserves her front parlour as an indicator of her social status, but when poverty forces her to transform it into a shoe shop, she discovers she has a flair for business. Monster of self-interest and malice, Mama, ambitious only for her sons, is ruthless with her daughters yet they come to recognise that she has at least given them 'character and faith in one's own self'.[29] Faced with inadequate or otherwise unhelpful parents, Boylan's daughter figures learn early on to deal with the outside world in their own ways: Janey flees to her grandmother's house in the slums and prospers, Daisy enters a convent, while Beth goes to live with a dressmaker and eventually learns enough to set herself up in a fashion house. Only the daughter at home, Weenie, fails to develop.

Opening in 1954, the year Ireland devoted to a celebration of Our Lady, *Room for a Single Lady* (1997) provides a telling juxtaposition between Catholic Ireland's idealisation of motherhood and women like Edie Rafferty engaged in the day-to-day task of mothering during poverty-stricken times. Edie is a thwarted artist, and the conditions of her life explain much about what held Irish women back during these years: poverty, lack of education, an unsupportive husband who, in measure as he is unable to provide the family income, compensates by exercising power over his wife and daughters, and an ideology of motherhood that expects women to sacrifice their lives outside the home. Edie is torn between encouraging her daughters to rebel against the constraints of their lives and fearing the consequences of non-conformity: 'Women have such little lives,' she tells her daughters, 'expected to do the small, unrewarding chores that must be done again tomorrow, to turn their talents to niggling skills like embroidery. No wonder there are so few great women artists. You girls are to express yourselves without restraint.'[30] During a carefree interlude when their father is absent from the home, Edie turns the clocks to the wall and encourages her daughters to paint on the kitchen walls.[31] As in Maeve Brennan's story 'The Sofa', it is as if mothers and daughters can only be free outside time, in an imaginary elsewhere.

At other times Edie warns her daughters: 'Women's lives are limited. That is how it is, especially in ordinary families.'[32] The Rafferty daughters learn how to negotiate their way round their society's restrictions on women from a series of eccentric lodgers taken in to supplement the family income. These include Sissy, who survives an unwanted pregnancy to get work as an air hostess (one of the few glamorous jobs open to Irish women in the 1950s), Minnie, who successfully runs businesses that chime in with the ideology of the times (baking, First Communions), and Dora, who swaps her unwanted baby for a prosperous future in the US. However, there is darkness too and an early indictment of Irish attitudes to child abuse in the secrecy over Selena's prolonged sexual abuse by her father, Edie remarking that it would be useless to tell the police, while the priest says without irony that it is 'a family matter'.[33]

In *Beloved Stranger* (1999), set in contemporary Dublin, Ruth, a reader of Simone de Beauvoir, Betty Friedan and Germaine Greer, observes her mother Lily's marital compromises with a sharp eye and rejects marriage, devoting herself instead to designing light, airy buildings as a protest against Dublin's dark oppressive houses that become places of captivity for women. Like all of Boylan's novels, *Beloved Stranger* possesses a comic touch that nevertheless does not conceal the tragedy of these characters' lives. By the 1990s such feminist themes were not uncommon in Irish women's writing but Boylan conveys her message with lightheartedness, attention to the details of everyday life and, particularly in *Room for a Single Lady*, a cast of colourful characters that engages the reader's attention. Realism in Boylan's quirky and witty novels constantly verges on the fantastic and the fairy tale.[34]

EDNA O'BRIEN

'From the mid-1960s to the early 1980s Irish literature contrived to suggest that lesbianism did not occur in the Republic.'[35] The 1980s was the decade when lesbianism became more visible in Ireland. In 1980, 'The Late Late Show' featured an interview with Joni Crone who spoke openly about her lesbianism, while in 1986 the Women's Community Press published *Out for Ourselves: The Lives of Irish Lesbians and Gay Men. The High Road* (1988), Edna O'Brien's only novel from this decade, portrays a lesbian relationship that, as in Kate O'Brien's *As Music and Splendour*, takes place outside Ireland. However, the relationship is more tentative in *The High Road* than in Kate O'Brien's novel. Since Spain, like Ireland, is portrayed as dominated by Roman Catholicism, the relationship between Anna, an Irish woman, and Catalina, a local Spanish girl, can take place only in a 'wilderness' space outside the patriarchal order. Despite talk of goddesses, of Christ as a woman, of breaking boundaries and transcending gender, in the end the forces of the patriarchy, of the family and Catholicism, prove too strong and the relationship between Anna and Catalina ends in tragedy. As a lesbian novel *The High Road*, like Molly Keane's *Devoted Ladies*, is somewhat dispiriting, though Helen Thompson, who has devoted more space than most critics to the theme of lesbianism in O'Brien's work, argues that O'Brien's exploration of lesbian sexuality challenges the rigid gender roles embedded in Irish nationalism even if the lesbian relationships that she depicts are not always emancipatory for her characters.[36]

Time and Tide (1992) returns to the world of *The Country Girls* in its depiction of Nell, a divorced Irish woman living in London. The novel opens as Nell's two grown-up sons leave her, one through a drowning accident on the Thames, reminiscent of the *Marchioness* disaster, the other to move in with his dead brother's pregnant girlfriend. Expanding on the story of Kate in *Girls in their Wedded Bliss*, the novel traces the trajectory of Nell's mothering, from her early years married to Walter, an aloof and controlling character resembling Eugene Gaillard, through divorce and her incestuous closeness to her sons in their early years. *Time and Tide* moves the story on by portraying the changing nature of their relationship as Nell's sons go off to boarding school, her affairs as a consequence of her loneliness, her breakdown and her sessions with a therapist, based on O'Brien's sessions with R.D. Laing.[37] Through it all weaves the story of Nell's relationship with her Irish Catholic mother and the values instilled by her rural Irish upbringing that she can never quite leave behind: 'always sooner or later, we are brought back to the dark stew of ourselves and the ancestry before us, back to the midnight of the race whose sins and whose songs we carry.'[38] Just as her mother seemed always to be a dark force drawing her back where she did not want to go, so Nell becomes 'an incubus'[39] for her sons as they grow away from her and she has to learn to let them go.

Although always more political than her reputation as a romantic novelist suggests, in the 1990s O'Brien began to focus specifically on national issues, producing a trilogy dealing, respectively, with the Northern Irish Troubles (*House of Splendid Isolation*), the 'X' case (*Down by the River*) and the land (*Wild Decembers*). *House of Splendid Isolation* (1994), written before the first ceasefire, aroused controversy for its sympathetic portrayal of Frank McGreevy, a republican gunman on the run, said to be modelled on Dominic McGlinchey, leader of the INLA, whom O'Brien visited several times in prison in the course of researching her book.[40] During this period, O'Brien's writing was moving towards more complex portrayals of Irish masculinity and examining the way in which Irish men too may be burdened by Ireland's gendered nationalism. McGreevy is trapped by a fixed interpretation of his country's history inculcated into him as a boy and by a concept of masculinity that urges him to fight for it. Rumours and stories have grown up around his commitment to armed struggle, ensnaring him in his own legend as pimpernel, buccaneer, desperado: 'If he quit and ran now, what would he do, what was there – nothing else, nothing else. His life was graphed by others.'[41]

Rather than the straightforward realism that the subject matter may seem to call for, *House of Splendid Isolation* is postmodernist in style (O'Brien has always been more experimental than she has been given credit for), drawing on diaries, poems and myth and written in a fractured, non-linear mode.[42] The hunt for McGreevy is interspersed with octogenarian Josie's traumatic memories of her early married life, her broken-off love affair with a priest, her abortion, and her uncle's Volunteer diary from 1921. Placing Josie's story alongside that of McGreevy allows O'Brien to explore the way in which Irish nationalism defines masculinity in terms of domination of the land and of women. Women are shown to collude in these gendered constructions: Josie's mother taunts her husband with being less than a man because he has not been able to hold on to their field.

The way Irish history is taught in schools is shown as encouraging Irish males to see their purpose as defending their country's heritage: inspired by stories of Irish rebels told to him by his teacher, the simple-minded Paud is persuaded to hide guns for the terrorists, and even some of the guards feel ambivalent about McGreevy, admiring his courage and half regretting having to kill him. When Josie's husband is shot by mistake, going to the aid of Paud, Josie feels that the violent history of her country will never end. As the opening of the novel proclaims: 'history is everywhere. It seeps into the soil, the sub-soil. Like rain, or hail, or snow, or blood. A house remembers. An outhouse remembers. A people ruminate. The tale differs with the teller.'[43]

Yet if there is a lesson in *House of Splendid Isolation* it is that all narratives are inadequate and that history should be laid to rest. The epilogue suggests that the land should be let be, that no more unreliable stories should be woven around it: 'the land cannot be taken. History has proved that. The land will never be taken. It is there.'[44] In the battered Big House, symbol of the shattered dreams of a united Ireland, Josie, who has fought her own battles for freedom from the Catholicism and masculinism of the Irish state embraced by her husband who treats her as a colonised subject, achieves a brief modus vivendi with the gunman whose violence she abhors but whose political commitment and personal suffering she has come to respect. The reader is left deliberately in suspense at the end of the novel, uncertain whether the cycle of violence in Ireland has come to an end, but suspecting that it has not.

The second novel of O'Brien's trilogy, *Down by the River* (1996), is loosely based on the 1992 'X' case in which a High Court order initially prevented fourteen-year-old Miss X, pregnant as the result of rape by a family friend, from travelling to England for an abortion. In *Down by the River*, Mary McNamara's pregnancy is the result of rape by her father and O'Brien thus picks up on the theme of father–daughter incest present in several novels by Irish women in this period, notably Dorothy Nelson's *In Night's City*. As Christine St Peter has observed, whereas Nelson's novel remains confined to private domestic space, in *Down by the River* incest moves into the public domain, reflecting greater public awareness of the issue in Ireland by the 1990s.[45]

In the ensuing national debate over whether Mary should be allowed to travel to England for an abortion, her body becomes the boundary by which the Irish nation defines itself.[46] Anti-abortionists argue that if the abortion is permitted, Ireland's integrity as a nation will be threatened. 'We're a Christian country … We're a model for the whole world,' declares one of the judges deciding Mary's case.[47] As various groups discuss what becomes known as 'Magdalene versus the nation', echoing the Catholic ideology that colours the discussion, it is clear that Mary's desire for an abortion threatens the very category of Irish woman as constructed by nationalist ideology. The debate does not entirely fall along gender lines. One of O'Brien's most interesting achievements in this novel is the polyphonic range she grants to her male characters. Some of the most virulent anti-abortionists are women. Some of the most sympathetic characters are men: Mary's headmaster, Luke, the Buddhist musician who gives her shelter, Cathal, her understanding lawyer, L'Estrange, her barrister, Frank, the judge who is prepared to listen to his daughter.

The Catholic and nationalist ideologies underpinning the Irish state do not regard Mary's pregnant body as autonomous. 'It's not your child,' a leading pro-lifer tells Mary, denying her a voice.[48] She is silenced also by the Virgin Mary, that impossible ideal of virgin and mother held up to her as a model. Nor can Mary tell her mother: Bridget, subject to beatings from her husband, does not see the abuse, or perhaps, since the servant Lizzie is aware of it, does not want to see it. Mary's rape is, literally, unspeakable. Only after her miscarriage is Mary able to break her silence and raise her voice in a song that unites her listeners:

> Her voice was low and tremulous at first, then it rose and caught,
> it soared and dipped and soared, a great crimson quiver of sound
> going up, up to the skies and they were silent then, plunged into
> a sudden and melting silence because what they were hearing was
> in answer to their own souls' innermost cries.[49]

Mary finds her voice, breaking through the various groups that have sought to silence her, and, the last line suggests, her nation responds.

In the final book of the trilogy, *Wild Decembers* (1999), Joseph Brennan's sense of identity is tied to his ancestral land and his masculinity bound up with defending his territory. O'Brien shows how the discourses of nation and gender leak into each other, ownership of the land and ownership of women becoming intertwined in Joseph's mind.[50] His proprietary attitudes not only involve him in a land war with his immigrant neighbour Michael Bugler, but also lead to him trying to control his sister Breege's sexuality. One of the consistent themes in O'Brien's work is a protest against the way in which rigid ideologies silence other voices in the Irish nation. As Mary in *Down by the River* is silenced by the situation in which she finds herself, so Breege is unable to speak of her love for Bugler. Maddened by what he regards as both personal and national betrayal, Joseph kills Bugler out of a sense of outrage that by impregnating Breege, Bugler has mixed his blood with that of the Brennans. The betrayal for him is both personal and racial: Bugler's baby threatens to adulterate the Brennans' Irish identity.

Like the previous novels in the trilogy, *Wild Decembers* ends on a tentative note of hope: the land becomes quiet and 'unfeuding' once more as Breege and Bugler's fiancée, Rosemary, occupy the two houses left empty by their men. Perhaps Breege will construct a different kind of mothering, one that does not tie her son to an obsession with ownership of the land. As in *House of Splendid Isolation*, the narrative is fractured, recounted through Irish legends, songs, letters, legal documents, third-person narrative and Breege's stream of consciousness as she struggles to move beyond myth to find her individual voice. *Wild Decembers* strains against mimetic realism, the characters taking on a symbolic significance that, despite its 1970s setting, makes the novel seem curiously timeless in the language and mores of its inhabitants so that in the end the struggle for land comes to possess the quality of myth or fairy tale.

JENNIFER JOHNSTON

Women finding their voice, particularly their artistic voice, is very much the theme of Jennifer Johnston's fiction during the 1980s when in the country as a whole women writers and artists were becoming more visible. In 1984, Róisín Conroy and Mary Paul Keane founded Attic Press specifically to promote women's writing, and in 1985, Arlen House published the landmark collection *Irish Women: Image and Achievement*, edited by Eiléan Ní Chuilleanáin. John Quinn's series of interviews with Irish women writers, broadcast on RTÉ radio in 1985 and subsequently published as *A Portrait of the Artist as a Young Girl* (1986), focused attention on the particular obstacles faced by female Irish writers. In his foreword to the collection, Seamus Heaney noted: 'overall there is a nice political edge to the book, insofar as it constitutes a spirited displacement of the aura of maleness which still tends to surround that hallowed word, "artist".'[51]

Reflecting this growing visibility of women writers, Johnston's first novel of this decade, *The Christmas Tree* (1981), is a portrait of a female Irish writer, albeit one who only gathers courage to insist on her vocation rather late in life. To some extent this mirrors Johnston's own situation since she once remarked how long it took her ('until I was thirty') to work out what her role in life was going to be. She related this to Irish society's lack of expectations for women:

> Most of my peers had no great expectations of life at the age of seventeen. They did secretarial courses, or became teachers, and eventually married and had children; but beyond that they never did anything with their lives. They had no expectations that they might do anything at all that was outside the normal course of traditional events.[52]

In *The Christmas Tree*, Constance adopts a marginalised position as a means of critiquing the Dublin middle-class Protestant world in which she was raised. Her failure to espouse Dublin 4 values brings her into conflict with her family: *The Christmas Tree* is not only a novel about the painful evolution of a female artist but also a story of a hostile mother–daughter relationship. Constance moves to London and attempts a career as a writer but is too easily discouraged by a male publisher. Her life seems about to repeat her father's thwarted writerly ambitions until a meeting with Jacob, a Polish Jew who chides her for her lack of courage, gives her confidence to start writing again. The novel's ending may be read in opposing ways. In an optimistic reading, Constance, unlike her father, has written her book and ensured that her daughter by Jacob will escape the kind of Protestant upbringing Constance found so constricting. In a more pessimistic interpretation, the struggle has cost Constance her life and delivered her child into two different patriarchies: Judaism, represented by Jacob, and Roman Catholicism, represented by Bridie.[53]

The Railway Station Man (1984), shortlisted for the Booker Prize, portrays a female artist, Helen, intent on creating her own space, a room of her own where she can develop her creativity unimpeded by the competing ideologies of her nation and the domestic demands of those around her. Recognising that she cannot remain in isolation from society, Helen regards her paintings as her means of dialogue with the outside world, much as Elizabeth Bowen in an earlier period declared that her writing was her way of connecting to society. *The Railway Station Man* depicts the lengthy process Helen, like many of Johnston's artist figures, undergoes before she finds her individual voice. The Northern Irish Troubles impinge on her life at various points. Her husband's murder by the IRA provides her with the necessary impetus to stop living her life according to other people's rules. At the end of the novel, after the explosion that kills her lover Roger, as well as her son who was peripherally involved in the nationalist struggle, Helen understands that her private space is not immune to the outside world, but nor will it be defeated by it. To rebuild and go on with her vision is her response to the deaths. In contrast to the violence in Northern Ireland that kills or maims the human body and to the Second World War that has left Roger physically and mentally damaged, Helen's sequence of four paintings celebrates the youthful healthy male body. Referencing Shelley's 'Ode to a Skylark', the novel makes the lark a recurring symbol of Helen's bid for artistic freedom.

In *Fool's Sanctuary* (1987), set during the War of Independence, Johnston turns back to the themes of her earlier novel *The Old Jest*, as Miranda struggles to attain adulthood amid the growing violence in her country. Like other Anglo-Irish heroines, Miranda is trapped in a hyphenated identity. She accuses her brother Andrew, who fought in the British Army during the First World War and has come over to Ireland to suppress those struggling for independence, of making no effort to understand the nationalists' point of view. Yet she also wants her lover Cathal to give up his participation on the nationalist side. Miranda is, like her father, a pacifist and like him sees their Big House, Termon, as a sanctuary for all sides. Such idealism is quickly defeated, however, by the realities of war.

Gender as well as class is responsible for Miranda's exclusion from political events in Ireland, as it was for Lois in Bowen's *The Last September*. While her father's work on land reclamation will remain to benefit the new Irish nation, Miranda has made no such contribution: 'I walked like King Wenceslas's page, in his footsteps leaving no trace of my own.'[54] When Cathal is killed, Miranda's story stops. Looking back over her life, she realises that the eruption of violence into her life has stunted her development: 'I never reached maturity. I never allowed myself that luxury.'[55] Her stasis is willed, a protest against a world that robbed her of her chance of love. Instead of confronting the 'brave new world' like her Shakespearean namesake and taking her place in the new Irish nation, she has chosen to remain isolated from the world in Termon. She hopes God will forgive her 'for the wilful destruction of myself'.[56]

Fool's Sanctuary is a portrait of female development cut off by an act of nationalist violence and as such it provides a telling comment on the stunting of women's lives in a country where nationalist narratives have celebrated male violence as male heroism. The novel, both in tone and content, becomes an elegy for female lives omitted from the narrative of Irish history. But, though Miranda remains excluded from the history of her nation and without a history of her own, her dying, fragmented ramblings interspersed with songs and quotations become her way of repossessing history and countering the heroic myths that have grown up around violence. Robert F. Garratt places *Fool's Sanctuary* and Johnston's following novel *The Invisible Worm* (1991) in the category of trauma novels in which characters attempt to recall a traumatic event in order to come to terms with it and move on.[57] For Miranda, death is the next stage, but for the middle-aged Laura there may be some hope of progress.

The Invisible Worm takes a similar theme to *Down by the River*, namely a daughter's rape at the hands of her father, which her mother is powerless to prevent. Though Laura's trauma is personal, Johnston's political preoccupations remain evident since Laura's father, a former IRA man turned senator, represents the new Irish establishment of the 1930s and '40s, intent on possessing power and control, particularly over women's bodies, while Laura's mother Harriet is Anglo-Irish and therefore on the losing side in the new Irish nation. Laura's rape has been interpreted as her father's act of revenge against her spirited Anglo-Irish mother whose life he has failed to control.[58] Like Mary in *Down by the River*, Laura has difficulty finding words to articulate her experience of abuse. Like Miranda, she lives with dreams, memories, and fragments of speech as she struggles to find her voice. She comes to symbolise all the abused children, battered women and incest survivors whose stories bear witness to the underside of Irish nationalism, stories that men like her father wish to suppress because they do not fit into the image of a glorious new nation: 'We have to keep our suffering to ourselves,' he tells her.[59]

Harriet's membership of the Ascendancy class has bestowed on her a certain prestige and glamour, not to mention financial security, and she is thus able to hand on to Laura more independence than Mary's Catholic country mother is able to bequeath her daughter in *Down by the River*. The house in which Laura lives is inherited from her mother and has passed down three generations of the female line. Laura stays faithful to her female genealogy by remaining in her mother's house and her mother's church. In the outside world, her father and her Catholic politician husband Maurice may be important, but by stubbornly clinging to her mother's house and her mother's world, Laura becomes an unsettling sign that not everyone in the nation agrees with their values. She chooses a very different sort of man, the ex-priest Dominic, to confess her trauma to. Dominic's listening ability allows space for Laura to come to terms with her rape. After telling her story, she surprises him with her energy as she burns down the summerhouse where the rape took place, thereby purging her home of her father's spirit. Laura's narrative becomes representative of those stories of rape, incest and domestic violence which, concealed in the life of the new Irish state, were coming to light in the 1990s. Johnston's novel ends on a note of hope. Having told her story and burned down the summerhouse, there is a chance Laura will come alive and 'begin to write my life' in a new and more liberating way.[60]

If Harriet's Anglo-Irish identity empowers her daughter, *The Illusionist* (1995), by contrast, demonstrates the extent to which nationality can get in the way of effective mothering. Stella's allegiance to her Irish nationality impedes her ability to mother her daughter Robin, who identifies with England and with Martyn, her English father. Stella's outsider status in England facilitates Martyn's seduction of Robin away from her and he reveals his doubts about the validity of Irish national identity when he insists that Robin must be educated in England: 'She's going to be assured, sure of who she is and proud of it.'[61] Though Martyn conceals from Stella any information about his family background and working life, his scorn for the Irish might have some bearing on the manner of his death (he is blown up by an IRA bomb).

Patterns of mothering are repeated in this novel: just as Stella has escaped to England to escape her mother's too-observant eye, so Robin resists her mother's nurturing, labelling it 'Motherspeak'.[62] As England will always be a foreign place for Stella, so Ireland is an alien country for Robin, and the fact that an IRA bomb is responsible for her father's death gives her an additional reason for hating her mother's nation. It is only as Stella matures that she learns to appreciate both her mother and her mother country. In portraying Robin's shock at discovering she is not the only daughter in her father's life, the novel leaves open the possibility that Stella and Robin may also at some future date be reconciled and that Robin may come to acknowledge the Irish part of her identity.

In *Two Moons* (1998), Johnston's exploration of the mother–daughter relationship extends across three generations with Grace, an actress, finding her life sandwiched between that of her sometimes hostile daughter Polly, in London, and Mimi, her frail, elderly mother who lives in Dublin. If Grace illustrates the tensions between women's caretaking role and their professional lives, in Mimi the novel highlights the invisibility of the elderly. Like the dying Miranda, Mimi is another of Johnston's liminal characters, on the threshold between life and death, sanity and insanity. During Grace's frequent absences at the theatre, Mimi communicates with an angel. *Hamlet* is a central intertext, reinforcing the theme of insanity and illuminating the scenes in which Grace, who is rehearsing the part of Gertrude, finds herself falling for Paul, Polly's boyfriend. As Gertrude's passionate obsession with Claudius is diverted by her son, so Grace's incipient passion for Paul is halted out of love for Polly. As indicated by the title, doubling is a feature of the novel, where Mimi's friendly messenger angel Bonifacio has a more threatening counterpart in the shape of her dead husband Benjamin. Mimi finally comprehends the reason for their unhappy marriage as Benjamin reveals his homosexuality, necessarily concealed in earlier decades. Sympathetic portraits of homosexuals are a feature of Johnston's later novels.

Two Moons gives a deeper portrayal of mother figures than Johnston's earlier novels: both Mimi and Grace are flawed mothers but access to their thoughts, dreams and imaginings allows us to understand why they have failed in their mothering. Mimi has provided too passive a role model for Grace and it is in reaction against her unhappy, helpless mother that Grace has neglected Polly's emotional needs in order to put her acting first. These mothers are far from ideal but they are a distinct improvement on the cauterising Anglo-Irish mothers of Johnston's early novels.

DEIRDRE MADDEN

Deirdre Madden (1960–) grew up in Toomebridge, County Antrim, the setting for some of her novels. Madden's experience of living for extended periods abroad in England, France and Italy is reflected in her fictional themes of identity and migration. In her first novel, *Hidden Symptoms* (1986), set in Belfast during the Troubles, Madden portrays a city paralysed by hatred and fear and underlines the impossibility of escape from sectarian divisions: the 'hidden symptoms' of the title refer to the discrimination and injustice that lay beneath the surface of everyday life in Northern Ireland even before the present explosion of violence. Twenty-two-year-old Theresa has been traumatised by the random sectarian killing of her twin brother Francis two years previously and she is unable to move beyond this. She retains her Catholic faith but refuses to be comforted by it. Her mental stasis is paralleled by that of the introverted city in which she lives, and the novel presents little hope of escape from the city's warring ideologies. Theresa tells the escapist intellectual Robert that abandoning his faith makes no difference, he will always be labelled Catholic: 'If you think that you can escape tribal loyalty in Belfast today you're betraying your people and fooling yourself.'[63] In a parallel trajectory, Theresa's rebellion against stereotypes of femininity (her refusal to wear make-up or to flatter men) leaves her in a state of paralysed uncertainty as to her identity.[64]

The Birds of the Innocent Wood (1988) draws on the Gothic to depict the buried traumas and repressions of family life in rural Ireland, relationships between sisters, and daughters' confusions of identity following the death of a parent, themes that Madden will explore in more depth and focus in the following decade in *One by One in the Darkness*. *The Birds of the Innocent Wood* is nevertheless memorable for its poetic evocation of the Irish countryside and for the development of Madden's trademark method of maintaining the reader's interest through gradual revelations about her characters' inner states of mind.

In *Remembering Light and Stone* (1992), Aisling is in flight not only from her country but from traumatic memories of a childhood with a violent father. Although the reader is given few precise details about Aisling's past, it is clear that she remains haunted by 'the psychic violence' that she associates with the landscape of her native region, the Burren.[65] The trauma is deep-seated enough for her to have preserved an instinct to flinch, as if expecting to be hit, and she flees any hint of aggression on the part of others. With a sense of reprieve, she settles in the small town of S. Giorgio in Umbria and proceeds to embrace the foreign culture, altering her behaviour and even her appearance to such an extent that she finds herself unrecognisable in old photographs from Ireland.

In the end, though, what is more significant than anything Aisling learns about Italy is the way in which living in a foreign culture begins the healing process which gradually leads her back to Ireland. Though the novel registers, through the character of Maria, significant reservations about the value of a perpetually cosmopolitan lifestyle, in Italy Aisling finds the necessary separation from Ireland to allow her to remember the past without becoming engulfed by it. And she is able, finally, to exorcise the pain of her childhood, as in the church of San Giorgio, in the fresco that so unsettles her, the blank-faced friar exorcises the devil. By the time Aisling revisits her family home, the threat of 'the psychic violence' that she associates with Ireland has vanished.

Nothing is Black (1994) returns to an Irish setting and foreshadows *Authenticity* in its contrast between the pressures of materialism in contemporary society and the integrity necessary for the artistic life. The cost and uncertain rewards of living out an artistic vocation are portrayed in the asceticism of Claire's life as a painter in Donegal. Claire's more materialistic cousin Nuala finds consumerism empty compensation for the loss of her mother, and her lack of confidence after her mother's death allows for development of a theme touched on in *Remembering Light and Stone*, namely an exploration of how life should be lived in the light of our own and others' mortality. In this slight novel, Madden raises a number of weighty themes that will be returned to in later novels, particularly concerning memory and the fluidity of identity. The complexities of the mother–daughter relationship that Nuala helps untangle for Claire's neighbour Anna feature centrally in Madden's next novel, *One by One in the Darkness* (1996).

In *Remembering Light and Stone*, Aisling's home has been destroyed by domestic violence; in *One by One in the Darkness*, the violence that disrupts the Quinn family life comes from outside the home and the novel moves between the 1960s and the 1990s in order to explore the impact of the Troubles on one ordinary Catholic family living in rural Northern Ireland. In an interview Madden explained:

> I wanted to write about the Troubles. Like the women in the book,
> I was a child in 1969 and I remember vividly that time and the
> years that followed. While aspects of that situation, such as the
> bomb scares, the endless checkpoints on the roads and the terrible

news night after night on television became familiar, they always remained abnormal and disturbing. And still normal life continued – school, exams, holidays, church, friendships and so on. I hope the book gives some sense of what it was like to live through that. So while it is a novel about a particular political conflict, it is also a book about ordinary life, about families, about parents and children, about how sisters relate to each other as the years pass.[66]

One by One in the Darkness portrays the growth to maturity of the three Catholic Quinn sisters and the traumatic impact on them of the murder of their father at the hands of loyalist paramilitaries. It goes back into the past to trace the childhood of the sisters' mother, Emily, already overshadowed, even before the Troubles, by the pressures of living as a member of a minority in Northern Ireland. Emily is doubly colonised since she has been obliged to give up her teaching job on marriage. She has a troubled relationship with her own mother, the forbidding Granny Kelly, and is only prevented from making the same mistakes with her daughters by her husband Charlie, one of the few attractive portrayals of a father figure in Irish women's fiction (another is Mr Wall in Emma Donoghue's *Hood*). The novel is set against the rise of the civil rights movement, the advent of the British Army and the growing violence in the North and registers a protest against the marginalisation of Catholics within the state. By taking an ordinary Catholic rural family as her subject, Madden emphasises the way in which the political situation impinged on daily life in Northern Ireland. Even Charlie, a tolerant Catholic who opposes militant republicanism, becomes increasingly politicised. After his death, home becomes a haunted place for all four women.

The sisters react to the Troubles in different ways. Cate escapes Northern Ireland and enters the glamorous world of London fashion magazines. After Charlie's death, Cate's London life comes to seem like 'an illusion' and she attempts to counter this by having a baby, feeling that at least this will be 'something real', yet recognising that her mother will have difficulty coming to terms with a pregnancy outside marriage.[67] In depicting the insecurity and sense of impermanence that underlie the outward glamour of Cate's London life, Madden indicates the way in which economic globalisation can abstract the self from place and community.

The life of Cate's elder sister Helen has been deformed by the pressure on her, as a member of the Catholic minority, to get a good education and do something to help her people. Reminiscent of the political differences between Helen Archer and Mother Mary Andrew in *The Land of Spices*, the two nuns at Helen's convent school give her differing advice: Sister Benedict urges her to choose a wider future outside Northern Ireland, while Derry-born Sister Philomena, a nationalist like Mother Mary Andrew, convinces her that Northern Ireland needs educated Catholic leaders. Helen becomes a Belfast lawyer specialising in terrorist cases, working out of the Falls Road, and her life, as Sister Benedict predicted, is increasingly bleak. The third sister, Sally, whose life has been colonised by their mother, remains at home and works as a primary school teacher. Despite the apparent narrowness of her life, Sally is the sister who, drawing on the emotional intelligence developed in her close bond with her mother, helps the family through the crisis provoked by Cate's pregnancy.

The novel's seemingly flat, realist narrative tone is disrupted, as often in Madden, by postmodernist features reflecting, as in *Hidden Symptoms*, the non-linear process of coming to terms with grief.[68] After Charlie's death, Emily becomes obsessed with growing flowers, using them as a way of attaching herself to the cyclical rhythm of the seasons rather than linear time, which she dreads. The four women's dreams and visions, expressing more than they are able to articulate in language, register a subconscious protest against the constraints of the political circumstances in which they are trapped. The female characters are drawn together also by their association with colour, which runs like a leitmotif through the novel. As if to register a protest against the grimness of their lives, Granny Kate and her granddaughter Cate have only brightly coloured clothes in their wardrobes. Granny Kate's subtle distinctions between colours contrast with the heavily politicised use of colour by the various political factions in Northern Ireland. Despite these brief moments of consolation, *One by One in the Darkness* ends, like *Hidden Symptoms*, on a vision of utter bleakness with Helen imagining the moment of her father's death against the backdrop of a dark and lonely universe.

NORTHERN IRELAND

As tensions heightened in the North, the 1980s and '90s brought renewed focus on the Troubles in women's writing.[69] *Sisters by Rite* (1984), a partly autobiographical novel by Joan Lingard (1932–), takes as its subject the shaping of identity by class, gender and religion. The novel traces the lives of three young girls, Rosie, a Protestant, Teresa, a Catholic, and Cora, a Christian Scientist (as Lingard was herself), living in east Belfast in the 1940s and '50s. Cora's Christian Science home establishes neutral territory where the other two can meet, and Cora is best situated to challenge the orthodoxies that surround the girls but in the end she only uses this knowledge to manipulate sectarianism to her own advantage when out of jealousy she alerts Rosie's Orange uncle to Rosie's love for Gerard, a Catholic. Despite the girls' bond of friendship, sectarian violence erupts into their private lives, bearing out the message of other women writers on Northern Ireland in this period that there was no safe private space from the violence.

Like Lingard, women writing on Northern Ireland often chose to depict the effect of the violence on young people. *The Dark Hole Days* (1984) by Una Woods portrays two teenagers reacting in different ways to the Troubles in Belfast: Joe joins the loyalist paramilitaries while Colette attempts to clear a space for herself, a psychological room of her own, by writing a diary. Like Madden's *Hidden Symptoms*, Woods's novella underlines the impossibility of evading the violence: Colette's opportunity to escape from Belfast is closed off by the random murder of her father by loyalist paramilitaries, while Joe ends up in hiding from both sides.

Frances Molloy's tragi-comic and subversive novel *No Mate for the Magpie* (1985) describes the life of Ann McGlone, a working-class Catholic girl growing up in Northern Ireland in the 1950s and '60s. Molloy was born in 1947 to an impoverished Catholic family in Derry and published only this one novel before her death in 1991. *No Mate for the Magpie*, related entirely in Northern Irish dialect, reveals the way in which Ann's life is restricted by gender, class and religion. She is kept off school by her mother to look after her younger siblings and when she gets a job in a supermarket as a bacon slicer her boss is delighted 'because he only had te give me half the pay a man would get'.[70] Ann eventually loses her job because her boss's wife is prejudiced against Catholics. After working both in Northern Ireland and in the Republic during the 1960s and '70s and concluding that misery, poverty and injustice flourish on both sides of the border, Ann follows the example of Anna Livia and turns her back on Ireland: 'A could see "Anna Livia" movin' beneath me, resolutely, determinedly, headin' outa Ireland, an' a knew then that a too must do the same an' go to a place where life resembled life more than it did here.'[71] Leading the reader through a variety of different scenes in picaresque fashion as Ann makes her way in the world – Catholic school, republican jail (where her father is imprisoned), Protestant factory, convent, a priest's house (where she is housekeeper for a while), a Dublin mental hospital and taking in the civil rights marches and anti-Vietnam war protests along the way – *No Mate for the Magpie* is a remarkable novel by any standards.[72]

To Stay Alive (1985) by Linda Anderson (1949–) is a harrowing portrayal of life in Belfast during the Troubles set in 1979, at a time when IRA prisoners were engaged in the 'dirty protest' that preceded the hunger strikes. Anderson's novel describes nineteen-year-old Rosaleen's attempts to stay alive, to stay human, in the face of a situation which seems calculated to crush both spirit and body. Even before the brutal sexual assault on her by four British soldiers, Rosaleen, born into a Catholic working-class family, has found her life constricted not only by poverty and violence but also by sexism. Despite her university ambitions, she is expected to care for her younger siblings while her mother nurses the latest baby and her long-term unemployed father is out drinking. At school the nuns, like the nuns in the convent school in Edna O'Brien's *The Country Girls*, equate young womanhood with chastity and humility and do little to aid Rosaleen's ambition to get to university. The only person who encourages Rosaleen's ambitions is Dan, a medical student, but by the time she has been accepted for Queen's she is pregnant by him. Due to the Catholic ban on contraception, instead of the freedom she had imagined at university, marriage and motherhood have become Rosaleen's fate.

Not only does Rosaleen challenge Catholic discourse concerning the female body, she also questions the nationalist assumptions of the Catholic working-class environment in which she has grown up. Echoing Eavan Boland, she argues that women may be powerful symbols in Irish music and poetry but in real life they are invisible: Irish men carry out violence on behalf of other Irish men while women and children get caught in the crossfire. She perceives the Irish nation as constructed by the nationalists to be male property and seeks escape from the constraints of her life through sex with Gerry, a British soldier newly arrived in the country. In the act of making love with Gerry, Rosaleen's rebellion against the ideologies constraining the female body (she should remain a faithful Catholic wife) and her resistance to nationalism (she should certainly not be unfaithful with a British soldier) come together, her body providing the means with which to express her dissent from the male-authored nationalism weighing on her community.

By the end of the novel, despite the assault on her by British soldiers, Rosaleen finds the courage to stay on in Belfast and become a symbol of resistance to the violent nationalisms of her environment. Her courage is matched by that of Dan, who returns from a brutal interrogation by the British Army determined not to be drawn into the war of guns. Though the novel ends on a note of hope, in the light of all that has gone before, the reader cannot help feeling that Rosaleen and Dan will have a terrible struggle ahead of them in their search for more fluid identities than their community allows them. However, as Madden's Cate Quinn discovered, exile is not always a solution to life in Northern Ireland: in Anderson's next novel, *Cuckoo* (1986), Fran takes refuge in London from the complexity of her life as a Northern Irish Protestant in Belfast but remains haunted by her memories of the violence in her native city.

Give Them Stones (1987) by Mary Beckett (1926–) traces Martha's more gradual disenchantment with the nationalist ideology that rules her working-class Catholic community and the violence it entails. Like Helen in *The Railway Station Man*, Martha moves towards creating her own space, a room of her own outside the competing ideologies of her nation, where she can develop her creativity, in this case her bread-making, unimpeded. Indeed, she concentrates on baking bread to such an extent that when a British soldier asks her whether she is a republican, she defines herself not in political terms but in economic: 'I was going to be a heroine but instead I said, "I am a home baker".'[73] Her bake house becomes more than an economic necessity: Martha's mothering of her sons has been a failure but she transfers her mothering skills outward into nurturing her community as the bake house draws the neighbourhood to her shop. For the stones thrown in violence on the streets outside, Martha substitutes her bread.

In 1983 Polly Devlin (1944–) published *All of Us There*, a haunting memoir about growing up in rural County Tyrone during the 1940s and '50s and the effect of living as a marginalised Catholic minority within Northern Ireland. Devlin drew on the same background for her novel *Dora, or the Shifts of the*

Heart (1990), in which Nora, a Catholic raised in rural Northern Ireland, moves to England at nineteen in order to avoid duplicating her mother's thwarted life. She changes her name to the more English-sounding Dora and, like Madden's heroine Cate, and like Devlin herself, begins to work in the glamorous world of fashion magazines. Set in the 1970s with flashbacks to Dora's childhood in the 1940s and '50s, the novel is close in atmosphere and time to Edna O'Brien's *Country Girls* trilogy. Like O'Brien's Caithleen, Dora is the daughter of a joyless, self-denying mother and has been educated at a convent school that inculcates an ethos of chastity, passivity and obedience into its girls. However, like O'Brien's heroines, Dora learns that neither her mother nor her mother country is easily left behind. She remains imperfectly translated into English life, ashamed of her Irish country origins, yet ready to defend her nation passionately against mistaken English assumptions. Only after many years is she finally able to come to terms with her dual identity as an Irish woman living in England. Exile helps Dora overcome mental barriers that might have remained in place if she had stayed at home, and her increasingly flexible notion of Irish identity allows her to avoid the limiting bitterness of her more sectarian countrymen.

Titanic Town: Memoirs of a Belfast Girlhood (1992), a semi-autobiographical novel by Mary Costello (1955–), portrays the strains of daily life in Andersonstown during the 1960s and '70s. The McPhelimy family lives in the heart of the violence and army raids and shooting in the streets are a nightly occurrence. Bernie McPhelimy, who is constantly afraid for her children's safety, allows Annie out only to go to school or to mass.[74] Like much women's fiction from Northern Ireland, Costello's novel emphasises that there is no safe domestic sphere: from her bedroom window, Annie can see 'the goings-on. The boys and the Brits, and the RUC.'[75] The killing of a local woman caught in cross-fire between the IRA and the British Army inspires Bernie and her friend Deirdre to attempt to negotiate a halt to the shooting, at least during the daytime. In keeping with the bleakly comic tone of the novel, the women's efforts are portrayed as farcical: though their wish for an end to the violence has great emotional appeal, they lack any political strategy to deal with its causes. Bernie and Deirdre end up being manipulated by all sides, by the media, by the Catholic Church, by the IRA who use them to present their demands to the British, demands they know have no chance of succeeding, and by the

British who turn the women's desire for peace into anti-IRA propaganda. Elmer Kennedy-Andrews comments:

> The Peace Women constitute an emblem of female energy, determination and commitment, but they are shown to be pathetically inadequate to deal with the establishment and counter-hegemonic power structures, both exclusively male, which would thwart, marginalise and take over those who seek to work through new channels.[76]

The weight of inherited narratives of Irish history and the difficulty of escaping from them is a central theme of the historiographic and metafictional novel *A Wreath Upon the Dead* (1993) by Briege Duffaud. The novel is recounted by Maureen Murphy, a Catholic brought up in Claghan, a town based on Duffaud's native Crossmaglen. Maureen has escaped Northern Ireland to live abroad and establish herself as a successful writer of romantic fiction. As is usual in works of historiographic metafiction, the novel employs ambiguity, irresolution, multiple viewpoints and unreliable narrative to emphasise the inaccessibility of the past. As in Madden's *Hidden Symptoms*, no escape is envisioned possible from the dead hand of Irish history, at least for the inhabitants of Claghan, where history re-emerges as violence with the reformation of the IRA.

Maureen intends her next novel to be about a pair of nineteenth-century lovers from Claghan, Cormac O'Flaherty from the Catholic peasantry and Marianne McLeod, daughter of a wealthy Protestant family. The house in which Cormac and Marianne took refuge has been saved from demolition by a group of liberal Protestants and preserved in the hope that it might become a place where Catholics and Protestants can reach across the sectarian divide. The fact that the house eventually collapses in on itself, blown apart from within by one of Cormac's descendants and from outside by the British Army, turns it into an (over-determined) symbol of the Northern Irish situation where future possibilities are portrayed as doomed in this novel by endless, and partial, recounting of old grievances. Not surprisingly, Maureen's novel never gets written. Duffaud's willingness to experiment with postmodern literary techniques in *A Wreath Upon the Dead* provides a welcome change from the predominantly realist mode used by female novelists to document the experience of living through the Troubles.[77]

POPULAR FICTION

The 1980s and '90s were a time when Irish women writers, taking up where their nineteenth-century predecessors left off, made a highly successful foray into the mass market. Their writing was not always confined to that traditional staple of women's mass-market reading, romance: indeed the opening of Maeve Binchy's best-selling novel *Light A Penny Candle* (1982) suggests that traditional romance was going out of fashion. Violet closes her library book feeling a sense of dissatisfaction at the romance plot's lack of connection with the circumstances of her own life. Like their nineteenth-century predecessors, women used the popular novel as a means of exploring social problems. Despite its predominantly sentimental and nostalgic tone, *Light A Penny Candle* features an abortion, illegal in the UK at the period in which the novel is set and in 1982 still illegal in Ireland. Binchy's novel also touches on dysfunctional families, alcoholism and sexual problems within marriage.[78]

Many popular Irish novels by women explored the theme of motherhood. Maura Richards's *Two to Tango* (1981) is a 'problem' novel centred on the predicament of the single pregnant woman in 1970s Dublin. In the face of her family's disapproval, Brig, like Rose in *Stars in the Daytime*, is determined to go through with the pregnancy and to show that it is possible, despite the enormous social and financial obstacles, to live as a single mother in Ireland. Richards's following novel *Interlude* (1982) was the luridly coloured paperback that alerted Emma Donoghue to the existence of Irish lesbian fiction.[79]

Mary Rose Callaghan's *Mothers* (1982), prefaced by the famous line from Woolf that 'we think back through our mothers if we are women', looks back at three generations of single mothers and the different dilemmas they have faced. Unwanted pregnancy also features in Emma Cooke's novels *A Single Sensation* (1981) and *Eve's Apple* (1985), the latter with a different twist: not a young girl but an older married woman faces the dilemma of what to do about an unplanned pregnancy in a country that is about to seal its opposition to abortion with a referendum. Caroline Blackwood's third novel *The Fate of*

Mary Rose (1981), a psychological thriller, portrays a mother whose cruelties and neuroses are visited on her young daughter to chilling effect. Ita Daly's *A Singular Attraction* (1987) charts the emotional development of a 38-year-old virgin, Pauline, after her mother's death. The novel, which has resonances with Janet McNeill's *The Maiden Dinosaur*, depicts Pauline gradually breaking away from a lifetime of hostility to her mother and beginning to experiment with sex. *A Singular Attraction* teeters on the brink of romance but finally resists the romantic ending in favour of presenting Pauline as a self-assured independent woman who has learned how to be comfortable in her own skin. In Maude Casey's *Over the Water* (1987), nationality impinges on the mothering task, as it does in Johnston's *The Illusionist*, and causes a division between Bridie, trying to raise her children according to Irish ways in London, and her children, who feel more at home in England.

Not all popular fiction by Irish women was confined to the domestic: Val Mulkerns's *Very Like A Whale: A Novel of Dublin Life* (1986) paints an uncompromising picture of a city ravaged by unscrupulous property developers and drug traffickers. Unemployment, violence and sexual abuse rule the lives of the children in the inner city school where Ben takes a job as a maths teacher. Also in this decade, Ruth Dudley Edwards began her career in popular fiction with her first detective story, *Corridors of Death* (1982), set, however, not in Ireland but in Whitehall in London. In the following decade, Catherine Brophy was to publish the first feminist science fiction novel by an Irish writer, *Dark Paradise* (1991).

By the end of the 1980s, a decade that had not on the whole been kind to Irish women, women's voices had become stronger and angrier. There was an increased willingness even in popular fiction to challenge Catholic notions of female behaviour and to expose the limitations of the family unit on which the Irish Constitution had been founded. Maeve Binchy's *Silver Wedding* (1988) takes apart the dark secrets lying behind the apparently happy family life of the Doyle family, while Ita Daly's more literary *Dangerous Fictions* (1989) exposes the insanity that lurks behind the dangerous fictions of the perfect wife and mother. Bearing some similarity to Elizabeth Bowen's *Death of the Heart* where an immaculate wife occupies a fashionable sitting room while her husband takes refuge drinking in the basement and a young girl on the brink of adulthood is damaged by the tensions between them, Daly's novel portrays distorted mother–daughter (and mother-in-law–daughter-in-law) relationships playing themselves out across the generations.

Mother–daughter relationships continued to feature centrally in 1990s popular fiction by Irish women but there was often now an attempt to portray the mother figure in a more favourable light.[80] In Clairr O'Connor's comic novel *Belonging* (1991), Deirdre, a lecturer in feminist literature, only develops as an adult when she begins to acknowledge her mother's influence. Deirdre turns her mother's sewing room into a study and, surrounded by samples of her mother's lace work hanging on the walls, starts to write her long-delayed book on Emily Dickinson, inspired by her mother's creative energies. Not only were mothers beginning to be portrayed more favourably, they were at last, as in Johnston's *Two Moons*, being given their own voice: in Lia Mills's *Another Alice* (1996), Alice recounts her attempts to overcome her childhood experiences at the hands of a violent, abusive father in order to avoid passing on the damage to her own daughter, while Mary O'Donnell's first novel *The Light-Makers* (1992) explores, through Hanna's voice, the experience of infertility.

Popular novels from the 1990s, such as Moya Roddy's *The Long Way Home* (1992), Eithne Strong's autobiographical novel *The Love Riddle* (1993), Aisling Maguire's *Breaking Out* (1996) and the lesbian novels of Linda Cullen (*The Kiss*, 1990) and Mary Dorcey (*Biography of Desire*, 1997), portray Irish women at odds with their culture and struggling to liberate themselves from an upbringing that no longer fits with the person they wish to become. Both *The Kiss* and *Biography of Desire* reveal the culture of secrecy that still weighed on the lives of Irish lesbians. June Levine's *A Season of Weddings* (1992) centres on a paradox that Nora, a supposedly liberated Irish woman, has coped less well with the constraints of her culture than Maya, who lives in the apparently more conservative society of India. Through her romantic friendship with Maya, Nora discovers that women have a universal culture that transcends national boundaries.

As well as exploring other cultures, women's fiction went back into Irish history. Aisling Foster's clever and funny novel *Safe in the Kitchen* (1993) spans half a century of Irish history, taking in some amusing vignettes of Éamon de Valera and the republican widows, in its account of IRA fundraisers in America who become involved in the fate of the Russian crown jewels. Kathleen Ferguson's *The Maid's Tale* (1994), recounted through the voice of Brigid Keen, housekeeper for thirty-three years to Father Mann in Derry, resembles a piece of oral history in its retelling of the tight hold the Catholic Church kept over women in Northern Ireland. Brought up in the 1950s in an orphanage run by the Sisters of Charity in Derry, Brigid is trained into obedience and humility till she loses all intellectual curiosity and becomes a shadow of the person she might have been. It takes Brigid fifty years to free herself from the church's influence and gain a sense of self and ownership of her life through telling her story.[81]

Mary O'Donnell portrays the clash between traditional and contemporary Ireland in *Virgin and the Boy* (1996) where The Guardians of Christian Destiny, defenders of conservative Catholic Ireland, do battle against the Irish female rock star, Virgin (Ginnie Maloney), on account of her sexually explicit stage performances. Like the anti-abortionists in *Down by the River*, The Guardians of Christian Destiny are determined to preserve de Valera's vision of Ireland's moral purity against the encroachments of the modern world, finding in their battle to root out moral corruption a power denied to them in their daily lives: before joining The Guardians, Hilary Dunne was a failed schoolteacher. *Virgin and the Boy* reveals the way in which Catholic imagery continues to influence, not just The Guardians, but characters like the misogynist Leo Kilgallen, politician and entrepreneur, and even the post-Catholic lives of Ginnie and 'the boy', her fan Luke. The novel lapses into melodrama as Hilary's perverted sexuality is revealed in her attempt to imprison Ginny and starve her into submission.

O'Donnell's *The Elysium Testament* (1999), a more accomplished novel, is an uncanny maternal narrative focused through the unreliable voice of Nina, mother of an epileptic son, Roland. By juxtaposing Nina's account with letters from Nina's daughter accusing her mother of physically and emotionally abusing Roland, O'Donnell raises questions about contemporary Irish parenting. Both Nina and her husband are too busy with their careers to pay proper attention to Roland, and in the modern Ireland of 'self-interest and doing', visionaries like Roland, or even Nina herself, are liable to be medicalised or shut up in mental hospitals.[82] The novel is both a comment on Celtic Tiger Ireland and an exploration of Nina's atavistic fears around motherhood.[83]

If *The Elysium Testament* depicts the uncanny emerging in domestic space, so too do Mullingar-born Josephine Hart's sparse, elegantly written novels evoking extreme states of mind that end either in madness, as in *The Stillest Day* (1998), or in silence as in *Damage* (1991), a horror story of sexual obsession on the scale of a Greek tragedy. Hart's combination of psychological thriller with Gothic horror creates unique and compelling worlds that blur the distinction between popular and literary fiction. In the following decade, in *The Truth About Love* (2009), Hart approached more directly the family tragedies that lay behind her fiction.

Kate O'Riordan also specialises in depicting psychological tensions within traumatised families. Sometimes, as in her first novel *Involved* (1995), portraying the O'Neills, a working-class Catholic family in Belfast during the Troubles, her writing spills over into a full-blown thriller. Beneath his respectable veneer of schoolteacher, Eamon O'Neill is an IRA hard man whose sadistic violence goes hand in hand with a puritanism that does not allow him to acknowledge the sexual thrill he gets from acts of cruelty. His father's early and violent death has left Eamon entangled in an oedipal relationship with his mother, Ma, a manipulative and hate-filled Mother Ireland figure who looks the other way as Eamon carries on his career of violence. Belfast during the Troubles is vividly evoked through the eyes of an outsider, Kitty, a doctor's daughter from a Big House in west Cork and girlfriend of Eamon's brother Danny, and an atmosphere of fear and suspense is built up as Kitty learns the hard way how difficult it is to escape being drawn into Belfast's violence and sectarianism.

O'Riordan's *The Boy in the Moon* (1997) portrays a private family trauma when the death of Brian's twin brother Noel in childhood finds its uncanny repetition in the next generation in the death of Brian's son Sam. Sam's death triggers post-traumatic stress disorder in Brian, who believes himself also responsible for Noel's death. Brian's wife Julia uncovers the truth of this traumatised family by listening to the concealed words of perhaps its most traumatised member, Brian's mother Margaret, who has died worn out by constant childbearing and drudgery. With the help of Margaret's journal, Julia comes to understand that the uncanny repetition of two accidental deaths at Brian's hands is only apparent: it was in fact his father Jeremiah who caused Noel's death and who is also indirectly responsible for Sam's death through instilling in Brian a belief that masculinity should be equated with fearlessness. Published at a time when revelations of the scale of child abuse in Ireland were beginning to emerge, *The Boy in the Moon* becomes, like Anne Enright's novel

The Gathering, an elegy for 'the blind, trusting love of constantly betrayed children everywhere'.[84]

EMMA DONOGHUE

Emma Donoghue's fiction is situated on the thin line between literary and popular fiction. Born in Dublin in 1969, Donoghue studied English and French at University College, Dublin before writing her doctoral thesis at Cambridge on the concept of friendship in eighteenth-century English fiction. Her first novel, *Stir-fry* (1994), is both a story of an innocent confronting the world and also a lesbian coming-out novel set in UCD student circles. Sharing a flat in Dublin with an older lesbian couple, seventeen-year-old Maria from the country learns to acknowledge her hitherto suppressed lesbian sexuality and to distinguish among the stir-fry of her emotions between lust and love. The novel ends with Maria on the verge of her first lesbian love affair but without, however, a public declaration of her sexual orientation, a declaration that will surely bring her into conflict with her conservative Catholic mother. In an interview, Donoghue explained: '*Stir-fry* is all about drifting into attraction, rather than discovering a crystal-clear sense of identity.'[85] The open ending conveys a sense of the fluidity of desire that is one of the main themes of this novel.

Hood (1995) is a bereavement novel that dwells on the attractions and comforts of the closeted lesbian life but also on the emotional and psychological dangers of not being out. Pen's preference for the closet (a necessity if she is to keep her teaching job at the Immaculate Conception Convent) catches up with her when her long-term partner, thirty-year-old Cara, is killed in a car accident and Pen has no means of openly expressing her grief. The novel focuses on a week in Pen's life after she has received news of Cara's death and culminates with her on the verge of coming out to her mother in an outpouring of grief. Yet *Hood* is far from lugubrious as Pen goes about her daily, closeted life in the everyday Dublin world of work, family and Catholicism while simultaneously recalling in a series of flashbacks her funny, warm, occasionally trying life with Cara. The novel is narrated through Pen's voice, thus drawing the reader in to experience the private life of a lesbian in a heterosexual world. *Hood* rejects politicised lesbian separatism, satirised in the Amazon Attic episodes, in favour of lesbian integration into mainstream Irish society.[86] The fact that lesbianism could now be openly taken as a subject in Irish writing reflects the increased visibility of gays and lesbians in Irish life after 1993, the year that homosexuality was finally declared legal.

Éilís Ní Dhuibhne

After gaining a doctorate in Folklore and Medieval Literature from UCD, Éilís Ní Dhuibhne (1954–) worked for many years as a keeper at the National Library of Ireland and lecturer on folklore. One of the most observant Irish writers of social change, Ní Dhuibhne combines sharp and often witty observations with a deep understanding of Irish history, values and mythology. Social comment as well as concern for environmental issues are to the fore in her first novel, *The Bray House* (1990), a dystopia set in the future after a nuclear disaster has devastated Ireland and Britain.[87] Observations on Ireland's lack of environment-friendly policies are set in the context of a quest novel (*Robinson Crusoe* is one of the many intertextual references). The novel's highly unreliable narrator, Robin Lagerlof, is a Swedish archaeo-anthropologist leading an initial exploratory expedition to Ireland. The landscape the expedition discovers in Ireland – ashes and cinders – reflects Robin's inner psychical landscape after a traumatic and neglected childhood and the novel raises questions about the anthropologist's role as Robin interprets her findings at the MacHugh house in Bray through the lens of her own experiences and prejudices. The appearance of a survivor, Maggie Byrne, further casts doubt on the reliability of Robin's methods.[88] *The Bray House* also explores more general issues of power and gender and skilfully mixes several discourses and narrative styles: Robin's mercilessly bleak and self-centred account of the voyage, her scientific but unwittingly humorous report on her findings at the Bray House, correspondence between the MacHugh family, newspaper extracts describing Ireland as an unequal, environmentally damaged society insouciant about the dangers of nuclear energy.

The Dancers Dancing (1999), shortlisted for the Orange Prize, continues the environmental theme and explores what is a central rite of passage in the lives of many young Irish as thirteen-year-old Orla spends a summer in the Gaeltacht studying Irish language and culture at Irish college. *The Dancers Dancing* is another example of an Irish female *Bildungsroman*, with nature in this case stimulating the heroine's awakening as Orla becomes aware of the gap between culture and nature and learns to inhabit and to celebrate that in-between space. *The Dancers Dancing* problematises divisions between urban and rural, male and female, adults and children, Gaelic and English speaking, Catholic and Protestant, North and South as her time in the west of Ireland leads Orla to question the repressive Catholic, patriarchal and class constraints of her upbringing in 1970s Dublin. The opening section of the novel, with its discussion of the unreliability of maps and the prejudices of map makers, alerts the reader to this question of the ideological constraints under which Orla lives.[89]

The influence of her urban culture on Orla gradually diminishes during her stay in the west. Her concern over details of social hierarchy, the shameful poverty of her home in comparison with Aisling's, for example, lessens. In contrast with life in Dublin, where girls are told what they must do so often that they lose all sense of themselves, immersion in nature reveals to Orla a primal, instinctual, fearless self. Ní Dhuibhne avoids an essentialist link between women and nature by the presence of an older Orla as narrator, commenting on the experiences of her younger self in a detached and ironic manner and pointing out the dangers Orla has ignored. Nature is harsh and unpredictable and women are tough too, and their power can be death-dealing: there is an echo of Keane's *Two Days in Aragon* in the scene where Orla discovers a heap of baby skulls and skeletons in the river, babies killed by desperate mothers. Orla discovers her own murderous potential when, out of a spurious sense of social shame, she abandons her sick old aunt Annie on the floor of her barn. Since Annie represents an older Irish culture and way of life, Ní Dhuibhne has likened Orla's action here to what has been done to the Irish language – not killing it but letting it slowly die out: 'Orla represents the postcolonial Irish who are ashamed of their Irishness.'[90]

The return to the 1990s at the end of the novel demonstrates how once again the landscape in the west of Ireland is threatened by economic and cultural forces from outside. A heritage centre now stands in the middle of Orla's wild valley. The wild raspberries Orla ate by the side of the burn are not 'a taste of a wonderful future', as she once thought, but 'a residue of a wild world that is past, or passing'.[91] The question *The Dancers Dancing* leaves us with, underlined by Ní Dhuibhne's use of Gerald Manley Hopkins's poem

'Inversnaid', is, if the west has been appropriated by tourism and by a heritage industry that threatens to congeal its identity, where will a girl like Orla go in the future to free herself from the restrictions of her environment? *The Dancers Dancing* interrogates the ethos of a nation which places such an emphasis on the land yet is a bad custodian of it.

POSTMODERNISM

Éilís Ní Dhuibhne's combination of postmodern literary techniques with older modes of storytelling is characteristic of the 1990s, when postmodernism became a feature of Irish women's fiction. We have already seen aspects of postmodernism in the novels of Edna O'Brien and Jennifer Johnston from this period.[92] Part fable, *Mother of Pearl* (1996) by Mary Morrissy (1957–) is set, possibly in the 1950s, against a generalised Irish background with many features – shipbuilding, biblical fundamentalism, the rise of sectarian violence – that evoke Northern Ireland. As Linden Peach suggests: 'the novel is not so much concerned with an identifiable, geographical environment, but a larger ideological environment.'[93] Christian ideology pervades the novel, from the title, 'Mother of Pearl', one of the names for Mary, to the many biblical allusions (Lot's wife, barren women, Samson's judgement on the two mothers, Moses's adoption by Pharoah's daughter, the Annunciation). Morrissy employs postmodern techniques to unpick idealised images of motherhood and replace them with descriptions of maternity based on female bodily experience. The mothering Irene receives from her Catholic mother Ellen is shaped by environmental factors: poverty and marriage to a violent husband have petrified Ellen's emotions so that when Irene is discovered to have TB, conscious of the social stigma attached to the disease, Ellen banishes her daughter from the family home. Catholic idealisations of the mother figure ring hollow in the face of a motherhood thwarted by poverty, while the portrait of eighteen-year-old Rita who resents her unborn baby for robbing her of her girlish identity provides an ironic commentary on the figure of the teenage Virgin Mary. Indeed, Rita's friend Imelda refers to Pearl's birth as a virgin birth: 'I mean, it was your first time, wasn't it?'[94]

By contrast, there is an instant physical and emotional bond between baby Pearl and Irene, who abducts her from the hospital. Irene, too, is a virgin mother, though one who is practised in giving sexual relief to men in the TB sanatorium where, in a parodic echo of Catholic worship of Mary, she becomes the focus of men's desires and aspirations. Marriage to the impotent Stanley ensures that Irene remains technically a virgin. Living in a society that expects wives to become mothers, Irene abducts Rita's baby in order to complete their 'holy family'. This lasts until Pearl is recognised and returned to the reluctant Rita, who renames the child Mary but cannot suppress the feeling that Mary is not the Hazel Mary she gave birth to but a stranger. Nor is this off-hand and indifferent Rita the mother that Pearl/Mary, with her submerged memory of Irene's calm, confident mothering, is looking for. The novel cuts a swathe through the notion of a biological mothering instinct. Rita's inability to provide Pearl/Mary with the mothering for which she yearns in turn affects her grown-up daughter's ability to mother. Lacking the resources to mother, Pearl terminates her pregnancy by Jeff. Pearl is doomed to be the daughter waiting for her mother to return while she tries in vain to mother the lost little girl inside herself. Meanwhile Irene, who waits across the river for her daughter to be found, displays, in the words of one critic, 'a maternal devotion that refuses to be corralled inside conventional human bonds'.[95] The portrayal of mothers and daughters in this complex and multi-layered novel disrupts the mother–son iconography central to the Christian religion and unravels Catholic myths of motherhood.

The postmodern novels of Emer Martin (1968–), *Breakfast in Babylon* (1995) and *More Bread or I'll Appear* (1999), portray a younger generation of Irish untrammelled by history or even by nationality. Isolt in *Breakfast in Babylon* is the young Irish woman as drifter, moving from one squat to another, associating with drug dealers, refugees and petty criminals. Unlike the earlier heroines of Kate and Edna O'Brien, Isolt never feels a pull back to Dublin; nor, unlike Madden's Aisling, has she left behind any great trauma. She has simply drifted away from home for a summer job in Paris and never stopped moving. In *More Bread or I'll Appear*, Ashling leads a similarly wandering life and her uncle observes: 'I suppose I saw her as part of the new generation in Ireland. We had grown up in the shadows, but here were Catholics raised with surety as the new dominant class. I don't know what happened to her. Why she didn't want anything. Why she ignored history.'[96]

On one level, *One Day As A Tiger* (1997) by Anne Haverty (1959–) positions itself at the heart of the Irish writing tradition, describing the beauty of the

Irish landscape and the slow rituals of country life as evocatively as any of John McGahern's books. On another level, it is Greek tragedy in the Irish countryside recounted in a playful postmodern style with a genetically modified lamb thrown into the mix. Marty's immature and self-deceiving narrative of his love for his sister-in-law Etti moves back and forth in time and contains many gaps and fissures. He deceives himself, for example, over his capacity for love, taking in and caring for Missy, a genetically engineered lamb, but abandoning her when she becomes an inconvenience. *One Day As A Tiger* moves beyond a rural Irish love story to embrace the comic, the weird and the cyborg. As Marty scrutinises Missy in order to work out what she lacks to be fully human, the novel becomes a meditation on what it means to be human in a postmodern age.[97]

ANNE ENRIGHT

One of the strongest new Irish voices of the 1990s was Anne Enright. Born in Dublin in 1962, Enright read English and philosophy at Trinity College, Dublin and subsequently studied creative writing at the University of East Anglia under Angela Carter. While she was working in RTÉ as a producer/ director her collection of short stories *The Portable Virgin* (1991) appeared and she was immediately hailed as 'a new voice in Irish fiction'.[98] Enright quickly established a reputation for a playful, innovative, postmodern even postfeminist style of writing and in her use of parody and pastiche she was perceived as following in the satirical tradition of Jonathan Swift and Flann O'Brien.[99] She has described her use of postmodernism as 'an attempt to be more honest and not less',[100] and regards her work as at odds with much of Irish mimetic realism:

> Irish prose tends to cling to the world in an unconfident way. This is a table, this is a chair … The world should be very ordinary and not to be doubted. Make fiction as close to fact as possible. But I don't think that fiction is fact. I feel like saying, you made it up, admit that you made it up, and you can make anything up.[101]

Despite her break with the realist mode, Enright's work echoes in a postmodern context many of the themes of Irish women's fiction from the 1980s and '90s, particularly in her attention to motherhood.

Enright's first novel *The Wig My Father Wore* (1995), set in contemporary Dublin, explores love, sex, the family, religion and redemption against the background of Grace's work on a tacky TV show, *LoveQuiz*, and her love for Stephen, an angel who turns up on her doorstep having committed suicide in Ontario in 1934. Like the stories in *The Portable Virgin*, *The Wig My Father Wore* cuts across gender binaries, challenges notions of fixed personal and national identities, and blurs the borders between fantasy and reality, sanity and insanity. The life Grace is leading is in every way inauthentic: television gives her access to money, power and sex but what she lacks, Stephen tells her, are 'purity, wisdom and grace'.[102] The wig worn by her father, which cannot be mentioned in front of him, becomes a metaphor for the secrets at the heart of Grace's family life. Under Stephen's influence, the world-weary and cynical Grace gradually undergoes a purifying experience until her body starts to resemble an idealised girlish body, while Stephen becomes more fleshly so that at the end they make love in what has been described as Enright's reworking of the Immaculate Conception, with Grace as an ironic Virgin Mary.[103] Pregnant, Grace gives up her television job and moves to the west of Ireland to become an alternative Mother Ireland. In this way Enright, like Morrissy in *Mother of Pearl*, not only deconstructs stereotypes of gender and Irish national identity, but also reclaims and reinvents myths around the Virgin Mary and Mother Ireland.

Enright explained of her early books: 'They dealt with ideas of purity, because the chastity of Irish women was one of the founding myths of the Nation State.'[104] She draws on her experience as a director to bring the conventions of television to fiction: the schedules, the credits, the camera angles, fast cutting and editing. In postmodernist style, *The Wig My Father Wore* employs pastiche, parody, magic realism, incongruous juxtapositions, fractured narrative, fragmented history, and an anarchic humour that relies on puns, word play and inversion. When the novel first appeared, reviewers used words like 'clever', 'unsettling', 'unpredictable' and 'immensely sophisticated' to describe it.

Enright's second novel *What Are You Like?* (2000) uses the subject of twins separated at birth to explore themes of loss, exile and the fragility of identity. Mirrored identities, or the lack of them, recur throughout the novel, lending it to analysis in terms of Lacan's mirror stage. Both twins lack a maternal mirror to give them a solid sense of identity; they live with a vacuum at the centre of their lives and an uncanny sense of their lives being off-kilter. Maria, raised in Dublin, 'had always felt like someone else. She had always felt like the wrong girl.'[105] In England, her twin sister Rose feels she was born with 'a hole in her life' and searches for the woman who gave her away.[106] Reunited at the end of the novel, the twins' individual identities become stronger and the novel has been interpreted as a comment on Irish emigration and the shadow cast by absent members on their families back home.[107]

What Are You Like? is, like much of Enright's work, about the secrets at the heart of Irish life: 'this incredible country,' thinks Rose. 'Where people did the most appalling things, and shut their mouths, and stayed put.'[108] Enright has used the term 'fragmented' to describe her early novels and she has linked this fragmentation to the political situation of Ireland in the 1980s: 'I lived in an incoherent country. They were slightly surreal, because Ireland was unreal.'[109] *What Are You Like?* is also, like so much Irish fiction in these decades, a comment on the iconisation of the mother in Irish nationalism at the expense of the realities of mothers' lives: the twins' mother Anna is sacrificed to a law that values the life of an unborn child over that of the mother. Only at the end of the novel does Anna speak from beyond the grave to tell her story.

Interviewed in 1995, the poet and short story writer Mary Dorcey commented: 'The Ireland I live in now is so far removed from the Ireland of twenty years ago it might be another country. And the Ireland of my childhood [1950s and '60s] remembered from this perspective seems like another planet.'[110] The same might be said of Irish women's fiction, which gained in confidence during this period with writers moving away from the angry and sometimes didactic feminism of 1970s and 1980s realist fiction into a more playful and risk-taking postmodernism. In the hands of writers like Mary Morrissy, Éilís Ní Dhuibhne, Anne Haverty and Anne Enright, the postmodernist novel picked apart assumptions about Irish lives, at the same time as it subjected the process of story telling itself to scrutiny.

The deeper artistic self-consciousness and greater attention to questions of aesthetics in Irish women's fiction noted in the previous chapter continued, as evidenced not only by postmodernist experimentalism but also by the reworking of myth and legend in the novels of Julia O'Faolain, Mary Morrissy and Éilís Ní Dhuibhne, the use of the unreliable narrator in the work of Molly Keane and Mary O'Donnell, Dorothy Nelson's experiments with narrative voice, Frances Molloy's use of dialect and the picaresque, and Briege Duffaud's historiographical metafiction. Diversity of form became the hallmark of Irish women's fiction as it had rarely been in the past. The rapid urbanisation, secularisation and consumerism of the Ireland of the late 1990s led to further diversity and experimentation in the novel of the Celtic Tiger era, discussed in the following chapter.

Chapter 7

THE NEW WOMAN IN THE CELTIC TIGER YEARS AND AFTER

CHICK LIT

Chick Lit: The New Woman's Fiction (2006), edited by Suzanne Ferris and Mallory Young, takes chick lit to be the new woman's fiction. However, chick lit, spawned from Helen Fielding's *Bridget Jones's Diary* (1996) in the UK and Candace Bushnell's *Sex and the City* (1996) in the US, is very different from its late nineteenth-century counterpart New Woman fiction that, as we saw in Chapter 2, offered inspiring and often angry portrayals of women's struggles to forge a life of their own in a patriarchal culture. In Ireland, chick lit is embodied by such names as Marian Keyes, Patricia Scanlan, Sheila O'Flanagan, Cathy Kelly and Cecilia Ahern and their novels often sell in hundreds of thousands. Like New Woman writing, chick lit is an international phenomenon but Irish chick lit novelists generally adapt the formula to suit the preoccupations and lifestyle of an Irish readership.

Despite arguments from its defenders that chick lit puts women's daily lives at its centre, speaks frankly about female sexuality, deals with important social issues such as domestic violence, drug addiction and alcoholism, and grants women commercial success in a male-dominated publishing world, many critics regard Irish chick lit as inextricably linked to the consumerism and self-obsession of the Celtic Tiger era (roughly 1994 to 2008).[1] Many Irish authors of chick lit have had careers in the media, journalism, modelling and advertising, and the genre's primary aim is to entertain rather than to provoke thought. Focusing on details of women's physical appearance and their search for the perfect male, chick lit ties in well with Naomi Wolf's analysis of women's postfeminist disempowerment in *The Beauty Myth* (1991), where Wolf argues that, though women may have equal access to education and employment, their oppression is now interiorised, and one element of this is the psychological pressure to possess the perfect body. Jessica Jernigan argues: 'Most chick lit is grounded in a jumbled, half-fantasy version of reality, a reality in which a better wardrobe, a better body, and a better man are not yet out of reach.'[2] The question is: does chick lit's obsession with fashion, appearance and named brands provide women with a means of expressing their identity, or does it simply buy into the capitalist consumer culture, at its height in Celtic Tiger Ireland, giving women freedom but only to consume? Certainly Debbie Ging has argued that unrestrained consumerism in Ireland during the Celtic Tiger years had a retrograde effect on gender roles: 'the increasingly commercial media-scape in Ireland has enabled deeply conservative images and ideologies of gender to proliferate.'[3] The commodification of everything has included gender roles.

Chick lit's defenders argue that the emphasis on clothes, shopping and dating are postfeminism's take on contemporary women's lives; in other words, feminism with the fun put back in. These novels, it is argued, show young women enjoying their femininity with a twist of knowing irony. The question remains: when is attention to the minutiae of appearance ironic and when does it segue into internalisation of an obsession with the ideal feminine shape as constant shopping, use of beauty products, and maintenance of a stern beauty regime become essential to chick lit heroines' self-presentation and self-fashioning? The genre raises questions about the re-emergence of gender stereotypes in the first decade of the twenty-first century, about young women's relations to feminism, to postfeminism and, not least, to each other, in the chick lit's heroine's constant monitoring, not only of her own appearance, but also that of other women.

Chick lit may be women's writing, but it is not women's literature, lacking as it does any imaginative use of language, inventive metaphors, layers of meaning, complex characters, innovative structures. The language employed is thin, accomplished only in its humour and its lively use of slang. In language, plot and depiction of women, the novels avoid posing a challenge to the reader; they are essentially for pleasure, escapism and self-indulgence, ideal reading for the beach or in bed. They may raise serious issues – Devlin's dilemma in Patricia Scanlan's *City Girl* (1990) as to whether to have an abortion – but, as in much nineteenth-century popular fiction by Irish women, the solutions provided are utopian in a way that only reinforces the *status quo*.[4] Like the nineteenth-century popular novel, Irish chick lit may prove of interest to future social commentators; for those concerned with literature, Anna Weinberg provides the clinching criticism of this genre: 'Inside their dust jackets covered with shopping bags, martini glasses, shoes or purses, many of these titles really are trash: trash that imitates other, better books that could have ushered in a new wave of smart, postfeminist writing.'[5] Fortunately Ireland has had a good number of smart postfeminist writers whose works cast a sharper eye on Irish life during the Celtic Tiger era than the authors of chick lit.

ÉILÍS NÍ DHUIBHNE

Conspicuous consumption as a theme did not enter Irish women's fiction in the Celtic Tiger era: writers could find precedents in Elizabeth Bowen's *Eva Trout* or Maria Edgeworth's *Belinda*, a novel that portrays fashionable society driven by a consumerism based largely on female extravagance. For her critique of the Celtic Tiger years in *Fox, Swallow, Scarecrow* (2007), Éilís Ní Dhuibhne drew inspiration from Tolstoy's *Anna Karenina* in order to juxtapose the life of Dublin-based Anna Kelly Sweeney, selfish and worldly writer of children's fiction, with Leo Kavanagh, idealistic owner of a small, subsidised, poetry publishing house devoted to the Irish language revival, who lives in the Gaeltacht. For readers familiar with Tolstoy's novel there are pleasures in tracing parallels with *Anna Karenina* in the progress of the adulterous affair between Anna and the war reporter Vincy, in her relations with her erring brother Gerry, and in her marriage to the reserved but highly successful property developer Alex. Levin in *Anna Karenina* is widely interpreted as representing Tolstoy himself, and his ideas on, for example, the superiority of country life to the city are not submitted to irony as Leo's are in Ní Dhuibhne's novel. In *Fox, Swallow, Scarecrow*, the Tolstoyan contrast between the hollowness of urban life and the authenticity of life in the country is a false one. The world inhabited by Leo is factitious: the Gaeltacht has been taken over by non-Irish-speaking foreigners and wealthy families from Dublin, the resulting loss of community means that Leo is often bored and lonely there, and in the end he readily sacrifices his devotion to the Irish language to his love for Kate, a non-Irish speaker.

The loss of the Irish language is just one of the many losses that lie behind the apparent gains of the Celtic Tiger years charted in *Fox, Swallow, Scarecrow*. In the opening pages, as Anna walks through Dublin to attend a fashionable book launch, Ní Dhuibhne pinpoints signs of consumerism in the clothes of the people on the street, their air of easy confidence, and the seductive window displays of high-class shops on Grafton Street. Beneath the surface glamour, though, are the Dubliners who are not participating in Ireland's success story – immigrants like Anna's Lithuanian cleaner Ludmilla, who rents a freezing boxroom in an ex-corporation house, the homeless man on the streets who follows Anna about, even Anna's brother Gerry, an undistinguished artist and middle-ranking civil servant priced out of the city centre property market.

The novel records other losses consequent on the Celtic Tiger lifestyle, for example the loss of the family unit: Alex, Anna and Rory live under the same roof, but lead such busy lives they barely meet and Rory is largely brought up by Ludmilla and Luz Mar, the Spanish au pair. Ireland's progress has led to environmental damage: Gerry and his wife argue whether it is right to cut down trees to make way for a new bus route. The frenetic pace of modern life leads to emotional shallowness: Anna doubts whether her love affair with Vincy could really be classed as a grand passion while Kate, a single woman with a frantically busy career, has no time to make friends. Other losses are highlighted: the loss of childhood innocence, the loss of imagination and, along with that, loss of originality. Anna realises that the children's book she has been writing is too much influenced by *Harry Potter* but that does not prevent her book in turn being plagiarised by her friend Lilian. There is a loss, too, of religious belief: Leo and Kate are obliged to attend a pre-marriage course arranged by the Catholic Church but this does not connect with their lives.

Fox, Swallow, Scarecrow portrays a society where consumers are never satiated and people lack meaningful inner lives. The end of the novel is ambivalent. Does it suggest Anna's loss of sanity in her inability to remember words, the tools of her trade? Or does her retreat to Annaghmakerrig represent a liberation from the hollowness of her life that will finally allow her to write something real?[6]

ANNE ENRIGHT

Anne Enright's *The Pleasure of Eliza Lynch* (2002) fictionalises the life of Eliza Lynch (1835–86) from County Cork who in the mid-nineteenth century became the mistress of Francisco Solano López, dictator of Paraguay, and mother of seven of his children. Historically, there have been two views of Eliza. She was either a national heroine who inspired Paraguayans during the devastating War of the Triple Alliance (1865–70) against Brazil, Argentina and Uruguay that wiped out 90 per cent of the male population or she was greedy and immoral, plundering Paraguay's wealth for herself and her family. Towards the end of the novel, Enright reveals that Eliza fled Ireland during the Famine, implying that memories of starvation in the Irish countryside are what drive her conspicuous consumption. This has led critics to suggest that the novel may be read as an oblique comment on the extravagances of Ireland's Celtic Tiger years, an interpretation confirmed by Enright in an interview.[7]

The novel is full of luscious, almost surreal, descriptions of the food, clothes and domestic interiors by which Eliza endeavours to consolidate her position as leading lady in Paraguay. Such conspicuous consumption serves to conceal the vacuum at the heart of Eliza's life: though she dazzles their husbands with imported French fashions and French food, Eliza is regarded by the wives of Paraguay as a fallen woman, an outsider to respectable bourgeois society, and her position as López's mistress, rather than wife, leaves her vulnerable to his increasingly insane whims. Eliza's transformation into a national icon for whom men are willing to lay down their lives is an indirect comment on the Mother Ireland topos that allows women to embody power but not to act on it. Eliza's surreal first-person narrative is juxtaposed to the dry, detached third-person narrative charting the Victorian masculinity of two male adventurers,

Dr Stewart and the engineer Whytehead, disintegrating under pressure from the foreignness of Paraguay.

The fractured narrative structure of *The Pleasure of Eliza Lynch*, chapters recounting the pregnant Eliza's river journey to Paraguay alternating with an account of her life there, serves to foreground Eliza's pregnant body and this may be interpreted as Enright's deliberate attempt to make visible the maternal body so often reduced to an object in discourses of the Irish nation.[8] Enright herself had given birth to her first child and was pregnant with her second while writing her next work, the non-fiction *Making Babies: Stumbling into Motherhood* (2004), in which her determined focus on her personal experience of the physical realities of childbirth and early motherhood and the socio-cultural context in which they took place may be seen as a political strategy to counter the discourses of maternity prevalent in Irish nationalism and Irish Catholicism, idealising mothers while censoring the female body and offering very little by way of practical help for mothers.

If *The Pleasure of Eliza Lynch* indirectly comments on the excessive consumption of the Celtic Tiger years, Enright's next novel *The Gathering* (2007) focuses on the dark side of Irish life as the secrets of four generations of the dysfunctional Hegarty family are filtered through the unreliable memory of Veronica Hegarty. Alcoholism, violence and child abuse have become standard themes in contemporary Irish fiction and this may be one of the reasons why, of all Enright's works, *The Gathering* has attracted most attention outside Ireland, winning the Man Booker Prize and finding an international readership. The main interest of the book lies, however, not so much in Veronica's bleak tale, but in her telling of it. Veronica's unreliability as narrator is related to her weak sense of self, passed down to her through several generations of Hegarty women. Uncertainty and doubt are the hallmarks of her narrative, together with the tricks memory plays: 'I would like to write down what happened in my grandmother's house the summer I was eight or nine, but I am not sure if it really did happen. I need to bear witness to an uncertain event.'[9]

At the heart of Veronica's narrative lies the childhood sexual abuse of her brother Liam by a family friend and Liam's subsequent suicide years later. Veronica's self-questioning stands in for the entire Irish nation's anguish in the 1990s at the revelations of child abuse carried out over decades in state- and church-run orphanages and, as in the work of Edna O'Brien, the traumatised family is made to represent the traumatised Irish nation. In 1998, Veronica may live a comfortable middle-class life with a husband who works in corporate finance, a convertible Saab and daughters who go to private schools, but the old Ireland continues to haunt her, as it haunted her compatriots throughout the Celtic Tiger years. 'This is the anatomy and mechanism of a family – a whole fucking country – drowning in shame,' she thinks.[10] Veronica's narrative explores the way it is possible to turn a blind eye to evidence of abuse and forget to remember for decades.

In *The Forgotten Waltz* (2011), Enright's challenge is to write in an original way about something as banal as a love affair with a married man set against the background of the lives of Dublin middle-class married thirty-somethings with children. Like Jeanette Winterson's *Written on the Body*, Enright's novel is a postmodern take on the romance plot: the chapter titles teasingly echo popular love songs, we know from the outset the course the love affair will take, Gina, the narrator, is not so much unreliable as uncertain about her feelings at any given moment: 'I can't be too bothered here, with chronology. The idea that if you tell it, one thing after another, then everything will make sense. It doesn't make sense.'[11] However, there are more moments of piercing tenderness and less flaunting of stylistic techniques than in the earlier novels and Enright has called this move towards her readers 'a more generous impulse'.[12]

The Forgotten Waltz is set between 2002 and 2009 and the marriages of Gina and Seán unravel in tandem with the Celtic Tiger economy, about which the narrator makes some caustic observations. At a pre-recession New Year's Day party: 'The Enniskerry husbands stood about and talked property: a three-pool complex in Bulgaria, a whole Irish block in Berlin.'[13] In the post Celtic Tiger era: 'If you listened to the car radio, all the money in the country had just evaporated, you could almost see it, rising off the rooftops like steam.'[14] The chief focus of the novel however is inward, on the details of the ebb and flow of the passion between Gina and Seán. The real truth of the story, signalled in the preface, only emerges at the end as Gina realises that the most important character has been not herself or Seán but Seán's fragile young daughter Evie, who in many ways may be said to have dictated the progress of her father's love affair. Childless, Gina has underestimated the bond between father and daughter, about which Enright writes here with sensitivity and perception. The novel writes beyond the romantic ending to the point where Gina finds herself taking responsibility for Evie while Seán is away possibly embarking on another affair.

By now, Enright has established a solid international reputation as one of Ireland's leading contemporary writers, noted for her clear eye for the truths about families, lovers, bodies, death and mothering that most people shy away from, for her voicing of the repressions of Irish culture and for the precision of her language.

POPULAR FICTION

Not all popular novels by women during this period can be classified as chick lit, and comparisons may be drawn between *The Pleasure of Eliza Lynch* and *The Story of Chicago May* (2005), a popular, fictionalised biography by Nuala O'Faolain (1940–2008).[15] Like Eliza Lynch, May Duignan emerged from rural Ireland (Edenmore in County Longford) to become internationally notorious as Chicago May (1874–1929). Less calculating than Enright's Eliza, and less ambitious, May was similarly motivated by greed: her first crime was to run off at nineteen with her family's life savings. Like Eliza, May lived a life of adventure, reinvention and grasping after money (though money never lasted long with May). If Eliza was a courtesan, May was frankly a streetwalker. Like Eliza, she was in danger of losing her identity behind the many different roles she performed.

At several points, the biography of this gangster and prostitute who wandered on the margins of society through Nebraska, New York, Chicago, Paris and London becomes specifically an Irish biography. May's years in Aylesbury jail for the attempted murder of a former lover allow O'Faolain to draw her into mainstream Irish women's history and imagine what it might have been like to have been an Irish woman incarcerated in an English jail during the First World War. She suggests that May would have met Constance Markiewicz, sent to Aylesbury prison in 1917 for her part in the Easter Rising, and that both women would have refused to go to chapel to pray for British victory. Adriana Bebiano is dubious about O'Faolain's wish to legitimise May here by linking her to the narrative of the Irish nation, pointing out that in the rest of her life May displayed little interest in questions of nationhood.[16] Nevertheless, for O'Faolain, her recuperation of May amounts to a political act. As Enright aimed to counter the kind of 'sneering excess' that Eliza Lynch provoked in her 'English-speaking biographers', so O'Faolain is similarly intent on rescuing Chicago May from previous biographers who tended to see her as an incarnation of evil: 'this or that ideologue goes to great pains to deny women like May a common humanity with the rest of us. She was excluded from every community. She was thrown out of memory. Well, I want her back in, and I want her such as she was.'[17]

The Celtic Tiger era is evoked in Kate O'Riordan's novel *The Memory Stones* (2003), through the observations of Nell Hennessy returning to Ireland after thirty years:

> Celtic Tiger, Riverdance, Bailey's Irish Cream, Guinness sexified, advertisements in French urging graduates *home* to work [...] Computer companies seeking support technicians, property developments in Dublin satellite towns. As far away as Leitrim is satellite now, Nell observes with astonishment. Celtic clothes, Celtic jewellery, Celtic glass, Celtic bars [...] Beautiful tinted photographs of islands off the west coast. Second homes in Portugal. Offshore investment companies. A country proudly selling itself. A country for sale.[18]

Like Enright in *The Gathering*, O'Riordan probes beneath this surface glamour to tell the story of a traumatised family extending over several generations. On one level, *The Memory Stones* depicts the 'simple' and 'obvious story' of Nell, a sixteen-year-old, pregnant, Irish girl sent over to England in 1970 to have her baby. Nell's case is rather different from the norm, however, for she is not propelled by the shame and guilt traditionally fostered on Irish unwed mothers (Nell's mother, Agnes, though disappointed, makes plans to accept the child into the family). Rather Nell uses this opportunity to reinvent herself abroad. She trains to become a wine expert and eventually moves to Paris where she buttons herself into an identity that superficially blends in with other smartly dressed Parisiennes of a certain age: 'Nevertheless, an invention. She will never be French. No matter how immaculately her tongue wraps round vowels, she is essentially a foreigner. In all the years she has lived here, there is no getting away from that.'[19] As in fiction by Edna O'Brien and

Deirdre Madden, *The Memory Stones* suggests that there is an essential Irish identity that cannot be erased.

Nell's determination to make something of herself has been pursued, the novel suggests, at the expense of her daughter Ali's happiness. A childhood of being moved at short notice to fit in with Nell's plans has left Ali with an emotional neediness, a resentful dependence on her mother in times of crisis, and low self-esteem that disrupts her relationship with her own daughter, Grace, leading to four generations of dysfunctional mothers and daughters in the novel. Nell's return to Ireland provides a turning point, allowing her to repair her fractured relationship with her daughter and to recognise that her mother, Agnes, did after all love her. What has been concealed and repressed in this family's life is brought into the light and, no longer a stranger in Ireland, Nell is able, finally, to bring the two parts of her life together, to translate between the two cultures in which she has lived. There is an early appearance of the immigrant theme as Nell contrasts her story with that of Bola, an asylum seeker from Nigeria who can never return home and yet for whom Ireland will always be a foreign place, though he hopes his daughter, or maybe his granddaughter, will come to think of Ireland as home.

Like *The Memory Stones*, Lia Mills's mass-market novel *Nothing Simple* (2005) takes for its theme an emigrant Irish mother. Ray leaves Ireland in the 1980s as a teenager to follow her husband Dermot to the US and the novel traces her developing maturity through raising four children. Unable to get a job because the US Immigration Service classifies her as a dependant, Ray becomes a sort of neighbourhood Irish mother. *Nothing Simple* juxtaposes the corporate world of big business, in which Dermot works as a cutting-edge computer scientist, with Ray's work of care and nurturance, childrearing and housekeeping that goes unregarded in Dermot's competitive world.[20]

Like their nineteenth-century predecessors, female Irish writers continued to use the novel form to highlight social problems. Mary Rose Callaghan's (1944–) *Billy, Come Home* (2007) exposes the underside of Celtic Tiger life, namely the appalling medical treatment handed out to the mentally ill. Billy is a schizophrenic and his sister Angela, who has acted as his caregiver since she was a child, reflects: 'No successful person in today's Ireland would dare admit that they suffered from depression, and people with schizophrenia were pariahs. Psycho was the word frequently used in the press.'[21]

Writing very readable but intelligent books, Christine Dwyer Hickey has successfully carved out a niche for herself in that difficult middle ground between literary and mass-market fiction with her portrayals of late twentieth-century Dublin through the voice of a young girl (*Tatty*, 2004) and a dying man (*The Cold Eye of Heaven*, 2011). In *Last Train from Liguria* (2010) Hickey updates a Kate O'Brien theme in the story of Bella Stuart, an Irish woman who works as governess to a Jewish Italian family amid a background of rising fascism in 1930s Italy.

Emma Donoghue

In Emma Donoghue's *The Landing* (2007), references to Celtic Tiger Ireland provide an ironic backdrop to the long-distance love affair between Síle, a globe-trotting cabin crew attendant for an Irish airline, and Jude, who lives in Ireland, Ontario, a small town that resembles rural Ireland of the 1940s and '50s rather than modern-day Ireland with its skinny lattes and sky-high property prices. In the main, however, recovering women's history became the focus of Donoghue's novels in this period. *Slammerkin* (2000), *Life Mask* (2004) and *The Sealed Letter* (2008) comprise a trilogy set in, respectively, the lower classes, upper classes and middle classes of British society. These are solid page-turners, steeped in their period, often focusing on a real historical event selected in order to unpick the operations of a patriarchal society in which women struggled to secure their independence and find their voice. At the same time the trilogy demonstrates postmodern scepticism about the way in which history is transmitted and the difficulty of arriving at a single truth.

Inspired by the story of Mary Saunders, a teenage prostitute hanged in 1764 for murdering her employer, *Slammerkin* portrays the lives of London prostitutes and Welsh seamstresses. Welsh-born Mary is instructed by a more knowing London prostitute, Doll, in the cultural significance of clothes and, like Eliza Lynch, learns which clothes to wear to attract men and which to mimic the appearance of a respectable woman. Like Eliza, Mary learns how to reinvent herself, presenting herself to her Monmouth employers as an innocent young girl. However, Mary lacks Eliza's status and financial resources and her love of finery is her undoing. Again there is an indirect comment on Celtic Tiger excesses, underlined by the Welsh setting, another Celtic periphery, and

Linden Peach suggests that in *Slammerkin* Donoghue is 'indirectly offering a feminist critique of late twentieth-century, capitalist society'.[22]

Life Mask, based on a love triangle between sculptress Anne Damer, Irish actress Eliza Farren and Lord Derby, explores the dangers of lesbian love in eighteenth-century society. *The Sealed Letter* also turns on suppressed lesbian feelings and is full of fascinating detail about mid-nineteenth-century feminism and the Langham Place Group. The central character, Emily Faithfull, was a historical figure involved in the first-wave British women's movement. The novel is based on the *Codrington v. Codrington* divorce case of 1858–66 in which Emily was called as a defence witness by Helen Codrington's lawyers, fled to avoid a subpoena, and subsequently returned to testify in Admiral Codrington's favour. The existence of the eponymous sealed letter and its contents was hinted at by contemporary observers of the trial and may have been used by the admiral to blackmail Emily into changing sides, but what exactly was in the letter remains a mystery. Drawing on Browning's correspondence, Donoghue suggests that the letter may have contained accusations of a lesbian relationship between Emily and Helen. In the novel, Emily suppresses the knowledge even to herself that her intense attachment to Helen is sexual. 'I'm interested in the fluidity and unpredictability of human sexuality,' Donoghue has said.[23] These are historical novels written with a modern sensibility.

Room (2010) is Donoghue's most successful novel to date, garnering an international readership and shortlisted for the Man Booker and Orange Prizes. *Room* draws on the harrowing cases of Sabine Dardenne, Natascha Kampusch and Elisabeth Fritzl, all abducted, imprisoned for varying lengths of time, repeatedly raped and in some cases giving birth to babies by their captors. The challenge for Donoghue was to find the language to tell the story through the voice of a five-year-old boy who has known nothing in his life but his mother and an eleven-foot square room. *Room*, a shocking and powerful book, underlines what has been evident from the beginning of Donoghue's career, namely her emotional intelligence as an author and her capacity for producing compelling fiction.

ANNE HAVERTY

Anne Haverty's fiction, like Donoghue's, includes both the contemporary and the historical. *The Far Side of a Kiss* (2000) is an account, through the first-person narrative of Sarah, a serving maid, of William Hazlitt's composition of *Liber Amoris* (1823). Constraints of gender and class put Sarah in a vulnerable position, somewhere between lady and streetwalker. The novel recreates early nineteenth-century London undergoing a generational shift from more liberated attitudes to a prudishness about sexuality that anticipates the Victorian era. Hazlitt's wild and romantic idealisations of women as angels in the house are a danger to Sarah, whose position requires that she be cautious and pragmatic in her loving.

In *The Free and Easy* (2006), Haverty employs the Jamesian device of an American innocent to portray Celtic Tiger Ireland as a country of excessive consumption and crooked businessmen brought before tribunals for cases that are never concluded and serve only to line the pockets of the lawyers. Tom has been sent to Ireland by his wealthy Irish American great-uncle Pender Gast, tormented by nightmares of his starving fellow countrymen beseeching him for help. Instead of the starving, in cosmopolitan Dublin Tom finds tanned and fit people who frequent gyms and art exhibitions and differ little from the natives of Manhattan:

> The various rooms of the Academy were thronged with sleek, well nourished and happy people. Any perceptible gauntness, any trace of pallor, was clearly due not to hunger but to the low-fat regimes and gymwork of the western urban dweller. Tom saw no sign of the kind of artist that he had naively half anticipated: ragged, and pale from intensity and disdain, eking out their impassioned days with potato meals. The busy cacophony of talk and laughter had the same timbre that you would find at such an event in Manhattan – the stamp of correct thinking and correct action leading, as night follows day, to achievement justly accompanied by prosperity.[24]

An acutely observed and funny novel, *The Free and Easy*, like Ní Dhuibhne's *Fox, Swallow, Scarecrow*, highlights the shallowness of Celtic Tiger Ireland.

HISTORICAL FICTION

Other Irish women writers during this period, besides Donoghue and Haverty, turned to historical fiction, some to give a pointed commentary on their own times, others to create works of historical reconstruction. Anne Barnett's *The Largest Baby in Ireland after the Famine* (2000) explores Irish experience of the First World War from the viewpoint of 1916 rural mid-Ulster, portraying the mores of a Protestant farming community with humour and compassion, while Monica Tracey's *Unweaving the Thread* (2001) describes life in Northern Ireland during the Second World War, charting her heroine's efforts to escape both the ideological rigidities of her 1940s upbringing in a Catholic republican family in Belfast and a traumatic sexual event in her past. Mary Morrissy's *The Pretender* (2000) probes postmodern issues of identity, memory and fantasy through imagining the early life of Franziska Schanzkowska, a Polish factory worker, who later claimed to be Anastasia, the fourth daughter of Tsar Nicholas II of Russia. The layered narrative of *The Pretender* suits the web of deceits that Franziska, like Enright's Eliza Lynch, weaves around her life as a means of survival. Like a Russian doll, Franziska's story unwinds backwards, 'her outer shell unravelling to reveal a small, then smaller, version of herself',[25] from her final years in America through wartime Berlin and her spell in an asylum, until we arrive at her origins, child of a peasant family in Poland. Each of these self-fashioned narratives seems utterly convincing, underlining the difficulty of separating truth from fiction.[26]

Clare Boylan developed her internationally successful novel *Emma Brown* (2003) from a work, provisionally titled 'Emma', left unfinished by Charlotte Brontë at her death in 1855. After Brontë's death, the first two chapters of 'Emma', which provide the opening of Boylan's novel, were published in the *Cornhill Magazine* with some alterations by her husband, Reverend Arthur Nicholls, which Boylan has retained. *Emma Brown* is a work of fiction but also of recuperation since Boylan makes extensive use of lines from Brontë's correspondence as well as a sequence from an earlier, abandoned novel introducing the character of Mr Ellin. The themes of *Emma Brown* were inspired by accounts of Brontë's growing preoccupation with social conditions in London: when Brontë stayed in the city after the success of *Jane Eyre*, she displayed an interest, dismaying to her hosts, in visiting prisons, Bethlehem Hospital and the Foundling Hospital. Boylan's novel portrays in detail the traffic in underage females and the lives of street children in nineteenth-century London. But *Emma Brown* also illustrates, as Boylan herself observed, 'two of my most common fictional themes – that of young girls on the verge of womanhood who are just beginning to get a clear picture of their identity when it becomes totally confused by adult expectations of the female; and that of powerful women powerless to command their own destinies'.[27]

The Fox's Walk (2003) by Annabel Davis-Goff opens in 1965 with the reburial of Roger Casement in Glasnevin cemetery and flashes back to the years 1912–16 when the narrator, Alice, was a child. Left on her grandmother's estate, Ballydavid, while her parents return to war-torn London, Alice comes into contact with her grandmother's Catholic neighbours who live down Fox's Row and realises that her Empire-loving grandmother's version of events can be countered and even corrected. Like Nancy in *The Old Jest*, Alice takes a crucial decision to protect the identity of a republican gunman: 'While I wouldn't side with the assassins, I no longer trusted the forces that would hunt them down if I spoke up.'[28] *The Fox's Walk* traces Alice's gradual awareness, through her conflicting feelings about Casement, of the way in which history can alter according to the teller and what gets lost in constructing a narrative. Her 1965 self provides an additional commentary on the revisionism of Irish history that was getting underway during the 1960s.

Julia O'Faolain's *Adam Gould* (2009) is set in an asylum in Passy run by Dr Emile Blanche who was responsible for treating several famous people, including the short story writer Guy de Maupassant. Like twenty-first-century Ireland, 1890s France is rapidly secularising and the presence in Dr Blanche's asylum of a Catholic priest caught up in a plot to restore the French monarchy allows for discussion of such issues as the balance of power between church and state and the church's role in education that were relevant to Ireland in 2009. An Irish strand is central to the novel in the presence of Adam Gould, spoilt priest and illegitimate heir of an Irish Catholic landlord, who comes to help in Dr Blanche's asylum. The novel ends with an ironic gesture towards Maria Edgeworth's theme of the absentee landlord since Adam's love for a Frenchwoman leads him to linger in Paris and leave all the improving work on his estate to his childhood friend, Con Keogh.

JENNIFER JOHNSTON

Amid the rise of new literary talent in the early years of the twenty-first century some familiar voices remained. Postmodernism has always been a discreet presence in Jennifer Johnston's work and many of her novels self-consciously draw attention to their fictionality, notably in her use of open endings, her first-person frameworks (there are no grand narratives in Johnston's work), diaries and frequent intertextuality in the many (too many for some readers) quotations from songs and poems. Postmodernist techniques are particularly evident in *This Is Not a Novel* (2002), a fractured narrative moving between several different pasts: Imogen's present, her 1950s childhood, her adolescence in the '60s, her stay in a nursing home in 1970, her father's diaries of her childhood, and her great-grandmother's notes and mementoes of Harry.[29] If this is not a novel, what is it? The narrator suggests that it is to be read as a *cri du coeur*: like Miranda in *Fool's Sanctuary* and Laura in *The Invisible Worm*, Imogen inhabits a border between sanity and insanity, reliving a trauma from her past. Sympathetic portraits of homosexuals are a feature of Johnston's later novels and *This is Not a Novel* portrays a line of troubled homosexuals stretching back to Imogen's great-uncle Harry and including her father and her brother Johnny. There is an echo of Keane's *Good Behaviour* as Imogen unwittingly acts as a cover for a homosexual relationship between her brother and Bruno.

Like many Johnston novels, *This is Not a Novel* is an exploration of family secrets and lies and the way they play out over time in the dynamics of family life. The same may be said of *Grace and Truth* (2005) in which Johnston returns to the theme of incest, this time in the topical context of clerical child abuse though, somewhat unusually, the abuser is not the standard Catholic celibate priest but a Church of Ireland bishop. Unlike Laura in *The Invisible Worm*, Ruth, the bishop's daughter, never tells the story of her abuse by her father and thus never finds healing. Consumed by self-hatred and depression, she casts a shadow over the life of her own daughter, Sally, who consequently rejects the mothering role for herself. Resisting the current Irish trend for positive mother–daughter stories, *Grace and Truth* is as disempowering a mother–daughter story as any found in the previous century.

Old age is a subject that Johnston has made her own and it comes to the fore again in *Foolish Mortals* (2007) in the portrayal of the irascible Tash raging against the waning of her artistic powers and the humiliating disintegrations of old age. With its Shakespearean title and cross-dressing twins, *Foolish Mortals* provides an indirect commentary on liberalising attitudes to homosexuality in Ireland. Henry has taken half a lifetime to accept his homosexuality while his son Donough talks frankly about his sexual orientation and lives as a couple with Brendan. Old age features again in *Truth or Fiction* (2009) in its portrait of Desmond Fitzmaurice, an ageing playwright, war correspondent and literary giant of the thirties. As with *This is Not a Novel*, the title, *Truth or Fiction*, suggests a postmodern questioning of the real and in fact Johnston's novel aroused controversy for the close resemblance of the ageing Desmond to the author's father, Denis Johnston, war correspondent, playwright, broadcaster and academic.[30] Like Denis Johnston, Desmond has had two wives, both actresses, and lives with his second wife in Sorrento Terrace in Dalkey where Denis and his second wife, Betty, lived for a time. Like Denis, Desmond confides his feelings about an ill-fated love affair to his tape recorder and secretly meets his first wife, Pamela, in pubs and coffee shops.[31] Johnston disputed that the novel was about her father but Desmond does share Denis's patriarchal attitudes towards women that were resisted by his first wife, Johnston's mother, Shelagh Richards, and are resisted in the novel by Pamela.

Such gestures towards postmodernism suggest that straightforward realism is not the best approach to Johnston's work which, at its most characteristic, is minimalist and poetic, focusing on the inner experience, emotions and perceptual subjectivity of her narrators. Criticisms concerning anachronisms, errors of detail, and recycling of themes are perhaps inevitable for a writer with such a constant output. At their best, her novels may be classified as literary impressionism. They endeavour to capture fleeting moments in the flux of life and, as in the work of literary impressionists, they privilege mood and atmosphere over plot, foreground point of view rather than omniscient narration, and insist on instability of personal identity, dissolution of plot, shifting time schemes, and the inadequacy of language. Nuances of characters' moods are evoked through dialogue, small gestures, expressive silences, and snatches of song and poetry, evoking Virginia Woolf's description of 'an ordinary mind on an ordinary day'.[32]

The fractured time schemes of Johnston's texts, particularly noticeable in *This Is Not a Novel* where Imogen's story moves between several pasts and the present, represent psychological as opposed to clock time. Johnston's protagonists refuse to be boxed in by other people's expectations. Their point of view may often be limited – by youth (Minnie in *The Gates*, Nancy in *The Old Jest*, Imogen in *This Is Not a Novel*), by ignorance (Sally in *Grace and Truth*,

Stella in *The Illusionist*) – but her protagonists struggle to disentangle themselves from the ghosts of the past in order to find their voice. Her narrators are often obsessed with words and the meanings of words but her novels also suggest that words are fallible, that language is unstable and inadequate to represent the world as her characters experience it. The periodic mutism of Imogen in *This Is Not a Novel* and Laura in *The Invisible Worm* suggest women silenced by the conditions of their lives. The ambiguous, relativistic and tenuous nature of experience is at the core of Johnston's novels, her characters like ghosts cling precariously to a sense of self.

EDNA O'BRIEN

In 2002, Edna O'Brien caused more than the usual outcry with the publication of *In the Forest* based on events that took place in 1994 in her native County Clare when Imelda Riney, her three-year-old son Liam and Father Joe Walsh were murdered by a disturbed young man, Brendan O'Donnell. O'Brien was criticised by, among others, Fintan O'Toole in the *Irish Times* for breaking an unspoken rule by intruding into private grief.[33] Others pointed to precedents set by novelists like John Banville in *The Book of Evidence* and defended O'Brien's right to describe incidents that happened in her native area.[34] O'Brien herself said: 'I have written a book to commemorate and perpetuate the story of this almost Greek tragedy which took place in a forest I happened to know.' In O'Brien's fictional portrayal, the victims are not only Eily, Maddie and Father John, but also, in a different sense, their murderer, Michen O'Kane, a young man brutalised by his upbringing at the hands of his violent father, by physical and sexual abuse at a detention centre run by priests and by being ostracised by his local community. Like Enright, O'Brien exposes the dark side of contemporary Irish life, raising questions about the way society treats young offenders and, rather remarkably, getting inside the mind of a psychopath while resisting any easy answers about what made him that way.

In the Forest may also be read as a culmination of O'Brien's evocation of Irish rural life, her interest in sacrificial women and violent men, and her unflinching portrayal of what she sees as the brutalities at the heart of Irish society. The novel raises questions both about the complacency of foreigners who move into rural communities and the unwillingness of those communities to accept outsiders: the guards drag their feet on investigating the disappearance of a foreign woman and her child until it becomes known that a priest is also missing. Yet the Ireland of O'Brien's novel is less a straightforwardly realistic portrayal than a poetic, and slightly surreal, evocation of people's hopes, dreams and nightmares, as one of their own turns into a legendary creature who haunts their sleeping and waking hours.

The Light of Evening (2006) provides a conclusion to the mother–daughter story in O'Brien's *oeuvre*. The tense relationship between the pious, poverty-stricken mother Dilly, who has lived all her life in rural Ireland and her cosmopolitan daughter Eleanora, who earns her living as a writer yet retains residual ties to Catholicism and to the Ireland of her childhood, reprises themes familiar from *The Country Girls* trilogy and *Time and Tide*. Here though the rural Irish mother is placed at the centre as Dilly tells the story, in her own words and letters, of her life before marriage as a young woman in domestic service in America and her doomed love affair. What is new in this novel is the insight into the lives, dreams and aspirations of Irish female immigrants in New York in the early 1920s. In this respect, *The Light of Evening* has similarities with Colm Tóibín's *Brooklyn* though receiving much less critical attention. Despite Dilly's distrust of her daughter's career, it is through writing that final understanding and reconciliation between mother and daughter comes about: Dilly reads Eleanora's diary and, after Dilly's death, Eleanora reads her mother's letters and through them the reader recognises that it is her voice that has inspired Eleanora/O'Brien as a writer. In an interview, O'Brien explained: 'I have hundreds of letters from my mother, which although they are not literary in the given sense, they are masterpieces.'[35] O'Brien's portrayal of the mother has moved from the matrophobia of her early work to a recognition of the influence of the mother's voice in shaping her life and writing.[36]

DEIRDRE MADDEN

Deirdre Madden has always been interested in exploring the life of the artist and the difficulty of remaining true to one's vocation. Reflections on the paintings and frescoes she encounters in Italy play a central part in Aisling's healing process in *Remembering Light and Stone*. In *Hidden Symptoms*, in contrast to Robert's dilettantish approach, Theresa looks on art as a calling akin in seriousness and commitment to the religious life and having as goals truth and authenticity. Madden picks up this theme in *Authenticity* (2002) where she examines the artistic vocation as an ethical choice through the grief of the middle-aged William for his unlived life. In the lives of Roderic, an established painter, and Julia, just embarking on her artistic career, Madden portrays the costs but also the joys of the authentically lived life. Throughout his drunken episodes and failed relationships, Roderic remains true to his gift in contrast to William who has never had the courage of his. A constant theme of Madden's work is how easy, and dangerous, it is to drift into social conformity and the unrealised lives that result.

Molly Fox's Birthday (2008) reprises the exploration of professional vocations against a general background of meditation on human identity. The unnamed narrator, a playwright, uses the birthday of her friend Molly Fox to reflect on the lives of herself and her two friends, Molly, an actor, and Andrew, an art historian. In the course of this, she is forced to ask herself questions about how well we know both ourselves and other people. All three – Molly, Andrew and the narrator – have found that their unswerving commitment to their vocations has led them away from their families and their original identities in order to become the people they needed to be. Andrew and the narrator share a Northern Irish background, albeit from different sides of the sectarian divide, and the Troubles briefly feature in the story of the involvement of Andrew's elder brother Billy with loyalist paramilitaries. The narrator's brother Tom, a Catholic priest, provides another strand in the novel's exploration of the cost and rewards of a vocation.

Madden's most recent novels are differently paced from her earlier ones and operate at a certain level of complexity, being meditative explorations around issues of identity and integrity in the artistic life. *Molly Fox's Birthday* in particular reveals a bravely unfashionable belief in the notion of an essential human self. As in *Authenticity*, the value of worldly success is questioned, the story of Molly's brother Fergus suggesting that a life regarded in social terms as a failure may be at least as admirable as a life filled with spectacular achievements.

CLAIRE KILROY

The creative life is also the focus of a trilogy by Claire Kilroy (1973–). 'Literary thriller' seems too slight a term to encompass all that Kilroy does in her novels, which combine exciting plot lines with stylistic precision and meditation on art, whether it be art restoration in *All Summer* (2003), music in *Tenderwire* (2006), or writing in *All Names Have Been Changed* (2009). *Tenderwire* in particular is a smartly paced thriller, with a compellingly unstable and unreliable narrator, which at the same time gives an insight into the professional life of a musician. *All Names Have Been Changed* is a witty deconstruction of the Great Irish (male) Writer in the figure of the blocked, self-pitying and self-indulgent Patrick Glynn. Kilroy, who took an MPhil in creative writing at Trinity College, Dublin, portrays the intense bonds and rivalries among five students in Glynn's writing class, one of whom ends up on a psychiatric ward. Almost more interesting than the story of Glynn's writing classes is the backdrop of recession-ridden Dublin in the 1980s. Kilroy vividly evokes a city of drug addicts and the unemployed, a place of random and unpredictable violence. In an interview she explained:

> The 1980s shaped me. I'm an architect's child and architects are the first to get hit in recessions. As children in the 1980s, we lived with the fear of ruin. In the end it didn't happen but it always felt like we were on the brink of emigration. It's a strange way to grow up, really.[37]

Written as Ireland was entering another crippling economic downturn, *All Names Have Been Changed* indicates the cyclical nature of Irish life. Irish women's fiction too has gone through cycles. After the late nineteenth and early twentieth century the number of professional women writers in Ireland fell sharply by mid-century and revived only in the 1970s with the advent of second-wave feminism. Not until the 1990s was Irish women's fiction the subject of serious critical attention. As Lia Mills has observed: 'a hundred years ago women were highly active in politics and writing; their popularity, or their exclusion, seems to come in waves of progress and regression. It doesn't do to be complacent.'[38] Though Irish women writers have become more visible in recent years and certainly more self-confident, the progress of Irish criticism reveals that inclusion in Irish literary histories can never be taken for granted and for this reason it has seemed to me important to record what Irish women have already achieved in fiction, highlighting points of connection and influence that I hope will open up future lines of inquiry. By now I hope it is clear that there exists in the Irish novel a solid body of work that reaches beyond masculine portrayals of women to give imaginative expression to Irish women's lives.

Stylistically, too, Irish women's fiction has gone through cycles. The formal experimentation of Maria Edgeworth in *Castle Rackrent* does not begin to be emulated with any thoroughness until Edna O'Brien's literary experiments of the 1970s and the appearance in the 1990s of the postmodern novels of Mary Morrissy, Éilís Ní Dhuibhne, Anne Haverty and Anne Enright. Within that period between Maria Edgeworth and Edna O'Brien certain New Woman writers such as George Egerton and Somerville and Ross paid attention to form while modernism's influence pointed the realist novel in the hands of writers like Elizabeth Bowen, Olivia Manning, Pamela Hinkson, Kathleen Coyle and later Jennifer Johnston and Deirdre Madden towards interiority, ambiguity, image patterns, time shifts and open-endedness. The black comedy of Molly Keane's fiction also called attention to its deliberate artistry. Such artistic self-consciousness, rare in the earlier periods, becomes the hallmark of Irish women's literary fiction from the 1990s onwards in a way that promises much for the future.

SELECT BIBLIOGRAPHY OF
SECONDARY SOURCES

Annat, A.L.S. 'Class, Nation, Gender and Self: Katharine Tynan and the Construction of Political Identities, 1880–1930', in F. Lane (ed.), *Politics, Society and the Middle Class in Modern Ireland* (London and New York: Palgrave, 2010), pp.194–211

Atkinson, C. and Atkinson, J. 'Maria Edgeworth, *Belinda* and Women's Rights', *Éire-Ireland: A Journal of Irish Studies*, 19, 4 (1984), pp.94–118

Backus, M. *The Gothic Family Romance: Heterosexuality, Child Sacrifice, and the Anglo-Irish Colonial Order* (Durham, NC: Duke University Press, 1999)

Belanger, J. (ed.), *The Irish Novel in the Nineteenth Century: Facts and Fictions* (Dublin: Four Courts Press, 2005)

Bennett, A. and Royle, N. *Elizabeth Bowen and the Dissolution of the Novel: Still Lives* (Basingstoke: Macmillan, 1995)

Benstock, S. 'The Masculine World of Jennifer Johnston', in T. Staly (ed.), *Twentieth-Century Women Novelists* (London: Macmillan, 1982), pp.191–217

Bourke, A., Kilfeather, S., Luddy, M., MacCurtain, M., Meaney, G., Ni Dhonnchadha, M., O'Dowd, S. and Wills, C. (eds), *The Field Day Anthology of Irish Writing*, vols 4 and 5 (Cork: Cork University Press, 2002)

Bourke, A. *Maeve Brennan: Homesick at the* New Yorker (London: Jonathan Cape, 2004)

Bradley, A. and Valiulis, M. (eds), *Gender and Sexuality in Modern Ireland* (Amherst, MA: University of Massachusetts Press, 1997)

Butler, M. *Maria Edgeworth: A Literary Biography* (Oxford: The Clarendon Press, 1972)

Cahill, S. *Irish Literature in the Celtic Tiger Years, 1990–2008* (London and New York: Continuum, 2011)

Canadian Journal of Irish Studies, The, Special Edition on Edna O'Brien, 22, 2 (1996)

Cardin, B. 'Reflections on Jennifer Johnston's *This is Not a Novel*', *The Canadian Journal of Irish Studies*, 31, 2 (2005), pp.34–41

Christensen, L. *Elizabeth Bowen: The Later Fiction* (Copenhagen: Museum Tusculanum Press, University of Copenhagen, 2001)

Clear, C. *Women of the House: Women's Household Work in Ireland, 1922–1961* (Dublin: Irish Academic Press, 2000)

Colletta, L. and O'Connor, M. (eds), *Wild Colonial Girl: Essays on Edna O'Brien* (Madison, WI: University of Wisconsin Press, 2006)

Colman, A. 'Far From Silent: Nineteenth-Century Irish Women Writers', in *Gender Perspectives in Nineteenth-Century Ireland: Public and Private Spheres* (Dublin: Irish Academic Press, 1997), pp.203–11

Connolly, L. *The Irish Women's Movement: From Revolution to Devolution* (Dublin: Lilliput Press, 2003)

Conradi, P. *Iris Murdoch: The Saint and the Artist* (London: Macmillan, 1989)

Conradi, P. *Iris Murdoch: A Life* (London and New York: HarperCollins, 2001)

Corcoran, N. *Elizabeth Bowen: The Enforced Return* (Oxford: Oxford University Press, 2004)

Coughlan, P. 'Irish Literature and Feminism in Postmodernity', *Hungarian Journal of English and American Studies*, 10, 1–2 (2004), pp.175–202

Coughlan P. and O'Toole, T. (eds), *Irish Literature: Feminist Perspectives* (Dublin: Carysfort Press, 2008)

Coulter, C. *The Hidden Tradition: Feminism, Women and Nationalism in Ireland* (Cork: Cork University Press, 1993)

Cullen, M. (ed.), *Girls Don't Do Honours: Irish Women in Education in the Nineteenth and Twentieth Centuries* (Dublin: Web, 1987)

Cullen, M. and Luddy, M. (eds), *Female Activists: Irish Women and Change, 1900–1960* (Dublin: The Woodfield Press, 2001)

Curtin, C., Jackson, P. and O'Connor, B. (eds), *Gender in Irish Society* (Galway: Galway University Press, 1987)

Cusick, C. (ed.), *Out of the Earth: Ecocritical Readings of Irish Texts* (Cork: Cork University Press, 2010)

D'hoker E., Ingelbien R. and Schwall H. (eds), *Irish Women Writers: New Critical Perspectives* (Bern: Peter Lang, 2011)

Donoghue, E. 'Noises from the Woodsheds: Tales of Irish Lesbians, 1886–1989', in I. O'Carroll and E. Collins (eds), *Lesbian and Gay Visions of Ireland* (London: Cassell, 1995), pp.158–70

Eckley, G. *Edna O'Brien* (Lewisburg, PA: Bucknell University Press, 1974)

Ellmann, M. *Elizabeth Bowen: The Shadow Across the Page* (Edinburgh: Edinburgh University Press, 2003)

Evason, E. *Against the Grain: The Contemporary Women's Movement in Northern Ireland* (Dublin: Attic Press, 1991)

Fauset, E. 'Studies in the Fiction of Jennifer Johnston and Mary Lavin', *Irish Studies Working Papers* (Fort Lauderdale: Nova Southeastern University, 1998), pp.7–12

Ferris, I. *The Romantic National Tale and the Question of Ireland* (Cambridge: Cambridge University Press, 2002)

Ferris S. and M. Young (eds), *Chick Lit: The New Woman's Fiction* (New York and London: Routledge, 2006)

Flanagan, T. *The Irish Novelists, 1800–1850* (New York: Columbia University Press, 1959)

Fogarty, A. '"Keynotes from Millstreet": Irish Women Novelists, 1800–1940', *Colby Library Quarterly*, 2 (June 2000), pp.145–56

Fogarty, A. 'Uncanny Families: Neo-Gothic Motifs and the Theme of Social Change in Contemporary Irish Women's Fiction', *Irish University Review*, 30, 1 (2000), pp.59–81

Fogarty, A. 'Deliberately Personal? The Politics of Identity in Contemporary Irish Women's Writing', *Nordic Irish Studies*, 1 (2001), pp.1–17

Fogarty, A. '"The Horror of the Unlived Life": Mother–Daughter Relationships in Contemporary Irish Women's Fiction', in A. Giorgio (ed.), *Writing Mothers and Daughters: Renegotiating the Mother in Western European Narratives by Women* (New York and Oxford: Berghahn, 2002), pp.85–117

Foster, J.W. (ed.), *The Cambridge Companion to the Irish Novel* (Cambridge: Cambridge University Press, 2006)

Foster, J.W. *Irish Novels, 1890–1940: New Bearings in Culture and Fiction* (Oxford: Oxford University Press, 2008)

Garratt, R.F. *Trauma and History in the Irish Novel: The Return of the Dead* (Basingstoke: Palgrave Macmillan, 2011)

Gibbons, L. *Transformations in Irish Culture* (Cork: Cork University Press, 1996)

Ging, D. 'New Gender Formations in Post-Celtic-Tiger Ireland', in M. Cronin, P. Kirby and D. Ging (eds), *Transforming Ireland: Challenges, Critiques, Resources* (Manchester: Manchester University Press, 2009), pp. 52–70

Glendinning, V. *Elizabeth Bowen: Portrait of a Writer* (London: Weidenfeld & Nicolson, 1977)

Gonzalez, A.G. (ed.), *Irish Women Writers: An A–Z Guide* (Westport CT: Greenwood, 2006)

Gray, K.M. 'The Attic Lips: Feminist Pamphleteering for the New Ireland', *Éire-Ireland: A Journal of Irish Studies*, 29, 1 (1994), pp.105–22

Greenwood, A. *Edna O'Brien* (Tavistock: Northcote House, 2003)

Grubgeld, E. *Anglo-Irish Autobiography: Class, Gender, and the Forms of Narrative* (Syracuse, NY: Syracuse University Press, 2004)

Haberstroh, P.B. and St Peter, C. (eds), *Opening the Field. Irish Women: Texts and Contexts* (Cork: Cork University Press, 2007)

Hand, D. 'Being Ordinary: Ireland from Elsewhere. A Reading of Éilís Ní Dhuibhne's *The Bray House*', *Irish University Review*, 30, 1 (2000), pp.103–16

Hand, D. *A History of the Irish Novel* (Cambridge: Cambridge University Press, 2011)

Hansson, H. *Emily Lawless, 1845–1913: Writing the Interspace* (Cork: Cork University Press, 2007)

Hansson, H. (ed.), *New Contexts: Re-Framing Nineteenth-Century Irish Women's Prose* (Cork: Cork University Press, 2008)

Hargreaves, T. 'Women's Consciousness and Identity in Four Irish Women Novelists', in M. Kenneally (ed.), *Cultural Contexts and Literary Idioms in Contemporary Irish Literature* (Gerrards Cross: Colin Smythe, 1998), pp.290–305

Harte, L. and Parker, M. (eds), *Contemporary Irish Fiction: Themes, Tropes, Theories* (Basingstoke: Macmillan Press, 2000)

Hayes, A. 'Big Women, Little Women: Toward a History of Second-Wave Commercial Feminist Publishing in Ireland', *Women's Studies Review*, 6 (1999), pp.139–50

Hayes, A. and Urquhart, D. (eds), *The Irish Woman's History Reader* (London and New York: Routledge, 2001)

Heaney, J. '"No Sanctuary from Hatred": A Re-appraisal of Mary Lavin's Outsiders', *Irish University Review*, 28, 2 (1998), pp.294–307

Heilmann, A. *New Woman Fiction: Women Writing First-Wave Feminism* (Basingstoke: Macmillan, 2000)

Herr, C. 'The Erotics of Irishness', *Critical Inquiry*, 17, 1, (1990), pp.1–34

Hill, M. *Women in Ireland: A Century of Change* (Belfast: Blackstaff Press, 2003)

Hoff, J. and Coulter, M. (eds), *Irish Women's Voices: Past and Present* (Bloomington: Indiana University Press, 1995)

Hoogland, R.C. *Elizabeth Bowen: A Reputation in Writing* (New York: New York University Press, 1994)

Ingman, H. *Twentieth-Century Fiction by Irish Women: Nation and Gender* (Aldershot and Burlington, VT: Ashgate, 2007)

Ingman, H. *A History of the Irish Short Story* (Cambridge: Cambridge University Press, 2009)

Innes, C.L. *Woman and Nation in Irish Literature and Society, 1880–1935* (New York and London: Harvester Wheatsheaf, 1993)

Jeffers, J.M. *The Irish Novel at the End of the Twentieth Century: Gender, Bodies and Power* (New York and Basingstoke: Palgrave, 2002)

Jordan, Heather Bryant, *How Will the Heart Endure: Elizabeth Bowen and the Landscape of War* (Michigan: University of Michigan Press, 1992)

Kahn, H.K. *Late Nineteenth-Century Ireland's Political and Religious Controversies in the Fiction of May Laffan Hartley* (Greensboro, NC: ELT Press, 2005)

Kelleher, M. (ed.), *The Feminization of Famine: Expressions of the Inexpressible?* (Cork: Cork University Press, 1997)

Kelleher, M. and Murphy, J.H. (eds), *Gender Perspectives in Nineteenth-Century Ireland: Public and Private Spaces* (Dublin: Irish Academic Press, 1997)

Kennedy-Andrews, E. (ed.), *Irish Fiction since the 1960s: A Collection of Critical Essays* (Dublin: Four Courts Press, 2002)

Kennedy-Andrews, E. *Fiction and the Northern Ireland Troubles since 1969: (De-) Constructing the North* (Dublin: Four Courts Press, 2003)

Kiberd, D. *Inventing Ireland: The Literature of the Modern Nation* (New York and London: Vintage, 1996)

Kiberd, D. *Irish Classics* (London: Granta, 2000)

Kickham, L. *Protestant Women Novelists and Irish Society, 1879–1922* (Lund: Lund University, 2004)

Kirby, P., Gibbons, L. and Cronin, M. (eds), *Reinventing Ireland: Culture, Society and the Global Economy* (London: Pluto Press, 2002)

Kirkpatrick, K. (ed.), *Border Crossings: Irish Women Writers and National Identities* (Tuscaloosa, AL: The University of Alabama Press, 2000)

Kreilkamp, V. 'The Persistent Pattern: Molly Keane's Recent Big House Fiction', *Massachusetts Review*, 28, 3 (1987), pp.458–60

Kreilkamp, V. *The Anglo-Irish Novel and the Big House* (Syracuse, NY: Syracuse University Press, 1998)

Laing, K., Mooney, S. and O'Connor, M. (eds), *Edna O'Brien: New Critical Perspectives* (Dublin: Carysfort Press, 2006)

Lane, L. *Rosamond Jacob: Third Person Singular* (Dublin: UCD Press, 2010)

Laracy, E. and Laracy, H. 'Beatrice Grimshaw: Pride and Prejudice in Papua', *The Journal of Pacific History*, 12, 3 (1977), pp.154–75

Lassner, P. *Elizabeth Bowen* (Basingstoke: Macmillan, 1990)

Lassner, P. and Derdiger, P. 'Domestic Gothic, the Global Primitive, and Gender Relations in Elizabeth Bowen's *The Last September* and *The House in Paris*', in M. McGarrity and C. Culleton (eds), *Irish Modernism and the Global Primitive* (New York: Palgrave Macmillan, 2009), pp.195–214

Ledger, S. *The New Woman: Fiction and Feminism at the Fin de Siècle* (Manchester: Manchester University Press, 1997)

Lee, H. *Elizabeth Bowen* (London: Vintage, 1999)

Levenson, L. *The Four Seasons of Mary Lavin* (Dublin: Marino, 1998)

Levine, J. *Sisters: The Personal Story of an Irish Feminist* (Dublin: Ward River Press, 1982)

Lewis, G. *Somerville and Ross: The World of the Irish RM* (Harmondsworth: Penguin, 1985)

Lewis, G. *Edith Somerville: A Biography* (Dublin: Four Courts Press, 2005)

Loeber, R. and Stouthamer-Loeber, M. 'Literary Absentees: Irish Women Authors in Nineteenth-Century England', in J. Belanger (ed.), *The Irish Novel in the Nineteenth Century: Facts and Fictions* (Dublin: Four Courts Press, 2005), pp.167–86

Loeber, R. and Stouthamer-Loeber, M. (eds), *A Guide to Irish Fiction, 1650–1900* (Dublin: Four Courts Press, 2006)

Lynch, R.J. '"A Land of Strange, Throttled, Sacrificial Women": Domestic Violence in the Short Fiction of Edna O'Brien', *The Canadian Journal of Irish Studies*, 19, 1 (1993), pp.36–48

McCarthy, A. '"Oh Mother Where Art Thou?" Irish Mothers and Irish Fiction in the Twentieth Century', in P. Kennedy (ed.), *Motherhood in Ireland: Creation and Context* (Cork: Mercier Press, 2004), pp.95–107

McCormack, W.J. *Dissolute Characters: Irish Literary History through Balzac, Sheridan Le Fanu, Yeats and Bowen* (Manchester: Manchester University Press, 1993)

McCotter, C. 'Woman Traveller/Colonial Tourist: Deconstructing the Great Divide in Beatrice Grimshaw's Travel Writing', *Irish Studies Review*, 5 (2007), pp.481–506

McCracken, S. 'A Novel from on the Margins: George Egerton's *Wheel of God*', in T.P. Foley, L. Pilkington, S. Ryder and E. Tilley (eds), *Gender and Colonialism* (Galway: Galway University Press, 1995), pp.139–57

Maher, E. and O'Brien, E. (eds), *Breaking the Mould: Literary Representations of Irish Catholicism* (New York and Frankfurt: Peter Lang, 2011)

Mahony, C.H. *Contemporary Irish Literature: Transforming Tradition* (New York: St Martin's Press, 1998)

Martin, A. 'Death of a Nation: Transnationalism, Bodies and Abortion in Late Twentieth-Century Ireland', in T. Mayer (ed.), *Gender Ironies of Nationalism: Sexing the Nation* (London and New York: Routledge, 2000), pp.65–86

Meaney, G. *Sex and Nation: Women in Irish Culture and Politics* (Dublin: Attic Press, 1991)

Meaney, G. *Gender, Ireland and Cultural Change: Race, Sex and Nation* (New York and London: Routledge, 2010)

Moloney, C. and Thompson, H. (eds), *Irish Women Writers Speak Out: Voices from the Field* (Syracuse, NY: Syracuse University Press, 2003)

Murphy, J.H. *Irish Novelists and the Victorian Age* (Oxford: Oxford University Press, 2011)

Murphy, J.H. (ed.), *The Irish Book in English, 1800–1891* (Oxford: Oxford University Press, 2011)

Napier, T.S. *Seeking a Country: Literary Autobiographies of Twentieth-Century Irishwomen* (Lanham, NY: University Press of America, 2001)

Nash, C, '"Embodying the Nation": The West of Ireland Landscape and Irish Identity', in Cronin, M. and O'Connor, B. (eds), *Tourism in Ireland* (Cork: Cork University Press, 1993), pp.86–112

Nash, J. (ed.), *New Essays on Maria Edgeworth* (Aldershot and Burlington, VT: Ashgate, 2006)

Ní Chuilleanáin, E. 'Woman as Writer: the Social Matrix', *Crane Bag*, 4, 1 (1980), pp. 101–5

Nolan, E. 'Postcolonial Literary Studies, Nationalism and Feminist Critique in Contemporary Ireland', *Éire-Ireland: A Journal of Irish Studies*, 42, 1–2 (2007), pp.336–61

O'Brien Johnson, T. and Cairns, D. (eds), *Gender in Irish Writing* (Milton Keynes: Open University Press, 1991)

O'Carroll, I. and Collins, E. (eds), *Lesbian and Gay Visions of Ireland* (London and New York: Cassell, 1995)

O'Connor, M. '"Becoming Animal" in the Novels of Edna O'Brien', in C. Cusick (ed.), *Out of the Earth: Ecocritical Readings of Irish Texts* (Cork: Cork University Press, 2010), pp.151–77

O'Connor, T. 'History, Gender, and the Postcolonial Condition: Julia O'Faolain's Comic Rewriting of *Finnegans Wake*', in T. O' Connor (ed.), *The Comic Tradition in Irish Women Writers* (Gainsville, FL: University Press of Florida, 1996), pp.124–48

O'Dowd, M. and Wichert, S. (eds), *Chattel, Servant or Citizen: Women's Status in Church, State and Society* (Belfast: Institute of Irish Studies, Belfast, 1995)

O'Faolain, N. *Are You Somebody? The Life and Times of Nuala O'Faolain* (Dublin: New Island Books, 1997)

Ó Gallchoir, C. *Maria Edgeworth: Women, Enlightenment and Nation* (Dublin: UCD Press, 2005)

O'Toole, T. (ed.), *Dictionary of Munster Women Writers, 1800–2000* (Cork: Cork University Press, 2005)

Parker, M. 'Shadows on a Glass: Self-Reflexivity in the Fiction of Deirdre Madden', *Irish University Review*, 30, 1 (2000), pp.82–102

Parker, M. (ed.), *Northern Irish Literature, 1975–2006* (Basingstoke: Palgrave Macmillan, 2007)

Parkes, S. *A Danger to the Men? A History of Women in Trinity College Dublin, 1904–2004* (Dublin: The Lilliput Press, 2004)

Patten, E. 'Women and Fiction, 1985–1990', *Krino*, 8–9 (1990), pp.1–7

Patten, E. 'Fiction in Conflict: Northern Ireland's Prodigal Novelists', in I.A. Bell (ed.), *Peripheral Visions: Images of Nationhood in Contemporary British Fiction* (Cardiff: University of Wales Press, 1995), pp.128–48

Patten, E. *Imperial Refugee: Olivia Manning's Fictions of War* (Cork: Cork University Press, 2011)

Peach, L. 'Contemporary Irish Women Writers and the Gendered Construction of Space', *Swansea Review* (1994), pp.450–61

Peach, L. *The Contemporary Irish Novel: Critical Readings* (New York and Basingstoke: Palgrave Macmillan, 2004)

Pelan, R. *Two Irelands: Literary Feminisms North and South* (Syracuse, NY: Syracuse University Press, 2005)

Pelan, R. (ed.), *Éilís Ní Dhuibhne: Perspectives* (Galway: Arlen House, 2009)

Pykett, L. *The 'Improper' Feminine: The Woman's Sensation Novel and The New Woman Writing* (London: Routledge, 1992)

Quinn, D. and Tighe-Mooney, S. (eds), *Essays in Irish Literary Criticism: Themes of Gender, Sexuality and Corporeality* (Lampeter: Edwin Mellen Press, 2009)

Quinn, J. (ed.), *A Portrait of the Artist as a Young Girl* (London: Methuen, 1986)

Rafroidi, P. and Harmon M. (eds), *The Irish Novel in Our Time* (Villeneuve-d'Ascq: Publications de l'Université de Lille III, 1975)

Richardson, A. and Willis, C. (eds), *The New Woman in Fiction and in Fact: Fin-de-Siècle Feminisms* (New York and Basingstoke: Palgrave, 2001)

Robinson, H. *Somerville and Ross: A Critical Appreciation* (Dublin: Gill & Macmillan, 1980)

Rooks-Hughes, L. 'The Family and the Female Body in the Novels of Edna O'Brien and Julia O'Faolain', *The Canadian Journal of Irish Studies*, 22, 2 (1996), pp.83–97

Rose, C. *The Female Experience: The Story of the Woman Movement in Ireland* (Galway: Arlen House, 1975)

Roulston, C. and Davies, C. (eds), *Gender, Democracy and Inclusion in Northern Ireland* (Basingstoke and New York: Palgrave, 2000)

Sales, R. *Women Divided: Gender, Religion and Politics in Northern Ireland* (London and New York: Routledge, 1997)

Scanlan, M. 'An Acceptable Level of Violence: Women, Fiction, and Northern Ireland', in T. D'haen and J. Lanters (eds), *Troubled Histories, Troubled Fictions: Twentieth-Century Anglo-Irish Prose* (Amsterdam-Atlanta: Editions Rodopi, 1995), pp.159–72

Showalter, E. *A Literature of Their Own: From Charlotte Brontë to Doris Lessing* (London: Virago, 1978)

Showalter, E. *Sexual Anarchy: Gender and Culture at the Fin de Siècle* (London: Virago, 1992)

Showalter, E. *Daughters of Decadence: Women Writers of the Fin de Siècle* (London: Virago, 1993)

Shumaker, J. 'Uncanny Doubles: The Fiction of Anne Enright', *New Hibernia Review*, 9, 3 (2005), pp.107–22

Smith, N.C. *Dorothy Macardle: A Life* (Dublin: The Woodfield Press, 2007)

Smyth, A. *Wildish Things: An Anthology of New Irish Women's Writing* (Dublin: Attic Press, 1989)

Smyth, A. (ed.), *Irish Women's Studies Reader* (Dublin: Attic Press, 1993)

Smyth, G. *The Novel and the Nation: Studies in the New Irish Fiction* (London: Pluto Press, 1997)

St Peter, C. *Changing Ireland: Strategies in Contemporary Women's Fiction* (Basingstoke and London: Macmillan Press, 2000)

Steel, J. 'Politicizing the Private: Women Writing the Troubles', in B. Cliff and E. Walshe (eds), *Representing the Troubles: Texts and Images, 1970–2000* (Dublin: Four Courts Press, 2004), pp.55–66

Stevens, J.A. *The Irish Scene in Somerville and Ross* (Dublin: Irish Academic Press, 2007)

Sullivan, M. 'Feminism, Postmodernism and the Subjects of Irish and Women's Studies', in P.J. Mathews (ed.), *New Voices in Irish Criticism* (Dublin: Four Courts Press, 2000), pp.243–51

Thompson, H. (ed.), *The Current Debate About the Irish Literary Canon: Essays Reassessing the Field Day Anthology of Irish Writing* (Lampeter: The Edwin Mellen Press, 2006)

Thompson, H. *The Role of Irish Women in the Writings of Edna O'Brien: Mothering the Continuation of the Irish Nation* (Lampeter: The Edwin Mellen Press, 2010)

Valiulis, M. and O'Dowd, M. (eds), *Women and Irish History* (Dublin: Wolfhound Press, 1997)

Wally, J. *Selected Twentieth-Century Anglo-Irish Autobiographies: Theories and Patterns of Self-Representation* (New York and Bern: Peter Lang, 2004)

Walshe, E. (ed.), *Ordinary People Dancing: Essays on Kate O'Brien* (Cork: Cork University Press, 1993)

Walshe, E. (ed.), *Sex, Nation and Dissent in Irish Writing* (Cork: Cork University Press, 1997)

Walshe, E. *Kate O'Brien: A Writing Life* (Dublin: Irish Academic Press, 2006)

Walshe, E. and Young, G. (eds), *Molly Keane: Essays in Contemporary Criticism* (Dublin: Four Courts Press, 2006)

Walshe, E. (ed.), *Elizabeth Bowen* (Dublin: Irish Academic Press, 2009)

Ward, M. *Unmanageable Revolutionaries: Women and Irish Nationalism* (London: Pluto Press, 1989)

Ward, M. (ed.), *In Their Own Voice: Women and Irish Nationalism* (Dublin: Attic Press, 1995)

Ward, M. *Hanna Sheehy Skeffington: A Life* (Dublin: Attic Press, 1997)

Weekes, A.O. *Irish Women Writers: An Uncharted Tradition* (Lexington, KY: University Press of Kentucky, 1990)

Weekes, A.O. *Unveiling Treasures: The Attic Guide to the Published Works of Irish Women Literary Authors* (Dublin: Attic Press, 1993)

White, J. 'Europe, Ireland, and Deirdre Madden', *World Literature Today*, 73, 3 (1999), pp.451–60

Wills, C. *That Neutral Island: A Cultural History of Ireland during the Second World War* (London: Faber, 2007)

NOTES

PREFACE

1   É. Ní Dhuibhne, *Fox, Swallow, Scarecrow* (Belfast: Blackstaff Press, 2007), p.16.

2   C. Ó Gallchoir, *Maria Edgeworth: Women, Enlightenment and Nation* (Dublin: UCD Press, 2005), p.8.

3   See, for example, the interviews in C. Moloney and H. Thompson (eds), *Irish Women Writers Speak Out: Voices from the Field* (New York: Syracuse University Press, 2003), particularly those with Anne Enright, Evelyn Conlon and Mary O'Donnell.

4   S. Cahill, *Irish Literature in the Celtic Tiger Years, 1990–2008* (London and New York: Continuum, 2011), pp.13–14.

5   H. Hansson (ed.), *New Contexts: Re-Framing Nineteenth-Century Irish Women's Prose* (Cork: Cork University Press, 2008), p.2.

6   Nuala O'Faolain reports the response of the general editor, Seamus Deane, whom she interviewed on the subject for RTÉ: 'He said words to the effect that he hadn't really noticed what he was doing. He just hadn't noticed' (N. O'Faolain, *Are You Somebody? The Life and Times of Nuala O'Faolain* (Dublin: New Island Books, 1997), p.112. For exploration of this controversy, see H. Thompson (ed.), *The Current Debate About the Irish Literary Canon: Essays Reassessing the Field Day Anthology of Irish Writing* (Lampeter: The Edwin Mellen Press, 2006).

7   H. Ingman, *Twentieth-Century Fiction by Irish Women: Nation and Gender* (Aldershot and Burlington, VT: Ashgate, 2007).

8   A. Fogarty, 'Uncanny Families: Neo-Gothic Motifs and the Theme of Social Change in Contemporary Irish Women's Fiction', *Irish University Review*, 30, 1 (2000), p.61. For a more extended discussion of the emblematic use of women in Irish studies, see M. Sullivan, 'Raising the Veil: Mystery, Myth, and Melancholia in Irish Studies', in P. Coughlan and T. O'Toole (eds), *Irish Literature: Feminist Perspectives* (Dublin: Carysfort Press, 2008), pp.245–77.

9   G. Spivak, *In Other Worlds: Essays in Cultural Politics* (London: Routledge, 1988), p.205.

10   E. Nolan, 'Postcolonial Literary Studies, Nationalism, and Feminist Critique in Contemporary Ireland', *Éire-Ireland, A Journal of Irish Studies*, 42, 1–2 (2007), pp.336–61.

11   I discuss Irish women's short stories across the centuries in *A History of the Irish Short Story* (Cambridge: Cambridge University Press, 2009).

12 Scholarly work in Irish children's literature is a rich and emergent field. To give some examples: K. O'Sullivan and V. Coghlan (eds), *Irish Children's Literature and Culture: New Perspectives on Contemporary Writing* (New York: Routledge, 2011), M.S. Thompson and V. Coghlan (eds), *Divided Worlds: Studies in Children's Literature* (Dublin: Four Courts Press, 2006), M.S. Thompson and C. Keenan (eds), *Treasure Islands: Studies in Children's Literature* (Dublin: Four Courts Press, 2005).

13 E. Bowen, 'Pictures and Conversations', in H. Lee (ed.), *The Mulberry Tree: Writings of Elizabeth Bowen* (Virago: London, 1999), p.297.

CHAPTER 1

1 Quoted in A. Hare (ed.), *The Life and Letters of Maria Edgeworth* (London: Edward Arnold, 1894), vol. 2, p.295.

2 Ibid., p.293.

3 C. Ó Gallchoir, *Maria Edgeworth: Women, Enlightenment and Nation* (Dublin: UCD Press, 2005), p.11.

4 See, for example, F.R. Botkin, 'Finding Her Own Voice or "Being on Her Own Bottom": A Community of Women in Maria Edgeworth's *Helen*', in J. Nash (ed.), *New Essays on Maria Edgeworth* (Aldershot and Burlington, VT: Ashgate, 2006), pp.93–108.

5 In *The Unappeasable Host: Studies in Irish Identities*, Robert Tracy finds in Thady's position as colonised servant echoes of Maria Edgeworth's dependent status in her father's home: 'I find it significant that a woman writer is the first to give a voice to the subject Irish at a time when women were essentially voiceless' (Dublin: UCD Press, 1998), pp.21–2.

6 Ó Gallchoir, *Maria Edgeworth*, pp.155–75.

7 See, for example, V. Kreilkamp, *The Anglo-Irish Novel and the Big House* (Syracuse, NY: Syracuse University Press, 1998), pp.26–69, and D. Kiberd, *Irish Classics* (London: Granta, 2000), pp.243–64.

8 M. Edgeworth, *Castle Rackrent and Ennui*, ed. M. Butler (Harmondsworth: Penguin, 1992), p.xlii.

9 Ó Gallchoir, *Maria Edgeworth*, p.63.

10 E. Somerville and M. Ross, *Stray-Aways* (London: Longmans, Green & Co., 1920), p.252.

11 A.O. Weekes, *Irish Women Writers: An Uncharted Tradition* (Lexington, KY: University Press of Kentucky, 1990), p.42.

12 Kreilkamp, *The Anglo-Irish Novel and the Big House*, p.69.

13 This ambivalence in Edgeworth's work is highlighted by several essays in Nash, *New Essays on Maria Edgeworth*; see particularly Alison Harvey's discussion of race in 'West Indian Obeah and English "Obee": Race, Femininity, and Questions of Colonial Consolidation in Maria Edgeworth's *Belinda*', pp.1–30.

14 Tracy, *The Unappeasable Host*, pp.25–40.

15 J.A. Miller, 'Acts of Union: Family Violence and National Courtship in Maria Edgeworth's *The Absentee* and Sydney Owenson's *The Wild Irish Girl*', in K. Kirkpatrick (ed.), *Border Crossings: Irish Women Writers and National Identities* (Tuscaloosa, AL: The University of Alabama Press, 2000), pp.13–37, and A. Fogarty, 'Imperfect Concord: Spectres of History in the Irish Novels of Maria Edgeworth and Lady Morgan', in M. Kelleher and J.H. Murphy (eds), *Gender Perspectives in Nineteenth-Century Ireland* (Dublin: Irish Academic Press, 1997), pp.116–26. See also C. Morin, '"Gothic" and "National"? Challenging the Formal Distinctions of Irish Romantic Fiction', in J. Kelly (ed.), *Ireland and Romanticism: Publics, Nations and Scenes of Cultural Production* (New York: Palgrave, 2011), pp.172–87.

16 Edgeworth's criticism of the marriage market in *Belinda* prompts comparison with *Canvassing* (1832?), published as part of John and Michael Banim's 'Tales of the O'Hara Family' but actually written

by Harriet Martin (1801–91). *Canvassing* writes beyond the concluding marriages to depict the consequences of marrying rashly and warn against worldly match-making mothers like Lady Anne. The novel advises consulting God before marrying (possibly code for trusting one's instincts) and Martin has some sharp comments on the restrictive nature of gender roles for upper-class women. See Heidi Hansson's discussion of this novel in 'Stuck on the Canvas: Harriet Martin's *Canvassing* and Locational Feminism', in P.B. Haberstroh and C. St Peter (eds), *Opening the Field. Irish Women: Texts and Contexts* (Cork: Cork University Press, 2007), pp.43–57.

17 'Dashers' spoke loudly and freely with lots of swearing, their behaviour intending to register a protest against passive femininity: see C. Atkinson and J. Atkinson, 'Maria Edgeworth, *Belinda* and Women's Rights', *Éire-Ireland, A Journal of Irish Studies*, 19, 4 (1984), pp.94–118.

18 M. Edgeworth, *Belinda*, ed. K.J. Kirkpatrick (Oxford: Oxford University Press, 1994), p.xviii.

19 Ibid., p.xxii. See also the discussion in Ó Gallchoir, *Maria Edgeworth*, pp.47–9.

20 M. Edgeworth, *Tales of Fashionable Life* (London: J. Johnson, 1809), p.iv.

21 S. Owenson, *Lady Morgan's Memoirs: Autobiography, Diaries and Correspondence* (London: W.H. Allen & Co., 1863), vol. 1, p.135. In Selina Bunbury's semi-autobiographical novel *Our Own Story*, Magda is similarly inspired in her writing career by the knowledge that Fanny Burney earned £1,500 for *Evelina* (London: Hurst & Blackett, 1856), vol. 2, p.11.

22 Owenson, *Lady Morgan's Memoirs*, vol. 1, p.211.

23 Ibid., p.254.

24 Ibid., pp.254–5.

25 Ibid., p.255.

26 C. Morin, 'Undermining Morality? National Destabilisation in *The Wild Irish Girl* and *Corinne ou L'Italie*', in E. D'hoker, R. Ingelbien and H. Schwall (eds), *Irish Women Writers: New Critical Perspectives* (Bern: Peter Lang, 2011), p.174.

27 S. Owenson, *Florence Macarthy: An Irish Tale*, introduction by R.L. Wolff (New York and London: Garland Publishers, 1979), vol. 4, p.38.

28 Quoted in I. Ferris, *The Romantic National Tale and the Question of Ireland* (Cambridge: Cambridge University Press, 2002), p.68.

29 For the publicity surrounding Owenson's novel, see C. Connolly, '"I Accuse Miss Owenson": *The Wild Irish Girl* as Media Event', *Colby Quarterly*, 36, 2, pp.98–115.

30 Owenson, *Florence Macarthy*, vol. 3, pp.264–5.

31 Ferris, *The Romantic National Tale*, p.72.

32 M. Burgess, 'The National Tale and Allied Genres, 1770s–1840s', in J.W. Foster (ed.), *The Cambridge Companion to the Irish Novel* (Cambridge: Cambridge University Press, 2006), p.54.

33 T. Flanagan, *The Irish Novelists, 1800–1850* (New York: Columbia University Press, 1959), p.125.

34 S. Owenson, *The Wild Irish Girl: A National Tale*, ed. K. Kirkpatrick (Oxford: Oxford University Press, 1999), p.250.

35 D. Hand, *A History of the Irish Novel* (Cambridge: Cambridge University Press, 2011), p.77.

36 Owenson, *Lady Morgan's Memoirs*, vol. 1, pp.293–4.

37 Quoted in M. Butler, *Maria Edgeworth: A Literary Biography* (Oxford: The Clarendon Press, 1972), p.448.

38 Owenson, *Florence Macarthy*, vol. 3, pp.273–4.

39 On this point see Anne Fogarty's comparison between Edgeworth and Owenson, 'Imperfect Concord: Spectres of History in the Irish Novels of Maria Edgeworth and Lady Morgan', in Kelleher and Murphy (eds), *Gender Perspectives in Nineteenth-Century Ireland*, pp.116–26.

40 Owenson, *Lady Morgan's Memoirs*, vol. 2, p.427. For Edgeworth's letter to her brother, see Hare, *The Life and Letters of Maria Edgeworth*, vol. 2, p.202.

41 H.C. Black, *Notable Women Authors of the Day* (London: Maclaren & Co., 1906), pp.16–17.

42 J.H. Riddell, *A Struggle for Fame* (London: Richard Bentley & Son, 1883), vol. 1, pp.229–30.

43 In Selina Bunbury's *Our Own Story* (1856), the narrator observes that Ireland is a 'land so under the ban of society that the scene even of a novel must be laid in any other if the book is to be published' (London: Hurst & Blackett, 1856), vol. 1, p.10.

44 L.H. Peterson, *Becoming a Woman of Letters: Myths of Authorship and Facts of the Victorian Market* (Princeton, NJ: Princeton University Press, 2009), pp.151–70.

45 M. Kelleher, 'Charlotte Riddell's *A Struggle for Fame*: The Field of Women's Literary Production', *Colby Quarterly*, 36, 2 (2000), p.120. See also N. Cross, *The Common Writer: Life in Nineteenth-Century Grub Street* (Cambridge: Cambridge University Press, 1985), pp.194–8.

46 A. Gregory, *Seventy Years* (Gerrards Cross: Colin Smythe, 1974), pp.4–5.

47 K. Tynan, *Twenty-Five Years: Reminiscences* (London: Smith Elder, 1913), p.39. This conflict between mothers and daughters over the latter's desire for an intellectual life continued into the twentieth century: see Enid Starkie's memoir *A Lady's Child* (1941), depicting her upbringing in Edwardian Dublin.

48 K. Tynan, *The Middle Years* (London: Constable, 1916), p.73.

49 For a balanced assessment of Tynan's feminism, see A.L.S. Annat, 'Class, Nation, Gender and Self: Katharine Tynan and the Construction of Political Identities, 1880–1930', in F. Lane (ed.), *Politics, Society and the Middle Class in Modern Ireland* (London and New York: Palgrave, 2010), pp.194–211.

50 H. Hansson, 'Selina Bunbury, Religion, and the Woman Writer', in J.H. Murphy (ed.), *The Irish Book in English, 1800–1891* (Oxford: Oxford University Press, 2011), pp.322–30.

51 For an account of Blessington's life and work, see R. O'Dwyer, 'Travels of a Lady of Fashion: The Literary Career of Lady Blessington (1789–1849)', in Hansson, *New Contexts*, pp.35–53, and see also J.H. Murphy, *Irish Novelists and the Victorian Age* (Oxford: Oxford University Press, 2011), pp.27–37.

52 For details of Hungerford's working life, see her interview in Black, *Notable Women Authors*, pp.107–19. For a recent critical re-evaluation of *Molly Bawn*, see E. Wennö, 'Hybridization as a Literary and Social Strategy: Mrs Hungerford's *Molly Bawn*', in Hansson, *New Contexts*, pp.92–108.

53 See M. Kelleher, 'Women's Fiction, 1845–1900', in A. Bourke *et al.* (eds), *The Field Day Anthology of Irish Writing*, 5 (Cork: Cork University Press, 2002), pp.924–5.

54 M. Brew, *The Chronicles of Castle Cloyne, or, Pictures of the Munster People* (London: Chapman & Hall, 1885), pp.286–7.

55 See J. Kavanagh, *Rachel Gray* (Leipzig: Bernhard Tauchnitz, 1856). For a discussion of Kavanagh's life and works, see E. Fauset, *The Politics of Writing: Julia Kavanagh, 1824–77* (Manchester: Manchester University Press, 2009).

56 This also holds true for some Protestant Evangelical writers: see H. Hansson, 'Selina Bunbury, the Pope and the Question of Location', in P. Coughlan and T. O'Toole (eds), *Irish Literature: Feminist Perspectives* (Dublin: Carysfort Press, 2008), pp.59–77.

57 J.W. Foster, *Irish Novels 1890–1940. New Bearings in Culture and Fiction* (Oxford: Oxford University Press, 2008), pp.97–106.

58 J.H. Murphy, '"Things Which Seem to You Unfeminine": Gender and Nationalism in the Fiction of Some Upper Middle Class Catholic Women Novelists, 1880–1910', in K. Kirkpatrick (ed.), *Border Crossings: Irish Women Writers and National Identities* (Tuscaloosa, AL: The University of Alabama Press, 2000), pp.58–78. See also Murphy, *Irish Novels and the Victorian Age*, pp.168–86.

59 Mulholland's experiences as an art student in London are reflected in volume 3 of *Dunmara*, an early novel by Mulholland published under the name Ruth Murray: see Murphy, *Irish Novelists and the Victorian Age*, p.245.

60 K. Tynan, *Memories* (London: Eveleigh Nash & Grayon, 1924), p.312.

61 Murphy, '"Things Which Seem to You Unfeminine"' in Kirkpatrick, *Border Crossings*, p.66.

62 M.E. Francis, *The Things of a Child* (London: W. Collins & Sons, 1918), p.22.

63   For a fuller analysis of this conflict, see H. Hansson, 'Patriot's Daughter, Politician's Wife: Gender and Nation in M.E. Francis's *Miss Erin*', in H. Hansson (ed.), *New Contexts: Re-Framing Nineteenth-Century Women's Prose* (Cork: Cork University Press, 2008), pp.109–24.

64   For details of Laffan's life and work, see Helena Kelleher Kahn, *Late Nineteenth-Century Ireland's Political and Religious Controversies in the Fiction of May Laffan Hartley* (Greensboro, NC: ELT Press, 2005).

65   May Laffan Hartley, *Christy Carew* (London: Richard Bentley, 1880), vol. 1, p.21.

66   Black, *Notable Women Authors*, p.60.

67   Ibid., p.65.

68   Ibid., p.65.

69   Mrs Alexander, *Kitty Costello* (Leipzig: Bernhard Tauchnitz, 1904), p.22.

70   Ibid., p.299.

71   L.T. Meade, *A Princess of the Gutter* (New York: Putnam's, 1896), p.162.

72   See J.W. Foster's judicious discussion of possible lesbianism in Meade's *The Princess of the Gutter* in *Irish Novels, 1890–1940*, pp.102–6.

73   E. MacMahon, *A New Note* (London: Hutchinson & Co., 1894), p.92.

74   Ibid., pp.120–1.

75   E. MacMahon, *A Modern Man* (London: J.M. Dent, 1895), p.89.

CHAPTER 2

1   E. Showalter, *Sexual Anarchy: Gender and Culture at the Fin de Siècle* (London: Virago, 1992), S. Ledger, *The New Woman: Fiction and Feminism at the Fin de Siècle* (Manchester: Manchester University Press, 1997), L. Pykett, *The 'Improper' Feminine: The Woman's Sensation Novel and The New Woman Writing* (London: Routledge, 1992), A. Heilmann, *New Woman Fiction: Women Writing First-Wave Feminism* (Basingstoke: Macmillan, 2000).

2   T. O'Toole, 'Ireland: The Terra Incognita of the New Woman Project', in H. Hansson (ed.), *New Contexts: Re-Framing Nineteenth-Century Irish Women's Prose* (Cork: Cork University Press, 2008), pp.125–41, A. Fogarty, '"Keynotes from Millstreet": Irish Women Novelists, 1800–1940', *Colby Library Quarterly*, 2 (June 2000), pp.145–56, G. Meaney, *Gender, Ireland and Cultural Change: Race, Sex, and Nation* (New York: Routledge, 2010), J.W. Foster, *Irish Novels, 1890–1940: New Bearings in Culture and Fiction* (Oxford: Oxford University Press, 2008), pp.276–309, J.H. Murphy, *Irish Novelists and the Victorian Age* (Oxford: Oxford University Press, 2011).

3   For details of the publishing careers of nineteenth-century Irish women writers in London, see R. Loeber and M. Stouthamer-Loeber, 'Literary Absentees: Irish Women Authors in Nineteenth-Century England', in J. Belanger (ed.), *The Irish Novel in the Nineteenth Century: Facts and Fictions* (Dublin: Four Courts Press, 2005), pp.167–86, Foster, *Irish Novels, 1890–1940*, pp.167–86, A. Colman, 'Far From Silent: Nineteenth-Century Irish Women Writers', in M. Kelleher and J. Murphy (eds), *Gender Perspectives in Nineteenth-Century Ireland: Public and Private Spheres* (Dublin: Irish Academic Press, 1997), pp.203–11.

4   O'Toole, 'Ireland: The Terra Incognita of the New Woman Project', p.129. See also Ledger, *The New Woman*, Chapter 6.

5   K. Tynan, *The Middle Years* (London: Constable, 1916), p.239.

6   K. Tynan, *The Wandering Years* (Boston and New York: Houghton Mifflin & Co., 1922), p.287.

7   E. Gordon, *The Winds of Time* (London: John Murray, 1934), p.61.

8   Ibid., p.61.

9   Kathleen Mannington Caffyn, *A Yellow Aster* (London: Hutchinson & Co., 1894), p.168.

10   'And if this fought-for climax is ever reached, and science, creeping along the path of experiment, so invades the realm of Nature that a blue chrysanthemum or a yellow aster can be produced at will, the question still remains, has Nature been made more beautiful thereby?' Caffyn, *A Yellow Aster*, n.p.

11   Iota, *Poor Max* (London: Hutchinson & Co., 1898), p.46.

12   Ibid., p.120.

13   Ibid., pp.233–4.

14   Ibid., p.232.

15   Ibid., p.334.

16   Countess of Fingall, *Seventy Years Young: Memories of Elizabeth, Countess of Fingall told to Pamela Hinkson* [1937] (Dublin: The Lilliput Press, 1991), p.175.

17   A. Gregory, *Lady Gregory's Journals, 1916–1930*, ed. L. Robinson (London: Putnam & Co., 1946), p.217. Lawless became addicted to heroin as a form of pain relief. This also may account for her languid appearance.

18   'A Chelsea Householder', *Spectator*, 4 November 1882. For more on the contemporary reception of Lawless's novel, see H. Hansson, *Emily Lawless, 1845–1913: Writing the Interspace* (Cork: Cork University Press, 2007), pp.36–8.

19   See Catherine Smith, '"Words! Words! Words!": Interrogations of Language and History in Emily Lawless's *With Essex in Ireland*', in E. D'hoker, R. Ingelbien and H. Schwall (eds), *Irish Women Writers: New Critical Perspectives* (Bern: Peter Lang, 2011), p.191.

20   Hansson, *Emily Lawless*, p.1.

21   J.M. Calahan, 'Forging a Tradition: Emily Lawless and the Irish Literary Tradition', in K. Kirkpatrick (ed.), *Border Crossings: Irish Women Writers and National Identities* (Tuscaloosa, AL: The University of Alabama Press, 2000), pp.38–57.

22   E. Lawless, *Grania: The Story of an Island* (New York and London: Macmillan & Co., 1892), p.146.

23   Lawless, *Grania*, p.146.

24   See Terry Eagleton: 'the sexual culture of the nation belonged to a complex economy of land and inheritance, property and procreation', *Heathcliff and the Great Hunger: Studies in Irish Culture* (London and New York: Verso, 1995), p.227.

25   See Meaney, *Gender, Ireland and Cultural Change*, pp.84–93.

26   G. Egerton, *Fantasias* (London: John Lane, 1898), p.124.

27   On spiritualism's empowerment of women, see T. Brown, *The Life of W.B. Yeats* (Dublin: Gill & Macmillan, 2001), p.39.

28   See, for example, Elaine Showalter, *Daughters of Decadence: Women Writers of the Fin de Siècle* (London: Virago, 1993), p.xiv.

29   George Egerton, *Keynotes and Discords*, ed. S. Ledger (London: Continuum, 2006), p.108.

30   George Egerton, 'A Keynote to Keynotes' (1932), quoted in Showalter, *Daughters of Decadence*, p.xiii.

31   G. O'Brien, 'Contemporary Prose in English: 1940–2000', in M. Kelleher and P. O'Leary (eds), *The Cambridge History of Irish Literature*, vol. 2, 1890–2000 (Cambridge: Cambridge University Press, 2006), p.422.

32   G. Egerton, *The Wheel of God* (London: Grant Richards, 1898), p.127.

33   Tynan, *The Middle Years*, p.380.

34   Ibid., p.380.

35   Sarah Grand, *Ideala* (Chicago: Donohue, Henneberry & Co., 1888), p.17.

36   Grand, *Ideala*, p.186.

37   E. Showalter, *A Literature of their Own: From Charlotte Brontë to Doris Lessing* (London: Virago, 1978), p.205.

38   Sarah Grand, *The Heavenly Twins* (New York: Cassell, 1893), p.39.

39   Ibid., p.349.

40 Sarah Grand, *The Beth Book*, introd. S. Mitchell (Bristol: Thoemmes Press, 1994), p.460.

41 For the link between *fin de siècle* Irish feminism and anti-vivisectionism, see M. O'Connor, '"I'm Meat for No Butcher!": The Female and the Species in Irish Women's Writing', in D'hoker, Ingelbien and Schwall (eds), *Irish Women Writers*, pp.133–50.

42 Grand, *The Beth Book*, p.368.

43 Ibid., p.418.

44 Ibid., p.527.

45 K. Tynan, *Twenty-Five Years: Reminiscences* (London: Smith, Elder & Co., 1913), p.78.

46 For details of her travels, see F. Binckes and K. Laing, 'A Vagabond's Scrutiny: Hannah Lynch in Europe', in D'hoker, Ingelbien and Schwall (eds), *Irish Women Writers*, pp.111–50. For her later, impoverished years, see J.H. Murphy, *Irish Novelists and the Victorian Age* (Oxford: Oxford University Press, 2011), pp.249–52.

47 K. de Forest, 'Recent Happenings in Paris', *Harper's Bazaar*, 36, 9 (1902), pp.812–13, quoted in D'hoker, Ingelbien and Schwall (eds), *Irish Women Writers*, p.128.

48 H. Lynch, *Autobiography of a Child* (Edinburgh and London: William Blackwood & Sons, 1899), p.217.

49 Foster, *Irish Novels, 1890–1940*, p.277.

50 Lynch, *Autobiography of a Child*, p.218.

51 Tynan, *Twenty-Five Years*, p.79.

52 See D'hoker, Ingelbien and Schwall (eds), *Irish Women Writers*, p.128.

53 See, for example, Meaney, *Gender, Ireland and Cultural Change*, pp.93–8, T. O'Toole, '"Nomadic Subjects" in Katherine Cecil Thurston's *Max*', in P. Coughlan and T. O'Toole (eds), *Irish Literature: Feminist Perspectives* (Dublin: Carysfort Press, 2008), pp.79–98.

54 *Irish Times*, 8 April 1910, p.7.

55 K. Thurston, *The Masquerader: A Novel* (New York and London: Harper & Brothers, 1905), p.86.

56 *Irish Times*, 8 July 1905, p.3.

57 K. Thurston, *The Fly on the Wheel* (New York: Dodd, Mead & Co., 1908), p.12.

58 Ibid., p.107.

59 Ibid., p.231.

60 Ibid., p.193.

61 Ibid., p.267.

62 K. Thurston, *Max* (London: Hutchinson & Co., 1910), p.64.

63 'How I Found Adventure', *Blue Book*, April 1939. See www.grimshaworigin.org/WebPages/BeatGrim accessed 2 September 2012

64 *Irish Times*, 6 May 1922, p.7. Claire McCotter has written extensively on Grimshaw's travel writing: see, for example, 'Woman Traveller/Colonial Tourist: Deconstructing the Great Divide in Beatrice Grimshaw's Travel Writing', *Irish Studies Review*, 5 (2007), pp.481–506. See also Eugenie and Hugh Laracy, 'Beatrice Grimshaw: Pride and Prejudice in Papua', *The Journal of Pacific History*, 12, 3 (1977), pp.154–75.

65 B. Grimshaw, *When the Red Gods Call* (London: Mills & Boon, 1911), p.57.

66 Ibid., p.350.

67 Grimshaw converted to Roman Catholicism in Dublin at the age of twenty-three.

68 G. Lewis, *Somerville and Ross: The World of the Irish RM* (Penguin: Harmondsworth, 1985), p.12.

69 E. Somerville and M. Ross, *Stray-Aways* (London: Longmans, Green & Co., 1920), p.230.

70 G. Lewis (ed.), *The Selected Letters of Somerville and Ross* (London: Faber & Faber, 1989), p.xxiii.

71 E. Somerville and M. Ross, *Irish Memories* (London: Longmans, Green & Co., 1917), p.326.

72 G. Lewis, *Edith Somerville: A Biography* (Dublin: Four Courts Press, 2005), p.251.

73 Somerville and Ross, *Irish Memories*, p.310.

74   Lewis, *Somerville and Ross*, p.66.

75   Somerville and Ross, *Irish Memories*, p.139.

76   Lewis, *Edith Somerville*, p.396.

77   Somerville and Ross, *Stray-Aways*, p.252.

78   Quoted in H. Robinson, *Somerville and Ross: A Critical Appreciation* (Dublin: Gill & Macmillan, 1980), p.37.

79   Lewis (ed.), *The Selected Letters of Somerville and Ross*, p.118.

80   Somerville and Ross, *Irish Memories*, p.134.

81   *The Observer*, 1 September 1889.

82   *The Daily Graphic*, 5 October 1891.

83   Somerville and Ross, *Irish Memories*, p.229.

84   E. Somerville and M. Ross, *The Real Charlotte* (Dublin: A. & A. Farmar, 1999), p.47.

85   *Lady's Pictorial*, 19 May 1894.

86   S. Gwynn, 'Lever's Successors', *The Edinburgh Review*, October 1921, pp. 346–57.

87   D. Kiberd, *Irish Classics* (London: Granta, 2000), pp.360–78.

88   See S.R. Mooney, '"Colliding Stars": Heterosexism in Biographical Representations of Somerville and Ross', *The Canadian Journal of Irish Studies*, 18, 1 (1992), pp.157–75.

89   Lewis, *Edith Somerville*, p.10.

90   E. Bowen, *The Mulberry Tree: Writings of Elizabeth Bowen*, ed. H. Lee (London: Virago, 1999), p.185.

91   Letters of 7 and 10 December 1915, quoted in Lewis, *Edith Somerville*, p.281.

92   Somerville and Ross, *Irish Memories*, p.324.

CHAPTER 3

1   F. Winthrop, *Callaghan* (Dublin: Martin Lester, 1920), p.73.

2   Ibid., p.174.

3   L. Lane, *Rosamond Jacob: Third Person Singular* (Dublin: UCD Press, 2010), p.85.

4   R. Jacob, *The Troubled House: A Novel of Dublin in the Twenties* (London: Harrap, 1938), p.29.

5   Ibid., p.91.

6   Ms 33,117. The manuscript is in four notebooks. The first is dated 21 January 1924.

7   Gerardine Meaney discusses this manuscript in *Gender, Ireland and Cultural Change: Race, Sex and Nation* (New York: Routledge, 2010), pp.110–13.

8   National Library of Ireland, MS 33,113/1.

9   F. Winthrop, *The Third Person Singular*, MS 33,113/1, p.82.

10   Meaney, *Gender, Ireland and Cultural Change*, p.120.

11   Lane, *Rosamond Jacob*, p.5.

12   E. Somerville and M. Ross, *The Big House at Inver* (Dublin: A. & A. Farmar, 1999), p.xvii.

13   V. Kreilkamp, *The Anglo-Irish Novel and the Big House* (Syracuse, NY: Syracuse University Press, 1998), p.123.

14   Somerville and Ross, *The Big House at Inver*, p.265.

15   B.M. Croker, *Lismoyle* (London: Hutchinson, 1914), p.208.

16   E. O'Brien, *Mother Ireland* (Penguin: Harmondsworth, 1978), p.55.

17   E. Conlon, *Stars in the Daytime* (Dublin: Attic Press, 1989), pp.41–2.

18   A.P. Smithson, *Her Irish Heritage* (Cork: Mercier Press, 1988), p.54.

19   K. Tynan, *The Years of the Shadow* (London: Constable, 1919), p.269.

20   K. Tynan, *The River* (London: The Literary Press, n.d.), p.25.

21   G. Cummins, *The Land They Loved* (London: Macmillan & Co., 1919), p.329.

22 G. Cummins, *Fires of Beltane* (London: Michael Joseph, 1936), p.133.

23 M. Alexander, *The Green Altar* (London and New York: Andrew Melrose, 1924), p.13.

24 See T. O'Toole (ed.), *Dictionary of Munster Women Writers, 1800–2000* (Cork: Cork University Press, 2005), p.15.

25 See D. Hand, *A History of the Irish Novel* (Cambridge: Cambridge University Press, 2011), pp.171–2.

26 N. Hoult, *Holy Ireland* (London: William Heinemann, 1935), p.186.

27 N. Hoult, *Coming from the Fair. Being Book II of Holy Ireland* (London: William Heinemann, 1937), p.337.

28 E. MacMahon, *Wind of Dawn* (London: The Bodley Head, 1927), p.74.

29 E. Bowen, *The Last September* (Penguin: Harmondsworth, 1987), p.62.

30 V. Glendinning with J. Robertson (eds), *Love's Civil War: Elizabeth Bowen and Charles Ritchie. Letters and Diaries, 1941–1973* (New York: Simon & Schuster, 2008), p.54.

31 H. Lee (ed.), *The Mulberry Tree: Writings of Elizabeth Bowen* (London: Virago, 1999), p.270.

32 Ibid., p.290.

33 Ibid., p.128.

34 Ibid., p.129.

35 Glendinning, *Love's Civil War*, p.25.

36 Lee, *The Mulberry Tree*, p.223.

37 E. Bowen, *English Novelists* (London: Collins, 1942), p.14.

38 Lee, *The Mulberry Tree*, p.125.

39 Ibid., p.87.

40 Ibid., p.118.

41 Ibid., p.118.

42 Ibid., p.119.

43 P. Craig, *Elizabeth Bowen* (Harmondsworth: Penguin, 1986), p.123.

44 Glendinning, *Love's Civil War*, p.92.

45 Lee, *The Mulberry Tree*, p.119.

46 E. Bowen, *The Hotel* (Harmondsworth: Penguin, 1987), p.18.

47 Glendinning, *Love's Civil War*, p.417.

48 E. Bowen, *The Little Girls* (Harmondsworth: Penguin, 1982), p.167.

49 Lee, *The Mulberry Tree*, p.123.

50 Ibid., p.124.

51 E. Bowen, *Pictures & Conversations* (New York: Alfred A. Knopf, 1974), p.34.

52 E. Bowen, *The Last September* (Harmondsworth: Penguin, 1987), p.7.

53 Ibid., p.49.

54 Lee, *The Mulberry Tree*, p.123.

55 M. Backus, *The Gothic Family Romance: Heterosexuality, Child Sacrifice, and the Anglo-Irish Colonial Order* (Durham, NC and London: Duke University Press, 1999), p.8.

56 Bowen, *The Last September*, p.166.

57 Ibid., p.66.

58 For more on the Anglo-Irish and style and, developing from this in connection with Bowen, the notion of the Anglo-Irish writer as dandy, see D. Kiberd, *Inventing Ireland: The Literature of the Modern Nation* (London: Vintage, 1996), pp.365–79.

59 Bowen, *The Last September*, p.60.

60 N. Corcoran, 'Discovery of a Lack: History and Ellipsis in Elizabeth Bowen's *The Last September*', *Irish University Review*, 31, 2 (2001), p.321.

61 Bowen, *The Last September*, p.203.

62 Ibid., p.89.

63 Ibid., p.89.
64 Ibid., p.99.
65 Ibid., p.74.
66 For a balanced assessment of the lesbian undertones in Lois's relationship with Marda, see Patricia Coughlan's essay on 'Women and Desire in the Work of Elizabeth Bowen', in E. Walshe (ed.), *Sex, Nation and Dissent in Irish Writing* (Cork: Cork University Press, 1997), pp.103–31.
67 Bowen, *The Last September*, p.128.
68 Ibid., p.60. For the open-endedness of Lois's fate, see Derek Hand's comments in *A History of the Irish Novel* (Cambridge: Cambridge University Press, 2011), pp.182–8.
69 Lee, *The Mulberry Tree*, p.121.
70 Ibid., p.124.
71 E. Bowen, 'The Art of Virginia Woolf', *Collected Impressions* (London: Longmans, 1950), p.81.
72 Glendinning, *Love's Civil War*, p.30.
73 K. Johnson, '"Phantasmagoric Hinterlands": Adolescence and Anglo-Ireland in Elizabeth Bowen's *The House in Paris* and *The Death of the Heart*', in E. D'hoker, R. Ingelbien and H. Schwall (eds), *Irish Women Writers: New Critical Perspectives* (Bern: Peter Lang, 2010), pp.207–26. See also Hand, *A History of the Irish Novel*, p.165.
74 'Meet Elizabeth Bowen', *Bell* 4 (September 1942), quoted in R.F. Foster, *Paddy and Mr Punch: Connections in Irish History and English History* (Harmondsworth: Penguin, 1995), p.118.
75 Bowen, 'What We Need in Writing', 1936, in A. Hepburn (ed.), *People, Places, Things: Essays by Elizabeth Bowen* (Edinburgh: Edinburgh University Press, 2008), p.309.
76 P. Lassner and P. Derdiger, 'Domestic Gothic, the Global Primitive, and Gender Relations in Elizabeth Bowen's *The Last September* and *The House in Paris*', in M. McGarrity and C. Culleton (eds), *Irish Modernism and the Global Primitive* (New York: Palgrave, 2009), pp.195–214.
77 E. Bowen, 'The Idea of France', in Hepburn (ed.), *People, Places, Things*, pp.61–5.
78 E. Bowen, *The House in Paris* (Harmondsworth: Penguin, 1976), p.76.
79 Ibid., p.89.
80 Lee, *The Mulberry Tree*, p.250.
81 Tynan, *The Years of the Shadow*, p.183.
82 L. Bardwell, *A Restless Life* (Dublin: Liberties Press, 2008), p.98.
83 Pamela Hinkson, *The Ladies' Road* (Harmondsworth: Penguin, 1946), p.278.
84 Ibid., p.284.
85 Ibid., p.284.
86 Ibid., p.319.
87 Glendinning, *Love's Civil War*, p.269.
88 A. Davis-Goff, *Walled Gardens: Scenes from an Anglo-Irish Childhood* (New York: Knopf, 1989), p.171.
89 A.O. Weekes, *Irish Women Writers: An Uncharted Tradition* (Lexington, KY: University Press of Kentucky, 1990), p.155.
90 Quoted in M. Breen, 'Piggies and Spoilers of Girls: The Representation of Sexuality in the Novels of Molly Keane', in E. Walshe and G. Young (eds), *Molly Keane: Centenary Essays* (Dublin: Four Courts Press, 2006), p.139.
91 M.J. Farrell, *Conversation Piece* (London: Virago, 1991): Polly Devlin, 'Interview with Molly Keane', unpaginated.
92 J. Quinn (ed.), *Portrait of the Artist as a Young Girl* (London: Methuen, 1986), p.76.
93 R.S. Lynch, 'Riding for a Fall: Molly Keane and the Equestrian Sublime', in Walshe and Young, *Molly Keane: Centenary Essays*, pp.36–48.
94 On this theme see A. Wessels, 'Resolving History: Negotiating the Past in Molly Keane's Big House Novels', in Walshe and Young, *Molly Keane*, pp.27–35 and S. McLemore, 'Big House Home

Improvements? Troubled Owners and Modern Renovations in *Mad Puppetstown*', in the same volume, pp.183–94.

95   M. Keane, *Devoted Ladies* (London: Virago, 1984), p.66.

96   M.E. Casey, 'Molly Keane's *Devoted Ladies*: The Apparitional Irish Lesbian', in Walshe and Young, *Molly Keane*, pp.169–80; see also in the same volume, M. Breen, 'Piggies and Spoilers of Girls: The Representation of Sexuality in the Novels of Molly Keane', pp.139–56. For general discussions of lesbianism in Irish women's fiction, see A.O. Weekes, 'A Trackless Road: Irish Nationalisms and Lesbian Writing', in K. Kirkpatrick (ed.), *Border Crossings: Irish Women Writers and National Identities* (Dublin: Wolfhound Press, 2000), pp.123–56 and E. Donoghue, 'Noises from the Woodsheds: Tales of Irish Lesbians, 1886–1989', in I. O'Carroll and E. Collins (eds), *Lesbian and Gay Visions of Ireland* (London: Cassell, 1995), pp.158–70.

97   G. Lewis, *Edith Somerville: A Biography* (Dublin: Four Courts Press, 2005), p.390.

98   See C. Lesnick, 'Untimeliness and the Big House Novel: Molly Keane's *Full House*', in Walshe and Young, *Molly Keane*, pp.61–72.

99   Keane, *Conversation Piece*, interview with Polly Devlin, unpaginated.

100   S. Mooney, '"Dark, Established Currents": Molly Keane's Gothic', in Walshe and Young, *Molly Keane*, p.205.

101   M. Keane, *The Rising Tide* (London: Virago, 1984), p.7.

102   Ibid., p.17.

103   O. Fielden, *Island Story* (London: Jonathan Cape, 1933), p.13.

104   Ibid., p.256.

105   A.R. White, *Gape Row* (Belfast: The White Row Press, 1988).

106   J.W. Foster, *Irish Novels, 1890–1940: New Bearings in Culture and Fiction* (Oxford: Oxford University Press, 2008), p.488.

107   D.G. Waring, *Nothing Irredeemable* (London: John Long Ltd., 1936), p.244.

108   Ibid., pp.30–1. Desmond qualifies for the Disbandment Pension because he has been an Auxiliary in the RIC.

109   K. Coyle, *A Flock of Birds* (New York: E.P. Dutton & Co., 1930), p.27.

110   Ibid., p.254.

111   Manning had previously published three serialised thrillers in 1929 under the name Jacob Morrow: see E. Patten, *Imperial Refugee: Olivia Manning's Fictions of War* (Cork: Cork University Press, 2011), p.15.

112   O. Manning, *The Wind Changes* (London: Virago, 1988), p.55.

113   Ibid., p.50.

114   Eve Patten poses the question as to how far Manning's 'links to Ireland by way of her mother and maternal grandfather, both from Ulster, help set the terms of her intermittent self-appointment to a political and national periphery' in Patten, *Imperial Refugee*, p.4.

115   M. Barrington, *My Cousin Justin* (Belfast: Blackstaff Press, 1990), p.234.

116   E. Walshe, *Kate O'Brien: A Writing Life* (Dublin: Irish Academic Press, 2006), p.50.

117   See E. Walshe, 'Wild(e) Ireland', in S. Brewster, V. Crossman, F. Becket and D. Alderson (eds), *Ireland in Proximity: History, Gender, Space* (London and New York: Routledge, 1999), pp.64–79.

118   Walshe, *Kate O'Brien*, p.44.

119   Ibid., pp.42–3.

120   For more on this theme, see my analysis in H. Ingman, *Twentieth-Century Fiction by Irish Women: Nation and Gender* (Burlington, VT: Ashgate, 2007), pp.122–5.

121   M. Hill, *Women in Ireland: A Century of Change* (Belfast: Blackstaff Press, 2003), pp.107–8. See also Hand, *A History of the Irish Novel*, pp.165–6.

122   K. O'Brien, *Mary Lavelle* (London: Virago, 1984), pp.204–5.

123   Máire Cruise O'Brien identifies the original of Mary Lavelle's Irish fiancé as Leo T. McCauley, head of the Irish Legation in Madrid during the period O'Brien was working there (1949–51): see M. Cruise O'Brien, *The Same Age as the State* (Dublin: The O'Brien Press, 2003), p.192.

124   Walshe, *Kate O'Brien*, p.69.

125   K. O'Brien, *Pray for the Wanderer* (New York: Doubleday, 1938), p.43.

126   Ibid., p.44.

127   See Sharon Tighe-Mooney's discussion of Una in 'Exploring the Irish Catholic Mother in Kate O'Brien's *Pray for the Wanderer*', in E. Maher and E. O'Brien (eds), *Breaking the Mould: Literary Representations of Irish Catholicism* (New York and Frankfurt: Peter Lang, 2011), pp.69–85.

128   O'Brien, *Pray for the Wanderer*, p.196.

129   E. Gordon, *The Winds of Time* (London: John Murray, 1934), p.267.

CHAPTER 4

1   *Irish Independent*, 8 June 1939, p.10.

2   These reports are most easily accessible in E. Walshe (ed.), *Elizabeth Bowen's Selected Irish Writings* (Cork: Cork University Press, 2011).

3   E. Bowen, 'Éire', in H. Lee (ed.), *The Mulberry Tree: Writings of Elizabeth Bowen* (London: Virago, 1986), pp.30–1.

4   Ibid., pp.32–3.

5   'Ireland Today' manuscript dated around 1952 or '53, published in A. Hepburn (ed.), *Listening In: Broadcasts, Speeches and Interviews by Elizabeth Bowen* (Edinburgh: Edinburgh University Press, 2010), p.120.

6   E. Bowen, 'The Short Story in England' (1945), in A. Hepburn (ed.), *People, Places, Things: Essays by Elizabeth Bowen* (Edinburgh: Edinburgh University Press, 2008), p.315.

7   Ibid., p.314.

8   E. Bowen, *The Heat of the Day* (Harmondsworth: Penguin, 1987), p.167.

9   E. Bowen, 'The Demon Lover', in Lee, *The Mulberry Tree*, p.97.

10   Bowen, *The Heat of the Day*, p.81.

11   Ibid., p.179.

12   O. Manning, *Artist Among the Missing* (London: William Heinemann, 1949), p. 249.

13   The border with Northern Ireland was hard to police and there were fears that workers from the South in the North would carry back information and pass it on to German spies: see C. Wills, *That Neutral Island: A Cultural History of Ireland during the Second World War* (London: Faber, 2007), p.147.

14   W.J. McCormack, *Dissolute Characters: Irish Literary History through Balzac, Sheridan Le Fanu, Yeats and Bowen* (Manchester: Manchester University Press, 1993).

15   'A Conversation Between Elizabeth Bowen and Jocelyn Brooke', in Hepburn, *Listening In*, p.283.

16   C. Wills, 'Half Different: The Vanishing Irish in *A World of Love*', in E. Walshe (ed.), *Elizabeth Bowen* (Dublin: Irish Academic Press, 2009), pp.133–49.

17   E. Bowen, 'Bowen's Court', in Hepburn, *People, Places, Things*, p.141.

18   For an exploration of Anglo-Irish themes in this novel, see R. Tracy, *The Unappeasable Host: Studies in Irish Identities* (Dublin: UCD Press, 1998), pp.242–55.

19   E. Bowen, 'Ireland Makes Irish', in Walshe, *Elizabeth Bowen's Selected Irish Writings*, p.131.

20   This is a criticism Bowen also voices in her essay 'How They Live in Ireland: Conquest by Cheque Book' (1946), reproduced in Walshe, *Elizabeth Bowen's Selected Irish Writings*, pp.131–4.

21   E. Bowen, *A World of Love* (London: Vintage, 1999), p.57.

22   V. Glendinning with J. Robertson (eds), *Love's Civil War: Elizabeth Bowen and Charles Ritchie. Letters and Diaries, 1941–1973* (New York: Simon & Schuster, 2008), pp.198–9.

23 Walshe, *Elizabeth Bowen's Selected Irish Writings*, p.17.

24 On this point see Wills, *That Neutral Island*, p.65.

25 K. O'Brien, *The Last of Summer* (London: Virago, 1990), p.179

26 E. Walshe, *Kate O'Brien: A Writing Life* (Dublin: Irish Academic Press, 2006), p.95.

27 K. O'Brien, *The Land of Spices* (London: Virago, 2000), p.14.

28 Ibid., p.168.

29 For Joycean echoes, see A.O. Weekes's discussion of *The Land of Spices* in *Irish Women Writers: An Uncharted Tradition* (Lexington, KY: University Press of Kentucky, 1990), pp.120–32.

30 O'Brien, *The Land of Spices*, p.199.

31 Weekes, *Irish Women Writers*, p.127.

32 E. Walshe (ed.), *Ordinary People Dancing: Essays on Kate O'Brien* (Cork: Cork University Press, 1993), p.165.

33 Ibid., p.164.

34 K. O'Brien, *The Flower of May* (London: William Heinemann, 1953), p.37.

35 Ibid., p.251.

36 On this point, see E. Donoghue, '"Out of Order": Kate O'Brien's Lesbian Fictions', in Walshe, *Ordinary People Dancing*, pp.48–9.

37 See F. Feehan, 'Kate O'Brien and the Splendour of Music', in Walshe, *Ordinary People Dancing*, p.122. For a detailed discussion of the use of operatic music in this novel, see A. Fogarty, 'The Ear of the Other: Dissident Voices in Kate O'Brien's *As Music and Splendour* and Mary Dorcey's *A Noise from the Woodshed*', in E. Walshe (ed.), *Sex, Nation and Dissent* (Cork: Cork University Press, 1997), pp.170–99.

38 K. O'Brien, *As Music and Splendour* (London and New York: Penguin, 2005), p.189.

39 Ibid., p.343.

40 Ibid., p.208.

41 Ibid., p.212.

42 M. Keane, *Devoted Ladies* (London: Virago, 1984), p.20.

43 D. Conyers, *Kicking Foxes* (London: Hutchinson, 1947), p.102.

44 There are interesting similarities with Mary Lavin's story 'Sarah', published in the same year. Was there perhaps a real Sarah?

45 M. Laverty, *No More Than Human* (London: Virago, 1986), p.14.

46 Wills, *That Neutral Island*, pp.259–62.

47 L. Gibbons, *Transformations in Irish Culture* (Cork: Cork University Press, 1996), p.53.

48 B. Fitzgerald, *We Are Besieged* (Bantry: Somerville Press, 2011), p.30.

49 B. Fitzgerald, *Footprint upon Water* (Belfast: Blackstaff Press, 1983), p.4.

50 Discussed by J.W. Foster in *Irish Novels, 1890–1940: New Bearings in Culture and Fiction* (Oxford: Oxford University Press, 2008), pp.78–113.

51 1942 was the date of the Canadian publication. The novel was originally published in the UK as *Uneasy Freehold*, 1941.

52 See N.C. Smith, *Dorothy Macardle: A Life* (Dublin: The Woodfield Press, 2007) and G. Meaney, *Gender, Ireland and Cultural Change: Race, Sex, and Nation* (New York and London: Routledge, 2010), pp.52–66.

53 Meaney, *Gender, Ireland and Cultural Change*, p.57.

54 D. Macardle, *The Uninvited* (Toronto: Reginald Saunders, 1942), p.238.

55 Ibid., p.144.

56 Ibid., p.235.

57 Smith, *Dorothy Macardle*, p.104.

58 Ibid., p.90.

59   D. Macardle, *Fantastic Summer* (London: Peter Davies, 1946), pp.12–13.

60   A link that is also made in Edna O'Brien's *In the Forest* (2002), which connects an artist and a murderer through their idealisations of Eily: see A. Greenwood, *Edna O'Brien* (Tavistock: Northcote House, 2003), p.105.

61   Smith, *Dorothy Macardle*, pp.114–15. In 1949, Macardle published her investigative study into children in post-war Europe, *Children of Europe*.

62   Smith, *Dorothy Macardle*, pp.129–30.

63   A. Bourke, *Maeve Brennan: Homesick at the* New Yorker (London: Jonathan Cape, 2004), p.131.

64   Ibid., p.154.

65   M. Brennan, *The Visitor* (London: Atlantic Books, 2001), p.8.

66   Bourke, *Maeve Brennan*, p.266.

67   Brennan, *The Visitor*, p.80.

68   M. Keane, *Two Days in Aragon* (London: Virago, 1985), p.139.

69   Ibid., p.88.

70   Ibid., p.ix.

71   See S.D. Fabre, 'Colonial Ireland in Retrospect in Somerville and Ross's *The Big House of Inver* and Keane's *Two Days in Aragon*', in E. Walshe and G. Young (eds), *Molly Keane: Centenary Essays* (Dublin: Four Courts Press, 2006), pp.75–84 and V. Kreilkamp, *The Anglo-Irish Novel and the Big House* (Syracuse, NY: Syracuse University Press, 1998), pp.174–94. See also Margot Backus's discussion of this novel in *The Gothic Family Romance: Heterosexuality, Child Sacrifice, and the Anglo-Irish Colonial Order* (Durham, NC: Duke University Press, 1999), pp.194–205.

72   For discussion of these, see J. Wally, *Selected Twentieth-Century Anglo-Irish Autobiographies: Theories and Patterns of Self-Representation* (New York and Bern: Peter Lang, 2004), T.S. Napier, *Seeking a Country: Literary Autobiographies of Twentieth-Century Irishwomen* (Lanham, NY: University Press of America, 2001), and E. Grubgeld, *Anglo-Irish Autobiography: Class, Gender, and the Forms of Narrative* (Syracuse, NY: Syracuse University Press, 2004).

73   K. Everett, *Bricks and Flowers* (London: Constable, 1949), p.1.

74   M. Keane, *Loving Without Tears* (London: Virago, 1988), p.108.

75   Ibid., p.170.

76   Ibid., p.8.

77   L. Levenson, *The Four Seasons of Mary Lavin* (Dublin: Marino, 1998), p.225.

78   M. Lavin, *Tales from Bective Bridge* (Dublin: Town & Country House, 1996), p.vii.

79   M. Lavin, *The House in Clewe Street* (London: Virago, 1987), p.257.

80   For analysis of the various ideologies that have been responsible for the suppression of the body in Irish society, see C. Herr, 'The Erotics of Irishness', *Critical Inquiry*, 17, 1 (1990), pp.1–34.

81   On this theme, see E. Fauset, 'Studies in the Fiction of Jennifer Johnston and Mary Lavin', *Irish Studies Working Papers* (Fort Lauderdale: Nova Southeastern University, 1998), pp.7–12.

82   See J. Heaney, '"No Sanctuary from Hatred": A Re-appraisal of Mary Lavin's Outsiders', *Irish University Review*, 28, 2 (1998), pp.294–307.

83   Thereafter, Lavin kept to the short story form, which she felt suited her temperament and fitted more easily than the novel into her busy life as mother of three growing daughters: see Levenson, *The Four Seasons of Mary Lavin*, p.79.

84   M. Lavin, *Mary O'Grady* (London: Virago, 1986), p.203.

85   See Anne Fogarty's insightful comments on this novel in '"The Horror of the Unlived Life": Mother–Daughter Relationships in Contemporary Irish Women's Fiction', in A. Giorgio (ed.), *Writing Mothers and Daughters: Renegotiating the Mother in Western European Narratives by Women* (New York and Oxford: Berghahn, 2002), pp.85–117.

86   V. Mulkerns, *A Time Outworn* (London: Chatto & Windus, 1951), p.69.

87 Ibid., p.216.
88 V. Mulkerns, *A Peacock Cry* (London: Hodder & Stoughton, 1954), p.63.
89 Ibid., p.83.
90 A. Crone, *Bridie Steen* (London: William Heinemann, 1949), p.328.
91 A. Crone, *This Pleasant Lea* (London: William Heinemann, 1952), p.23.
92 A. Crone, *My Heart and I* (London: William Heinemann, 1955), p.277.
93 Ibid., p.291.
94 J. McNeill, *Tea at Four O'Clock* (London: Virago, 1988), p.27.
95 J.W. Foster, *Forces and Themes in Ulster Fiction* (Dublin: Gill & Macmillan, 1974), p.242.

CHAPTER 5

1 'Interview with Mary Dorcey', in I. O'Carroll and E. Collins (eds), *Lesbian and Gay Visions of Ireland* (London and New York: Cassell, 1995), p.38.
2 R. Pelan, 'Reflections on a Connemara Dietrich', in K. Laing, S. Mooney and M. O'Connor (eds), *Edna O'Brien: New Critical Perspectives* (Dublin: Carysfort Press, 2006), p.18.
3 N. Wroe, 'Saturday Review', *Guardian*, 2 October 1999. For discussion of O'Brien's stage persona, see Pelan, 'Reflections on a Connemara Dietrich' and M. O'Connor, 'Edna O'Brien, Irish Dandy', in Laing, Mooney and O'Connor, *Edna O'Brien*, pp.12–37 and pp.38–53.
4 E.J. Dickson, 'Weekend', *The Times*, 1 February 2003, p.6.
5 Quoted in M. O'Connor, '"Becoming Animal" in the Novels of Edna O'Brien', in C. Cusick (ed.), *Out of the Earth: Ecocritical Readings of Irish Texts* (Cork: Cork University Press, 2010), p.176.
6 Laing, Mooney and O'Connor, *Edna O'Brien* and L. Colletta and M. O'Connor (eds), *Wild Colonial Girl: Essays on Edna O'Brien* (Madison, WI: University of Wisconsin Press, 2006).
7 R. Cooke, 'The First Lady of Irish Fiction', *Observer*, 6 February 2011, p.11. O'Brien's memoir, *Country Girl* (London: Faber and Faber, 2012) mentions a bailiff's visit and an episode with her drunken father and a revolver.
8 C. Gébler, *Father and I: A Memoir* (London: Abacus, 2000), p.48.
9 For a comparison between their careers, see M. Woods, 'Red, Un-Read, and Edna: Ernest Gébler and Edna O'Brien', in Laing, Mooney and O'Connor, *Edna O'Brien*, pp.54–67.
10 Quoted in G. Eckley, *Edna O'Brien* (Lewisburg, PA: Bucknell University Press, 1974), p.26.
11 E. O'Brien, *Mother Ireland* (Harmondsworth: Penguin, 1978), p.19.
12 E. O'Brien, *The Country Girls Trilogy* (Harmondsworth: Penguin, 1987), p.27.
13 For a discussion of mother–daughter relations in O'Brien's fiction, see A.O. Weekes, 'Figuring the Mother in Contemporary Irish Fiction', in L. Harte and M. Parker (eds), *Contemporary Irish Fiction: Themes, Tropes, Theories* (Basingstoke: Macmillan Press, 2000), pp.100–23 and A. Fogarty, '"The Horror of the Unlived Life": Mother–Daughter Relationships in Contemporary Irish Women's Fiction', in A. Giorgio (ed.), *Writing Mothers and Daughters: Renegotiating the Mother in Western European Narratives by Women* (New York and Oxford: Berghahn, 2002), pp.104–9.
14 In *Country Girl*, O'Brien describes the convent school where she and her fellow boarders learned 'to be immune to passions, to mortify ourselves in every way and to put up with our chilblains', p.62.
15 In *Country Girl* O'Brien reveals that Sean McBride was the original Mr Gentleman (p. 89). In 'Madame Cassandra' (*Saints and Sinners*, 2011), O'Brien returned to the story of Mr Gentleman, recounted this time from the point of view of his wife.
16 See R. Pelan's elaboration of this point in 'Edna O'Brien's "Love Objects"', in Colletta and O'Connor, *Wild Colonial Girl*, pp.58–77 and also S. Peterson, '"Meaniacs" and Martyrs: Sadomasochistic Desire in O'Brien's *The Country Girls Trilogy*', in Laing, Mooney and O'Connor, *Edna O'Brien*, pp.150–70.

17 For further discussion of O'Brien's subversion of the romance plot, see A. Greenwood, *Edna O'Brien* (Tavistock: Northcote House, 2003), pp.21–34.

18 The title was changed to *Girl with Green Eyes* for American editions.

19 O'Brien's memoir, *Country Girl*, reveals how much of the material in this novel, and indeed the entire trilogy, is drawn directly from life.

20 O'Brien, *The Country Girls Trilogy*, p.252.

21 C. Herr, 'The Family and the Female Body in the Novels of Edna O'Brien and Julia O'Faolain', *Canadian Journal of Irish Studies*, 22, 2 (1996), p.88.

22 O'Brien, *The Country Girls Trilogy*, p.523. K. Byron's discussion of the trilogy pays particular attention to the epilogue: see '"In the Name of the Mother": Reading and Revision in Edna O'Brien's *Country Girls Trilogy and Epilogue*', in Colletta and O'Connor, *Wild Colonial Girl*, pp.14–30.

23 O'Brien, *The Country Girls Trilogy*, p.440.

24 Ibid., p.525.

25 Eckley, *Edna O'Brien*, p.24.

26 E. O'Brien, *August is a Wicked Month* (London: Jonathan Cape, 1965), p.34.

27 Ibid., p.120.

28 Ibid., p.136.

29 See M. Burke, 'Famished: Alienation and Appetite in Edna O'Brien's Early Novels', in Laing, Mooney and O'Connor, *Edna O'Brien*, pp.219–41.

30 E. O'Brien, *Casualties of Peace* (London: Jonathan Cape, 1966), p.75.

31 Ibid., p.138. On this question of clothes, see S. Mooney, '"Sacramental Sleeves": Fashioning the Female Subject in the Fiction of Edna O'Brien', in Laing, Mooney and O'Connor, *Edna O'Brien*, pp.196–218.

32 O'Brien, *Casualties of Peace*, p.122.

33 Pelan, 'Reflections on a Connemara Dietrich', in Laing, Mooney and O'Connor, *Edna O'Brien*, p.20.

34 O'Brien, *Country Girl*, p.197.

35 E. O'Brien, *Night* (London: Weidenfeld & Nicolson, 1972), p.114.

36 Ibid., p.58.

37 Ibid., p.7.

38 Ibid., p.150.

39 Ibid., p.150.

40 H. Thompson, 'Hysterical Hooliganism: O'Brien, Freud, Joyce', in Colletta and O'Connor (eds) *Wild Colonial Girl*, pp.31–57 and Pelan, 'Reflections on a Connemara Dietrich', in Laing, Mooney and O'Connor, *Edna O'Brien*, pp.31–4.

41 E. O'Brien, *James Joyce* (London: Phoenix, 2000), p.2.

42 E. O'Brien, *Johnny, I Hardly Knew You* (London: Weidenfeld & Nicolson, 1977), p.10.

43 Ibid., p.119.

44 Greenwood, *Edna O'Brien*, p.22.

45 On the significance of epigraphs in O'Brien's work, see B. Cardin, 'Words Apart: Epigraphs in Edna O'Brien's Novels', in Laing, Mooney and O'Connor, *Edna O'Brien*, pp.68–82.

46 J. O'Faolain, *Godded & Codded* (London: Faber & Faber, 1970), p.170.

47 O'Faolain, *Godded & Codded*, p.105.

48 Ibid., p.32.

49 Ibid., p.33.

50 Ibid., p.102.

51 Ibid., p.57.

52 J. O'Faolain, *Women in the Wall* (New York: Carroll & Graf, 1988), p.11.

53 Ibid., p.162.

54   J. Casey, *The Horse of Selene* (Dublin: The Dolmen Press, 1971), p.97.

55   Ibid., p.98.

56   E. Bowen, *The Little Girls* (Harmondsworth: Penguin, 1982), p.163.

57   V. Glendinning with J. Robertson (eds), *Love's Civil War: Elizabeth Bowen and Charles Ritchie. Letters and Diaries, 1941–1973* (New York: Simon & Schuster, 2008), p.352.

58   Ibid., p.308.

59   Ibid., p.309.

60   Ibid., p.350.

61   Ibid., p.351.

62   Ibid., p.398.

63   Ibid., p.405.

64   H. Lee (ed.), *The Mulberry Tree: Writings of Elizabeth Bowen* (London: Vintage, 1999), pp.279–80.

65   Glendinning and Robertson, *Love's Civil War*, p.358.

66   Ibid., p.422.

67   Quoted in V. Glendinning, *Elizabeth Bowen: Portrait of a Writer* (London: Weidenfeld & Nicolson, 1977), p.22.

68   Glendinning and Robertson, *Love's Civil War*, p.435.

69   Ibid., p.463.

70   Ibid., p.389.

71   Ibid., p.303.

72   The article is reprinted in A. Hepburn (ed.), *People, Places, Things: Essays by Elizabeth Bowen* (Edinburgh: Edinburgh University Press, 2008), pp.377–9.

73   T. O'Toole, 'Angels and Monsters: Embodiment and Desire in *Eva Trout*', in E. Walshe (ed.), *Elizabeth Bowen* (Dublin: Irish Academic Press, 2009), pp.162–78.

74   Glendinning and Robertson, *Love's Civil War*, p.418.

75   E. Bowen, *Eva Trout, or Changing Scenes* (London: Vintage, 1999), p.12.

76   J. Baudrillard, 'The System of Objects', *Selected Writings* (Cambridge: Polity Press, 2001), p.30.

77   Bowen, *Eva Trout*, p.222.

78   Glendinning and Robertson, *Love's Civil War*, p.302.

79   Ibid., pp.243–4.

80   Ibid., p.419.

81   I. Murdoch, *The Unicorn* (Harmondsworth: Penguin, 1966), p.98.

82   P. Conradi, *Iris Murdoch: The Saint and the Artist* (London: Macmillan, 1989), p.113.

83   I. Murdoch, *The Red and the Green* (London: Chatto & Windus, 1965), p.32. Murdoch herself apparently identified with Frances: see *Iris Murdoch Newsletter*, 14 (Autumn 2000), p.12.

84   In his discussion of *The Red and the Green* Derek Hand makes a similar observation of Frances, but it is actually more applicable to Millicent, see D. Hand, *A History of the Irish Novel* (Cambridge: Cambridge University Press, 2011), pp.229–30.

85   See Conradi, *Iris Murdoch*, p.464.

86   C. St Peter, 'Jennifer Johnston's Irish Troubles: A Materialist-Feminist Reading', in T. O'Brien Johnson and D. Cairns (eds), *Gender in Irish Writing* (Milton Keynes: Open University Press, 1991), pp.112–27.

87   R. Imhof, 'Review of *The Invisible Worm*', *Linen Hall Review*, April 1990, p.28.

88   M. McKeone, 'Roddy Doyle puts birthday boot into "Joyce industry"', *Sunday Tribune*, 8 February 2004, p.3.

89   J. Quinn (ed.), *A Portrait of the Artist as a Young Girl* (London: Methuen, 1986), p.59.

90   E. Battersby, 'A Shaper of Sophisticated Stories', *Irish Times*, 9 January 2010.

91   V. Kreilkamp, *The Anglo-Irish Novel and the Big House* (Syracuse, NY: Syracuse University Press, 1998), p.201.

92 Quinn, *A Portrait of the Artist as a Young Girl*, p.57.

93 Ibid., p.59.

94 Kreilkamp, *The Anglo-Irish Novel*, pp.195–221.

95 C. Moloney and H. Thompson (eds), *Irish Women Speak Out: Voices from the Field* (Syracuse, NY: Syracuse University Press, 2003), p.68.

96 J. Johnston, *The Captains and the Kings* (London: Fontana, 1982), p.103.

97 R.F. Garratt, *Trauma and History in the Irish Novel: The Return of the Dead* (Basingstoke: Palgrave Macmillan, 2011), pp.69–83.

98 *Fortnight*, April 1995, pp.36–7.

99 J. Johnston, *The Old Jest* (London: Fontana, 1984), p.27.

100 S. Benstock, 'The Masculine World of Jennifer Johnston', in T. Staly (ed.), *Twentieth-Century Women Novelists* (London: Macmillan, 1982), pp.191–217.

101 A.O. Weekes, *Irish Women's Writing: An Uncharted Tradition* (Lexington, KY: University Press of Kentucky, 1990), p.202.

102 R.S. Lynch, 'Public Spaces, Private Lives: Irish Identity and Female Selfhood in the Novels of Jennifer Johnston', in K. Kirkpatrick (ed.), *Border Crossings: Irish Women Writers and National Identities* (Dublin: Wolfhound Press, 2000), pp.250–68.

103 J. Johnston, *Shadows on Our Skin* (Harmondsworth: Penguin, 1991), p.154.

104 For more on the theme of border crossing in Johnston's work, see Lynch, 'Public Spaces, Private Lives', in Kirkpatrick, *Border Crossings*, pp.250–68.

105 L. Bardwell, *A Restless Life* (Dublin: Liberties Press, 2008), p.98.

106 Ibid., p.254.

107 Ibid., p.213.

108 N. O'Faolain, *Are You Somebody? The Life and Times of Nuala O'Faolain* (Dublin: New Island Books, 1997), p.67.

109 Bardwell, *A Restless Life*, pp.132–40.

110 L. Bardwell, *Girl on a Bicycle* (Dublin: Irish Writers' Co-Operative, 1977), p.56.

111 Interview with Caroline Walsh, *Irish Times*, 7 November 1975, p.8.

112 Bardwell, *Girl on a Bicycle*, p.52.

113 Ibid., p.79.

114 C. Blackwood, *Great Granny Webster* (New York: New York Review of Books, 2002), p.66.

115 Ibid., p.68.

116 Bardwell, *Girl on a Bicycle*, p.79.

117 J. McNeill, *The Maiden Dinosaur* (London: Geoffrey Bles, 1964), p.177.

118 Ibid., p.135.

119 Ibid., p.9.

120 Ibid., p.18.

121 See I. O'Carroll and E. Collins (eds), *Lesbian and Gay Visions of Ireland* (London and New York: Cassell, 1995), pp.164–5.

122 For more details, see Alan Hayes, 'Big Women, Little Women: Toward a History of Second-Wave Commercial Feminist Publishing in Ireland', *Women's Studies Review*, 6 (1999), pp.139–50.

123 For more on the developing research into Irish women's history, see the chapters by Mary O'Dowd, Mary Cullen and Cliona Murphy in A. Hayes and D. Urquhart (eds), *The Irish Women's History Reader* (London: Routledge, 2001), pp.7–25.

124 For further discussion, see C. St Peter, *Changing Ireland: Strategies in Contemporary Women's Fiction* (Basingstoke and London: Macmillan Press, 2000), pp.70–2.

125 E. Patten, *Imperial Refugee: Olivia Manning's Fictions of War* (Cork: Cork University Press, 2011), p.54.

CHAPTER 6

1   Julia O'Faolain, *No Country for Young Men* (London: Allen Lane, 1980), p.101. For a discussion of the Diarmuid and Grainne myth in this novel, see A.O. Weekes, *Irish Women Writers: An Uncharted Tradition* (Lexington, KY: University Press of Kentucky, 1990), pp.174–90. For a reading of the novel as intertextual with *Finnegans Wake*, see T. O'Connor, 'History, Gender, and the Postcolonial Condition: Julia O'Faolain's Comic Rewriting of *Finnegans Wake*', in T. O' Connor (ed.), *The Comic Tradition in Irish Women Writers* (Gainsville, FL: University of Florida Press, 1996), pp.124–48. For an emphasis on the trauma theme, see R.F. Garratt, *Trauma and History in the Irish Novel: The Return of the Dead* (New York: Palgrave, 2011), pp.37–49.

2   O'Faolain, *No Country for Young Men*, p.297.

3   J. O'Faolain, *The Obedient Wife* (Harmondsworth: Penguin, 1983), p.30.

4   Ibid., pp.147–8.

5   Ibid., p.226.

6   See L. Rooks-Hughes's discussion of this novel in 'The Family and the Female Body in the Novels of Edna O'Brien and Julia O'Faolain', *The Canadian Journal of Irish Studies*, 22, 2 (1996), pp.83–97 and also A. Fogarty, '"The Horror of the Unlived Life": Mother–Daughter Relationships in Contemporary Irish Women's fiction', in A. Giorgio (ed.), *Writing Mothers and Daughters: Renegotiating the Mother in Western European Narratives by Women* (New York and Oxford: Berghahn, 2002), pp.85–117.

7   On this subject see E. O'Brien, 'Abjection and Molly Keane's "Very Nasty" Novels', in E. Walshe and G. Young (eds), *Molly Keane: Centenary Essays* (Dublin: Four Courts Press, 2006), pp.101–24 and K.J.S. McGovern, 'Fattening Out Memories: Big House Daughters and Abjection in Molly Keane's *Good Behaviour* and *Loving and Giving*' in the same volume, pp.125–36.

8   E. Walshe, '"Now the Day is Over": Bourgeois Education, Effeminacy and the Fall of Temple Alice', in Walshe and Young, *Molly Keane*, pp.157–68.

9   See A.O. Weekes' discussion of *Good Behaviour* in Weekes, *Irish Women Writers*, pp.154–73.

10 M. Keane, *Time After Time* (London: Sphere, 1984), p.11.

11 For parallels between Leda's storytelling and Keane's, see E.M. Wolff, 'Narrating Anglo-Ireland: Molly Keane's *Time After Time*', in Walshe and Young, *Molly Keane*, p.60.

12 M. Keane, *The Knight of Cheerful Countenance* (London: Virago, 1993), p.5.

13 M. Keane, *Loving and Giving* (London: Virago, 2001), p.172.

14 On Keane's ambivalence towards the Anglo-Irish, see especially Wolff, 'Narrating Anglo-Ireland', in Walshe and Young, *Molly Keane*, pp.49–60.

15 L. Bardwell, *The House* (Belfast: Blackstaff Press, 2006), p.60.

16 L. Bardwell, *A Restless Life* (Dublin: Liberties Press, 2008), p.73. The best known of the Collis brothers was Robert ('Bob') Collis, a paediatrician at the Rotunda Hospital, on whom Richard is based. The character of Cedric is based on Bob's elder brother Maurice, who worked for many years in Burma and later published several books on Southeast Asia.

17 Bardwell, *A Restless Life*, p.257. The collection was *Different Kinds of Love* (1987).

18 D. Nelson, *In Night's City* (Dublin: Wolfhound, 1982), p.64.

19 D. Nelson, *Tar and Feathers* (Normal, IL and London: Dalkey Archive Press, 2004), p.99.

20 J. McMinn, 'The Necessary Female View', *Fortnight*, 222 (1985), pp.17–18.

21 M. Kelly, *Necessary Treasons* (Belfast: Blackstaff Press, 1991), p.240.

22 M. Kelly, *Florrie's Girls* (London: Michael Joseph, 1989), p.1.

23 Ibid., p.246.

24 E. Conlon, *Stars in the Daytime* (Dublin: Attic Press, 1989), p.148.

25 Ibid., p.130.

26 Bennett's letter is quoted in D. Ferriter, *Judging Dev: A Reassessment of the Life and Legacy of Éamon de Valera* (Dublin: Royal Irish Academy, 2007), p.239.

27 Conlon, *Stars in the Daytime*, p.171.

28 M. Leland, *Approaching Priests* (London: Sinclair-Stevenson, 1991), pp.290–1.

29 C. Boylan, *Home Rule* (London: Abacus, 1997), p.224.

30 C. Boylan, *Room for a Single Lady* (London: Abacus, 1998), pp.25–6.

31 This episode draws on Boylan's own childhood: see J. Quinn (ed.), *A Portrait of the Artist as a Young Girl* (London: Methuen, 1986), p.21.

32 Boylan, *Room for a Single Lady*, p.295.

33 Ibid., p.222.

34 See G. Tallone, '"Once Upon a Time": Fabulists and Storytellers in Clare Boylan's Fiction', in E. D'hoker, R. Ingelbien and H. Schwall (eds), *Irish Women Writers: New Critical Perspectives* (Bern: Peter Lang, 2011), pp.269–84.

35 A. Quinn, 'New Noises from the Woodshed: The Novels of Emma Donoghue', in L. Harte and M. Parker (eds), *Contemporary Irish Fiction: Themes, Tropes, Theories* (Basingstoke: Macmillan Press, 2000), p.146.

36 H. Thompson, *The Role of Irish Women in the Writings of Edna O'Brien: Mothering the Continuation of the Irish Nation* (Lampeter: The Edwin Mellen Press, 2010), pp.117–78.

37 E. O'Brien, *Country Girl: A Memoir* (London: Faber & Faber, 2012), pp.189–97.

38 E. O'Brien, *Time and Tide* (Harmondsworth: Penguin, 1993), p.260.

39 Ibid., p.216.

40 E. Kennedy-Andrews, *Fiction and the Northern Ireland Troubles since 1969: (De-) Constructing the North* (Dublin: Four Courts Press, 2003), p.248. Details of O'Brien's research for this novel are given in *Country Girl*, pp.236–49.

41 E. O'Brien, *House of Splendid Isolation* (London: Orion, 1995), p.35.

42 For a discussion of postmodernism in this novel, see M. Harris, 'Outside History: Relocation and Dislocation in Edna O'Brien's *House of Splendid Isolation*', in K. Laing, S. Mooney and M. O'Connor (eds), *Edna O'Brien: New Critical Perspectives* (Dublin: Carysfort Press, 2006), pp.122–37. See also D. Farquharson and B. Schrank, 'Blurring Boundaries, Intersecting Lives: History, Gender and Violence in Edna O'Brien's *House of Splendid Isolation*', in L. Colletta and M. O'Connor (eds), *Wild Colonial Girl: Essays on Edna O'Brien* (Madison, WI: University of Wisconsin Press, 2006), pp.110–42. For a discussion of the entire trilogy, see S. Hillan, 'On the Side of Life: Edna O'Brien's Trilogy of Contemporary Ireland', in Colletta and M. O'Connor, *Wild Colonial Girl*, pp.143–61.

43 O'Brien, *House of Splendid Isolation*, p.3.

44 Ibid., p.215.

45 See C. St Peter's discussion of these two novels in 'Petrifying Time: Incest Narratives from Contemporary Ireland', in Harte and Parker, *Contemporary Irish Fiction*, pp.125–43.

46 See A. Martin's analysis of the 'X' case in 'Death of a Nation: Transnationalism, Bodies and Abortion in Late Twentieth-Century Ireland', in T. Mayer (ed.), *Gender Ironies of Nationalism: Sexing the Nation* (London and New York: Routledge, 2000), pp.65–86.

47 E. O'Brien, *Down by the River* (London: Orion, 1997), p.285.

48 Ibid., p.175.

49 Ibid., pp.297–8.

50 See Eve Stoddard's discussion of this novel in 'Sexuality, Nation and Land in the Postcolonial Novels of Edna O'Brien and Jamaica Kincaid', in Laing, Mooney and O'Connor (eds), *Edna O'Brien*, pp.104–21.

51 S. Heaney, 'Foreword', in Quinn, *A Portrait of the Artist as a Young Girl*, p.xii.

52 Quinn, *A Portrait of the Artist as a Young Girl*, p.59.

53 See differing interpretations of this novel by C. St Peter, *Changing Ireland: Strategies in Contemporary Women's Fiction* (Basingstoke: Macmillan, 2000), pp.20–6, R.S. Lynch, 'Public Spaces, Private Lives:

Irish Identity and Female Selfhood in the Novels of Jennifer Johnston', in K. Kirkpatrick (ed.), *Border Crossings: Irish Women Writers and National Identities* (Tuscaloosa, AL: The University of Alabama Press, 2000), pp.250–51, and Weekes, *Irish Women Writers*, p. 210.

54   J. Johnston, *Fool's Sanctuary* (Harmondsworth: Penguin, 1988), p.6.

55   Ibid., p.35.

56   Ibid., p.132.

57   R.F. Garratt, *Trauma and History in the Irish Novel: The Return of the Dead* (New York and Basingstoke: Palgrave Macmillan, 2011), pp.69– 83.

58   See R.S. Lynch, 'Public Spaces, Private Lives', in Kirkpatrick, *Border Crossings*, pp.250–68, and also M. Backus, *The Gothic Family Romance: Heterosexuality, Child Sacrifice, and the Anglo-Irish Colonial Order* (Durham, NC: Duke University Press, 1999), pp.225–38.

59   J. Johnston, *The Invisible Worm* (Harmondsworth: Penguin, 1992), p.57.

60   Ibid., p.181.

61   J. Johnston, *The Illusionist* (London: Minerva, 1996), p.170.

62   Ibid., p.38.

63   D. Madden, *Hidden Symptoms* (London: Faber, 1988), p.46.

64   S. Mikowski makes a similar point in her discussion of Madden's work, 'Deirdre Madden's Novels: Searching for Authentic Woman', in D'hoker, Ingelbien and Schwall (eds), *Irish Women Writers*, pp.245–54.

65   D. Madden, *Remembering Light and Stone* (London: Faber, 1992), p.32.

66   Http://english.slss.ie/Magazine–Spring2003Madden.html, accessed 17 June 2012.

67   D. Madden, *One by One in the Darkness* (London: Faber, 1997), p.93.

68   For discussion of Madden's postmodernism, see M. Parker, 'Shadows on a Glass: Self-Reflexivity in the Fiction of Deirdre Madden', *Irish University Review*, 30, 1 (2000), pp.82–192. See also E. Kennedy-Andrews, *Fiction and the Northern Ireland Troubles since 1969: (De-) Constructing the North* (Dublin: Four Courts Press, 2003), pp.151–61, and J. Steel, 'Politicizing the Private: Women Writing the Troubles', in B. Cliff and E. Walshe (eds), *Representing the Troubles: Texts and Images, 1970–2000* (Dublin: Four Courts Press, 2004), pp.55–66.

69   There is a particularly useful chapter on Northern Irish women's writing in Kennedy-Andrews, *Fiction and the Northern Ireland Troubles since 1969*, pp.224–68.

70   F. Molloy, *No Mate for the Magpie* (London: Virago, 1985), p.110.

71   Ibid., p.170.

72   *No Mate for the Magpie* lends itself to a variety of critical approaches: see particularly Kennedy-Andrews's discussion of the novel in terms of Bakhtinian carnival in *Fiction and the Northern Ireland Troubles since 1969*, pp.172–7.

73   M. Beckett, *Give Them Stones* (London: Bloomsbury, 1987), p.123. For a reading that underlines Martha's shift from nationalism to a gender-based class politics, see M. Sullivan, '"Instead I Said I Am a Home Baker": Nationalist Ideology and Materialist Politics in Mary Beckett's *Give Them Stones*', in Kirkpatrick (ed.), *Border Crossings*, pp.227–49.

74   Compare Colette's mother in Una Woods's *The Dark Hole Days*: 'Mam says she doesn't rest till the door's closed and we're all safe' (Belfast: Blackstaff Press, 1984), p.1.

75   M. Costello, *Titanic Town* (London: Methuen, 1992), p.3.

76   Kennedy-Andrews, *Fiction and the Northern Ireland Troubles since 1969*, p.266. Jennifer Jeffers accurately regards Helen in *One by One in the Darkness* as representing a later generation of educated, professional Northern Irish Catholic women who were better able than Bernie and her friend to deal with the judicial system: see J. Jeffers, *The Irish Novel at the End of the Twentieth Century: Gender, Bodies, and Power* (New York: Palgrave, 2002), p.73.

77   See Eve Patten's criticism of women writers' reliance on realism in 'Women and Fiction, 1985–1990', *Krino*, 8–9 (1990), pp.1–7, and her more specific criticism of Northern Irish novelists in this respect:

'Fiction in conflict: Northern Ireland's Prodigal Novelists', in I.A. Bell (ed.), *Peripheral Visions: Images of Nationhood in Contemporary British Fiction* (Cardiff: University of Wales Press, 1995), pp.128–48. For a defence of the radical potential of realism in the hands of women writers, see R. Pelan, *Two Irelands: Literary Feminisms North and South* (Syracuse, NY: Syracuse University Press, 2005), pp.116–22.

78   For a balanced assessment of Binchy's novels, see St Peter, *Changing Ireland*, pp.135–46.

79   E. Donoghue, 'Noises from the Woodsheds: Tales of Irish Lesbians, 1886–1989', in I. O'Carroll and E. Collins (eds), *Lesbian and Gay Visions of Ireland* (London: Cassell, 1995), pp.165–6.

80   For general discussions of the literary portrayal of the mother–daughter relationship during this period, see A. McCarthy, '"Oh Mother Where Art Thou?" Irish Mothers and Irish Fiction in the Twentieth Century', in P. Kennedy (ed.), *Motherhood in Ireland: Creation & Context* (Cork: Mercier Press, 2004), pp.95–107, A.O. Weekes, 'Figuring the Mother in Contemporary Irish Fiction', in Harte and Parker, *Contemporary Irish Fiction*, pp.100–23, A. Fogarty, '"The Horror of the Unlived Life": Mother–Daughter Relationships in Contemporary Irish Women's Fiction', in Giorgio (ed.), *Writing Mothers and Daughters*, pp.85–117.

81   There is a detailed discussion of this novel in L. Peach, *The Contemporary Irish Novel: Critical Readings* (Basingstoke and New York: Palgrave, 2004), pp.115–25; and see also H. Hansson, 'To Say "I": Female Identity in *The Maid's Tale* and *The Wig My Father Wore*', in E. Kennedy-Andrews (ed.), *Irish Fiction since the 1960s: A Collection of Critical Essays* (Dublin: Four Courts Press, 2002), pp.137–49.

82   M. O'Donnell, *The Elysium Testament* (London: Trident Press, 1999), p.124.

83   See Anne Fogarty's discussion of the Gothic as expressive of anxiety around the changing nature of the Irish family and female roles in this and other 1990s novels by Irish women in 'Uncanny Families: Neo-Gothic Motifs and the Theme of Social Change in Contemporary Irish Women's Fiction', *Irish University Review*, 30, 1 (2000), pp.59–81.

84   K. O'Riordan, *The Boy in the Moon* (London: Flamingo, 1997), p.278.

85   'Emma Donoghue', in C. Moloney and H. Thompson (eds), *Irish Women Writers Speak Out: Voices from the Field* (Syracuse, NY: Syracuse University Press, 2003), p.173.

86   On this point, see A. Quinn, 'New Noises from the Woodshed', in Harte and Parker, *Contemporary Irish Fiction*, pp.159–65.

87   Ní Dhuibhne subsequently revised *Bray House* in the light of the Chernobyl disaster to emphasise the environmental theme: see D. Perry (ed.), *Backtalk: Women Writers Speak out* (New Brunswick: Rutgers University Press, 1993), p.252.

88   See Susan Cahill's discussion of *Bray House* in S. Cahill, *Irish Literature in the Celtic Tiger Years, 1990–2008: Gender, Bodies, Memory* (London and New York: Continuum, 2011), pp.29–43, and also G. Tallone, 'The Unwritten Land: The Dynamic of Space in Éilís Ní Dhuibhne's *The Bray House*', in R. Pelan (ed.), *Éilís Ní Dhuibhne: Perspectives* (Galway: Arlen House, 2009), pp.49–68, D. Hand, 'Being Ordinary. Ireland from Elsewhere: A Reading of Éilís Ní Dhuibhne's *The Bray House*', *Irish University Review*, Spring/Summer 2000, pp.103–16.

89   See C. St Peter, 'Burn, Road, Dance: Éilís Ní Dhuibhne's *Bildungsreise*', in Pelan, *Éilís Ní Dhuibhne*, pp.29–48.

90   'Éilís Ní Dhuibhne', in Moloney and Thompson, *Irish Women Writers Speak Out*, p.104.

91   É. Ní Dhuibhne, *The Dancers Dancing* (London: Review, 2001), p.72.

92   Though Heidi Hansson has argued that even some nineteenth-century fiction by Irish women displays postmodernist features and, to that extent, postmodernism may be regarded as a female literary tradition, see Hansson, 'To Say "I"', in Kennedy-Andrews, *Irish Fiction since the 1960s*, pp.137–49.

93   Peach, *The Contemporary Irish Novel*, p.156. See also A.O. Weekes' account, '"Diving into the Wreck": Mary Morrissy's *Mother of Pearl*', in P.B. Haberstroh and C. St Peter (eds), *Opening the Field. Irish Women: Texts & Contexts* (Cork: Cork University Press, 2007), pp.134–45.

94   M. Morrissy, *Mother of Pearl* (London: Vintage, 1997), p.118.

95   Fogarty, 'Uncanny Families', *Irish University Review*, p.66.

96   E. Martin, *More Bread or I'll Appear* (New York: Anchor Books, 2000), p.193.

97   See also Gerry Smyth's ecocritical perspective on this novel in 'Shite and Sheep: An Ecocritical Perspective on Two Recent Irish Novels', *Irish University Review*, 30, 1 (2000), pp.163–78.

98   *Irish Times*, 25 February 1991.

99   S.E. Senson, 'Anne Enright', in A.G. Gonzalez (ed.), *Irish Women Writers: An A–Z Guide* (Westport, CT: Greenwood, 2006), p.121.

100   C. Bracken and S. Cahill (eds), *Anne Enright* (Dublin: Irish Academic Press, 2011), p.18.

101   'Anne Enright', in Moloney and Thompson, *Irish Women Writers Speak Out*, p.55.

102   A. Enright, *The Wig My Father Wore* (London: Vintage, 2007), p.4.

103   E. D'hoker, 'Reclaiming Feminine Identities: Anne Enright's *The Wig My Father Wore*', in P. Coughlan and T. O'Toole (eds), *Irish Literature: Feminist Perspectives* (Dublin: Carysfort Press, 2008), p.188.

104   A. Enright, *Making Babies: Stumbling into Motherhood* (London: Vintage, 2005), p.194.

105   A. Enright, *What Are You Like?* (London: Vintage, 2001), p.37.

106   Ibid., p.140.

107   K. Ewins, '"History is Only Biological": History, Bodies and National Identity in *The Gathering* and "Switzerland"', in Bracken and Cahill, *Anne Enright*, pp.127–44.

108   Enright, *What Are You Like?*, p.22.

109   Enright, *Making Babies*, p.194.

110   'Interview with Mary Dorcey', in I. O'Carroll and E. Collins (eds), *Lesbian and Gay Visions of Ireland* (London and New York: Cassell, 1995), p.25.

CHAPTER 7

1   See, for example, R. Pelan, *Two Irelands: Literary Feminisms North and South* (Syracuse, NY: Syracuse University Press, 2005), p.xiii. Studies of the Celtic Tiger era include C. Kuhling and K. Keohane (eds), *Cosmopolitan Ireland: Globalisation and Quality of Life* (London: Pluto Press, 2007) and C. Coulter and S. Coleman (eds), *The End of History? Critical Reflections on the Celtic Tiger* (Manchester: Manchester University Press, 2003).

2   J. Jernigan, 'Slings and Arrows: Chick Lit Comes of Age', *Bitch*, Summer 2004, p.74.

3   D. Ging, 'New Gender Formations in Post-Celtic-Tiger Ireland', in M. Cronin, P. Kirby and D. Ging (eds), *Transforming Ireland: Challenges, Critiques, Resources* (Manchester: Manchester University Press, 2009), p.69. See also Kristen Mascia's unpublished TCD MPhil dissertation (2011), for a perceptive discussion of Irish chick lit: 'Celtic Tiger "Chicks": Female Subjectivity in the "Postfeminist" Popular Fiction of Marian Keyes and Patricia Scanlon.'

4   See C. St Peter's discussion of Scanlan's fiction in *Changing Ireland: Strategies in Contemporary Women's Fiction* (Basingstoke: Macmillan, 2000), pp.127–35.

5   Quoted in S. Ferris and M. Young (eds), *Chick Lit: The New Woman's Fiction* (New York and London: Routledge, 2006), p.9.

6   See R. Pelan (ed.), *Éilís Ní Dhuibhne: Perspectives* (Galway: Arlen House, 2009), pp.24–5 and S. Cahill, *Irish Literature in the Celtic Tiger Years, 1990–2008: Gender, Bodies, Memory* (London and New York: Continuum, 2011), p.174 for alternative readings of the ending of *Fox, Swallow, Scarecrow*.

7   'Anne Enright', in C. Moloney and H. Thompson (eds), *Irish Women Writers Speak Out: Voices from the Field* (Syracuse, NY: Syracuse University Press, 2003), p.28. For illuminating readings of *The Pleasure of Eliza Lynch*, see S. Cahill, '"A Greedy Girl" and a "National Thing": Gender and History in Anne Enright's *The Pleasure of Eliza Lynch*', in P. Coughlan and T. O'Toole (eds), *Irish Literature: Feminist Perspectives* (Dublin: Carysfort Press, 2008), pp.203–222 and P. Coughlan, '"Without a Blink of her Lovely Eye": *The Pleasure of Eliza Lynch* and Visionary Scepticism', in C. Bracken and S. Cahill (eds), *Anne Enright* (Dublin: Irish Academic Press, 2011), pp.107–27.

8 Eliza's position as a pregnant, immigrant woman has been related to anxiety in Ireland over pregnant African women culminating in the 2004 Citizenship Referendum: see Cahill, '"A Greedy Girl" and a "National Thing"', in Coughlan and O'Toole, *Irish Literature: Feminist Perspectives*, p.208.

9 A. Enright, *The Gathering* (London: Jonathan Cape, 2007), p.1.

10 Ibid., p. 168.

11 A. Enright, *The Forgotten Waltz* (London: Jonathan Cape, 2011), p.46.

12 Bracken and Cahill, *Anne Enright*, p.17.

13 Enright, *The Forgotten Waltz*, p.85.

14 Ibid., p.207.

15 Adriana Bebiano situates both novels in the picaresque tradition: see A. Bebiano, '"Mad, Bad, and Dangerous to Know": The Stories of Chicago May and Eliza Lynch', in E. D'hoker, R. Ingelbien and H. Schwall (eds), *Irish Women Writers: New Critical Perspectives* (Bern: Peter Lang, 2010), pp.255–68.

16 Ibid., p.262.

17 N. O'Faolain, *The Story of Chicago May* (London: Michael Joseph, 2005), pp.303–4.

18 K. O'Riordan, *The Memory Stones* (London and New York: Pocket Books, 2003), p.40.

19 Ibid., p.13.

20 For an extended discussion of this novel, see Bridget Hogan, 'Is the Mother Re-Visioned in Contemporary Irish Women's Literature?', unpublished PhD thesis, University of Limerick, 2012.

21 M.R. Callaghan, *Billy, Come Home* (Dingle and London: Brandon, 2007), p.31.

22 L. Peach, *The Contemporary Irish Novel: Critical Readings* (Basingstoke and New York: Palgrave, 2004), p.12.

23 Moloney and Thompson, *Irish Women Writers Speak Out*, p.175.

24 A. Haverty, *The Free and Easy* (London: Vintage, 2007), p.64.

25 M. Morrissy, *The Pretender* (London: Jonathan Cape, 2000), p.200.

26 On this point, see A. Fogarty's discussion of this novel in 'Deliberately Personal? The Politics of Identity in Contemporary Irish Women's Writing', *Nordic Irish Studies* 1 (2001), pp.1–17. See also A. Fogarty, 'Feminism and Postmodernism: Representations of Identity in Mary Morrissy's *The Pretender*', in P.B. Haberstroh and C. St Peter (eds), *Opening the Field. Irish Women: Texts & Contexts* (Cork: Cork University Press, 2007), pp.147–63.

27 C. Boylan, *Emma Brown* (London: Abacus, 2004), p.441.

28 A. Davis-Goff, *The Fox's Walk* (Orlando: Harcourt, 2003), p.319.

29 See B. Cardin, 'Reflections in Jennifer Johnston's *This is Not a Novel*', *The Canadian Journal of Irish Studies*, 31, 2, (2005), pp.34–41.

30 P. Smyth, 'Riveting truth in a "non-memoir"', *Irish Times*, 31 October 2009.

31 For Denis Johnston's life, see B. Adams, *Denis Johnston: A Life* (Dublin: Lilliput Press, 2002).

32 V. Woolf, 'Modern Fiction', *The Crowded Dance of Modern Life* (Harmondsworth: Penguin, 1993), p.8.

33 F. O'Toole, 'A fiction too far', *Irish Times*, 2 March 2002, p.37.

34 R. Pelan, 'Reflections on a Connemara Dietrich', in K. Laing, S. Mooney and M. O'Connor (eds), *Edna O'Brien: New Critical Perspectives* (Dublin: Carysfort Press, 2006), pp.12–18.

35 UCD/SC, O'Brien Papers, OB/572, p.3.

36 Ellen McWilliams, who has reached the same conclusion as myself on the evolution of the mother figure in O'Brien, explores this in Chapter 3 of her study *Women and Exile in Contemporary Irish Fiction* (New York: Palgrave, 2012).

37 *Sunday Tribune*, 30 January 2011.

38 Moloney and Thompson, *Irish Women Writers Speak Out*, p.188.

INDEX